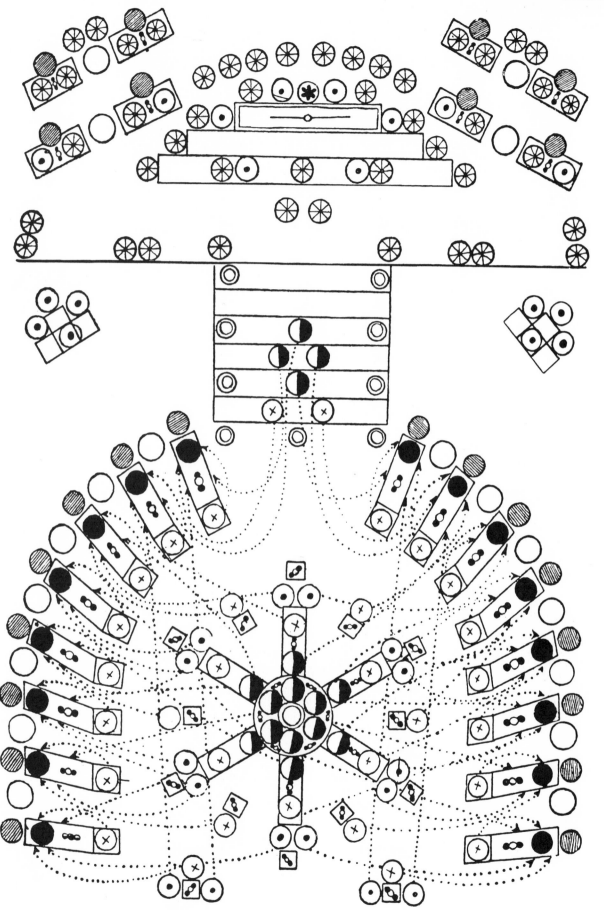

B

FOUR CENTURIES OF

BALLET

FIFTY MASTERWORKS

FOUR CENTURIES OF
BALLET
FIFTY MASTERWORKS

LINCOLN KIRSTEIN

DOVER PUBLICATIONS, INC.
NEW YORK

Frontispiece. Human movement analyzed. Italy, c. 1579.

Published in Canada by General Publishing Company, Ltd.,
30 Lesmill Road, Don Mills, Toronto, Ontario.
Published in the United Kingdom by Constable and Company, Ltd.

This Dover edition, first published in 1984, is an unabridged,
corrected republication of the work originally published in 1970
by Praeger Publishers, Inc., New York, under the title *Movement & Metaphor: Four Centuries of Ballet.*

Manufactured in the United States of America
Dover Publications, Inc., 31 East 2nd Street, Mineola, N.Y.
11501

Library of Congress Cataloging in Publication Data

Kirstein, Lincoln, 1907–
    Four centuries of ballet.

    Reprint. Originally published: Movement & metaphor. New
York : Praeger, 1970.
    Bibliography: p.
    Includes index.
    1. Ballet—History.   I. Title.
GV1787.K513   1984   792.8'09   83-20596
ISBN 0-486-24631-0

She sees a Mob of Metaphors advance,
Pleas'd with the Madness of the mazy dance.
                              —Alexander Pope

This is a sketch of classical theatrical dancing involving iconography and metaphor. Is this pretentious? Working ballet masters are not bothered by erudition, having no need to be conscious of sources, since they eat and breathe them. However, only if we deem ballet trivial can we ignore background and masters, upon which, by apostolic succession, it has been built. Image and metaphor clarify the old and place the new. In defining the Greek *metapherein* as "transference" (in the psychoanalytical sense), Professor Gombrich sums up the method of analysts from Diderot, Gautier, and Mallarmé to Cocteau and Jacques Rivière:

"The possibility of metaphor springs from the infinite elasticity of the human mind; it testifies to its capacity to perceive and assimilate new experiences as modifications of earlier ones, of finding equivalences in the most disparate phenomena, and of substituting one for another. Without this constant substitution, neither language nor art, nor indeed civilized life, would be possible."*

This book may also be read as a cast of archetypes providing male dancers with leading roles: God, King, Courtier, Soldier, Sailor, Gentleman, Barbarian, Peasant, Puppet, Common Man, Athlete, Artist; finally—Dancer. Since the start, ladies were Amorous, Capricious, Haunting, Jealous, Vengeful; but first, last, always—Ballerinas. Men wore different masks; girls different costumes.

There are no claims to completeness here; how could there be for our size and scope? Many matters are largely unmentioned—audience, impresario, critics, the rela-

tionship of Mannerist art to ballet style, biomorphic considerations, the psychology of self-exhibition rooted in performers, choreographers as teachers, the development of individual steps. More drastically, the last forty years—those most familiar—will seem scantily treated. But a tenth of the story could easily have taken ten times the space.

Here is sketched the long issue of academic theatrical dancing by surveying fifty separate works. Ballets chosen define tradition at a given period or extend it through some crucial enlargement. In this, personalities are minimized; many eminent performers are not noted when their performances, however cherished, were not matched by the quality of choreography that was their basis. The cult of glamorous stars obscures two vital factors: the role of the *corps de ballet*—not a group of subservient dancers, but a collective organism—and the responsibility of ballet masters as choreographers and preceptors. In the last half-century, companies emerge as collective stars; individual interpreters—soloists—are important, but impotent without their institutional frame. Thus, dancing, not dancers, is presented.

If there is a hero, it is choreography. Dance design is not simply one element; it is that without which ballet cannot exist. As aria is to opera, words to poetry, color to painting, so sequences in steps—their syntax, idiom, vocabulary—are the stuff of stage dancing.

Ballet was not independent at its start; it shared the

---

* E. H. Gombrich, *Meditations on a Hobby Horse* (1963).

scene with song for more than a century. Only in the last fifty years has choreography, liberated from parade, padding, pantomime, staff painters, and hack composers, emerged as autonomous, parallel in possibility to other plastic arts. Whether or not its constructs are comparable in depth or quality to architecture, painting, or sculpture need not detain us. Ballet makes up in immediate intensity for what it loses through its ephemeral nature.

This book outlines certain ballets by relating them to society, art, and ideas. Each may be seen as a lens fixed on lyric imagination in its epoch. For every one described, others might have been substituted. Of fifty chosen, there are fifteen concerning which extensive monographs might profitably be published. Telegraphic treatment is mandatory. What we need is an ample general encyclopedia honoring a field rich in documentation, increasingly illuminated by international scholarship. However, there are no good books in English covering Viennese or Italian ballet; Dutch, Czech, Slavic, and Scandinavian coverage is inadequate or lacking.

Thus, limitations of the present study are manifold. For whom is it written? For the "general audience," which presumably knows little and would like to learn more? How much can one presuppose, covering a broad historical process? What names and dates need be included? What omitted? Is a "general" audience the so-called dance public, already familiar with a fair-sized, repetitive bibliography, which doesn't need to be reminded who Nijinsky was or Balanchine is? Can one omit primary definitions distinguishing Renaissance from Baroque? Rococo from Neoclassic? Must one analyze Romanticism again? What is lacking all but equals what manages to get mentioned. A number of nominally eminent areas find no place at all. Has "nothing" happened on the European continent in the last forty years? No word for Russia, France, Italy, Scandinavia, Central Europe? All have been active, but it is hard to find key works that mark lasting additions to autonomous choreography, although individual performances gave pleasure and acquired prestige.

So, finally, this book is *not* for the general reader, but for those who, self-chosen, enjoy ballet. Enjoyment may be sharpened if they learn, in some depth, what they watch, through some of its history. A number of youthful spectators say they are tired of our available repertory. Perhaps their own vision is limited and their range can be enlarged, not only in the visual realm. The most tiresome enthusiasm of our expendable advance-guards is their rejection of historicity. History, they fume, is a recitation of failure. They seek an uninterrupted series of instant triumphs, without precedent, each the product of revolutionary virgin genius. Here they will find triumphs, but few of the ballets described are "original"; something in each was tried before. Much in most used old material in new ways, which amounts to invention when great gifts are given.

L.K.

New Year's Day, 1970.

CONTENTS

FOUR CENTURIES OF
BALLET
FIFTY MASTERWORKS

1. 2. 3.

1. The soldier. Italy, c. 1450.

2. The acrobat. Italy, c. 1550.

3. The dancer. France, 1849.

4.

5.

6.

4. Spartan youth at games. France, 1860.

5. Sword dance. Rome, c. 150 B.C.

6. School of swordsmanship. France, 1623.

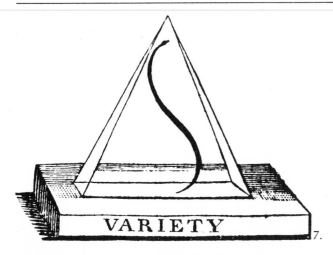

VARIETY

7.

Bodies

Choreography is a map of movement—patterns for action that ballet masters ordain by design. Its composition depends on human bodies schooled in a grammar of movement whose end is legible virtuosity. Four centuries have intervened from the beginnings of theatrical dancing to its present condition, during which choreography, at first wedded to verse and song, has become autonomous. In this autonomy, it exists as cousin to music, architecture, painting, and sculpture.

Ballet dancing differs in kind from folk and ballroom dancing, as well as from various independent, individual schools of national dances. Folk dancing once served magical ends: as guarantee of crops, victory in battle, continuation of the tribe. Social dances of country and city peoples in the open air or dance halls are still more for fun than to make a show. Isolated artists with vivid personalities have, by chance or choice, composed grammars of movement suitable to themselves, which they have briefly taught to companies of students who supported them in public appearances. Since such studios seldom survive the retirement of the teacher (Ruth St. Denis, Isadora Duncan, Rudolph von Laban, Mary Wigman, Kurt Jooss, Doris Humphrey), they contribute little to that tradition which has established and maintained the academic theatrical classic dance—ballet—for four hundred years as the orthodox school of Western virtuosity.

Acrobacy—extreme physical versatility controlled by rigid discipline—is what attracts the great public to all spectator events, from bull fights and ballgames to ballet. Expressive and spectacular virtuosity is the aim of the classical dancer's instruction and eventual deployment, and the minds and bodies of persons groomed for ballet differ in kind and quality from those developed for other intense physical activities. Heterodox schools outside the classic academy instruct toward limited virtuosity, since aspirants magnetized by the

several dominant personalities operative within their decades are polarized more by ideas than by spectacle. These performers appeal to a genuine if restricted audience that is drawn to their idiosyncratic alternatives to "mere" physical brilliance. Verbally they have some ingenuity as acrobats; physically they are naive and incompletely schooled (they begin to dance ten to fifteen years after most ballet students). Over the last seventy years they have neither provided a unified, legible method, a repertory that can be shared, nor a strong inheritance beyond the originators of the so-called modern dance mentioned above.

All soldiers, athletes, and dancers stand, walk, run, and jump. Soldiers are schooled for combat, athletes for competition, dancers for spectacle. Combat and competition are incidentally spectacular; stage dancing alone is focused from its start toward a display of bodies in movement expressing fictive emotion or contrived design.

1. *

2.

3.

Consider military activity in the metaphor of mock combat: boxing, wrestling, or fencing. Of these, the last is the most legible, its rules of stance and profile closest to a dancer's. Whether with light foil, dueling sword, or saber, fencing has one purpose: to touch an opponent without being touched; touching is symbolic of drawing blood. Fencing's supple economy of action, its elegant sequent silhouettes, the physical and moral eloquence in its economical dialogue are determined by weight of weapon, legal limitation of a vulnerable target area, and the metamorphosis of symbolic murder into sport. It is beautiful to watch, but its spectacle is secondary.

5.

6.

Athletes are competitors in public or private games. Their aim is to win according to established rules. They run or jump, not only against others, but against the cumulative performance of past record-breakers. Training is long, hard, and logically specialized for particular contests; disciplines devoted to breaking records often result in professional deformation. Sport is riveting to watch, although not primarily designed as spectacle, and an Olympic athlete may, incidentally, possess grace of body in addition to muscular supremacy. Yet, however extreme an expenditure of moral or physical energy, sport's limits in total legibility for a spectator are rigid, restricted, and repetitive.

2.

387.

To make war may be an art; if so, generals can be choreographers. Describing Waterloo, Wellington said, "The history of battle is not unlike the history of a ball." Certain tactics, strategy, and the maneuvering of bodies in mass have discernible patterns. Sport, in its strictness, measure, and morality, is closer to dance, but finally it expresses itself fully only in moments of crisis. Dancers may be seen as absolute athletes or acrobats who are also fitted to express designed emo-

99.

100.

---

7. "Line of Beauty."

* Numbers in the margins refer to relevant illustrations.

tion in climates of extreme motion. This extra dimension permits them to be ranked as artists. Soldiers and athletes, using artful skills, are not, exactly, artists.

The dancer, then, is an expressive as well as a physical performer. Certain exercises enable him, as specialist, to whet his instrument and craft, body and idiom. With lovely logic his schooling has developed over four hundred years. His academy teaches positions and steps, then their combination, moving from static placements to the kinetic and dynamic. The criterion is three-dimensional plasticity; governing principles are directed toward rendering an active spectacle legible to a passive audience.

In atomic war, the individual soldier's art is vestigial. In foot races, competing bodies reach physiological limits; climaxes are confused, needing a camera eye for ajudication. In theatrical dancing, since its stuff is the human body moving in space, measured by music and ordered by a ballet master's imagination, possibilities are still unlimited; figurations borrowed from combat or competition can be combined for continual poetic or metaphysical analysis and pleasure.

Instruction

The basis for such possibility is formal and fixed. It depends on the dancer's traditional language, which is inlaid in an alphabet of movement taught in much the same daily, weekly, and annual order in classrooms the world over. Training in body mechanics has been forged into a system of practice exercises based on absolute standards of theatrical legibility. The daily lesson, lasting an hour and a half, is not a rehearsal, but a training session, identical in progression for both beginners and accomplished professionals. It commences slowly, with the body supported by a bar, permitting canonical correctness impossible without this aid. Later, students are released into the hall for center practice. Slow movements are followed by faster (adagio to allegro). The lesson ends with practice in toe shoes for girls and aerial action for boys. Mirrors aid in diagnosis of error, but native narcissism forgives much. The teacher is the ultimate criterion, or rather, masters chosen by individual dancers as their preferred judges guide the aspirant's necessary self-fascination.

At no stage in this instruction is there room for improvisation, experiment, or doubt. Practice is comparable to finger exercises for violin, flute, or piano, but extends to the entire body. At the start, the sole aim is correctness. Only after degrees of facility lead to virtuosity may aspirants be permitted that restricted freedom in which shadings of personal conviction are determined.

The pupil grasps the bar. Before moving, one must stand well. Pelvis is centered, neither tipped back nor forward. Abdomen is drawn in, diaphragm raised. Shoulders drop naturally; head is straight, eyes front. Arms are carried downward, rounded from shoulders to finger tips. The desired "turn-out," in which, with heels together, the feet are spread to form an angle of 180 degrees, supporting the erect upper body, is only slowly gained. Muscles eventually accommodate it without strain, but this is neither a swift nor easy process. However, the turn-out offers maximum base and support for any ensuing movement; it is the bedrock of ballet style and practice.

Each exercise is planned to prepare one part of the body for ultimate virtuoso requirements. The deep bend (plié) stretches the Achilles' tendon; pointing with leg extended, knee straight (battement tendu), stretches the foot; the high kick (grand battement) frees the entire leg from the hips. These exercises are repeated often, usually in four directions in units of eight—front, side, back, and side. Dancers are trained to be completely ambidextrous. Lessons liberate the body from instinctive muscular habit. In its stoic simplicity, daily schooling, as spectacle, possesses the lean elegance of a well laid-out palette, colors freshly squeezed, or a perfectly controlled chromatic scale fingered on the piano.

13.

Five positions of feet and arms support the subsequent academic vocabulary. All traditional schooled action starts and stops with these positions, which have their subliminal logic in the carrying of torso by legs and feet, and in initiating movement for every key hinge in the body. Starting with the five positions in succession, practice at the bar commences with half-bends (demi-pliés), slow continuous lowering and straightening of the knees, followed by the deeper full bends (grands pliés), in which the heels leave the ground. Arms coordinate in large sweeps with the deeply sinking and fully rising body. Port de bras, or carriage of the arms, frames the body as, next, it dips forward and back. A large family of elementary "beats" (battements tendus simples, battements jetés, petits battements, frappés, soutenus) forms the substructure for smaller movements of the feet that, when mastered, permit the further fractioning into sharp and rapid movements later required for acrobatic brilliance in turns and jumps.

21.

When the class shifts onto the open floor, exercises from the bar—but now without its help—are repeated and developed. Movement progresses off the floor into the air, as the separate male or female specialties are accentuated. (Men do not dance on toe; girls do not jump very high.) Girls, on toe-point, move almost imperceptibly in feathery runs (pas de bourrée). Boys

23.

20.

8. 9.

10. 11.

8. Dancer. Asia Minor, c. 150 B.C.

9. Dancer. Florence, 1485–86.

10. Dancer. Paris, c. 1760.

11. Dancer. 20th century.

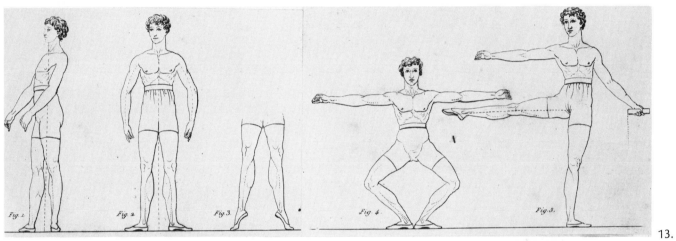

12. Social dance positions. France, 1725.

13. Ballet positions. Italy, 1820.

14. Mercury. Italy, c. 1590.

15. *Attitude*. London, 1830.

16. Dancer. Italy, c. 1806–9.

18.

17.

19.

20.

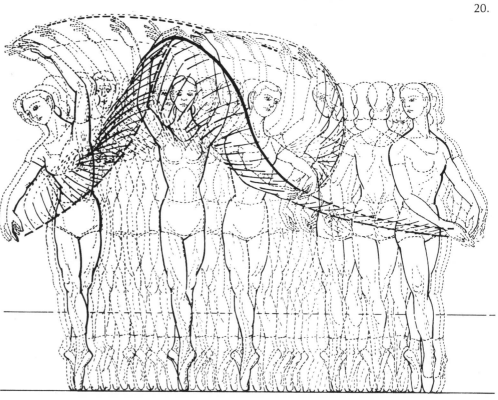

17. Toe dance. Netherlands, 1812.

18. Ballet skirts. France and England, 1838.

19. Toe shoe, c. 1916.

20. *Pas de bourrée.*

22.

21.

23.

21. Dancing school. France, c. 1580.

22. Ballet master. Denmark, c. 1840.

23. Ballet school. New York, c. 1916.

start to execute multiple turns (*pirouettes*) and broad leaps (*grands jetés*). *Petite batterie,* or small jumps with beats (*changements de pieds, royales, brisés*), in which feet, held close together, change neatly and briskly, inches off the ground, lead to *entrechats,* the familiar interlacing beats that, when multiplied, are the spectacular trademarks of male dancers.

Schools

Beginning in the mid-nineteenth century, a very few ballet schools—notably the Russian—shared security and prestige equal to other national-service academies. Russian state pupils were uniformed; on their collars naval cadets wore anchors; army students crossed sabers; aspiring dancers (and musicians) Apollo's lyre. The Soviets continue an imperial tradition in which tsars maintained ballet out of their privy purse at the cost of some two million dollars yearly by the end of the last century. Russian students, up to the First World War, felt that they were included within the aura of an imperial household; in Moscow today the official prestige of ballet still surpasses opera or drama. The Russian situation, deriving from Louis XIV's initial patronage, is now widely approximated in Eastern Europe. In London and Copenhagen royal ballet companies keep their own schools, secured by national support, while enjoying a symbolic connection with what is still numinous in crown charters. In the United States, on a far less official or secure level, schools back civic companies with community funds and foundation grants.

The quality of schools determines companies. Retired dancers enrich the teaching force. There are two types of teacher: instructors by analysis and models through example; it is unusual to find a patient analyst and a brilliant stylist in the same body. In America, and England also, due to historic circumstance of academic deprivation, many self-taught teachers without stage experience or contact with a professional company set themselves up as instructors. Their practice is not only incorrect and useless, but dangerous. Too early promotion to *pointe*-work for instance, may be permanently damaging. If a child wishes to become professional, he should start with lessons at least once a week by the age of nine. Within five years classes should be daily, and by fifteen a promising pupil has eyes on connection with a company. Dancers perform well into their fifties, and teach brilliantly into their seventies; they are notoriously long-lived.

Not every child who wishes to may become a dancer. Cruel physical jokes are played on many bodies in adolescence; dwarfs and giants are equally impractical as performers. More importantly, there is the question of temperament. Ballet dancers are a self-chosen elite. To survive and surmount years of disciplinary preparation and seasons of even more arduous performance requires rigid determination and almost mindless self-abnegation. One other factor is difficult to predetermine: without a certain admixture of hysteria—sometimes masking as self-obsession, sometimes even counterfeiting incipient madness—performers, at once acrobats, artists, and animals, make little public impression.

Increasingly, however, what pleases our audience is repertory—illuminated, to be sure, by well-trained dancers. This depends more on choreography than personalities, since repertories are molded by ballet masters, not by stars. Today the quality of repertory marks the institution. Stars are replaceable by emergent students; choreography, in repetition, persists.

Choreography

The problem of arranging dances may be seen at its simplest level in composing exercises for daily class: the teacher puts together a series of steps from the academic vocabulary, not for beauty, but to strengthen a particular muscular response. On a more sophisticated level, the dancing master creates new positions and steps from the classroom dictionary and arranges them in a grammatical sequence governed by the metric and physical dynamics of his chosen music, which usually has a marked rhythm and overmastering melody.

The single-focus, relatively simple solo dance, or variation, can be redesigned for two complementary figures, thus becoming a *pas de deux* and introducing contrasts inherent in a male-female partnership. Traditionally, the man supports or lifts his partner at emphatic or accented moments. He raises her in a broad trajectory, enabling her to give an impression of height and balance she could not attain alone. If he is an able partner, he unobtrusively enhances her presence; as a personality he disappears. In a more complex arrangement, the *pas de deux* may be framed by a group of dancers, or *corps de ballet,* whose members dance in unison or contrapuntally, undifferentiated as personalities. Visibility, or legible plasticity, must be maintained, however numerous the *corps* or complex its maneuvers. The contrast in movement that soloists provide against a *corps* engages an additional plastic richness.

In the beginning, in sixteenth-century court entries and masquerades, pattern was largely planimetric. An ideal spectator would have been a bird looking down on an open plaza, where cavaliers guided their mounts through knotty designs. On ballroom floors, dancing masters might form the initials of the princes they were paid to praise, or make danced ciphers that were rebus or riddle flattering the virtues of their patrons. Pattern was backed by metaphysics. The ancient metaphor of the labyrinth applied to ravelled and unravelling choreography; knot-figures held their science of morality and could be read as riddles and emblems. The nine muses, for example, had each her knot.*

261.

62.

29.

87.

42.

103.

---

* See Edgar Wind, *Giorgione's "Tempesta"* (London, 1969), p. 29, for an ingenious exercise in iconographical history and method.

Often the audience sat on three or even four sides of the floor, looking down from above onto a *parterre*, which was, in reality, a background. Later, scenery was set out in dispersed permanent or movable pieces. The stage still had no central focus or framing proscenium.

When proscenia became permanent (by 1640), the audience was shifted to one end of the house, its seats now more or less level with the performing area, and planimetric formulas gave way to stereometric patterns in depth. Dancers were seen, not as from above, but head-on, and, later, with raked (slanted) stages, from slightly below. Choreographers still started with a floor plan, but their frontal compositions, like high reliefs in sculpture, were what the public saw first.

While an indispensable factor in the development of choreography, apart from dancers' augmented technique, was orchestra and instrumentation, promulgation of aesthetics in the visual arts had strong effects. If we generalize about pattern governing group dances in the late sixteenth and early seventeenth century, we may risk that they were four-sided: symmetrical or quadrilateral. From engravings we deduce that when the *corps de ballet* was broken up, it fragmented into smaller, similar figures—squares and diamonds—usually balanced and roughly equal. There were transitional formations, forming V's, A's, K's, S's, and Z's; the aim seems to have been to keep the stage filled with busy, evenly modulated movement, in figurations not unlike statuary lining a formal promenade. By the mid-seventeenth century, the quadrilaterals were replaced by long curves and increased bilateral transverse asymmetry.

But by the first quarter of the eighteenth century, no ideal canon, no single criterion, no absolute taste in dance existed, as it did in the other plastic arts. However, the writings of the painter William Hogarth (apologist of the academic Baroque aesthetic in his prose if not in his pictures) undeniably affected the new *ballet d'action*, or dramatic ballet, as choreographed and staged by the important international ballet master and reformer Jean Georges Noverre (1727–1810) and his colleagues in Lyons, Stuttgart, Vienna, Milan, London, Paris, and Petersburg. (Although one cannot posit much evidence for the direct influence of Hogarth's writing on Noverre, his ideas were probably transmitted through the English actor David Garrick, of whom Hogarth painted an intimate portrait with his wife, a dance pupil of Franz Hilferding van Wewen, Noverre's predecessor. Garrick was Noverre's impresario during his London days, and his permanent model for theatrical deportment.)

Formulas based on fanciful interpretations or resurrections of antiquity were already outworn; now Hogarth,

synthesizing the thought and practice of Italian painters, presented a new plastic philosophy. In *The Analysis of Beauty* (1753) he demonstrated the curve as governing desirable structures. This curve should not be complex or overcharged, doubled like an S (as in Rubens), but open, simple, like a C (as in the curvilinear forms of Sir Christopher Wren's architectural detail). He proposed a two-dimensional serpentine "line of beauty" and, as though coiled around a cone, a three-dimensional "line of grace." This, "by its waving and winding at the same time different ways, leads the eye in a pleasing manner along the continuity of its variety."

"Serpentine" was a word also applied to elements in the informal, or "natural" English garden; compare the strict symmetry, the static choreography of Le Nôtre's gardens at Versailles with the pruned freedom of the *Englischer Garten* in Munich. The curve of Hogarth's "line of beauty," its canonization in sinuous variations, and its surprising supple turns and twisty spirals attacked the former rectilinear standard. The revolution from formal, preconceived arrangements to realistic observation and detail in naturalistic painting, of which Hogarth was a commander, "hated straight lines"; there were *no* straight lines in nature. Hogarth established a humane explanation for human variety, or, as he called it, "composed variety": "Though in nature's work the line of beauty is often neglected, or mixt with *plain* lines, yet so far are they from being defective on this account that by this means there is exhibited that infinite variety of human form, which always distinguishes the hand of nature from the limited and insufficient one of art."

Dancing masters for court ballets until the eighteenth century had an abstract ideal of plastic perfection: late Greek or Roman sculpture. Their dancers aspired toward monumental plasticity, which was perforce static; dressed as they were and commanding but a rudimentary accuracy, they did not—or could not—move much or fast. A century later, choreographers for *ballets d'action* had at their disposal dancers of considerable virtuosity with an enlarged idiom. They moved to music monumentally still, but with admixtures of mimicry and expressive posture that reflected human habit rather than some established carved, cast, or conceptual ideal. This geometrical proliferation from right angles to curves, circles, and spirals was increasingly reflected also in the fragmented composition of orchestration as projected from Lully through Rameau, to Gluck, Weber, Wagner, Delibes, Debussy, and Stravinsky.

In the nineteenth century, mathematical divisions in the *corps de ballet* were increasingly diversified. In Paul Taglioni's drawings for *Le Diable à Quatre* (Berlin, 1861), we find long transverse formations—asym-

7.

430.

5.

29.

24.

25.

26.

24. Social dance (allemande). Germany, 1768.

25. Ballroom dance. France, 1763.

26. Staged dance. France, c. 1780.

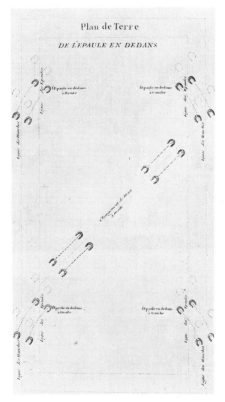

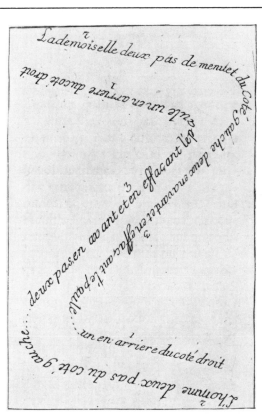

27. 28.

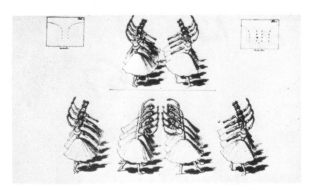

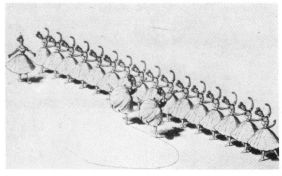

29. 30.

31. 32.

27. Horse choreography. France, 1753.

28. Social dance choreography. France, 1725.

29–32. Ballet choreography. France and Germany, c. 1860.

33. 34.

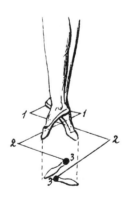
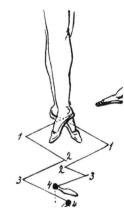

35. 36.

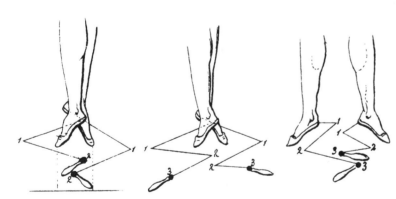

37.

33. *Entrechat.* Italy, c. 1603.

34. *Entrechat.* Italy, 1634.

35. *Entrechat.* Germany, 1716.

36. *Entrechat.* Germany, 1717.

37. *Entrechat.* Germany, 1887.

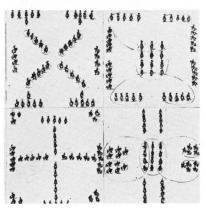

38. Gentlemanly arts. Germany, 1742.

39. Riding academy. Vienna, 1729.

40. Horse ballet. Italy, 1652.

41. Court ballet. France, 1617.

42. Court ballet. Italy, 1637.

metrical, interrupted—together with familiar quartered figures—adaptations of patterns at least four decades old. Of course, such designs never map the whole pattern; they are only signposts, with bridging sequences omitted.

In the twentieth century, fragmentation of the *corps de ballet* becomes unlimited. We now imagine pattern as mosaic in depth rather than as high relief or linear geometry. Iron filings pulled toward an invisible magnet, ice fronds on a windowpane, particles in an atomic chamber propose themselves as underlying structure, since our informed vision (and hearing) has been extended by radical metrics—telescope, microscope, and electronics—past all visual imaginings and hearings of our ancestors. Armatures of movement in action may be reduced to diagrams, but when actually seen in several theatrical dimensions, they are as severely variable as an asymmetrical kaleidoscope. Ballet masters can extract their primary elements from toys, games, or sport and through them make personal, magical anagrams.

Let us distinguish here between choreographers and ballet masters. Such nomenclature is hardly binding; terms overlap, but a distinction between respective services can be almost precise. All fifty ballets further noted herein may be labeled the work of ballet *masters*. Choreographers put steps together from a syntax they receive; from this, they compose rather than invent dances. Such dances may be linked together to form ballets. Choreographers are simple carpenters; ballet masters are cabinetmakers; some of them—the most gifted—sculptors. Ballet masters have the capacity to conceive unusual or novel movement beyond the range of the academy. Not only do they increase repertories with memorable work, but they also extend the academic idiom by new orientations and analyses. Every author of the ballets further mentioned, at least commencing with the mid-eighteenth century, was, to some degree, an innovator. For every one such, there were some fifty others working in a vernacular, from Stockholm to Naples, Lyons to Warsaw, using a practical vocabulary with more or less grace. They took what was given them, providing much pleasure from many capable performances. They still do. Efficient, attractive, unmemorable, their combined steps served a purpose and can be constantly recomposed for needs of opera houses or dancers.

Choreography by a ballet master is characterized by those personal traits that transcend, subvert, or overturn the academy, although these magicians or revolutionists act only through a mastery of an academic language that must be digested to be rejected. Ballet masters are also administrators and teachers; otherwise their work would never be staged. When new movements are proposed, it is likely they go against the grain of school correctness. Schools exist to be violated. They survive dent, bruise, and fracture simply because their consequent and cumulative system has its fatal and final logic on which to build, not composition, not choreography, but trained bodies that will encompass any and every familiar or unfamiliar action whenever needed.

With an increased rising to half-toe (*demi pointe*) and the presupposition of toe shoes after 1815–25, a new area of movement for both male and female dancers was opened. The Romantic ballet of the 'thirties and 'forties also brought innovations in partnering. Dancers were not only upheld by partners, they leapt onto their shoulders and into their arms, as tricks long used in the circus were grafted onto school practice. Folk dances from Spain, Italy, Central Europe, and the Near East, which violated the turn-out by reversing it, adding outlandish rhythms and accents with heeled boots or bare feet, enlarged the idiom, first as a special department of opera-house practice known as character dancing, then as an integrated supplement involving expressiveness beyond mere divertissement. Ballet masters had long been quick to expropriate any hint of new movement from exotic dances, increasingly glimpsed at international exhibitions after 1850, and from virtuoso entertainers in street fairs, music halls, vaudeville houses, and, later, night clubs and films.

17.

312.

46.

424.

In the twentieth century, the half-dozen ballet masters responsible for our present international repertory have been susceptible to unprecedented influence outside their inherited traditional vocabulary. The most resilient of them have been equipped to digest these immediately. Early in our century, Isadora Duncan (1878–1927), an unschooled primitive with keen musical instinct and a supremely permissive crusading philosophy, which amalgamated Plato, Whitman, Wagner, Nietzsche, and Gordon Craig, proclaimed, and to a degree demonstrated, a license in movement (but more particularly in music and costume) that revitalized decadent or atrophied opera-house dancing. Her personality rather than her technique or teaching announced new directions, but a solid basis for reform within the academy had already been sounded by Michel Fokine (1880–1942). While painting, sculpture, architecture, poetry, and music had benefited by the Romantic revolution, ballet existed as a contained province, little affected by progressive music or painting. Not until Serge Diaghilev (1872–1929) composed his repertory for export to Paris before the First World War did autonomous choreography enjoy some parity with the other plastic arts.

349.

388.

Since then, the academy persists, strengthened and in many cases (notably in the United States and Great Britain, but also in Holland, Germany, and Canada) institutionalized and made fruitful where little was before. Choreographers exist, as they always have, in some supply. Ballet masters, as always, are rare. Innovations made in the last thirty years have depended primarily not on the inspiration of poetry (as in the nineteenth century), or on painting (as in the first third of the twentieth), but on music. Extraordinary activity in the aural area commencing with Debussy and Stravinsky and more recently involving Schönberg, Berg, Webern, Ives, Copland, Britten, and Xenakis, has forced or inspired ballet masters to extremes unconsidered before them, impossible to conceive without them.

Choreography, at least in independent, progressive ballet companies, is a far less collaborative art than was projected fifty years ago. It was then anticipated that Richard Wagner's proposed comprehensive artwork would be achieved by equal contributions from librettist, composer, decorator, and choreographer. What happened was that first musicians dominated (Debussy, Stravinsky, Satie, Prokofiev), then painters (Picasso, Braque, Juan Gris, Max Ernst). But increasingly, after the death of Diaghilev (1929), the autonomy of choreography emerged; today, ballet masters are in charge, not impresarios. Painting has assumed its traditional secondary role; painters have tossed in every gadget and gimmick including Pop and Op, but their support for choreography has not been impressive. They wish to compete with choreographers and defeat ballet masters. Few succeed. In music, however, recent developments in advanced structuring or non-structures, electronic music, and computerized sonorities, with elements of probability or chance as suggestive bases, are beginning to be reflected in ballet, although the results often are less impressive on stage than in the pit.

So, at the end of four centuries, after ambiguous partnerships with the operatic establishment, choreography today is recognized as independent, capable of being molded, in the hands of ballet masters, into masterwork. The classic dance is a language, and ballets are its constructs, comparable to others formed in other idioms. The battle picture, still life, landscape; the comedy of manners, heroic tragedy; the novel of society or psychological observation create worlds based on tradition, observation, and craft. The universe projected by ballet in its brief temporal duration draws on analogous sources and is capable of maintaining similar metaphors.

Ballet is conservative. While it has organized a fluent flexible language, there are psychological, indeed physiological, limitations, which those who are attracted to it gratefully accept. *Haute école* riding—dressage by the Viennese Hochreitschule—is not a vestigial reminder of the Baroque; it is a present and immediate

monumental activity in Baroque's liveliest style. Olympic fencing, Spanish bullfighting, Japanese *sumo*, *kendo*, other ritual martial sports, and the Noh itself are more than survivals; they are extant exemplars. Thus, the ballet, which has been quite unaffected by social eruptions—political, religious, or technological—and has survived the French Revolution of 1789, European revolts of 1848, and the Russian Revolutions of 1905 and 1917 as a court style, is, in essence, untouched. Idiosyncratic innovators outside academic discipline, from Isadora Duncan to Mary Wigman, Martha Graham, and their epigones, have had fringe effects far weaker than the impact of parallel developments in music or the lyric imagination. W. H. Auden says of opera in *Secondary Worlds* (1968): "To possess the vocal cords which can make sounds which other people want to listen to is a gift granted to very few. Singing, like classical ballet dancing, is a virtuoso art. A virtuoso art can be tragic or comic, but it has only one style, the high style; a low or humble style and virtuosity are incompatible." Further, what Auden writes of *verismo* opera is also true of naturalistic ballet, a genre attempted only when classic dancing is impoverished or choreography incompetent, and which has left few traces in repertory: "The so-called *verismo* operas are simply drama in which exotic settings and characters have replaced the gods and courtesans . . . of the courtly Baroque; both are secondary worlds very far removed from the primary world of our everyday experience."

This hardly denies a continued relevance of opera and ballet, or their elevated virtuosity. On the contrary, high style, whether at the hands of a violinist, soprano, or dancer, is one of the few permanent visible signals of possible perfection in immediate human capacity. Ambitions of the dancer transcend those of soldier or athlete. Self-elected, he is trained to survive only on his own terms. If a dancer is judged, it is against performance within tradition—a tradition that provides each artist with a personal opportunity for unique coloration. Other expertise may be more popular or exacting; analysis, military or athletic, responsible for lunar conquest has a collective majesty at its base, star performance only at its peak. But the excitement inherent in the moving human body, untouched by any mechanism save its own perfected anatomy, nervous system, and personal grace, released in legible plasticity on opera-house stages, is still an incomparable metaphor of humane possibility, mastered by mind and muscle, schooled by history, reincarnated in styles and visions of a hundred generations of repertories.

43.
44.

45.
46.

43. Peasant dance. Northern Europe, c. 1500.

44. Social dance. England, 1753.

45. Balleticized folk dance. Italy, c. 1855.

46. Balleticized folk dance. France, 1861.

47. 48.

49.
50.

47. *Pas de deux*. Germany, 1790.

48. *Pas de deux*. Vienna, 1823.

49. *Pas de deux*. France, 1841.

50. Acrobatic adagio. France, 1843.

GESTURE AND MIME

51.

From around 1700, as ballet began to separate from song, projecting choreography toward its autonomy, need grew for a rationale of gesture that would make sequences of mute dramatic action more comprehensible. When court ballet ceased being masquerade, divertissement, or interlude and began to aim at an heroic potential for itself, links were needed to connect danced portions with narrative explication. Danced steps already had their nomenclature; thus they could be repeated and taught with some exactness. Attempts to codify gesture in a similar manner resulted in handbooks that structured bodily signals, but since these descriptions were based neither on floor plans nor musical notation, considerable allowance had to be made for interpretation. Forms of gesture can hardly be equated with the precision of steps: mimicry is general, loose, unstable; academic dancing arbitrary, strict, and firm. However, by 1750, elementary conventions were fixed, serving ballet pantomime until about 1900. In addition to the accretions of theatrical tradition for professional mimicry, the language was enriched by borrowings from museums, spoken drama, amateur innovators. Practice exercises often originated as theoretical instruction for orators, preachers, actors, and singers.

In the Middle Ages, Rhetoric, third of the Liberal Arts, with an academic tradition extending back to Cicero's and Quintilian's essays on oratory, taught skill in using persuasive language, determining eloquent speech as well as writing. In addition to mouthed words, it

included the body's mute language; elocution was analyzed for bodily as well as vocal declamation. Quintilian claimed the eye stronger than the ear; Cicero that the eloquence of the body entire can be as convincing as words. "Histrionical rhetoric" was described by the German writer and physician Cornelius Agrippa (1575) as "Rhetorical daunsing, not unlike that of stage players but not so vehement." Thus in attempting to define *ballet d'action* (fl. 1750–80) and *choreodramma* (fl. 1810–20), both exalters of pantomime over dance, we begin by knowing Rhetoric and Action went hand in hand.

In 1604, Thomas Wright's *Passions of the Mind* defined Action as "either a certaine visible eloquence, or an eloquence of the bodie, or a comely grace in delivering conceits, or an externall image of the internall mind. . . . Action then universally is a natural or artificial moderation, qualification, modification or composition of the voice, countenance and gesture of the bodie proceeding from some passion, and apt to stir up the like."

In 1644, John Bulwer, interested in education for the deaf and dumb, distinguished between *chirologia* and *chironomia*. The former differentiated "the Speaking Motions and Discoursing Gestures" expressing "the pathetical motions of the mind." He described sixty-four such gestures, illustrating forty-eight separate positions for arm, hand, and fingers. *Chironomia* displays the artificial uses of the hand by which natural gesture is regulated, extended, or intensified. *Dactylogia* is the dialect of fingers alone (twenty-five examples). *Actio* was apt action, "in a certaine moderation of the voice and qualification of gesture," with differing accentuation and emphasis for prose or metrical verse. *Pronuntiatio* was not only shaping the tongue, but gestural framing for the whole body. *Decorum* (and with it, an observation of models) ordered gesture for social and aesthetic consideration.

170.

Heroes, gods, kings, and soldiers acted with grandeur and smoothness. Peasants, clowns, and other low life moved awkwardly, angularly, abruptly—grotesquely. In Molière's comedy with ballet interludes, *Le Bourgeois Gentilhomme* (1670), a dancing master attempts to teach upper-class deportment to an aspiring lower middle-class boor. More subtly, town gentlemen in palaces moved otherwise than country gentry in châteaux.

59.

Naturally, hands provoked the greatest attention. Consider common parlance: close-fisted, open-handed, under-handed, light-fingered. Guilty Pilate and Lady Macbeth wring their hands as they wash them. Youths (and Italians) have emphatic hands; old men slow, waggly fingers. When masks were discarded (c. 1665–

170.

51. Tragic acting. England, 1776.

70), physiognomy joined the play: rolling eyes, curling lips, grimace, frown, and smile. Mime became a virtuoso display, comparable in its relation to pure dance as aria is to recitative in opera. A certain decorum of gesture was maintained; stage use differed from that of pulpit or rostrum. Certain movements, efficient in pantomime, were indecorous for sermon or oration. Bulwer wrote: "The trembling hand is scenicall, and belongs more to theater than to forum. . . . To strike the breast with the hand is scenicall."

The English were particularly disposed toward rationalizing pantomime. John Weaver (1673–1760), dancing master and author of several excellent studies, will be mentioned further concerning his *Loves of Mars and Venus;* in 1712, his *Essay Towards an History of Dancing* organized available information that pertained specifically to theatrical as opposed to social dancing. He understood anatomy, body mechanics, and facial expression: "The Face may not improperly be term'd the Image of the Soul; Anger and Scorn are seated in the Brow; the Eyes express the Sentiments of the Heart; and every Passion of the Mind is discover'd in the Countenance." English criteria were established by actors rather than dancers; moreover, the influence of English dramatic acting affected European ballet chiefly through French and German dancers. However, no national British school for instruction developed when everything seemed just ripe for it, comparable to academies of dance and song on the Continent.

In Lully's operas, there was music accompanying not only dance passages, but those that were purely mime. Such *jeux-muets* were arranged by the Abbé Olivet, a specialist for very young dancers innocent of a rigid style of heroic operatic convention. In Paris, at the St. Laurent and St. Germain fairs, *pièces à la muette,* solo virtuoso numbers, framed pantomime as separate from danced portions. In 1719, the Abbé Dubois' *Critical Reflections on Poetry and Painting* declared ballet was not solely leg exercises, but the aesthetic and physical equal of spoken drama, opera, and dance. Each theatrically expressive passion was endowed with its specific gesture, facial expression, and, in vocal drama, even its own pitch. He warned against blind dependence on antique precedent; the old Roman *saltatio,* which bracketed dance to pantomime, had no contact with present needs. At first the Romans had been read for limited empirical requirements and for borrowing prestige by association with legitimate precedent. But it was impossible to interpret the texts that were unaccompanied by pictures. Gesture cannot be sprung by formula; it depends on an individual player's emotion. Also, "action surpasses pictorial art; models of feeling cannot be found in paint or marble."

In the eighteenth century there was a growing search for a richer mimic style; as more interest was manifest in dancing with stronger drama, ballet masters looked to the Comédie Française, where, after the resounding, crystalline classicism of Corneille and Racine, a new repertory was initiated by Voltaire (beginning with *Mérope,* his first success, 1743). The pace of his metric seemed more rapid, his style less lapidary than that of his canonized predecessors. He sounded more a part of the present. Similarly, still acknowledging ancient precedent, ballet masters sought new justifications in old forms, exploring the musical aspects of Greek tragedy and developing increased mobility in dumb show. Reforms in costume (1735–50)—shortened skirts, lighter materials, easier shoes—slight as they seem to us, somewhat liberated the dancing body; reforms in management, such as the exclusion of spectators from the stage itself (1759), gave more space for movement. In drama, the actor-producer Lekain (Henri-Louis Kain) introduced incidental music into tragedy; he had already developed a new picturesque, or quasi-expressionist, style of formal exaggeration. His sustained poses —artfully designed profiles—were widely imitated. His colleagues, the actresses Clairon and Dumesnil, carefully detailed pantomime, which had become perfunctory, by psychological richness in observation, smaller movements, and greater fragmented detail. Garrick, the greatest English actor of his epoch, had considerable direct influence on the development of dramatic continuity in dance. Noverre, chief persuader for the *ballet d'action,* who had worked for him, admitted his own ballets had merit only after he saw Garrick, who visited Paris (1764–65) and impressed the French theatrical profession in private demonstration.

In spite of successive published theories, the progressive enlargement and codification of pantomime as a demi-science, and studies in physiognomical anatomy (these were little undertaken until masks were abandoned), there were few academies where fixed methods were taught. One of these was the acting school organized in 1588 by the Spanish dramatist Lope de Vega; then, around 1610, the learned landgrave Maurice of Hesse hired English players to instruct his students. In 1770, the ballet school in Stuttgart taught young dancers acting as well as music. But what little mime technique most dancers acquired they picked up from dramatic theaters or book illustrations, such as the royal painter Charles Le Brun's *Method of Delineating the Passions* (1667), a series of handsome engravings of the swollen extremities of rage, grief, and joy, legible from the proscenium arch as from the frescoed ceilings. The Dutch, who supported important theaters, provided a number of manuals not alone in play-house engineering but in patterns of body mechanics. In the painter Gérard de Lairesse's encyclopedic *Groot Schilderboek* ("Master Book of Painters," 1707), peasants fumble mugs while gentry sip their wine. In 1727, a brilliant catalogue of Jesuit techniques appeared in

64.

163.

230.

53.

Father Franciscus Lang's *Dissertation on Scenic Action*. He advised avoidance of conventional histrionics, since professionals—preachers as well as stage artists—were already deformed by habit. One should go observantly to the heart of nature. Gestures of command were described down to the imperious index finger.

The development of science aided the craft of gesture and physiognomy. Articles in Diderot's *Encyclopedia* leaned heavily on Buffon, the naturalist, who noted that of all the animals man alone gesticulates, although higher apes approximate him. The Swiss Lavater produced a massive study on physiognomy (1772–83), followed by the work of Sir Charles Bell, an anatomist. The classic book remains Charles Darwin's *Expression of Emotion in Men and Animals* (1872).

While a rationale of stagecraft in the era of the Encyclopedists would nominally favor naturalism, nature was still artifice; to most stage producers, the so-called natural, which was actually an ideal nature, could be found sooner in the Louvre than in a tavern. In *Paradoxe sur les Comédiens* (c. 1778) Diderot wrote that the stage should be considered a framed picture; its inhabitants tastefully composed a unique theatrical reality larger than life—a superrealism of expressively enhanced action. He particularly admired psychological descriptions in Richardson's novels and the picturesque sentiment in paintings by Greuze. Voltaire, however, alarmed by the direction that his reaction against the verbal dramatic tradition had taken, wrote that four fine verses with feelings were worth forty lovely attitudes on stage. The ballet master and dance historian Louis de Cahusac's *Ancient and Modern Dancing* (1754) demanded more characterization in the form of the *pas héroïque*, the danced and mimed self-description of godlike characters rooted in the spirit of the Baroque. He pleaded for a *danse d'action* of separate significant movements rather than canonical steps. He proposed that the vitality inherent in *la danse comique* would intensify serious dancing if properly appropriated. The term "pantomime" as a stage direction appears often in Rameau's scores after 1750, due in part to the innovations of Noverre, who was influenced by Cahusac and who tried to enliven opera-ballet with more expressive pantomimic action. There was general impatience with the academic dance and its routine choreography, mechanically executed; this Noverre's new *ballet d'action* ostensibly would redeem.

Almost as important as direct or indirect influence of aestheticians or actors on well-educated ballet masters had been the live tradition of pantomiming actors, dancers, and acrobats descended from the seventeenth-century Italian improvisors of the *commedia dell'arte* ("comedy of skill"). Their total effect on the *danse d'école* is difficult to establish exactly. By their spontaneity they fertilized dancing by spirit and example more than by fixed method. The comedians contributed new acrobatic techniques—lifts, holds, jumps—a widening and freeing of gesture, alacrity, and vitality, although their contributions were consistently denied by masters upholding the dignity of dance as a craft whose independent authority had only just been gained. (Garrick was criticized for too much playing Harlequin, or, in other words, for adopting too many Italianate gestures). But it is clear that while actors of the Comédie furnished models for tragic mimicry, virtuosos of the *commedia* enriched comic dumb show. From the start of the sixteenth century, local individualized stock characters had put on the grotesque masks of Pantaloon, the Venetian merchant; the old Doctor from Bologna; Pulcinella from Naples; Harlequin from Bergamo. These were universalized into stereotypes throughout Europe. In dancing they continued that thrusting, angular, provocative, sensual, outrageous movement of the medieval moresque (the lively grotesque dance executed to vocal accompaniment). The comedians performed on semi-temporary stages in open fairs, far from palaces of ballet and opera. Before the start of the seventeenth century, they lent their personages, half-masks, tight costumes, and loose tricks to interludes in court ballet. Since their system was improvisatory, based on assigned scenarios and a repertory of carefully rehearsed physical repartee, their performance was personal, and it is unlikely that court dancers used much more than the skin of their style.

But their presence was impossible to ignore. In the next century, from 1740 to 1750, there was a veritable mania for pantomime in Paris. A famous Italian star, Luigi Riccoboni, played at the Théâtre Italien; English companies appeared at the St. Laurent and St. Germain fairs. While mute narrative gesture was allocated to both tragic and comic styles, physical virtuosity was naturally identified with comic alacrity, due in large part to the practice of Italian or Italianate professionals. Divine grace, regal majesty, and military authority were neither as supple nor humane as that ferocious rapid fragmentation of gesture that mocked such noble attitudes by overt obscenity or abrupt somersaults, techniques reaching back to the ancient origins of theater. Molière adored the comedians; they spoke his words, danced his divertissements. They grew so overweening from success that they drew the wrath of Madame de Maintenon; in a famous political incident involving presumed libel, they were put out of Paris, and France was deprived for years. We find them in Watteau's paintings, as he imagined them in exile, wistful and pert, touched with a faintly tragic aura, lurking in languid exasperation and suppressed hysterical irony. Restrictions on their speech and song, enforced by jealous official singers and dancers, and their ensuing lack of legal license gave them their mute rebellious manner. They persisted in a cultural underground well into the next century as monitors of the bad conscience of an

177.

61.

174.

59.

60.

148.

186.

academic correctness and legitimacy that they always mocked.

Despite the occasional theatrical philosopher and philosophizing dancing master, the observation of natural man was not generally useful to the operatic bureaucracy. Throughout the Renaissance and well past the Baroque, difference was drawn between *istoria*—not the historical process, but the selective depiction of elevated, didactic themes from antiquity or the Bible—and genre—views of low life as exemplified in Dutch and Flemish minor masters for comic vulgarity. While the brothers Le Nain in the seventeenth and Chardin in the eighteenth century painted pathos and dignity in poverty, a more common strain, with the bawdy peasant as protagonist, derived from the works of Jan Steen, Adriaen van Ostade, Adriaen Brouwer, and David Teniers.

As for gesture, Rococo practice was lighter, more balletic than Baroque. Index fingers were no longer imperiously pointed, but provocatively, delicately crooked. Hogarth, theoretician as well as master painter, advised actors to move their hands so beautifully in all directions that graceful movements would be natural to their arms. Salons, not throne rooms, provided the models of manners for theater. Intimately observant of drama, in the streets as well as on stage, Hogarth wrote in his *Analysis of Beauty* that the comic is *essentially* expressive. His observations of the English cousin of the Italian Arlecchino tell us something of how Harlequin and his companions danced:

"The attitudes of the harlequin are ingeniously composed of certain little, quick movements of the head, hands and feet, some of which shoot out as it were from the body in straight lines, or are twirled about in little circles.

"Scaramouch is gravely absurd as the character is intended, in over-stretch'd tedious movements of unnatural length of lines. Pierrot's movements and attitudes are chiefly in perpendiculars and parallels, so is his figure and dress.

"Punchinello is droll, he being the reverse of all elegance. . . . His limbs are raised and let fall almost together at one time, in parallel directions, as if his seeming fewer joints than ordinary, were no better than the hinges of a door."

In our day, ballet, while based as always on an academy, is so free in pattern as to be entirely eclectic. With us, any gesture, spasmic to elegant, prompted from gut or head, is equally commanding; no rigid forms frame movement. This was not true until Michel Fokine's reforms started over fifty years ago. In the eighteenth century, ballet, while it aroused a middle-class audience, was still conceived in a court atmosphere. In spite of innovators or propagandists for pan-

tomime-oriented ballet—Jean-Baptiste de Hesse (1705–59), Franz Hilferding van Wewen (1710–68), Jean Georges Noverre, Gasparo Angiolini (1731–1803), and later, Salvatore Viganò (1769–1821)—dancing in opera houses depended on mimic manner that might seem to us restricted, mannered, overstylized. However, school steps increased in variety while retaining an inherited nomenclature, and new extremes in technique for one generation were norms for the next. Gesture remained a far less precise language. *Corps de ballet* had little need to learn much more than steps; first-dancers moved as ordered, adding a dash of idiosyncratic embellishment, but a dancing chorus was hardly asked to act.

August Wilhelm Iffland (1759–1814) may be mentioned as prototype for his epoch. He was actor, dramatist, and producer; with Iffland, as with Hogarth, curves dominated. He recommended that *port de bras* be prepared by swinging semicircular exercises. Soft, rounded arms should *never* be lowered violently, and when raised they remain still; only at phrase ends may they gracefully fall. Wrists are never bent or twisted; arms move with hands, *never* hands with arms. The whole body suggests freedom and harmony by subtle inclination of head and upper torso. Arms are *never* raised above eye-level (citing Quintilian's definition of the "normal" angle of observation). If the head is lowered, arms may seem higher when lifted than they really are. By combining multiplicity (fragmentation of motion) with simplicity (grand linear curves), one arrives at Garrick's style: what he called conventional, and what we might recognize as formal, beauty. Iffland cited the French actor La Rive in Rousseau's mimodrama *Pygmalion* (produced by Goethe, 1772), who conveyed a whole mute *tirade* or mimed aria simply by shading one significant gesture into another.

As for stage manners, France established a standard François-Joseph Talma, Napoleon's instructor and favorite, was the greatest French actor of his time, as well as a reformer of costume and an innovator in staging. He found new meanings in facial control and fluid sequences of monumental profiles; he turned his back on his audience while still speaking; he did not arrest action at the end of a long speech, waiting suggestively for his public to applaud. The French moved with measured calm on leaving the scene. Germans made exits abruptly and prolonged fixed poses, compensating by pedantic traditional correctness for what they may have lacked in expressive nobility. The Spanish style was the most flamboyant, but it approached a parody of itself. Stage manners were measured finally by French practice.

In the nineteenth century, mime was taught in ballet schools. Auguste Bournonville (1805–79), master of the

190.

229.

261.

259.

171.

195.

163.

52.

22.

52. 53.

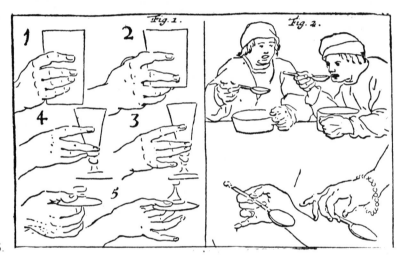 

54. 55.

56. 57. 58.

52. Gesture. Germany, 1727.

58. Gesture: Delsarte, 1889.

53, 54. Gesture. Netherlands, 1707.

55–57. Gesture. Germany, 1785.

59. 60.

61. 62.

59. Grotesque movement. Germany, 1480.

60. Grotesque movement. Italy, 1616.

61. Harlequin. England, 1753.

62. Gesture. Netherlands, 1827.

Danish ballet in its most productive era, recalled his predecessor, Vincenzo Galeotti (1733–1816), a pupil of Angiolini and Noverre:

"Galeotti had the traditional discipline of the Italian ballet, the stereotypes of whose pantomime are preserved in opera houses and popular harlequinades. It is mostly characterized by high grade rhythmic precision and kaleidoscopic symmetry. Italian pantomime has its own methods, comprising a whole vocabulary of habitual manual motions taken from the Roman and Neapolitan common folk. . . .

"Pantomime is neither dialogue nor conventional gesture, but a harmonious and rhythmic sequence of picturesque attitudes taken from nature and classic models, suitable to character, costume, nation and epoch. The sequence of postures and movement composes a type of dance, but without the turn-out (en dehors) of ballet. Its attitudes are aimed at effects of plasticity and characterization entirely apart from virtuoso academic technique."

In nineteenth-century Russian schools, then the best in the world, courses in pantomime were mandatory for seven years, followed by more specialized training in "perfection" classes. But this does not signify much; schooling was less intense then and performances less frequent. Today the relics of mimic tradition, as exemplified in the extant repertory, seem to us more like silent movies without subtitles than a plastic language with kinesthetic efficiency. An interest in what is advertised as traditional mime for its own sake vestigially exists, as with Marcel Marceau; its relation to the classic academic dancer's present use is neither lively nor necessary.

There were other exterior influences on gesture. We can imagine ballet behavior as a grammar that can be spoken only in one inherited class accent, applicable only to certain sites or occasions. With this attitude we may attempt to reconstruct the contemporary shock at new eruptions. (Today, few surprises are possible; shock has become merely evidence of various idiosyncratic styles of incompetent virtuosity). In 1768 an Indian *bayadère* (Portuguese *bailadeira*—"dancer") appeared in Paris; her name was Bebaiourn and she performed "shawl dances"; she ended up in a convent. Her arms, feet, and belly moved in ways heretofore unknown to the West. If one may generalize, occidental dance forms tend toward positions that are open or centrifugal, oriental forms closed or centripetal. Here was a new-found land of movement potential, and Bebaiourn inspired a succession of themes based on her exotic origin. In the 1780's, Emma Hart, later Lady Hamilton, Admiral Nelson's mistress, learned to arrange herself in sculptural poses while serving as model to George Romney, the painter. In translucent "antique" draperies, within a large picture frame, can-

dles behind her, she appeared in her private repertory of graceful mimo-plastic poses, engravings of which were widely published. She owed something to wall paintings uncovered at Herculaneum and Pompeii and to famous antique marbles, but Goethe, seeing her in 1787, felt she derived more from *tableaux vivants* arranged for the Neapolitan Christmas, imitating terra cotta figures of the adoration of Christ's Nativity. Her direct influence on ballet is dubious, although her looseness in dress and morals established a certain extratheatrical excitement that served as one suggestion for reformation in decadent opera-house habit.

Far more important than Emma, a century later, was Isadora Duncan. A Californian, motivated more at the outset by what she could read of Delsarte than by ideas of Greece, she cast the gravest doubts on the results of moribund academic ballet training, which was becoming more common in provincial America, where it was already an echo of the worst Franco-Italian practice. Through her, the public, or a critical part of it, became interested in the roots of dance action—in body movement—rather than in historic styles of theatrical habit. However, here, as with all else linking free gesture, expressive mimicry, and the academic dance, it is not easy to allocate debts incurred or paid. Duncan's antiacademic, idiosyncratic movement, her use of the floor to lie on as well as move on, her plasticity in uncanonical arm movements have been claimed as the seminal influence on Michel Fokine, the first important choreographer of the twentieth century. However, it is likely that his particular adaptation of freer arm movements and a loosening of the whole body was affected also by a troupe of Siamese temple and palace dancers, who had appeared in Petersburg by 1900, five years before Isadora arrived. But at the least, she was incarnate corroboration of what both he and Stanislavsky, his great colleague in theatrical reformation, knew was needed. Also, she was the right person at the right time in the right place: prerevolutionary Russia. She was a real aid, indirectly but powerfully, to Diaghilev.

Great international exhibitions began to be organized in Paris and other European capitals after 1850. Choreographers saw exotic provincial and colonial dances. They could increase authentic borrowings, since designers had gained more knowledge from scientific archeology and research in unfamiliar architectural styles. Spain and Italy had long been admired for their ancient native dances. Folk music was imported with accompanying steps and measured not only dancing but (as in the tarantella) pantomime as well. However, the problem in structuring mime was its lack of musical base; music might loosely indicate, but could not strictly control, gesture. It is significant that the two most profound analysts of theatrical gesture in the nineteenth century were primarily musicians.

69.

58.

349.

45.

François Delsarte (1811–71), a singer, lost his voice and turned to teaching, but not singers alone. He invented an elaborate anatomy of movement directed toward a discipline of the whole body in physiological (and ethical) terms. Among his pupils, apart from famous opera stars, were the actress Rachel, the tragedian Macready, and the preachers Père Hyacinthe and Lacordaire. Delsarte devised a rationale of biomechanics, but his inheritance is dubious, since he left few personal documents, and students codified his method in very unsatisfactory manuals. Isadora Duncan carried one of these in her luggage; on her early cards was printed "Professor of Delsarte." The pioneer American male dancer Ted Shawn has written a fascinating study of Delsarte's complex, sensible, if elusive proposals (*Every Little Movement*, 1910). But Delsarte's direct influence on dance hardly penetrated past Isadora's personal use of his theories.

The effect of Émile Jaques-Dalcroze (1865–1950), composer, musicologist, and educator, through the choreography of Vaslav Nijinsky (1890–1950), is indisputable historically although difficult to determine in depth. It will be analyzed further in descriptions of Nijinsky's choreography. Dalcroze proposed a mechanical translation of musical rhythm to all parts of the human body, each note corresponding to a transferred movement. His simple but very profoundly analytical gymnastics taught students to count with complete awareness of musical structure. His designs in themselves were limited, monotonous, untheatrical. He did not claim them as spectacular, but as preparation for further specialized analysis; as such they surely proved very useful to one dancer of genius, Nijinsky. The method lost wide acceptance after 1914, but George Balanchine (b. 1904) is one teacher who credits its usefulness. Delsarte and Dalcroze made the last serious contributions to a putative science of gesture of interest to ballet masters. Neither has been explored or exploited commensurate with their many suggestive insights. Today choreographers and teachers discover means for mime in their own instinctive movements, without elevating them into formal order.

In our current repertory, gesture and movement—motions of the hand and whole body, steps of the feet—are integrated so closely that one hardly determines, as in ballets by Antony Tudor (b. 1909), Sir Frederick Ashton (b. 1906), or Jerome Robbins (b. 1918), where dance starts or mime stops. Formal separated pantomime surviving in revivals of *Giselle, Coppélia,* or *Swan Lake,* are vestigial rituals approaching dim parodies of lost originals. Pointing, defensive, threatening hands and arms or wanly shaken hands sketch their perfunctory signals—obvious, hollow, unnecessary—approaching that realm of sacred silliness we dignify as camp. Alfred Jarry, pataphysician and founding father of the Theater of the Absurd, which supplants

Stanislavsky's "method" as our latest academy, wrote, before 1900, on *The Futility of the "Theatrical" in Theatre.* He recommended using masks again, full face and profile, as worn by puppets; this, long after Heinrich von Kleist's supermarionette, but before Gordon Craig's hope for puppets entirely dominated by a director:

61.

161.

"[Masks] are simply expressive; therefore, universal. Modern mime makes the huge error of employing the conventional idiom of mimicry which is boring and meaningless. As example—the hand indicating a vertical ellipse about the visage, and a kiss stuck on to it —to suggest a lovely lady plus love. An example of universal gesture is the puppet demonstrating its amazement by leaping wildly back and smacking its head against the scenery."

Models of contemporary mime, mimo-dance, or dance-drama are Fokine's *Petrouchka* (1911); the quartet of lovers in Tudor's *Lilac Garden* (1936); the duet of Dark Angel and Poet in Balanchine's *Orpheus* (1947). In each case, plastic mimicry depends on musical impulse.

369.

439.

451.

While pantomime may be designed on beat, off it, or against it, it is today woven inextricably into an overall texture of patterned metrical action, drawing no attention to itself as prose speech apart. Its expression comes from manipulating a few legible motions that have come to represent a general truth, and which, from documentation, seem to have changed little in three thousand years. Mime in ballet can no longer be considered as a separate grammar, but rather as an extension of dance movement for intermittent narrative, as opposed to virtuosic, purposes. Its basic phrases are few, its skeleton simple, but this does not limit its expressiveness. Correct usage is rarely taught in classrooms; rather, mimicry evolves in an alchemy of composition and rehearsal, when observation from life, art, and craft is rectified from ancient and inexhaustible ore to new coin.

While it is possible to summarize development in stage architecture, scenery, or theatrical dancing, it is impossible to summarize the role of music. Music is partner; floor not frame. Without orchestras over the last four centuries, ballet is unthinkable. Dances were invented before music and have been created to no music, but in few cases were the results significant. Ballet masters are grateful for rhythmic propulsion and sonorous dynamics; most capable choreographers are generally sight readers who play violin or piano. A few fortunate ones have collaborated with composers of genius who have not considered ballet less productive than opera or symphony. Of these there have been only a handful, from the time dancers first shared opera orchestras—musicians captivated by, as well as gifted for, dance as theater.

Dance forms are so various, their identical nomenclature at different times so confusing, that a lexicon is necessary to allocate precedent and practice. Just to fix origins and mutation in the dance suite from 1650 calls for a book bigger than this. With the introduction of folk forms from Central Europe, confusion is compounded: dances known as French, Spanish, Italian, and German will be found to be English, Flemish, Austrian or American. The minuet changed every generation for a century; where does one focus an epitome of the waltz?

The development of dance music may be seen as corollary to the history of orchestration. As soon as architects allocated a set space for bandsmen below the stage (c. 1630), we find, not exactly a beginning, but at least a place to start. There were bands before the development of the pit, but they became a prime factor after 1625 when indoor stages were raised to increase visual and acoustical efficiency, and sonority needed to be enlarged to fill new spaces, now bigger than most ballrooms. Music was required to distract from shifting scenery, to describe transformations, to command processions, to heighten climaxes, to emphasize individual specialties. An augmented vocabulary in the academic dance depended on more varied rhythmic devices, whatever their origin in previous folk or court practice. Choreographic structure and its musical accompaniment altered as their function evolved from the generally participant to the specifically spectacular; audiences no longer joined performers even at the end of performances, but sat still facing the framed stage to look, listen, and applaud.

One is surprised to find how few composers of quality in the nineteenth century were attracted to ballet. Although the twentieth century borrows from Berlioz, Bizet, Brahms, Chopin, Chabrier, Elgar, Liszt, Lanner, Mendelssohn, Schubert, the Strausses, and Weber, few of these, however indebted to dance rhythms, wrote directly for dancing, except incidentally for minor oc-

casions in opera or spoken drama. (Similarly, very few important easel-painters, until 1917, designed for ballet). Ballet music was a special province, commissioned and supervised by self-protective bureaucrats. Not all staff musicians were hacks, but the nature of the job—fulfillment of subscription schedules and deadlines, instant novelty, catering to tyrannical stars—was no great inducement to genius occupied with the enlargement of its own talent.

Instead of attempting to outline the complex descent of music for theatrical dancing, profiles follow of composers who made key contributions, and whose ballets are further documented. Some half-dozen composers have written specific ballets still danced. Adolphe Adam left one; Delibes (of three composed) two; Tchaikovsky three. Gluck wrote two, of which one is remembered; Beethoven one, known chiefly for the fact that he wrote it. Today, except in a well-endowed music school, one can hardly imagine full length revivals of *Le Ballet-Comique de la Royne,* which is usually called the first of its form, or an entire opera-ballet of Lully, or a ballet-opera by Rameau. Fortunately for our epoch, we have Stravinsky's ample repertory of pieces written as dances or expropriated for dancing. This master has provided so many springboards in syncopation, metrical variety, sonority, and silence measured by sound, that they have not begun to be exhausted. And it transpires that Bach, Handel, Haydn, Vivaldi, Corelli, and Mozart wrote for our present ballet repertory, serving us more than their contemporaries. Survival of a ballet seems to depend almost as much on music as dancing. Many ballets earned oblivion by the laxity of their scores; it is more than possible that the eighty-odd ballets of Petipa and Ivanov no longer mounted held choreographic morsels as appetizing as their mere three with scores by Tchaikovsky.

Recent contemporary indications from composers propose a preponderance of massive sonority. Serial indications give way to electronic or computer-projected, in which kinetic impulse with obvious rhythmic pulse is of slight importance. Such sounds supply a dense, shifty background, an ambiguous base for dancing. They are often received in a manner that might be frustrating to their producers—regarded as mechanical and repetitive rather than suggestive or inspiring. But ballet will continue to depend on what choreographers make of their aural floor. Music, semi-improvised, built on chance, with novel organization or disorganization, neither denies the basis of academic dance nor promises inevitable masterpieces. Varèse, Stockhausen, Messiaen, Boulez, Penderecki, Cage, and other explorers in the aural arena have theatrical interests and have occasionally benefited dance designers.

Seventeenth Century: Court Ballet
Jean Baptiste Lully (1632–87), of obscure Italian birth,

became the most eminent French composer of his time, formulator of ballet-opera and founder of academies of music and dance, whose aesthetic and repertory dominated into the eighteenth century. In his youth he knew the *commedia dell'arte* and performed as comic dancer and mime. At the age of fourteen, he was placed in the *grande bande* of twenty-four violins by Louis XIV; later (1656) he was charged with a new orchestra of sixteen strings, *les petits violons*, whose fresh virtuosity surpassed the larger group. He danced beside the king in some thirty ballets, beginning with *Le Ballet de la Nuit* (1653); as courtier and collaborator, he enjoyed royal confidences. Energetic and ambitious, Lully was a virtuoso violinist, harpsichordist, composer-conductor, and musical administrator. Above all, he was a skilled theatrical operator. He created a new manner in French opera and a national style of instrumentation leading to our modern orchestra.

Lully's ballets were not intended to frame individual dancing virtuosos, of whom there were few. They were a focused reflection of political etiquette. His music provided a sonorous base and background for danced statements of pyramidal political order, with, at a choreographic peak, the prince. His music—clear cut, logical, deliberate, authoritative—suited the firm symmetry of Versailles. It embodied solid glory and formal joy.

Lully cultivated rhythmic precision that propelled dances, shearing away traditional French embroidery that blunted melody. In his own day he was criticized for overinsistence on dance rhythms—for that *baladinage* ("danciness") that pervaded even his vocal and instrumental passages. He worked with available forms of dance music (passepied, rigaudon, bourrée, and others) whose names remained from an earlier age, but whose shape and tempos altered drastically from decade to decade. Although Lully's music for many dances may now seem monotonous, its differences all but indistinguishable, in his day the slightest novelty was noticed.

In the new *comédie-ballet* (conceived by Molière), he revolutionized the music of the earlier *ballet de cour* by inserting a number of Italian devices—secco recitative, buffo scenes, the affective manner—and replacing generally slow sections by faster numbers, propelling quicker turns. After 1670, upon his notation, women would commence multiple pirouettes. His *airs de vitesse* began to characterize individuals in especially assigned rhythms, with instrumentation richer and fuller than Italian or Austrian. Parallel to new uses for soloists and *corps de ballet*, Lully developed, as a French specialty, interior dialogues between his entire orchestra and smaller groupings—large sections contrasted against smaller, woodwinds against strings. Instead of treating themes as simple melodies with accompaniment, in the prevailing Italian manner, Lully analyzed his orchestra,

reinforcing all voices and balancing harmony and counterpoint so that each instrument retained an individuality.

In each section of Lully's ballets, there are suggestions for choreographic blocking and structural sequence. Despite much research and attempted reconstruction of the dancing, actual practice remains vague; we can only guess at the exact expression of a lost language. Descriptions read very like; there seems to have been a sameness no matter what action demanded, reinforced by Lully's methodically consistent accompaniment, which deviated little from superior routine efficiency over thirty active years. Yet we know that what was danced, and the manner in which it was danced, did indeed change, due to the shift in performance around 1670 from noble amateurs to paid professionals.

Eighteenth Century: Opera-Ballet

Jean-Philippe Rameau (1683–1764) was, after Lully, the most gifted contributor to French dance music. Rameau did not enter the opera house until he was forty, a short time after his influential *Treatise on Harmony* appeared in 1722. His first successful opera, based on Racine's *Phèdre* (1733), was followed two years later by the opera-ballet *Les Indes Galantes*, of which one act in an adaptation will later be described. He always acknowledged Lully, but Rameau's orchestration is more dynamic, free, full; accompaniments more elaborate, symphonic proportions more melodramatic. A rational gentleman of the middle-class Enlightenment rather than a courtier, friend to Voltaire, his *airs de danse* were as studied as his *symphonies dramatiques*.

221.

216.

Simultaneous with Rameau's ascendant professionalism, there came a new craze for theatrical dancing. However, taste dictated that divertissements must have some theatrical logic; dances should not break the story or last too long. Thus, librettists for composers developed a special craft: *faire entrer les danses*, or how to accommodate dance music appropriately. French opera, unlike Italian, assigned an integral place to dancers; and from 1750 there were indications that ballet would ultimately declare independence. By about 1735, the then-outworn Baroque *danse noble* disappeared, unregretted by the ballet master Noverre, who thought it "old, languorous, characterless, designed for an age when dancing was tranquil."

186.

Rameau arrived when Lully's inheritance was threadbare, his formulas suiting only a dead past. Although he was not, like Lully, a trained dancer, he understood kinetic propulsion. He added local color, variety, and specified individual characterizations, articulate melody, and, especially, novel rhythms that "seemed to take dancers by the hand."

Monotonous symmetry had rooted figured dancing to the floor; Rameau's music opened a path to elevate it above the boards, toward acrobacy, with more turns, beats, and jumps. With Lully he shared highly cultivated taste. He detailed vivid, atmospheric, descriptive pieces using, for instance, authentic horns for hunting scenes. "Before Rameau," wrote Diderot, "no one distinguished delicate nuances that separated the tender from the voluptuous, voluptuous from passionate, ardor from the lascivious." Each traditional *air de danse* had its proper atmosphere, which Rameau rendered suitable for specific situations or reactions of individual characters.

Some forms disappeared: allemande and courante were no longer popular. Sarabandes became more tender while staying seductive. There were new overtones of whim, nostalgia, piquancy, and provocativeness, and more subtle psychological inflections. Lully's foursquare ponderous authority was fragmented toward lightness, asymmetry, and contrast. In ballrooms minuets stayed slow and grew even slower; on stage faster. Of the forms in duple time, the gavotte, inherited from Lully, was now either fast or slow, expressing grace, sweetness, and naive joy. Bourrées were quicker; bourrées, minuets, gavottes went often in contrasting pairs. The rigaudon, a lively Provençal form popular at the end of the previous century, was used for general rejoicings. Also from Provence came the tambourin, which was originally accompanied by recorder and small drum (still heard in Stravinsky's *Petrouchka*, 1911). The ballerina Marie Camargo endowed it with recommendations for jumps. For pastoral scenes, contrasting with palace or town, musettes echoed rustic bagpipes; marches remained deliberate, for regal, divine, or warlike entrance or exit. Final numbers displaying the company in extended evolutions were set to contredanses (once English country dances) or passacaglia (passecaille) and chaconne, twin forms in ¾ time, of Italian or Spanish (the latter possibly of West Indian) origin, constructed on a ground bass. Rameau amplified these forms so that he could bring down the curtain on crowds or group formations. Gluck's opera-ballet *Orfeo ed Euridice* ends with a grandiose chaconne.

Rameau was a violin specialist; he reduced string sections in his orchestra from five to four, a concentration achieved half a century earlier in Italy, Germany, and Austria. Brisk, neat, polished, he was not so much an innovator as an idiosyncratic master with Gallic wit and lyricism. He was the first French-born composer predominantly interested in instrumentation. Since French music, dancing, and visual art would provide criteria in Europe over the next century, and since the necessary luxury of orchestral sound supports ballet wherever, Rameau's importance cannot be overestimated.

Eighteenth Century: Ballet Drama

Christoph Willibald Ritter von Gluck (1714–87) was more opera than ballet composer, but his contribution to orchestration, his reform of music drama involving dancing, his ballet score *Don Juan*, and the dances in his opera *Orfeo* demand grateful attention. His name is Czech rather than Austro-German; he studied in Prague, Vienna, and Italy. In 1761, collaborating with the reform-minded Raniero Calzabigi as librettist, with Angiolini as ballet master, and supported by Count Durazzo, who had charge of the Imperial Theaters in Vienna, he wrote *Don Juan*, whose score may represent the desired yet seldom fulfilled aims of *ballet d'action*— coherent mimo-drama, proposed to elevate dancing above naive divertissement or conventional stage behavior and opera-house practice. In 1762, with *Orfeo*, for which he took material from *Don Juan*, Gluck started new directions in opera. Here he used the French chorus and ballet, but dispensed with formal rhetoric or mere pretext for display, stripping action to essential pathos, evoking powerful sentiment free of stylized pseudoarcheological or national considerations. Gluck's influence on ballet was delayed and indirect. His scores were considered ponderous, too pretentious for so gracile a language as dance; too symphonic. Similarly, a century later Tchaikovsky's and Chabrier's ballet music would be called "too Wagnerian." All three composers were generously restive and proceeded beyond current norms.

Gluck was perhaps the first composer to impose timeless and placeless unity. "Simplicity, truth, naturalism [*le naturel*] are beauty's prime principles. I search by noble, sensitive, and naturally melodic means for precise declamation fitting the prosody of each tongue and the character of each people, to posit a method proper to all lands, obliterating these ridiculous distinctions in nationalistic music." Of opera instrumentation he wrote what is also applicable to ballet: "Instrumentation should be introduced in proportion to the degree of interest and passion in the words [for 'words' read 'dynamics of movement']; instruments are to be employed not according to players' dexterity, but the dramatic propriety of their tonality." Exigencies of action determine instrumentation; orchestration governs or impels what can be danced. *Don Juan* was the concentrated equivalent in music of Molière's *Le Festin de Pierre*, from which it derived. Gluck charged his music by italicizing the dynamic structure with little rhetoric, parade, or divertissement; even the entertainment at Juan's banquet propels the plot. In Gluck's day, nothing was easier than to mock the preposterous tyranny of Italian opera—professional deformation of *castrati*, vanity of singers, perfunctory pantomime—the whole mindless ritual redeemed only by electric performance. Gluck rejected the whole convention. Influenced perhaps by meeting Rameau in Paris, he worked within the tradition of French opera, while extending it, as

223.

224.

Noverre and his colleagues embraced Franco-Italian ballet but enlarged it. When in 1774 he rewrote *Orfeo* for the Paris Opéra, he took his final hell scene's "Dance of Furies" from *Don Juan*. The minuet for "Blessed Spirits in the Elysian Fields" no longer merely echoes court custom. The dances are serene, imperturbable, celestially elegant whether in heaven, limbo, or hell. Visually they present no familiar echo of Baroque, Regency, or Rococo; palace practice is transcended. We seem to be hearing dances designed for some airless lunar landscape by Piero della Francesca or Nicolas Poussin. Gluck's coloration, harmonic strength, solidity prophesy a future; his spirit was closer to Carl Maria von Weber than to such neighbors as Handel or Bach. He omitted the controlling harpsichord, added harps, and used clarinets and trombones, strengthening chromatics. Dance music before Gluck, whatever its qualitative excellence, sounds thin. However transparent, Gluck's sonority is dense. Just as he underlined clear declamation in song, so he projected dramatic movement in dance. Mozart (who borrowed from *Don Juan* for his own *Don Giovanni*), Beethoven, Berlioz, and Wagner (who produced Gluck's *Iphigénie en Aulide*, 1847) felt his enduring influence. So did Dalcroze and Isadora Duncan. Balanchine has directed notable revivals of *Orfeo* (New York, 1937; Hamburg, 1964). Stravinsky's own *Orpheus* (with Balanchine's choreography) cannot be imagined without Gluck as ancestor.

Nineteenth Century: Toward Symphonism

Adolphe Charles Adam (1803–56), composer of *Giselle* and other Romantic ballet scores now best remembered from libretto or lithograph, was the son of a pianist-composer. Success in *opéra-comique* allied him to ballet. Few of his generation efficient in light opera possessed his instinct for dance or served dancers with such speed, tact, or grace. His experience with the voice characteristics of individuals, his familiarity with the limits of opera-house orchestras, and, chiefly, the pleasure he seemed to take in ballet itself were unusual; for him dance music was not workaday drudgery, but pure delight. He admired Ferdinand Hérold (1791–1833), whose *La Somnambule* (1827) and reworking of *La Fille Mal Gardée* (1828) animated comic and dramatic pantomime with devices from popular Italian opera. Against common practice, Hérold tried not to warm over familiar tunes his audiences were already humming; he invented his own new ones.

While the Paris Grand Opéra enjoyed subvention and prestige as the first lyric theater in Europe (when Milan lost eminence in dance), it was an official institution with the continual disadvantages of a bureaucratic agency, at the mercy of rough, nonmusical politics. The several commercial musical theaters of the *grands boulevards* served as a kind of Off-Broadway in reverse, forcing the Opéra to progressive reform in stage effects,

the hiring of foreign personalities, and new music. The direction of the house was determined to build and keep a ballet public second to none.

The new dance audience commanded a richer aural background for a new race of ballerinas. Adam was suited to theater by temperament; his first ballet, *La Fille du Danube* (1836), was written for the ballerina Marie Taglioni in five weeks (he liked to be hurried). A leading critic found it nothing but a suite of contredanses, nicely composed but offering too little opportunity for pantomime; in fact, "too musical." In 1841, the piano score for *Giselle*, whose libretto enchanted him, seems to have been finished in about a week. (On close terms with choreographer and ballerina, he made practical suggestions altering the final curtain: Giselle should not merely *bourrée* backward to her grave; she should collapse, stage center, to be borne back by Albrecht, who would deposit her on a bed of blossoms, which sank through the floor.)

289.

Adam may not have been the first to assign identifiable melodies to individual characters, but in *Giselle* (1841) there is an expressive transmutation of leading themes (leitmotivs) for the same dancers in various situations. The superior quality of his score was recognized at once; François-Antoine Habeneck, chief conductor at the Opéra, chose to lead its première, instead of assigning it to a subordinate as was normal for ballet music. A critique appeared in *La France Musicale*, welcoming so seriously conceived a score. It compared the first act waltzes favorably with those of the elder Strauss and applauded the unusual use of horns. In the second act, the Queen of the Wilis entered "to arpeggi on the harps, four muted first violins playing in their highest register a four-part melody the effect of which is really magical. . . . Then follow several dance tunes whose rhythm is always varied without the fantastical coloring ceasing for a minute. It is the first time we have seen the fantastic treated with a regard for grace and charm."

286.

In the first half of the nineteenth century, the orchestra matured through both invention and refinement by instrument-makers, together with the growing abilities of composers in novel instrumentation. Mechanical improvements were made in flute, saxophone, clarinet, bassoon; the entry of valved horns and trumpets was useful to Meyerbeer, Berlioz, and, later, Wagner. Opera-house orchestras became symphonic, producing heavier and more luxurious sound supporting dancers; all that was needed were good composers willing to provide notes to prompt steps, and able choreographers to be appropriately prompted. The latter, as always, were seldom available. When Wagner's opening "Bacchanal" in *Tannhäuser* (added for its Paris production, 1861) was howled down, it was not due to chauvinism alone; choreography itself had not kept pace with orchestra-

433.

tion. And as importantly, male dancers had disappeared. The Romantic revolution in ballet was finished. While what was heard often seemed unprecedented, what was seen was repetitious and hollow.

Léo Delibes (1836–91) was Adolphe Adam's pupil. His ballets still in repertory are *Coppélia* (1870) and *Sylvia* (1876). Entering the Opéra as under-choirmaster, he was far more musically gifted than Adam, but might have become a hack like many colleagues had not his gift for melody, his skillful manipulation of ethnic material, and his genius for shaping dances through his commanding rhythms saved him. At a time when dancing in Paris was decadent, he maintained an ideal for dance music. Tchaikovsky, no less than Dalcroze and Stravinsky, studied him carefully. Delibes was Parisian, like Gounod and Bizet, but unlike them, friendly to the heavier density of Berlioz and Wagner. His taste for clarity, rhythmic precision, transparency, discretion, and theatrical tact goes back, by divergent paths, to Rameau and Lully. His was the clear classical school, like *la danse d'école*—that French academy divested of rhetoric and vulgarism which would dominate ballet in its next mutation, the absolute criterion of the Russian academy. In the early nineteenth century, influential Italians writing music for Paris were showy and noisy; France was grateful for their theatricality. Paris owed something to Vienna, but Germanic heaviness and opacity were always antipathetic and antiballetic. Théophile Gautier, poet, librettist, and critic, thought he detected a Teutonic tinge to Delibes; but then, he asked, is not ballet a mimed symphony?

It is impossible to deny the effect of Wagner on Emmanuel Chabrier (1841–94); yet, in spite of his opera *Gwendoline*, with its homage to Bayreuth, one could never take him for a German. His music for the opera *Le Roi Malgré Lui* (1887), with its sung and danced Polish festival, an apotheosis of opera-ballet at the end of a two-hundred-year-old tradition, is one of the most splendid frames for theatrical dancing ever conceived. Since 1932, Balanchine has continually used some dozen of his orchestral or piano pieces. Chabrier has been well compared for his sunny solidity with Manet and Renoir; for his wry irony and sinister odd rhythmic and melodic bite with Toulouse-Lautrec.

Following Chabrier, the most important French music for ballet was produced by Claude Debussy (1862–1918). His *Prélude à l'Après-Midi d'un Faune* (1894) served Nijinsky for revolutionary plastique (1911), although its essential relevance to dancing is arbitrary, exceptional, and ambiguous. Debussy's orchestration, as also for Nijinsky's *Jeux* (1913), is almost too delicate, complex, and elusive—ballet was nearly too broad a language for such fragility. The coarser rhythms and franker colors of Maurice Ravel (1875–1937) had more immediate acceptance. Debussy, in the concert hall,

suggests shimmering tapestries of evanescence, metamorphosis, flow, and splendor, which need no dancing; when supporting dancing, his pieces, lacking a symphonic underpinning, shrink and fade. Debussy calls for complete listening, not a compromise in fused hearing and seeing, which music when servant-inspirer of dancing permits.

Peter Ilitch Tchaikovsky (1840–93), composer of three of the chief surviving nineteenth-century ballets, is also responsible for much other music not originally intended for dancers, which has subsequently served them. *Swan Lake* (1877) was, after its first failure, revived posthumously as only a partial success, but it became the signature of the art form universally. The *Sleeping Beauty* (1890) and the *Nutcracker* (1892) came at the end of his career. This triad, in portions at least, persists as the most popular and persuasive music written for dancing, and revivals can be quite untarnished by familiarity. Their serious strength, despite suffocating vulgarization in sight and sound, remains a criterion for the classic academic dance; variations and group numbers are absorbed in classrooms from the first ballet lessons. No composer of durable ballet ignores him as master, whether debts are direct or tangential. Both in rhythmic generosity and melodic support, he, like Rameau, "takes dancers by the hand." A considerable case can be made for his specifically Russian coloration; similar claims can be made for Russian-derived classical choreography after 1890. Although we recognize his patrimony, embodied in devotion to Glinka and Pushkin, he, like Gluck, transcends nationalism. He provided ballet music for the world; taking three centuries of invention in instrumentation, he suggested new dimensions, divisions, and action.

On his mother's side Tchaikovsky descended from French *émigrés;* he was always aware of France and French music. He was a member of the first class of the Petersburg Conservatory (1862); four years later he became professor of harmony at the new Moscow school where he taught twelve years. Moscow was considered a provincial town; had *Swan Lake* been produced by Petipa or Ivanov at the official Marinsky Theatre of imperial St. Petersburg, it might possibly not have failed at first. While there is little of his symphonic music that does not suggest dancing, *Romeo and Juliet*, *Francesca da Rimini*, *Hamlet*, *Mozartiana*, the piano concertos, several of his symphonies, and many of his suites have actually been used to project ballets. When a colleague suggested that his Fourth Symphony sounded "too much like ballet music," he replied that such in itself was not bad, citing Delibes' *Sylvia*. He spent far more effort on opera; his ballets came quickly, without pain. He welcomed excessively detailed instructions from the choreographer Marius Petipa, and no writer for films ever received more

31.

333.

328.

325.

strict directions accompanying footage. He embraced choreographic suggestion, including precise indications, for he understood dance as theater, and his extraordinary technical and musical gift profited by professional promptings. His gloomy personal life hardly tinctures his dances; *Swan Lake* has its operatic grandeur, more melodramatic than tragic. *Nutcracker* is filled with delicious comic details, and the contrast between children dancing with and without grownups recalls Tchaikovsky's beautiful distinction between a provincial party and the great Petersburg polonaise in his opera *Eugene Onegin*.

Twentieth Century: Stravinsky

The founding of conservatories in Petersburg (1862) and Moscow (1866) provided a training ground for Russian composers, instrumentalists, and musical performers comparable to that offered by their twin-sister dancing academies during the preceding century. Russia had produced good dancers but few were seen in the West. Similarly with music after Glinka; it received hearings before and after Tchaikovsky, but not until Diaghilev's conquest of Paris and London, beginning in 1908 with productions of operas by Moussorgsky, Borodin, and Rimsky-Korsakov, did it become internationally known. In the vanguard of a new generation was Igor Stravinsky (b. 1882), son of a prominent basso at the Marinsky. With no formal conservatory training, he was advised in 1902 by Rimsky-Korsakov (1844–1908) to continue law school, since he had not been overly precocious in music. But in 1905, Rimsky, a masterful technician, agreed to teach him composition and orchestration. Stravinsky admired two native masters, Tchaikovsky and Alexander Glazounov. He was also attracted to Chabrier and, particularly, Debussy, who had lived in Russia. Hearing Stravinsky's orchestral *Fireworks* (1908), Diaghilev asked him to orchestrate two piano pieces for Fokine's *Les Sylphides* (opening "Nocturne"; closing "Grande Valse Brillante") for his 1909 Paris debut. He composed on commission for Diaghilev over the next two decades; in his whole long life rarely have two years passed when he has not produced scores directly or indirectly useful for dancing. His association with Balanchine, commencing with a version of *Pulcinella* (1920) before the choreographer left Russia in 1924, has been one of ballet's most profitable partnerships.

Stravinsky's career is massively documented and his scores amply recorded, so that it is unnecessary here to more than mention landmarks in his huge and unique repertory. Early works, notably *Firebird* (1910), *Petrouchka* (1911), *Le Sacre du Printemps* (1913), and *Les Noces* (1923), were imbued with a national color; Stravinsky presented himself as legitimate heir to every Russian after Glinka. He then began to represent international music; increasingly he speaks for his century. *Apollon Musagète* (1928) involved itself

first in recapitulation, then in instigation of rhythmic materials, projecting the first extension of academic classic choreography in twenty years (since *Les Sylphides*). *Apollon* wove a fabric from dance music's most luminous strands—Lully through Handel, Gluck to Glinka, Delibes, Tchaikovsky. It is no anthology, but a glorious anatomizing and transformation of rhythmic contrasts and imperious melodies, factors that always support ballet at its clearest, at once reminiscent and contemporary. No one has written more evocatively for dancing, neither in so grand a variety of metrical insinuation, nor with such an elevated luxury in restricted instrumentation (here, strings alone). Stravinsky's opulence is deceptive; in his last thirty years, it is the absolute yet laconic or stoic spareness of discrete sound. His dance music is conceived for a function: to support legible and wholly entertaining human movement. His earlier, more lavish instrumentation is revealed better in concert hall than on stage. *Petrouchka* was an announcement of a new practice. It is now odd to remember that this score once seemed profoundly disturbing; orchestras protested it was unplayable, full of "wrong" notes. To us today, whatever its historical novelty, it seems to look back—toward Rimsky-Korsakov. *Le Sacre* retains its initial shock from sheer crushing density. Each rehearing proves its incontestable impact and influence. Too big for ballet, it permits no theatrical additive. Later beauties—*Le Baiser de la Fée* (1928), *Jeu de Cartes* (1937), *Scènes de Ballet* (1943)—suffer from reverse factors. Their scoring is almost too exquisite, rhythmic irregularities too finely delineated, subtle, sophisticated to ensure a crass success with choreographers possessing less than comparable musicality, or with a public spoiled by successions of larger, harsher, or louder sounds.

Often, with Balanchine, Stravinsky scores not originally proposed for dancing have been strikingly effective, such as *Ragtime* (1918), *Capriccio* (1929), *Monumentum pro Gesualdo* (1960), and *Movements for Piano and Orchestra* (1958–59). It is impossible to sketch Stravinsky's many orchestral innovations that Balanchine embodied in ballet. Typical of these (seen in *Agon*, 1957) is the brief, strategically placed silence, alternating with moments of paper-thin mandolin accompaniment that last only seconds in clock time, which, in sequence with inset movement, frame action or designed inertia in arresting and disconcerting duration. Concentrated semi-silences permit no rest or relaxation; indeed, dancers often move on silence, as sometimes they stay quiet on focuses of sound. Motivation from aural discontinuity in a metrical structure pinpoints movement, clearing our often blurred or inattentive eyes from familiar or expected combinations. Miniature shocks, like small short circuits, clear the eye and ear, demanding closer viewing. Stravinsky's late scores are without plot or pretext; they are "about" music and, incidentally, —but not accidentally—movement.

434.

375.

397.

462.

While similar principles for architecture and scenic decoration govern dance, opera, and spoken drama, this is not true of costume. The requirements of dress for ballet are peculiar to dance alone. A dancer's whole voiceless body is his instrument; what is worn should not impede physical possibility; it must describe it in relation to absolute physical freedom. Around 1550, before professionals were schooled to exploit a developed idiom, noble amateurs in the more ostentatious court shows paraded mutely in costumes adapted from Roman armor. A half-imagined antiquity provided every precedent, to be invoked for any departure. There was one licensed period: Roman. There was one formula: how Rome (a late, triumphal, imperial Rome) might translate armor into some ideal India, Africa, America. Auden says, "to the ignorant the past is simultaneous." For the more informal burlesque and grotesque dances, however, fantastic detail was invented according to individual imagination, while still maintaining the waistline and general silhouette of antique precedent.

After 1750, designers were less ignorant of geography. Scientific archeology banished a singular fictive Rome. With a growing historical sense and more precise knowledge of foreign places, authentic costume (in theatrical translation) became mandatory. Myth died; allegory was retold in everyday anecdote. Once everyone "knew" what the Romans looked like; then came discoveries that there were numerous ancient peoples—Greek, Cretan, Egyptian, Phoenician, Italian; even Etruscan. At the same time the immediate present, along with a verifiable past, was admitted to theatrical history; contemporary civil dress, with its own hem, neck, and waistline, became the frequent basis for stage costume.

Greece
The dress of ancient Greece, as seen cut in stone or painted on baked clay, provided precedent for much theatrical costume around 1800. Since 1900 it has often been used to evoke timelessness and placelessness on ballet or dramatic stage. In Greece, weather permitted outdoor performance in light clothing denied northern nations. Since drama was also ceremony, stage dress was more elaborate and formal than daily. After Alexander the Great's Indian campaign (327 B.C.), cotton and silk were imported; these, mixed with flax, were woven into semi-transparent gauze, later embroidered with metal. Such material enhanced motion, reinforcing or echoing dynamics in metric and mimicry; shifting folds accentuated contrast between arrest, repose, and movement. Anatomical detail was concealed, but bodies and gestures were rendered monumentally legible, as demanded by the distances in huge amphitheaters. Stage cloaks had bright patterns with symbolic color: royalty wore purple, mourners black. Choruses—

frogs, birds, wasps—were masked, in dramatic reminiscence of a primitive era, before hunting and battle rites became stylized for the theater. Greek dance should be imagined under open skies with accident of sun and cloud—not in monochrome, as on surviving vase or cut marble, but vivid in dye and paint.

379.

Renaissance and Baroque: A Dominance of Rome
When Rome fell, large-scale dramatic spectacle (outside court circles) disappeared for a thousand years, until the building of new theaters—on imagined Roman models. The aspect of imperial Rome triumphant was then renewed, determining heroic theatrical dress for three centuries. Roman armor, hammered onto molds of pectorals and bellies, was revived to become the uniform of Renaissance soldiers, singers, actors, and dancers.

154.

Italy, where dance steps began to be codified after 1450, was filled with monuments for reference: no need to dig or reconstruct. From 1550, at the beginning of the Baroque, aim in stage fashion was pictorial rather than plastic. Glorified civil dress was not intended to license swift or free movement; manipulation of voluminous skirts and graceful handling of heavy yardage in silk or velvet was an integral part of social dance instruction. While neckline, waistline, hem and hair style from daily custom served as basis for the actor's dress, as soon as ballet quit the ballroom (c. 1625), exaggeration was intensified within the proscenium frame. Silhouettes were swollen for ostentation and legibility. The nude was not thought provocative, but, rather, unadorned and unimproved—hence, unprincely, poor. Male dress on stage was a dream of ancient armor, complete with cape, helmet, and plumes, as realized in the plush velours and metal-shot brocades of the Renaissance court. The outfit also included something never seen in ancient Rome: the *tonnelet*, a full hooped skirt of mid-thigh length that was to remain a standard feature in the costume of the male dancer in the high style through the greater part of the eighteenth century. For women, after 1670, similar artificial padding—bone, wire, or canvas—allowed lighter but seemingly massive expansion. Their bodices were decorated with simulated Roman armor or other fanciful motifs.

10.

65.

Deliberate amplification of the performing presence by corselet and cuirasse, plus helmeted goat- or horsehair high-piled wigs, was a burden professional dancers learned to bear. Molded leather, metal cloth, heeled and laced high boots, masks, plumes, and gloves encased them in gorgeous strait jackets. In addition, specific characters in the ballets were weighted down with attributes and symbols: shoemakers were covered with shoes; musicians with musical instruments, including,

220.

in one case, a large hat in the shape of a violin. Folly wore a hundred tinkling bells, while marine gods and goddesses labored under stereotyped headdresses of sea shells and coral. Until these were discarded, there would be small leeway for virtuosity and acrobatics. A start was made when male dancers shed buskins for shoes and stockings, but this did not occur until the 1760's.

Famous Italian painters, working a century before academic ballet was established, had conceived beautiful dresses that described dancers in ideal motion, rather than merely displaying them, like pieces of scenery, for ephemeral entries. Festive clothes in the paintings of Botticelli, Mantegna, Leonardo, Foppa, Cossa, Vasari, Arcimboldo are simpler yet more stylish than their French successors, but we must remember to translate paintings into a theatrical realization if we would learn what dancers actually wore.

Régence and Rococo

Renaissance and Baroque had added an extra, superior dimension to the clad figure, making it, at its peak, heroic, approaching sculpture. Rococo ended this aim, replacing it by an exquisitely appropriate elegance, still somewhat overblown for the bare body, but approximating a human scale. Although rational artists of the time inveighed against even this stylized excess, there was little willingness to abandon its transparent charm in court circles until the French Revolution made a clean, overnight sweep.

In the early eighteenth century, dancing emerged as a profession, and the creation of dance costume was recognized as a specialized and exacting art. Master tailors serving designers had shops in every opera house. Dancing dresses, to survive stress, stretch, and sweat had to be engineered with skill. To be seen from a distance and under the brighter lights that the stage demands, details of court dress became more gross.

After the death of Louis XIV (1715), a Regency (régence) under the Duc d'Orléans ruled during the minority of Louis XV, the Sun King's great-grandson. The Baroque—symmetrical and grandiose (incarnate in the irregular curves of monster pearls)—gave way to the Rococo (from rocaille), based on plant or rock shapes and particularly on shells, from which were derived abstract ornaments in S- and C-forms—asymmetrical, lighter, more capricious. The Regency developed its own taste, in reaction against the loaded splendor of Versailles—less formal, if no less artificial or restrictive, than that of Louis XIV, which had been typified by the gorgeous and sophisticated costumes of the elder Jean Bérain, chief designer for Lully's repertory. Outstanding among the Rococo heirs of the

younger Bérain were the painters Louis-Simon Boquet, François Boucher, Jean-Baptiste Martin, and the painter-engraver Claude Gillot. Antoine Watteau, finest artist of his epoch, painted theater at one remove; his vision suggests the essence of an era better than documents. He hardly saw the exiled comedians he depicted, deriving them from drawings by Gillot, his master.

209.
212.

188.

Around 1720, the panier ("pannier," a hooped petticoat) appeared in Paris, apparently from London, although its ancestor was the Spanish farthingale, familiar from Velázquez's enormously skirted infantas. Panniers raised skirts, now of lighter materials, a few important inches off the ground.

The engraver Jacques Callot was the first (c. 1630) to accurately record Italian popular comedians in action. A century later, many of their stereotypes, along with their distinctive dress, had been absorbed into opera-ballet, although the close-fitting kaleidoscope tights of Harlequin and the loose skirts of Columbine initially contradicted official opera-house style. The influence of oriental exploration, which had begun to appear in books and prints, also found its way into design of costume ornament, along with new modes for skirt, bodice, hat, and jacket, inspired by the East but transformed into Parisian chic. For indications of color range we have pale water-color sketches by Boucher and Boquet and the changeable silks and watery moires in the paintings of Watteau, Lancret, and Pater. The palette was pastel—pink, pale azure, grey, silver, citron, pistachio, peach. No more the brazen grandeur of the Baroque, with dark coppery browns, maroons, and purples.

60.

188.
186.

187.

After 1740, the full Rococo asserted itself: S- and C-shapes in scroll and leaf were not only broken but twisted; earlier circular domed panniers were now flattened out, front and back. Grandes toilettes encouraged skirts four yards at the hem; this allowed partners in a minuet to bow or curtsy face to face, but ladies could only pass sideways through a door.

190.

Wigs, smaller and tighter, were powdered with meal; white hair made the young provocatively mature, the old younger by artifice. Half-masks were still being worn into the 1770's. When facial make-up replaced them, it was lead white with carmine dabs; naturalistic maquillage, as we know it, was reserved for ladies of pleasure.

162.

Exaggeration in dress and headdress was more flattering—not to say appropriate—to static singing than to free dancing. The chief impediments to movement, against which such reformers as Noverre railed but accomplished little, were heeled shoes, corseted bodices, and vast skirts, whose stiff stretched expanses were

229.

63.

64. 65.

63. Court ballet. France, 1581.

64. Male dancer. France, c. 1680.

65. Male dancer. France, 1752.

66. 67.

68. 69.

66. Ballerina. France, c. 1755.

67. Opera dancer. France, 1790.

68. Ballerina. France, 1860.

69. Isadora Duncan, 1916.

festooned with flowers, flounces, lace, and ribbons. Prompted spasmodically by daring individuals, ballet skirts became centimeters shorter during the eighteenth century, worn sometimes with precautionary pantaloons. In 1722 in London, Mrs. Santlow, in *A Masque of Deities,* with hair loose and deerskin across her breast, danced with "her purple gown tucked up to her knees." Around 1730 Marie Camargo's legs in motion could be seen up to her underdrawers; in repose, her skirt fell just above her instep. Mariette, a skirt-dancer, raised hers "so her *entrechats* would crackle." Marie Sallé appeared (London, 1734), wigless and with her own unjeweled hair down her back, "like a Greek [sculpture]."

Panniers and *tonnelets* were abolished neither by Noverre nor the Grand Opéra, but by the more progressive Comédie Française, in the persons of its chief actress, Mademoiselle Clairon, and the actor Lekain, who tentatively discarded them about 1750 (although we see from prints that their use persisted for another thirty years). Then, in 1779, in Noverre's *Toilette de Vénus,* fauns danced in tiger skins without *tonnelets.* Beginning in 1780, there were instances of naked limbs; the dancer Charles Louis Didelot, in other respects more important as choreographer and teacher, wore pink tights in 1791 and a transparent tunic in 1793; undoubtedly there were unrecorded occasions of partial nudity before. But it was not until 1902 that Isadora Duncan danced corsetless and barefoot in Vienna.

Neoclassicism

The roots of Neoclassicism were laid in the mid-Rococo, sparked by the unearthing of the buried Roman towns of Herculaneum (1737) and Pompeii (1748). Findings from these excavations were fully documented and widely published. The German archeologist and aesthetician Winckelmann proclaimed a "noble simplicity and calm grandeur," or rather, a more authentic antiquity unadorned by decorative deformation. Under Louis XVI (reigned 1774–93), Rococo persisted as a court style, but in other spheres—not alone in literature, theater, and garden landscape, but also in civil dress casually styled for country houses—there was heavy influence from English naturalism. British tailors developed what remains, with modification, the modern male habit: trousers instead of knee breeches; well-cut coats; sobriety in stuff and color. Women's dress à l'anglaise was worn after 1780, almost for the first time in unrelieved white. Typically it was a simple unhooped cylinder of material, tightened just below the bust and with a low neckline. Corsets were abandoned (temporarily). The male waistline was also raised. Before long these habits found a place on stage in light or comic ballets.

Le style antique remained fashionable; rich ladies spoke

less of being well dressed than beautifully draped. In the heroic ballet, if the Baroque stage costume was à la romaine, under the Directory and Empire it was à la grecque—recalling a Greece not of painted vases or polychromed pediments, but of blank white statuary (from Hellenistic copies or sculptural imitations by Antonio Canova). With scientific archeology and exploration, at first focused on the Mediterranean, and the growth of museums, libraries, and publications (backed by Napoleon after his Egyptian campaign, 1799), costume-designers relied less on inherited stereotypes and more on documents. China was no longer imaginary Cathay, but a land where travelers voyaged and made drawings; so were Brazil, Peru, the Near East, and all the Russias. Ballet masters from Paris practiced in Petersburg; there was a new authenticity, tinged, to be sure, by every fleeting fad in civil dress, but ethnic materials were now at hand; originality was less invention than translation.

For the noble style of dancing, the new fashions were revelation and reformation. Human bodies, clad in Greek draperies, at last had full capacity for movement, aided by wires that flew dancers and by the development of heelless slippers, which would become toe shoes (1790–1815), augmenting movement and balance. In Neoclassic ballets of the first quarter of the nineteenth century, male dancers wore versions of the Greek chiton, with bare legs and sandals; the ballerinas' semi-transparent gauzes were sometimes sprayed, since clinging wet fabrics emphasized the body beneath.

As for frank expressions of the nude, kept alive by painters, which a combination of Greek precedent and lighter dresses might have licensed—bare bodies had been fairly slow to appear. Since before the elder Bérain, dancers wore fleshings; earlier still, Queen Elizabeth's maids of honor had silk stockings. About 1810, Maillot, a tailor at the Opéra, knitted improved tights; in the Papal States, at least, these were protectively dyed blue to reduce suggestiveness. After the Bourbon Restoration (1815), there was sporadic Parisian censorship in the name of "decency"; it failed, mainly because there was no real interest in nudity, and by 1825 corsets had made their stubborn comeback, until banished for good by Isadora.

In addition to the dancers in the heroic style, by the 1820's there were two other distinct types, each with their own ballets and their own costumes: dancers of *demi-caractère,* a genre midway between the heroic academy and opera-house national dances (*caractère*), wore doublet and hose with plumed round caps, loosely derived from Renaissance fashion. Character dancers wore versions of peasant dress: men in open shirts, braces, and short jackets; girls in laced bodices and bouffant skirts.

Romanticism and Revivalism
In the eighteen-twenties, male opera dancers appeared still in doublet and hose, labeled with no accuracy *le style troubadour;* Gothic shadings were promised, but these did not flower with much flavor until *Esmeralda* (1844). The "troubadour" costume displayed the body elegantly, without exaggeration. There were indications of puffing at the shoulders, slashed trunks, and details from Renaissance styles, but these did not obscure the natural silhouette.

In 1831 the ballet interlude of lapsed nuns in Meyerbeer's opera *Robert le Diable* launched Marie Taglioni as queen-star of Romantic ballet. When Taglioni appeared the next year as *La Sylphide,* the costume she wore became the habit of a new order of devoted, disciplined aspirants: ballerinas. Her sylph's dress—a vision in layers of white gauze—became stereotyped; no matter what pretext was danced or character represented, principal ladies began to appear as ethereal sylphs, in clouds of white, pale blue, and pale pink. Their silhouette was the ballgown of the 'thirties, tight and low-cut in the bodice, with the hint of a sleeve, and full skirts shortened to show feet, now permanently toe-shod. Adoption of this dress was due to Taglioni's infectious magic and durable prestige; dancers who wore similar skirts shared, to some degree, her fame. Later in the century, in Italy, Russia, and France, the many-layered tarlatan would be drastically abbreviated to reveal the entire leg. The *tutu* (Parisian nurses' parlance for their babies' bottoms) is still canonical. While archeology suggested details for lesser members of a cast, ballerinas wore this conventional uniform inviolate, until reforms proposed by Michel Fokine at the start of this century. Fokine was a student of art history and rejected conventional ballet costume in favor of a more correct stylization, which, however, without such able designers as Bakst and Benois, was almost as dry and as dead as former opera-house practice.

Isadora Duncan's unique appearances from about 1900, coinciding with the movement for women's suffrage, freed civil dress as much as theatrical; after her, laced corsets even for stylish women would be increasingly unfashionable. Gordon Craig wrote that Isadora "threw away ballet skirts and ballet thoughts. She discarded shoes and stockings too. She put on some bits of stuff which, when hung upon a peg, looked more like torn rags than anything else; when she put them on they became transformed. Stage dresses usually transform the performers—but in her case it was these bits that became transformed by her putting them on. . . ." But Duncan's homage to or borrowings from Greece remained outside official theater practice for nearly a decade and were mainly relevant to her own body in performance.

Stage costume as we know it today depends on the use Serge Diaghilev made of principal designers during the twenty years (1909–29) of his Ballets Russes. His first and most professional costumers were Alexandre Benois and Léon Bakst, artist-craftsmen and erudite amateurs of art history. Benois, by his *émigré* inheritance, favored French palace styles. Bakst, a Jew, was gifted in manipulating oriental models. He also loved Greece, and, unlike designers in previous periods, had actually toured the country—not alone the Parthenon, but Crete and the islands as well. Both Bakst and Benois were rapid, skillful, and accurate draftsmen; their sketches were more than stylish indication, instructing costumers exactly how materials must be cut, draped, and sewn. They rifled history, reviving the past with little idiosyncratic commentary; their art derived from print room and library. They were masters of museum theater. They were brought up on ballet; they served dance even more than theater. This was not true of famous easel-painters working later who left execution to professional costumers. But Diaghilev grew bored with the familiar and pedantic precision of Bakst and Benois, with their relentless reminiscence of past tastes. He came to prefer vague flashier sketches by new painters, in whose interpretation he might be permitted to participate, and who reflected the present epoch.

Easel-Painters
In spite of interest in theater shared by David, Delacroix, Daumier, Degas, Seurat, and Toulouse-Lautrec, master painters in the nineteenth century were only tangentially interested in stage investiture. Stage design, like music, was a professional province of opera houses. Bureaucracy dispensed with outside intruders, who did not know the business and who might make, with pressing programs and schedules, "impossible" or "inconvenient" demands. Then Diaghilev arrived with vague ideas of visual reforms, prompted by Beardsley, Appia, and Craig, which were realized in part by Benois and Bakst. He made a manner of modernity; exploring studios of the School of Paris, he incidentally launched the public careers of galaxies of schools; Cubists, Constructivists, Surrealists, neo-Romantics, and Sunday painters.

The chief historical development in costume since Diaghilev's death (1929) is the persistent use of rehearsal practice clothes in public performance, as in George Balanchine's repertory after 1934. Balanchine has returned bodies to primary starkness. A stripped style, or an impoverished style, it is enriched only by structures in choreography; would decorative adornment for such constructs be an advantage?

374.

80.

381.

81.

407.

460.

70.

Over four centuries choreography has been adorned, but infrequently enriched, by interior decoration. On few occasions has a perfect balance been attained between music, dance, and décor, although this ideal is still piously pursued. Choreography requires a maximum of flat, unencumbered surface, with unlimited access off and onto the dancing floor. Scenery should be suggestive but splendidly tactful, to avoid insistence, competition, or confusion with the elusive kinetic metamorphosis that is spectacular dancing.

Since their joint birth, ballet and opera have been dressed in similar styles of quasi-realistic or fantastic décor. Before there were permanent playhouses (c. 1580), with elevated, framed stages, professional performers, and the need to store repertory, scenery was often a series of three-dimensional structures—houses, portals, pavilions—built as solid stationary backgrounds against which action was focused. A suite of scenes was viewed simultaneously, from Heavenly Gates at the left to Jaws of Hell at the right. During the Early Renaissance in Italy, when parade entries and carnival masquerades were combined in secular shows—broadly in the open air, with more careful detail in roofed rooms—costumed bands of players were drawn in a series of fantastic cars by disguised stagehands. Plump sea monsters and vast pearl shells provided both a sculptured frame and a background from which maskers descended to perform.

In sixteenth-century France, when such shows were held in halls primarily designed to house parliaments or tennis players, there was a combination of fixed and mobile units; stationary town fronts or groves of gilded trees were constructed with openings for the entrance of wheeled fountains or billowing chariots filled with musical tritons, the last a vestige of the antique Roman triumphal processions, when Victory trumpeted above chariots hauled by captives. Another characteristic of the propaganda entry, which persisted into the Baroque

era, was the street parade arch that framed or supported *tableaux vivants*—the Three Graces, the Judgment of Paris, Mars and Venus. Beautiful drawings and pictures of stage designs from Botticelli and Leonardo to Rubens, Bernini, and Inigo Jones show the love, artistry, and cash lavished on such ephemera. The prime motive was display and embellishment—the compliments in a glorious, lively, mythical if static ambience to the patron—rather than provision, invention, or extension of space useful for performing large patterns of movement.

94.
9.
92.

The Farnese Theater, Parma (1619), by Giovanni Battista Aleotti (c. 1546–1636), has been called the earliest modern theater. For the first time a proscenium hid a grid and flies; backstage space held movable scenery; a broad parterre extended into the auditorium, permitting parades or dancing to descend from the stage for joint social and theatrical dancing at the end of performances. The decorative double arcades at the rear of banked seats promised eventual galleries and boxes. The influence of the early Italian theaters can be exaggerated; Palladio's Olympian Theater at Vicenza (1580–84) was a dead end rather than a prototype, and even the Farnese was rarely used for ten years after its construction. Temporary playhouses began to be set up from Paris to Prague, at first inside large existing chambers.

82.

In 1640, Richelieu commissioned a galleried hall in Paris, designed by Jacques le Mercier. First called the Hall of the Palais Cardinal, when given to the king it became the Palais Royal. In the beginning it held chairs only for the cardinal and royal family; later, when inherited by Molière's troupe, seats and boxes were added. Enlarged in 1671, it became the official Opéra.

75.

Italian architects, engineers, and machinists were the principal innovators in theater and scenic design. A pupil of Aleotti, Giacomo Torelli (1608–78), had a profound effect on stage space. Aleotti's side wings in Parma needed a man on each to shift them; in 1641 Torelli invented a system that could be controlled by one stagehand. Gasparo Vigarini (c. 1586–c. 1633), who designed the splendid park theater in Versailles, also constructed the Hall of Machines in the left wing of the Tuileries Palace, Paris (1662–64), a rectangular room equipped for changing elaborate scenery.

142.

Since theaters were built of wood, and illumination came from exposed or ill-protected flame, destructive fires were frequent. Like surgery on battle fields, design and construction improved vastly through the use of whatever expedient was at hand and from the constant need to start anew. In 1710, Emperor Joseph I erected the Kärntnertor Theater in Vienna for common civilians rather than for a court or high-bourgeois audience. Small and magnificently elegant court theaters con-

196.

70. Scenery. Italy, c. 1730.

tinued to be built, a dozen of which survive in good condition, notably at Bayreuth, Drottningholm, Munich, Leningrad (Hermitage), and Moscow (Ostankino). Apart from their increasingly lavish decoration, which made an important contribution to the pleasures of an evening—mirrors tripling the illusion of space, crystal chandeliers competing with the brilliance of stages, gilt, plasterwork, painted ceilings, drapes, festoons—theaters of today are more hygienic and physically comfortable, but hardly aesthetically improved. Advantages have been gained in stage illumination and fireproofing. From the start of the nineteenth century, large popular theaters were built to accommodate a mass public, but the Paris Grand Opéra, planned early in the sixties, was designed as an exceptionally large court theater. As frames in which ballet can be seen under optimum circumstances (plus enjoyable intermissions), perhaps the finest theaters today are in Bordeaux, Vienna (Theater an der Wien), Venice (La Fenice), Naples (San Carlo), Paris (Champs Elysées), Leningrad (Kirov), Chicago (Auditorium), the Academies of Music in Philadelphia and Brooklyn, and the New York State Theater.

The productions of the Baroque were not at first intended for repertory, but for splendid isolated occasions; then, increasingly toward the last quarter of the seventeenth century, the same spectacle might be repeated in several palaces, and the need for permanent performing areas was established. When theaters framed raised and raked stages within an elaborate unchanging proscenium, floors were cleared for dancing. At first, however, ingenious engineering transformations—marble palace to armored port, encampment, or prison, break-away walls for earthquakes, conflagrations, cloud effects—had a metamorphic movement and energy more magical than most of the dancing. Seventeenth-century stage decoration supplied elemental splendor by suggestions of architecture or artificial forms simulating rock, garden, grotto, drapery in an overcharged grandiose monotony. Neither archeological research nor more than superficial attention to geography determined historical or local color, a specific site, or allusive atmosphere. The embellished background was supertheatrical, past any human scale—busy, heavy, crushing. What rudimentary dancing there was need not have suffered; an overwhelming impression of ornament—miracles of machinery, flying figures, and floating clouds—was far more memorable than the primary measures that were performed.

Methods of rendering or suggesting forms in space were inherited from Italian architects, painters, and mathematicians who, early in the fifteenth century, wished to depict solid structures free-standing in air at various simulated distances from a beholder's eye. The science of perspective, linear—the manipulation of vanishing points on an imaginary horizon—and

aerial—the precipitation of forms seen from many angles, above and below—developed as an obsession. Skill in fooling the eye by control of cast shadows from rigidly determined sources of artificial light became a pretext for a special grammar of ornament. Plane surfaces worried with a confusion of detail were substituted for permanent, three-dimensional formal architectural elements; flat canvas and wood side wings and backdrops that could be hung and rolled afforded maximum mobility for changes as well as frequent entries and exits. An unencumbered central area gave dancers clearance; for such nonrealistic spectacle as ballet, this floor plan has not altered substantially since around 1630.

By about 1700 the symmetry of High Baroque stage design had mutated into new means for suggesting space. What was depicted no longer showed a head-on, four-square view—a room, as it were, bluntly facing the public with a transparent fourth wall. Now, due in large part to Andrea Pozzo (1642–1709), a great Jesuit designer of décor for church fetes and ceremonies, and to the genius of the Bibiena family (c. 1675–1770), scenes were sliced at an angle, to encompass deep space that appeared to penetrate the back wall of the stage house. Courtyards, corridors, and colonnades precipitated backward in a sequence of solid geometrical abstractions; here, at least, the fondest dreams of architects were momentarily realized in paint, freed from restrictions of treasury or chancellery, which always delayed or altered planned monuments of bronze or marble. From existing engravings it is safe to say that the general impression of opera-house décor well into the nineteenth century was linear, with the geometrical armature of elements—syncopated broken cornice or columnar processional, draped baldachin or dungeon bars—washed by pale tones that, even now, might to us seem faded. Clean, undimmed drawings and extant eighteenth-century scenery in Sweden and Czechoslovakia show muted umber, gamboge, lilac, rose, pale blues and bisters. Yellow was sulphur, not citron; green was sage, not grass; red rust, not crimson. Underpainting in grisaille played down local tints on top, which provided, in their very lack of contrast, both a fusion of forms for an enveloping atmosphere, and a flattering muted foundation for the flash of metallic brocade in costumes.

Stage lighting, at first torches or tallow dips, was later provided by candles or oil lamps, equally difficult to focus or localize. Lights were lowered or raised and footlights could be dimmed by metal shades, but it was not until around 1784, with the invention of the Argand lamp, that stage illumination benefited by controlled chiaroscuro. Later, gas allowed some contrasts of black and light, characteristic of lithography, that were stronger than the pale differences of shadings in steel engravings. With limelight and, later, elec-

78.

79.

216.

71.

72.

73.   74.

71. Perspective. Italy, c. 1475.   73, 74. Décor. France, 1581.

72. Perspective. Italy, c. 1540.

42

75.

76. 77.

75. Permanent theater. France, 1641.

76. Proscenium and auditorium. Italy, 1616–17.

77. Transformation. France, 1686.

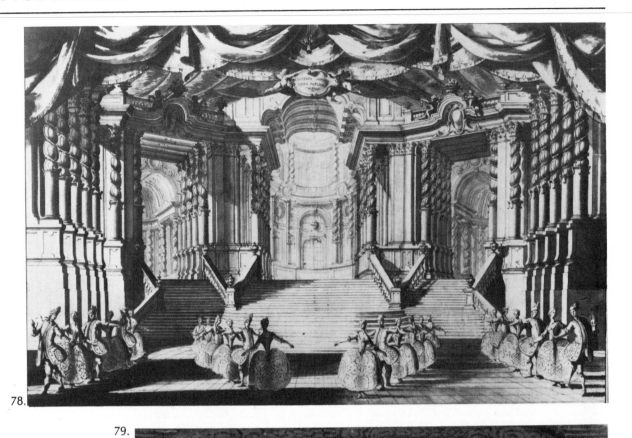

78.

79.

78. Symmetry. Italy, c. 1725.

79. Asymmetry. France, c. 1745.

80.

81.

80. *Ballets Russes*, 1910.

81. *Ballets Russes*, 1929.

tricity by the end of the nineteenth century, individual performers could be picked out and followed. But the specific science of lighting dancers can be attributed to Diaghilev, whose ubiquitous presence was sometimes a mystery: "But what do you actually *do*, M. Diaghilev?," journalists would ask, since he neither danced, designed, nor composed music. "*Moi? Je règle les lumières.*"

In the eighteenth century, the lavish occasional format of court ballet was reduced to town practicality. City theaters began to be built that could keep suites of scenery to accommodate seasonal repertory. While the means of rendering foliage, waves, and drapery was more playful, flakier, or lighter than before, the governing principles of design did not change much. Local color—authentic detail from archeological evacuation or explorers' sketches—assumed a new flavor benefiting from a more domestic format and a brighter view of the dancing. Halfway through the century, the public was excluded from sitting on stage, and this gave maximum space to the dancers. Innovations in design, when they came, were in the nature of ingenious cut-out scenes, back lighting, and transparencies. The experimental palettes of the great easel-painters would have little effect on contemporary opera-house practice.

Ballet as a theatrical spectacle became, in the nineteenth century, a special opera-house province. Scene-painter, costumier, machinist, dance-designer, dance-conductor and -composer ran their bureaus with relative efficiency, if mechanical style. The Italian Alessandro Sanquirico, who was engaged by La Scala from 1806 to 1832, served Viganò ably, working in a manner still largely Baroque, and was perhaps the outstanding lyric theater designer of the century. In Paris, Pierre-Luc Charles Ciceri set a Romantic atmosphere of pallid fantasy (1820–35); in London, the families of Grieve and Teblin furnished vernacular scenes, lacy foliate borders, and coarse architectural detail to meet workaday needs. Few designers aspired to individual vision, or seemed ever to have felt repercussions from Romantic painting, which from Baron Gros and Géricault to Delacroix and Courbet was transforming into newer visions the academic concepts that had so long guided official art. With the wisdom of afterthought (or appetites stimulated by Diaghilev), one may wonder why Blake was never called to dress ballet, or Delacroix to decorate—rather than only illustrate—Shakespeare. The English water colorists, the Pre-Raphaelites, Turner of the *Liber Studiorum* had no contact with stagescape. Reading notices of nineteenth-century ballet, one is struck by the haphazard frequency with which visual (or aural) aspects elicit much attention. The personality of a ballerina, her difference from other dancers, her charm, even her qualitative efficiency, yes; but what she appeared against, in what dress, what design supported her pantomime or gave glow to her gifts—barely a word.

We have observed how few progressive musicians who loved dance rhythms composed directly for the dance. Few painters who loved theater—Daumier, Doré, Gavarni, Degas, to Lautrec and Seurat—worked in it on any lasting basis. The opera house was administered by licensed intendants who never doubted that painters should keep to their places—studio or salon. Scenic decorators were hardly artists; the arcana of stagecraft, since it was all they possessed, was jealously guarded, and, since ballet in Western Europe greatly declined after 1850, painters considered it merely picturesque subject matter, a metaphor for the decadence of pubescent female mindlessness, a proprietary bourgeois brothel, or, at best, innocent frou frou, as in the posters of Jules Chéret.

After 1880, on certain advance-guard stages, the gifts of easel-painters began to be sought. In the private opera of the Muscovite Maecenas Sava Mamontov, a cousin of Stanislavsky, Post-Impressionist practice would be adapted by the Russian artists Vrubel, Korovin, and Golovin, laying groundwork for Diaghilev's later commissions. Gauguin's application of paint would reappear in Scythian disguise in Nicholas Roerich's cloths for *Prince Igor* and *Le Sacre du Printemps*. From 1887 to 1894, at André Antoine's Théâtre Libre in Paris, Lautrec, Bonnard, Munch, Vuillard, Redon, Maurice Denis, and K. X. Roussel designed single productions. There were significant technical differences between methods of executing Russian and French scenery. The French used a paint-frame that slid up and down, on the principle of an easel; the painter rendered a squared canvas for his sketch. Russians often spread their cloths on the floor and allowed a free flow, blot, and pooling, which gave vitality and vibration to their enlargements, making them, unlike the run of French work, less dry, tight, and thin. It must be remembered that the great Russian collections of Post-Impressionist and Fauve paintings were made before the début of the Ballets Russes, while Rouault's and Matisse's coarse boldness was still discounted in Paris as eccentric nonsense; their handling of paint was put to good use by the Russians in rendering scenery. But it was neither Impressionism, the Nabis, Post-Impressionism, nor the Fauves that first suggested new ideas for décor to Diaghilev and his two chief early collaborators, Alexandre Benois and Léon Bakst. Rather it was the graphic shock of Aubrey Beardsley, Frank Brangwyn, and other illustrators who followed William Morris in England and Austria during the 'eighties and 'nineties. Young Diaghilev tried to buy Beardsley drawings when the sick draftsman was in Dieppe. Although always immediately sensitive to music, Diaghilev genuinely loved Russian and Italian religious painting and provincial

276.
407.

81.

343.

80.

eighteenth-century Russian portraiture; a deeper visual appreciation came later, when he commissioned designs from leading contemporary artists, primarily for their novelty. Whereas the advance-guard in music, represented by Stravinsky, had been with him from the start, Diaghilev made no use of the Fauves or Cubists until 1917, when Jean Cocteau brought in Picasso for *Parade,* but by then he had been involved with Italian Futurism. Léon Bakst (1866–1924), who gave up his ambitions as an easel-painter to devote himself to theater, quickly understood the theatrical uses of French researches into luminosity, simultaneous contrasts, and the vibration of chromatics; for his triumphant *Schéhérazade* (1910), he appropriated the discoveries of Impressionism, including as well homage to Delacroix. He did no fully Pointillíst décors, however. An erudite stylist, he knew archaic as well as classical Greece and Crete first hand. Alexandre Benois (1870–1960) was more museum-oriented, a delicate and skillful illustrator in the Baroque and Rococo tradition of French, Scottish, and Italian architects and sculptors who raised Peter the Great's grand window on the West. Both men were experienced in theater and mastered the scale of opera houses and the specific needs of dancers. Intrinsically they were conservative and traditional; as such, Diaghilev was not slow to repudiate them. Yet they forged a strong, widely imitated style, giving the Ballets Russes its earliest familiar stamp.

With the outbreak of the First World War, separated from Russia, then his sole source of dancers, and prompted by Stravinsky's exploitation of Slav resources, Diaghilev made use of the vivid cloths of Larionov and Gontcharova, easel-painters in the advance-guard of a Russian renaissance, who transformed motifs from folk art through an adapted Fauve and Cubist idiom.

Picasso's ballets, particularly those supported by Satie, Stravinsky, and De Falla, were skillfully and wittily achieved. Picasso, the complete professional, was interested in the given problem and recognized that his responsibility differed between opera house and art gallery. Diaghilev had far less success, save for the cachet of names, with Matisse, Braque, Max Ernst, Juan Gris, and Vlaminck. For example, when Matisse delivered his rough drawings for Stravinsky's *Rossignol* in 1920, he had hoped for a new incarnation of *chinoiserie,* but what he was handed resembled, he complained, ordinary chinaware from the usual shops. But he had a shrewdness for survival; knowing his provision for dancers was weak during the 1920's, he engaged Paris' foremost easel-painters to dress his novelties. What he did from expediency has since been claimed as a model method. Apart from the work of Larionov, Picasso, Gontcharova, and André Derain, which was always produced with immaculate professionalism, he extracted what was useful to him from loose and cursory sketches offered him as samples of

painters' individual styles. Skillful technicians—scene-painters and dressmakers—then took over these scrappy indications and realized them for the actual stage, of which the artists had slight knowledge. In offering easel-painters' idiosyncratic sketches blown up to backdrop dimensions, with every accident of blot and scumble literally magnified, Diaghilev gave novel scale and style to the backgrounds against which dancers moved. The contrast in orientalism from Bakst's *Schéhérazade* to Rouault's *Prodigal Son* (1929) shows the shift in rendering from start to finish of an era. This was essentially a transference from the formulas of three-dimensional Baroque scenography (in Post-Impressionist painterly terms) suggesting enclosed space to the immediately recognizable, coarse, posterlike thumbprint of Fauve mannerism for one-dimensional enlarged paintings.

80.
81.

From around 1905, Isadora Duncan danced against deep blue-black or grey velour drapes, whose heavy folds lent her a rich neutral background with maximum focus on her movement and her then-extraordinary choice of important music. She was not visually motivated; few dancers or choreographers are. (Fokine talked constantly about museum art, but his own salon portraits betray his real taste.) Some theater artists, however, are so plastically or kinetically conscious, that taste—good, bad, or indifferent—is of slight importance. Isadora knew what was good for her. Gordon Craig's experiments with operatic décor (1900–1902) certainly made an impression. He sought scale and surface tactility through manipulation of vast screens; however, his ambitions were never viable in opera-house repertory. Craig offered Diaghilev a project in 1911; there was no issue. Craig was interested in his scenery far more than in dancers, and practical considerations irritated him. He was an innovator above all, demanding special conditions that no traveling troupe could provide. Neither could Diaghilev use Adolphe Appia, a noble designer who had made massive flights of abstract steps for Dalcroze dancers.

350.

Since Diaghilev's death, the situation remains more or less constant.* In France and England easel-painters have been attracted to ballet, rarely with notable results, although isolated creations have often surpassed the normal practice of professional designers. The demands of producing repertory on small subsidies with time-and-a-half overtime schedules, as much as the restrictions of the Scenic Designers Union—which systematically discourages American easel-painters from working in a field dominated by Broadway theater and TV—are not conducive to the involvement of easel-painters in ballet or opera. The inspiration for stage design today usually derives from two steady sources: museum, library, or print room, and one-man shows of contemporary artists, whose researches or styles can be borrowed.

---

* Since then, the exceptional décor of Pavel Tchelitchew, using light within screens rather than paint, and of Christian Bérard, using paint with a highly personal wit, have been in the spirit of Diaghilev's taste for elegant novelty. The sculptor Isamu Noguchi, designing particularly for Martha Graham, has suggested a new plastic ambiance with strong forms and reflective surfaces somewhat derived from Miró, Gabo, and Pevsner, who

had designed for Diaghilev. In the line of Diaghilev's practice, Marc Chagall has painted a series of attractive cloths in his popular palette with his familiar repertory of Russian-Jewish birds and beasts from folklore. Eugene Berman, from 1935 to 1955, continued the tradition of Baroque opera-house decoration in stylish pastiche.

82.

240.

274.

313.

Descriptions are only suggestive, here greatly reduced from detailed sources; a bibliography indicates the extent of available documentation. The music of many ballets can be played on pianos or heard on records. Pictorial testimony is spotty, even with photography. For reasons of space, names of collaborators are omitted except when memorable. Choreography, the map of movement as a developing process, its syntax and structure, is stressed. The following chart only outlines the growth of ballet over four centuries.

Priority:
A work is cited if it makes an initial, culminating, or archetypical statement. Ballets exceptional in form or style are those that affect tradition. When there was choice, it fell on works having the most vivid pictures.

Precedent:
No masterpiece proves a virginal novelty; seeds are in the past, however original, shocking, or surprising fresh work may first appear. Echoes or memories from prose, poetry, and plastic art combine in many ballets. A recurrence of similar elements in every epoch testifies to what is constant, useful, or necessary in tradition.

82. Proscenium stage. Italy, 1619.

6.

413.

83.

Politics:

Manipulation of power—by royalty, theater management, or private patronage—vitally affects the spectacle produced. Social and economic backgrounds of companies are crucial, as are the personal characters of dancers, teachers, and ballet masters. The caliber of administration plus the available treasury determine engagements and repertory.

Plot or Pretext:

When librettos propose dance action, they are indicated, but plots never describe dances. Studied in combination with pictures, they may help us to deduce style, presupposing a knowledge of the music. Narrative rarely suggests movement or design; iconography has always been more attentive to individual performers than to choreographic pattern.

Production:

Details of performances are noted, with minimal reference to individual performers, except as they are specially used. Choreography, rather than the success of great dancers, is the focus. Authority is given to initial occasions rather than revivals, except where one is definitive, although in most cases it will share with the original production only pretext and music.

83. Metaphor of movement. Italy, 1624.

84.

LE BALLET DES POLONAIS
(The Polish Ballet)
August 19, 1573
Paris
Palace of the Tuileries

Priority:

This indoor palace fete, loosely termed a "ballet," included spoken verse and song of greater importance than dance, embodying elements already familiar in Franco-Italian court shows. While its several components had been used before, *Le Ballet des Polonais* displays the marked French taste for figured dancing that would develop over the next century to become the dominant continental school. North-Italian dancing masters attracted to the Valois court brought a syntax of steps codified during the previous hundred and fifty years. Their French colleagues would learn this vocabulary and, with additions, translate it into their own style. International nomenclature for music (and the plastic arts) remained Italian; for dancing (diplomacy and cooking), France took over. In Italy, impetus in opera-ballet would be toward vocal virtuosity—aria into music-drama. France was more dance-oriented from the beginning, although after *Le Ballet des Polonais* more than a century would pass before dance completely disengaged itself from song. When it did, ballet emerged as a form approaching an autonomous art.

Precedent:

In ancient days, processions of symbolic floats on cars were voted by Roman senates to honor triumphant generals. Since the early Renaissance, adapting antiquity and following models sculptured on surviving triumphal arches, corps of singing and dancing citizens, costumed or disguised, hailed prince and soldier in superb parades. Honorific decorations contained niches framing living pictures that presented allegorical compliments. Success in battle, signature of treaties, royal births, coronations, and funerals were celebrated by designed feasts. Entries, interludes, and divertissements praised and amused the patron. In open-air tourney and equestrian show, as in banquet hall, tennis court, and parliamentary rooms transformed into temporary theaters, dance was as much a social as a spectacular activity. Medieval theater had been largely religious, controlled by craft guilds holding hereditary rights to perform portions of the Scripture in the ceremonial Christian calendar. Renaissance celebrations were secular. Medieval dumb show was adapted and developed into formal pantomime with expressive gesture more legible than spoken Latin. Dance and mimicry, partners, would keep step in complex measure for centuries.

Politics:

Le Ballet des Polonais, more focused than many court shows or private masquerades carefully produced for a single occasion in provincial châteaux, was no popular spectacle. It impressed an influential yet limited audience of courtiers and diplomats. The Massacre of St. Bartholomew's, climax of the strife between Catholic and Protestant, had occurred the year before, and court functions had been curtailed for months. Now Catherine de Médicis, the Queen Mother, wished to celebrate the election of her second son, Henri of Anjou, as King of Poland. The "ballet" was a collaboration of French poets and

a Flemish musician following Italian models, with an Italian dancing master guiding French amateurs. In spite of invoked models, it had nothing to do with antiquity; ballet's roots extend back only to Italy from the fourteenth to the sixteenth centuries. Due to competitive Italian courts, a rich cultural climate, a native impulse in music toward movement, formulation and codification had been largely Italian. An outstanding composer provided the score: the Italian-trained Fleming, Roland de Lassus (Orlando di Lasso), came to Paris in 1571, recommended by Bavarian dukes whom he had well served. With a European reputation, he was already published in France. By this time, the technique of engraving music, as well as pictures, had accelerated the spread of ideas far past hand-copying. Lassus arrived with two songs to words by the fine court poet Pierre Ronsard; the first, originally addressed to Henri II, was now transferred to the living Charles IX; the second was longer and praised the Queen Mother far more highly than the reigning monarch. Leader of the Pléiade, a constellation of court poets, Ronsard in his own time was praised on the level of Homer and Virgil.

91.

85.

Plot or Pretext:

In a large temporary theater, erected for the show, there was a small stage at one end from which steps led down to an expansive dance

87.

---

84. Royal medal. France, 1575.

85. *Apollon*. France, 1581.

floor. Spectators seated in garlanded arcades on three sides crowded the performers. First France, Peace, and Prosperity, personified by court ladies, celebrated their solemn rites. Toward the king, centrally seated, Silenus with four satyrs pushed a huge silver-gilt rock of lathe and canvas, twenty-six feet high, on which perched sixteen of the queen's ladies-in-waiting, representing the French provinces. These recited "eighty-nine Latin verses . . . well sung, though ill-composed," then descended from their mount for a formal measure, adapting popular ballroom steps to theatrical usage, moving about the central area. Finally the nymphs presented the king and important guests with gilt plaques engraved with pictures of appropriate produce from each province. General dancing by performers and the public followed.

Production:
It took an hour. Latin verses based on pedantic Italian formulas and ostensibly reconstructed from ancient metric were rendered into court French by Ronsard, then set to music by Lassus. Ronsard conceived allegory as *philosophia moralis,* or "the truth disguised under a mantle of fable." Dancers were instructed by Balthasar de Beaujoyeulx (born Baldassarino di Belgioioso), "the finest violin in Christendom," who is credited as founder of French court ballet. There were no professional performers. Brantôme, author of scandalous and revealing contemporary court memoirs, describes how, after having made a circuit of the floor, the nymphs, again seated on their rock as in a military encampment, stepped down, forming small battalions for maneuvers of "bizarre intention." This martial allusion derives from the medieval tourneys and prearranged land and water fights, which were more brilliantly produced in Florence than in France. A band of thirty viols accompanied the dancers, who,

88.

86.

"without one false step, to a lovely cadence," drew up before the king for ingenious figures, turns, turnabouts, counter-turns, interlacings, stops, and starts, in which "not one lady failed to memorize their order, all participants having solid judgment and excellent memories!"

After 1550, Italian dancing masters in Paris popularized unfamiliar forms, including the *brando,* a more complex spectacular theater dance, as well as the *ballo* and the *balletto,* which anticipated the contredanse and the quadrille. Such fantastic or grotesque entries in sequence produced divertissements loosely called "ballets." These would later be enhanced by professional execution, allowing pretexts for virtuosity and enlarging the idiom of the academic theatrical dance. The room's space

determined pattern; music measured the steps. Slow dances were followed by fast ones; low dances on the floor contrasted with leaping ones off of it. The practice of individual masters began to limit and define the language as elegant, stylized, natural movement; there was as yet little mimic gesture. Promptness, precision, correct placement of legs, feet, and arms laid the groundwork for an emergent school.

86. Social dance. France, c. 1582.

87.

87. Ballet finale, 1573.

88.

89.

88, 89. Social dance. France, 1581.

COURT BALLET: A Culmination

90.

BALLET-COMIQUE
DE LA ROYNE LOUISE
*(Queen Louise's Ballet
Entertainment)*
October 15, 1581
Paris
Salle Bourbon, Louvre

Priority:
"*Comique*" does not signify "comic," but rather "dramatic"—that designed to involve mind, sight, and hearing in a unity of allegorical action. The *Ballet-Comique de la Royne Louise* is one of the first efforts to realize a coherent choreographic spectacle, as proposed by court aestheticians on principles of reconstructed antiquity. In this collaboration, using talent of the highest level, dancing, at least from the published title, seems to have been memorable, although in seventy pages of music, but twenty were for ballet. *Ballet-comique* was closer to *opéra-comique* than to *ballet de cour*, and as an independent genre, its life was brief. It was too expensive; spoken and sung tirades too long and tiresome. Publication of the complete libretto with description, music, verse, and pictures gave it fame; it was widely imitated.

Precedent:
There had been many less gorgeous examples in the pastoral style, such as *Le Ballet des Polonais*, 1573, but these lacked scale or diversity. For Queen Louise's spectacle the subject matter, mythology culled from

Politian's *Orfeo* and Tasso's *Aminta*, was familiar to the ballet's cultivated audience, which could translate Italianate myth into current French events. Pagan legend had replaced Christian miracles and moralities a century before: In Bruges, 1468, a royal wedding party viewed the "Twelve Labors of Hercules"; Milan, 1489, saw "Jason and his Argonauts." As for spectacular dancing, England and Germany, throughout the sixteenth century, had mimed interludes in which patterned measures were a part.

Politics:
The ballet celebrated the marriage of the queen's sister, Margaret of Lorraine, to the Duc de Joyeuse. After recent painful religious civil wars, here was a proposal to heal old wounds, restore peace, and solidify central royal authority, which would lead to prosperity and national security. Allegory and dance were under Italian influence; music, décor—over-all taste—were French. At the end of the ballet, performers presented honored guests with symbolic emblems. The queen gave the king a disc blazoned with the emblem of a dolphin (a play on *dauphin*, which also means "heir apparent") over the motto "*Delphinum ut delphinem rependat*" ("A dolphin is given to receive a dauphin"). The political symbolism behind such occasions was stated succinctly by such iconography. Medals remained as souvenirs. Politian had provided emblematic *imprese* for Giuliano de' Medici; Shakespeare conceived an *impresa* for the Earl of Rutland, March 24, 1613, celebrating the anniversary of James I's accession. *Emblemata* (1531) was the first of many collections of pictorial cryptograms hiding moral meanings.

Plot or Pretext:
Ulysses, escaping from the enchantress Circe, throws himself (literally) at the feet of the centrally seated king, begging him to summon

Peace, Harmony, and a new Golden Age, in order to free him (Intelligent Man) and his bewitched companions from Evil. Circe complains of his escape, then retires disdainfully. In the first interlude three sirens and a triton sing while parading around the hall. A three-tiered fountain bears musical naiads and tritons. In a centered loge sit the queen and maids of honor. The fountain vanishes. Enter, by two trellised arches, in white satin and aigrettes, ten viols who play for the first "ballet": twelve pages dance with twelve naiads in spiral and triangular figures. Circe, daughter of Sun and Sea (corruption of one matter, generation of another) controls the cycle of the Seasons (an endless chain dance, with hands interlinked). While Ulysses can use his own intelligence, his companions cannot use theirs. Divine Intelligence is required. Jupiter, Pan, and Mercury, with dryads (earth spirits), attack Circe's castle; she is taken prisoner. Athena (Divine Intelligence) honors the (real) queen, spouse of the French Jupiter.

Production:
Staged in a vast hall of the old palace, the ballet lasted from ten at night until three in the morning. Scenery was distributed in isolated stations around the floor; there was no proscenium or separate stage area. Décor in set pieces gave chances for direct confrontations between actors and audience; the playing space was three-quarters in-the-round. At the rear were Circe's palace and garden; behind them, a perspective townscape. On the right stood Pan's grove and grotto, from which an organ sounded. At the left was a gilded vault, which hid "ten concerts of music." Mythological personages appeared on chariot-floats, dragged in by costumed stagehands who could be converted to chorus or *corps de ballet*. Exchanges of sung and spoken dialogue directly facing the royal party focused the spectacle with intense realism, since

73.

137.

93.

90. Dolphin (*dauphin*). France, 1581.

54

The circle, self-enclosed, with no angles—endless, infinite, unfocused —was celestial. Neoplatonists of the Renaissance, following a tradition from Pythagoras, read geometry not only as abstract measure but as symbolic speech. Methods to square the circle, and the resultant approximation of the octagon, spelled fusion of earth and heaven. In pictorial terms, the fountain, or font, meant baptismal grace, purity—the washing away of sin. The fountain of youth stood for sexual potency; fountains in paradise gardens spouted wisdom as well as oblivion. The warm-blooded dolphin, an unfishlike mammal, swam in pure waters. While there was slight attempt at virtuosity—few high leaps or quick turns—discipline was strict and manners elegant. The dance language was rudimentary; future impulse would be toward speed and elevation, increased brilliance and showmanship.

95.

Orchestration moved toward protosymphonism. There were limitations in using courtiers as chorus and *corps de ballet*, untrained though well rehearsed: although French and Italian derived from Latin, the chorus could not retain the strict quantities of antique syllabic meters, an alternation of long and short units regulating prosody, which imposed an artificial rhythm on music and restricted tempi in dancing. While all these contributing elements are complex, we are still only at a beginning.

royalty were the recipients of the laudatory action.

The dancing master, Beaujoyeulx (Baldassarino), claimed ballet as "a modern invention," or, at least, unknown since the ancients. Choreography, his map of movement, was "a geometrical arrangement of several persons dancing together, to the diverse harmonies of numerous instruments." His finale, or *grand ballet*, was danced by sixteen courtiers "in forty passages of geometric figures, neatly formed in diameter; some square, others round or oval . . . also triangular patterns accompanied by others subdivided into smaller quartets . . . so it reminded those who saw it of a combat army corps. So well was order kept, so cleverly each dancer studied and observed his rank and cadence . . . that Archimedes could not have better imagined geometric proportion than these princesses and ladies practiced in ballet." Preparations and

rehearsals could not have been simple or inexpensive. Direction was professional, but all performers save the instrumentalists were noble amateurs.

Since the public mostly sat on three sides of the hall, in double galleries looking down on the performers, it was afforded a clear impression of dance pattern, as seen against the floor. The floor, in fact, rather than the dispersed constructed décor, was the ballet's background. Certain choreographic figures were deemed to hold virtue by their very geometry and were titled according to sympathetic magic. Others were based on a "recently discovered" Druid alphabet that few could read. One ballet master was inspired by chickens running after scattered corn. The square, with its perfect formal symmetry, signified earth's solidity, the four cardinal compass points, the four seasons, and the four elements: earth, air, fire, and water.

91. Roland de Lassus, 1565.

92.

93.

92. Neptune, 1504.

93. Tritons. France, 1581.

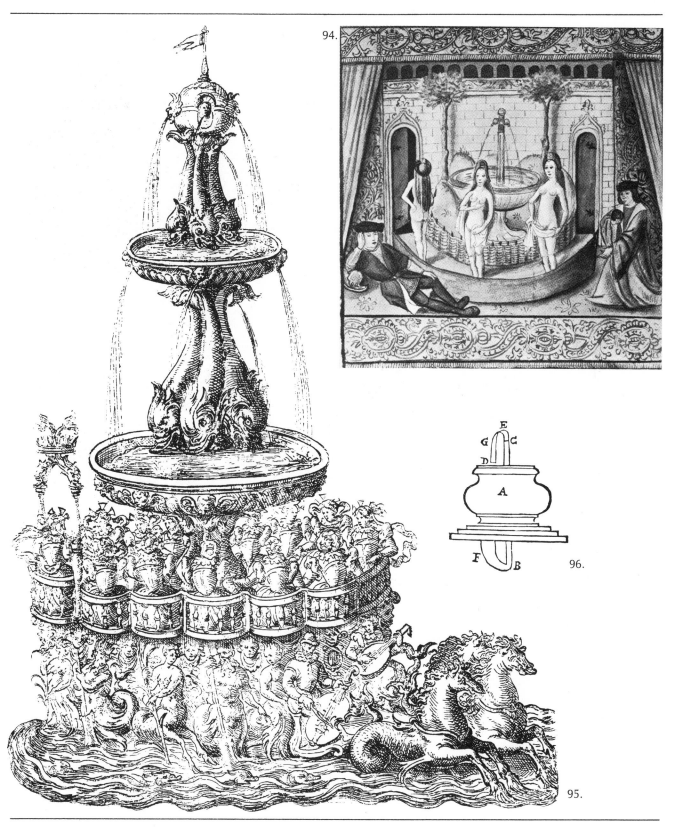

94.

96.

95.

94. Street show. Brussels, *c.* 1496.

95. Fountain décor. France, 1581.

96. Fountain machine. Italy, 1637–38.

97.

LA LIBERAZIONE DI TIRRENO E D'ARNEA, AUTORI DEL SANGUE TOSCANO

(The Liberation of Tyrsenus and Arnea, Seeds of the Tuscan Race)
February 6, 1616
Florence
Teatro Ducale, Uffizi Palace

Priority:

This is perhaps the first ballet to be documented by an artist. of quality, Jacques Callot (1592–1635), whose three engravings provide a vivid picture of a typical Florentine fete, to be widely imitated from Paris to Prague. The publication of such engravings was an important element in the dissemination of ballet.

Precedent:

The theater in the Uffizi opened in 1586 with an elaborate mytho-logical spectacle (including a scene from Dante's *Inferno*). A series of other shows followed, emphasizing musical and, particularly, visual elements, arranged by gifted Medici designers and engineers. The Uffizi was also the scene of complicated equestrian ballets and military tournaments, splendidly produced, in which dance had its incidental part. Here, as in the *Ballet-Comique of Queen Louise*, Circe, enchant-ress of Ulysses, is villainess.

Politics:

This *veglia* ("night vigil"), during which the ballet was performed, was held during Carnival and celebrated the wedding of Ferdinando Gonzaga, Duke of Mantua, to Caterina de' Medici, sister of Grand Duke Cosimo II. The author of the libretto, a court poet, borrowed his legend from Hesiod, tracing how Etruscans, original settlers of Tuscany (now ruled by Cosimo), came from Asia Minor to Italy, led by their prince, Tyrsenus. Such entertainments were more festival than theater, shows for a single occasion.

During the entire seventeenth century, France and Italy increasingly developed ballet. In Paris, Turin, or Florence, dancers were recruited chiefly from the ranks of courtiers; the main interest was the praise and prestige of princes, not performing skills. However, important musical and visual developments were pursued by professional artists, not amateurs. There was significant innovation, as expert musicians, designers, or dancers assumed increasing authority.

98.

76.

58

Plot or Pretext:

Prince Tyrsenus never appears. The libretto, a mélange from Ovidian mythology and Ariosto's *Orlando Furioso*, is a mere pretext for spectacle. Somehow, Circe, Hercules, and the island of Ischia had to be connected for song, dance, and staged fights. The audience was first informed that its Etruscan or Tuscan ancestors were imprisoned by Circe on Ischia, to be liberated by Hercules, aided by Jupiter, his father. The ballet starts with the arrival of Hercules; in the background, a smoking volcano. The imprisonment of the Etruscans is explained; Hercules promises aid, if his father agrees. Circe is drawn by dragons and gloats over the imprisoned Tyrsenus. Mars and Jupiter appear on a cloud machine; the volcano erupts. Thunderbolts are hurled against the mountain, which splits. The scene changes to hell (a Dantesque Inferno), where Circe begs Pluto, lord of hell, to aid her against the power of Love. Inconstancy appears on a wheel of fortune, opposite Faithfulness. Pluto is umpire of an ensuing combat-at-the-barrier between the armies of Circe and Tyrsenus. At the climax, Love himself appears, and the scene changes to his realm, a pillared courtyard. Amor and the chorus chant "No more war; no more fury!," the three Graces sing a madrigal, and the vigil closes with a ballet of elaborate choreographic floor pattern.

Production:

One of Callot's engravings depicts the moment when the mountain is split. Out of the fragments step a dozen dancers—*i cavalieri del balletto*; after they have executed an introduction, they are joined by twelve ladies, a chorus of Hamadryads, with Hercules. This was "a most beautiful ballet danced by twelve gentlemen, first on stage; then by the same twelve and by twelve richly dressed ladies in the center of the auditorium. The Grand Duke danced among the gentlemen, the Archduchess among the ladies." Dancers passed from the stage by two ramps and curved steps onto the main floor, where, after the finale, the performers would join with the public in social dancing. After the second intermezzo was sung, "two squadrons of gentlemen, twelve in each, performed various forms of combat, some with swords, others with pikes. The spectacle was over in some forty minutes, done with such gusto and beauty that everyone applauded, because one is all too aware of the horror which the length of such combats entail. . . . Finally, a ballet of forty ladies and forty gentlemen; to these were added jousters."

France was to develop ballet as a language, building on the base set in Italy during the fourteenth century in dance-songs called *balletti*, which were performed in the street or in palaces. In Lombardy, the Veneto, and elsewhere in northern Italy, *canzoni a ballo* ("songs for dancing") included a soloist, an alternating chorus, dances, and perhaps elements of recited verse; these were later adapted for use in court figures, which began to follow the music more strictly. Improvisation and suggestions from folk dancing helped court dancing masters name steps and arrange their sequence in an increasingly fluent syntax. Choreographic rules were formulated, such as the alternation of fast and slow, high and low, activity and repose. The basis of the future academic dance was laid in two categories: "natural" bodily movements—simple and double steps, enhanced by noble presence or physical bearing; the bow and curtsy; turn, half-turn, and jump; and "accidental" movements—running steps, small beating movements of the feet; the ability to manage a partner's robe and skirt. Accidental gave variety to natural. The codification of these fundamental steps has been compared to notes in the musical scale, which opened an evolution for the suite, sonata, and symphony. Italian dancing masters of the Renaissance did not depend heavily on mimicry or pantomime, but analyzed movement sequences in themselves, as they moved in their own interest and dignity toward abstraction of gesture. Dancing masters began to be treated as artists rather than entertainers.

The Milanese were welcome everywhere. Their school was not known as Italian, but as ballet dancing; their academy was imposed on many European provincial courts. The tradition took on a unity, flavored to some degree by national characteristics, but dominated by the French, due to specific encouragement by royalty and an increasing support of an official professional academy.

98.

98. Etruscan warrior, 4th century B.C.

59

99.

100.

99. Armed dancers. Greece, c. 510 B.C.

100. Pyrrhic dance. Greece, 4th century B.C.

101. *Tirreno*. Interlude II.

102. *Tirreno*. Finale.

LA DÉLIVRANCE DE RENAUD
(The Liberation of Rinaldo)
January 29, 1617
Paris
Grande Salle, Louvre

Priority:
A presentation in person of the sovereign, Louis XIII, as demi-god, central power over disruption, and first-dancer, depicting in fantastic terms the triumph of order over anarchy. Elements of recitative in rhetorical verse were reduced in favor of more dancing. Action explained itself, and decoration was now less important than choreography. *Le Ballet-Comique's* stationary free-standing scenery had been dispersed about the hall. *Renaud,* by contrast, used shifting scenery enclosed within a proscenium. In the former, movement was processional, around the room; in the latter, it was framed and focused at one end.

The high style of late Renaissance and Baroque art lent its heroic grand manners to shape ballet, which, once purely a court function, today retains echoes of such behavior. Virtuoso singing and dancing demand a style larger than life. Naturalism, the comic, ironic, or grotesque add spice to pantomime, but the classic dancer's prime roles are most gratefully tragic or fantastic, metaphors of man's mortality and possibility. For subject matter, Arthurian or Carolingian epics, combined with legends of classical antiquity, now replaced the Biblical symbolism mandatory during the Middle Ages. Present also in *Renaud* were dominant ideas from contemporary literature.

Ariosto's *Orlando Furioso* (1516), followed by Tasso's *Gerusalemme Liberata* (finished 1575; published 1580–81), married classical myth and epic romance with Christian philosophy. Ignoring hackneyed Biblical allusion, this seemed a fresh expression, glorifying modern Europe as Homer exalted

Greece or Virgil Rome. Tasso's Jerusalem is the City of God; his poem revives the ancient tension between town and country, organized society against anarchic nature. The sacred city is contrasted with tempting magic gardens. Here nature is a lovely trap for soldiers who would better be besieging Jerusalem. The Crusader, a pious, dedicated knight, by defeating the Saracens gains salvation for Christ's city and his own soul. The garden is illusory, frustrating, corrupting—more beautiful the more evil. The perilous ambivalence of physical versus moral perfection, metaphor of long traditions of contest between classical and Christian culture, shows also the eternal struggle between illusion and reality, love and duty, sex and God. City is superior to garden, mind to matter, salvation to enjoyment. It is more suitable for the king's subjects to live in a condition of divine grace than in a state of prelapsarian nature.

Precedent:
Le Ballet de Madame (1615) had purportedly celebrated the king's coming-of-age, but actually was a frank statement of the power of his Queen Mother, Marie de Médicis. *Le Ballet de Monsieur Vendosme* (1610) was a political allegory using characters from Ariosto's *Orlando Furioso*, with burlesque features—owls, dwarves, Turks (Saracens).

Gerusalemme Liberata, within a decade of publication, supplied subjects for painters, musicians, and dancing masters. Its first illustrated edition (Castello: Genoa, 1590) may have suggested costumes, scenery, and groups. Another edition by the same artist (1617), coming after preparations for this ballet had begun, could serve subsequent producers of a now popular theme, who were always conscious of available iconography; pictorial tradition is as important as poetic and musical. One of the earliest illustrations (if

not the very earliest) of a court show (1378), given before the Holy Roman Emperor, displayed the conquest of Jerusalem by Godefroy de Bouillon (1099). Peter the Hermit is seen praying in his ship, which floated in and out on rollers.

Politics:
Prevented by a strong-willed mother from participation in state affairs, Louis XIII confined himself to music and hunting with his favorite, Charles d'Albert, Duc de Luynes. The *Renaud* production suggested the king was asserting authority to re-establish central royal power. Louis' public performance was also to reassure Spanish and Austrian ambassadors (his wife's partisans) that his marriage was successful in spite of de Luynes' and his apparent frigidity.

With Cardinal Richelieu as his prime minister, a *ballet à grand spectacle* would be a systematic means of exalting the image of monarchy. The king chose the plot (used before) and danced its lead; he had performed in public once previously. His dancing, a reflection of his regal essence, was dignified by his role as the Demon of Fire (equivalent to Apollo, the Sun God) whose manifest wisdom might please the Protestant opposition, humor jealous princes, warn enemy nations, and legitimize central authority from Paris over the provinces. Behind the fictive show, there was drama aplenty. The young sovereign stammered, pretending boredom and idleness. Few noticed he was now come of age, his own man. Underneath his impersonation he had a style of his own—energetic, intelligent, cruel, and quite capable of the death of his mother's favorite. *Renaud* frames him, aged sixteen, on the verge of taking over. The following April 26 he had Concini, Maréchal de l'Ancre, the Queen's creature, assassinated. On May 3 he exiled the Queen Mother to Blois. Richelieu, for the mo-

109

75.

ment, retired. The political significance of this ballet, as of many to come, was lost on neither performers or public.

Plot or Pretext:
In Tasso's *Gerusalemme Liberata*, Armida (cousin to Circe or Medea), niece and adept of the wizard king of Damascus, infiltrates the Crusader camp, sets fire to its tents, and takes prisoner the entire Christian élite. Rinaldo *(Renaud)* alone resists. Furious, she manages to enchant him by her earthly or daemonic charms. In his absence from battle the Christians lose; but when her powers fail, he escapes to deliver Jerusalem (Christendom).

After a brief prelude, scored for sixty-four voices, twenty-eight viols, and fourteen lutes, the curtain, painted with a grand perspective of a palace in deep landscape, fell (rather than rose) to reveal a mountain, in whose niched grotto is enthroned the Demon of Fire. At the base of the mount lies Rinaldo (de Luynes, the favorite). To viol music Demons of Air descend into the hall to dance. Rinaldo follows; Fire scolds him for having left without his permission. The scene changes to Armida's enchanted garden with three gushing fountains. Two soldiers, ancient Romans, watch a radiant nymph rise from the water, but they resist her magic, and she disappears. Enter monsters, owls, a grotesque lawyer, a peasant with dog's legs and head, two monkey chambermaids. But neither beauty nor ugliness can sway true Christian hearts. Now Rinaldo, obsessed by passion for Armida, praises earthly lust. The two soldiers force him to gaze into a crystal mirror in which he beholds the faults of his wasted youth, laziness, and pride. Overcome with shame he casts away his rich jewels, symbols of waste and vanity. Armida, furious at such remorse of conscience, summons all her basest earth-trained creatures—snails, crayfish, lobsters, turtles—who are transformed into

idiotic old men. They parody Armida's futile rage. The scene changes; antique ruins: a car rolls in bearing a grove of trees, with, behind each trunk, a Crusader. With Peter the Hermit, inspirer of the Crusade, these celebrate Rinaldo's liberation from his sinful self. Mortal Passion is overcome by Divine Reason. Two gilded palms shoot up; ninety-two voices and forty-five instruments hymn Rinaldo's triumph. As Godefroy de Bouillon (transformed from the Demon of Fire) once freed Jerusalem from the Saracens, so Louis frees France from disorder. All Europe does homage to this God-protected king, now apotheosized in the final general dance.

Louis represents divine authority on earth: *le prince absolu*. Armida stands for man's undifferentiated appetite, lustful, energetic, mindless. Rinaldo is knightly human youth, whose unlimited capacity must be directed by such as Peter the Hermit, representing both humane intelligence and divine reason. The opening and closing *grands ballets* demonstrate harmonious order; these are divided by bizarre, grotesque, ignoble, and disorderly measures.

Production:
The king and his suite entered the Louvre's Salle Bourbon around eleven at night. There were maddening delays. He started the performance at two-thirty a.m.; it lasted until five in the morning. The big room was hazy with drifting smoke from lamps and torches, which added a fortuitous magic to fresh paint, embroidery, and gilding, on scenery, armor, and fountains. Male dancers were masked, partly in imitation of the antique, partly because they were "amateurs in facial expression." French music of the early seventeenth century derived from Italian, but was already enlarging its own lyric stimulus, which was more descriptive, clear, and humane. The French were less occupied with academic

prosody, based on interpretive analyses of Greek and Roman metrics, which obsessed the Italians and led them more in the direction of vocal music-drama than dancing. French melody propelled movement and action; repeats were rare. The final *grand ballet*, excluding women and all commoners, exalted the legitimacy of an aristocracy, immutable, absolute, consisting of grave, noble *terre à terre* steps, simple turns, and glides; little elevation, no acrobatics nor mimicry, all within the stiff capacity of high-heeled shoes. Costumes were heavily embroidered, brocaded, padded—unsuitable for quick movement. *Renaud* was notable for its new system of changing scenery: painted panels were moved onto a fixed frame in slots; the central unit revolved on a small turntable.

41.

103.

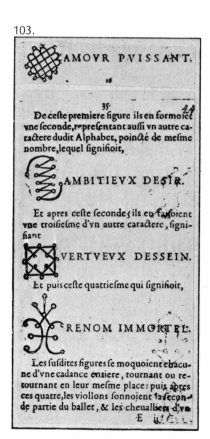

103. Choreography moralized. France, 1610.

104.

105.

106.

104. River festival. Italy, 1608.

105. Armida and earth demons. Paris, 1617.

106. Crusaders. Paris, 1617.

107.

108.

110.

109.

107. Medieval round dance. Netherlands, c. 1480.

110. Rinaldo and Armida. Italy, c. 1590.

108. *Renaud.* Sixth ballet entry.

109. Marriage of Louis XIII, 1624.

THE ENGLISH COURT MASQUE

111.

SALMACIDA SPOLIA
(Spoils of the Fount Salmacis)
January 21, 1640
London
Whitehall

Priority:

This, the last of the English court masques, may be cited as typical of the local adaptation of Franco-Italian models, employing dancing to a lesser degree than verse, music, or machinery. Librettos of French ballets were printed early; Prague, Stockholm, Warsaw, or Madrid made their own versions, often within a short time of the Paris production. In England during the early seventeenth century, two pre-eminent collaborators, the poet Ben Jonson and the architect Inigo Jones, raised the masque into a particular genre that included theatrical dance as subsidiary feature; it was characteristically richer in ideas and decoration than in dance.

The masque also focuses the historical position of ballet in England. Henry VIII, Elizabeth I, and Charles I loved to dance. French and English performers exchanged appearances before the end of the

sixteenth century. However, we know little of dancing or dancers in Shakespeare's plays, although he included masques, and we assume his actors danced. The pantomime of the Italian virtuosos was assimilated—characters from the *commedia dell'arte* are found in *Salmacida Spolia*—and, generally, the dominant criteria remained Continental rather than local.

There was no national academy until the twentieth century, and only in the last fifty years has Britain consistently provided professional dancers of international caliber. England's primacy in dramatic literature makes this seem strange, yet logical. Her poets and playwrights led Europe, and from earliest times there was preference for spoken narrative. What dancing there was in anti-masques, or interludes, grew increasingly gestural, leading to the mixture of music with pantomime that, in the nineteenth century, became a characteristic national tradition, and is still to be seen in Christmas extravaganzas. English composers were not attracted to ballet.

Precedent:

Masques derived from medieval folk custom in which fantastically disguised mummers sang, danced, and, as a final act, invited spectators to join. Christmas revels, rooted in antiquity, included the carol, a danced song probably from Provence, and the morris, once a sword dance, possibly of Moorish origin.

These were vehicles for folk figures —Robin Hood, Maid Marian, Little John. Features from Burgundian court tourneys were borrowed by the Tudors; in 1545, there was a Master of Revels, and Ben Jonson became court poet for the revels in 1603. He tried to maintain a verbal logic as a foil for the overwhelming Italianate mechanical and pictorial ingenuity of Inigo Jones, whose scenic genius stands with Torelli's. Movement patterns

followed those in European dance manuals, with additions from local country dances. There were few foreign ballet masters at the English court. Around 1609, the anti-masque was introduced; this was a danced and mimed interlude that contrasted with a formal sung or spoken section. In France, the *grand ballet* was the finale; the English version occurred in the middle of the work.

41.

The source of the story of the Salmacian spring, which has traces of Orphic myth and which Davenant read in Ovid's version, is obscure and tangential to the masque, but demonstrates how a specific show was triggered by a tale that attracted a learned poet, to be transformed in the telling, with some aspects suppressed, others enlarged, and ornament added. Hermaphroditus, of dubious sex, son of Hermes and Aphrodite, was given to dryads on Mount Ida to conceal his anomaly. He grew up wild and rude. In Caria (Asia Minor), he came to a pond ruled by the nymph Salmacis. He repulsed her; she cursed him. They fell in love, merged to become one body, and he who bathed in their water lost his virility.

In the pretexts for its entries, the ballet of *Salmacida Spolia* also derives in part from *Le Ballet de la Foire de Saint Germain*, given in Paris, 1612.

Politics:

Charles I's final struggle with Parliament had begun; the Thirty Years' War, starting in Bohemia (1618) and involving all Europe, now threatened England with civil and religious strife. Despite this and harsh differences with Scotland, Charles ignored the facts. "The King is dayly so imployed about the Maske, as till it be over, we shall think of little else," a courtier noted on January 9, 1640. Sir William Davenant's verses for *Salmacida Spolia* pleaded unity, dispersal of discord, defense of the

114.

111. Fury. England, 1640.

throne against an unruly people, an overweening priesthood, and foreign threats. Only in the twenty danced anti-masques were current events forgotten or ignored. The exile, Marie de Médicis, mother-in-law of Charles, was in the audience of this last artistic statement of the divine right of kings.

Plot or Pretext:
Aside from the roles taken by the king (called Philogenes, "lover of his people") and the queen, the characters were Fury, the Good Genius of Britain, Concord, and a choir of Beloved People. The pretext referred to Salmacis, an antique fountain that attracted a tavern-keeper to set up his inn nearby. Its pure waters appealed to barbarians, who were transformed by its crystalline liquor to adopt the mildness of Greek manners. Salmacian spoils, gained without bloodshed, are preferable to victories in which

anarchy descends on victor and vanquished alike. The Good Genius of Britain, with Concord, "being arrived at the earth and descended from the chariot, . . . incite the beloved people to honest pleasures and recreations, ever peculiar to this nation." The twenty anti-masques included: "Confection of Hope and Fear to entertain lovers"; "Julep of fruition, to recreate the hot fevers of love"; "A subtle quintessence drawn from mathematical points and lines, filtered through a melancholy brain to make eunuchs engender"; "Spirit of Satyrus' high capers and Bacchus' whirling vertigos to make one dance well." (In the French libretto, upon which this last entry was based, this read: "Spirit of the *caprioles* of Saturn, the *entrechats* of Vulcan, the *pirouettes* of Bacchus"; so specific a reference to the academic dance vocabulary might have been less clear in Britain.)

112.

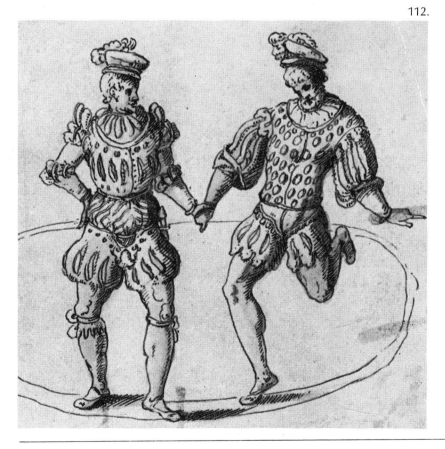

112. Fays. England, 1611.

Production:
Salmacida Spolia is fully documented by text and Jones's beautiful drawings and working plans. It cost fourteen-hundred pounds, a large sum. The highest nobility performed, with no professionals. The dances are unattributed, and there is no indication of choreography, but numerous references to expression in face masks and dumb show. Patterns generally followed meander, square, circle, triangle. Twelve dancers as nymphs spelled out the name of Anne of Denmark, "Anna Regina." (Francis Bacon wrote: "Turning dances into figures is a childish curiosity.") In the eighteenth entry—"Three Swisses, one a little Swiss who played the wag with them as they slept"—the court dwarf, Sir Geoffrey Hudson, danced the Little Swiss. He had already played Tom Thumb in Ben Jonson's *Fortunate Isles*. Inigo Jones introduced from Italy (and France) not only the picture-frame proscenium and scenery that could be changed, including painted perspective flats sliding in grooves and turntables mounted with many-faceted constructions, but also a vast wit and richness in costume, less extravagant than French dress design, but more elegant and better adapted to body movement.

103.

42.

67

113. Furies. England, 1640.

114. Philogenes. England, 1640.

115.

116.

117.

115. *Salmacida Spolia*. Scene 5.

116. *Salmacida Spolia*. Anti-masque I.

117. Masquers borrowed from *commedia*. London, 1640.

118.

LA FINTA PAZZA
(LA FOLLE SUPPOSÉE)
(The Maiden Feigning Madness)
September 19, 1645
Paris
Salle du Petit Bourbon, Louvre

Priority:

In inviting Giacomo Torelli, the scenic designer and engineer, to Paris, Cardinal Mazarin, Richelieu's successor (and an Italian), borrowed the greatest talent available, irrespective of nationality. Torelli immediately established the proscenium arch as a frame for spectacle, eliminating forever dancing areas on auditorium floors. This permitted elaborate movable scenery and the developed use, in Paris, of stage machinery heretofore possible only in Florence and Venice.

Precedent:

La Finta Pazza, a *dramma per musica*, or opera with interludes, had been produced in Venice (1641), featuring the first important décor of Giacomo Torelli, perhaps the most original scenic designer of the seventeenth century. Basing his work on that of Italian Renaissance artists—easel-painters as well as decorators—Torelli established a language of fictive magnificence, creating architecture and landscape in a style that would become the common expression of the Baroque, to be inherited by Bérain in France, the Bibiena in Italy and Austria. Improvised theaters in palace ballrooms could hardly accommodate the new shifting perspective scenery—painted canvas hung on ropes or guided in slots—equipped with machinery to make clouds support choirs. For the Venice production, Torelli linked eight pairs of wings to counterweights that "one boy aged 15" could manage; flats were hung on frames that moved back and forth on a trolley under the stage, all connected by ropes to a central drum.

The Indians, ostriches, parakeets, and monkeys of the several ballet entries reflected a century of world voyages, the beginnings of imperial colonization in India, America, and Africa. The monkey, in particular, as a parody of man, was a favorite for comic roles; painters and ceramicists would make a special genre of *singerie* ("monkey tricks"). In a lovely miniature at Chantilly, attributed to Geoffrey Tory (c. 1532), François I is shown with his monkey pet at table. Aesop's *Fables* had been repeatedly illustrated since 1476. On February 18, 1613, John Chamberlain, the letter-writer, noted the marriage of Princess Elizabeth of England to the Prince Palatine: "The twelve maskers with their torch-bearers and pages rode likewise upon horses exceedingly well trapped and furnished, beside a dozen little boys dressed like baboons that served for an antimasque (and they say performed it exceedingly well). . . ." *Danina, or Jocko, the Brazilian Ape* was a popular ballet-pantomime from 1825 when Charles Mazurier, a famous character dancer, first performed it in Paris. A portrait of Marius Petipa, the great Franco-Russian ballet master, shows him as a boy with his monkey pet. George Balanchine's first role at the Marinsky Theater was as a monkey in Petipa's *La Fille du Pharaon* (1917).

87.

118.

304.

305.

118. Morisco. Germany, 1500.

Politics:

Mazarin, as a matter of political prestige, popularized Italian opera and theater in Paris. The queen of France requested the duke of Parma to send her his ballet master, Giovanni Battista Balbi (c. 1600–1655), and Torelli, his scenic designer. Parma had had its fine permanent theater, with resources for moving slotted scenery, since 1619. Now the duke sent Torelli and Balbi to Paris, where Italian companies had been playing since 1571. Balbi and Torelli at first felt badly treated, since, instead of being attached to the queen, they were merely on the actors' payroll. Balbi, known as Il Tasquino ("the tease"), said his dances aimed at little but to please Louis XIV, a seven-year-old child-king. Possibly Balbi sensed pathos in his situation; fatherless, ill-kempt, ignored, unloved, the lonely boy was once pulled out of a pool in the Palais Royal, half-drowned.

Plot or Pretext:

Achilles is disguised as a woman by his mother, who fears he will be slain if he goes to the siege of Troy. When the gods arrive to persuade him to fight, the maiden Deidamia, by whom he has a son, feigns madness to hold him. Jove aids her, and everyone credits her insanity except her father who, discovering the deceit, imprisons her in a garden. At the end, Achilles agrees to marry her, and a heavenly choir sings the praise of reason restored.

Production:

The Paris production took place on a stage bigger than the Venetian. A prologue was added; cuts and other adjustments made. Balbi's ballets seem, from engravings, to have been in the free style of the Italian popular comedians, with their fixed routines of apparently improvised but well rehearsed tricks, set to music and often linked by dance steps. Unlike the run of French ballet divertissements, they have little to do with

the plot. When the female disguise of Achilles is first discovered, the first dance is for four eunuchs (a possible reference to his impersonation?), four bears, and four monkeys. Turbaned Turks (harem guardians?) sprinkle the floor, mop it, and lead in bears who dance to their own drumbeats. At the end of the second act, six ostriches, disturbed by Deidamia's madness, enter two by two, pecking; they drink from a fountain. In the finale when Achilles decides to get married, a boat filled with eight plumed Indians arrives; they congratulate the bridal pair and dance to tambourines with cymbals and parasols. Crossing swords, they release five parrots. The dances resemble those later to be called *danses de caractère*, those based on characteristic regional or occupational steps, with costumes and hand props extending the definition. Symmetry seems to have been a main formal element, as it was in scenery, which was of fantastic magnificence. Virtuosity was displayed less in dancing than in overwhelming décor. The Italians used some ten types of scenic

119.

decoration that repeatedly served opera or ballet; these included palace courtyards; harbors; seascapes; palace rooms (large and small); prisons; gardens (with and without formal flower beds); forests (deep or shallow); and military encampments. In *La Finta Pazza*, the Prologue was set in the Garden of Flora, with trees in perspective; a harbor showed in its background an actual Parisian scene—the Pont Neuf with the beak of the Ile de la Cité, the equestrian statue of Henri IV commissioned by Marie de Médicis, and the flèche of La Sainte Chapelle. There was little sense of locale, since scenery made for one ballet was often adapted to another. Grandeur, the illusion of space, rich ornament, and a huge scale were most desired. A curtain was not lowered between the acts.

We may imagine early dances were slow and sedate; there were also fast ones. Italian masters of the late sixteenth and early seventeenth centuries had established a skeleton, which time would flesh out to our full vocabulary. Already, two paramount principles were presupposed, the turn-out of the legs and the full *plié*, or deep knee bend. Five steps in the galliard (a form usually in 3/2 time, from the fifteenth century) may have determined the five basic foot positions of the academy. A set preparation for the turn (*pirouette*), with rounded arms, was already established.

70.

143.

12.

119. *Commedia.* Netherlands, 1696.

120–29. *La Finta Pazza,* entries.

126.

127.

128.

129.

130.

LE BALLET DE LA NUIT
(The Ballet of Night)
February 23, 1653
Paris
Salle du Petit Bourbon, Louvre

Priority:
Louis XIV, aged fourteen, presents himself as *Roi Soleil*, Sun King, his favorite role at court and before the world. *Le métier du roi*, "the craft of kingship," enhanced his image as abstract symbol incarnate in living performer. This ballet makes early use of a specific setting, not only as décor, but integrated with dancing.

Under the influence of Jesuit instruction, theater was designed to teach rather than merely amuse. A didactic tool was the cloaking of morality by myth. To begin with, the Society of Jesus compared itself to Mercury, messenger of the gods. La Fontaine, the great fabulist, said that moralizing without adornment was a bore, but that its embodiment in myth made a point acceptable. Hence, unlike numerous Italian spectacles, in the more rational French court shows myth and allegory were not perfunctory.

Mythology was taught methodically; manuals detailed the canonical accoutrements of divinity (*les équipages des dieux*). Boccaccio's *Genealogy of the Gods* (1372) linked the legendary lives of the Olympians, half-forgotten through the Dark and Middle Ages to the Renaissance. This was supplemented by handbooks that provided programs for Italian frescoes and pretexts for French opera-ballets. Hence, the grammar of mythical metaphor, absorbed by courtiers from school days, was not farfetched, but, in the hands of court poets and painters, apposite and legible.

Precedent:
The Triumph of Time was a subject familiar from antiquity. Chronos with hourglass and Father Time with scythe go back far past medieval picturing. *La Déliverance de Renaud* (1617) had found a similar frame for the King of Fire as a flaming divinity. Thirty-six years later, the star of *Le Ballet de la Nuit* was flattered as his father's heir when he danced as the Sun. In *Le Ballet du Chasteau de Bicêtre* (Paris, 1632) counterfeiters danced, spangled with coins, hats, and jackets dripping with metal plaques —base lead not gold—ready to be minted. Familiar street scenes were shown in a provincial ballet called *Les Rues de Paris* (1647). Popular imagery with precise pantomime served as contrast to exalt the grandiose manner and atmosphere of formal ballet.

Politics:
There had been continual resistance to the throne. The Paris *parlement*, the middle class, and the peasantry were joined against Anne of Austria, the Queen Mother, and Giulio Mazarini, her first minister. Cardinal Mazarin called the *parlement* slingshots (*frondes*) who broke his windows. The Frondeurs wore hat cords knotted like slings. High taxes and general misery made allies of bourgeois and worker. In 1651, the year of Louis XIV's majority, a mob invaded the Palais Royal; two years later the Fronde was defeated and absolute monarchy ensured.

Mazarin remained in Paris, but he is unmentioned in this libretto. Normal life was restored to the capital; the first *récit* of this ballet praised Anne, the victress. Sung and spoken verse prophesied the uncrowned king's expected prowess in love and war. He appeared in six roles, among them a Flame and the Rising Sun. At Louis' birth (1638), a medal had been struck with the motto *"Orbis Solis Gallici"* —"the Risen Sun of Gaul." Caesar identified himself with the sun; Pharaoh had been Ra, Re, or *roi*. The king was to live in full view, not alone in public entries, visits,

130. Royal ballet. France, 1651.

and battles, but in his private *lever, diner, souper,* and *coucher.* His every action was staged. He impersonated and incarnated *Gloire,* instructing his grandson: "The Nation is not the same as France; it resides entirely in the *Person* of the King." Benserade, his librettist, gave him the line: "*Je suis l'astre des Roys,*" "I am the star of kings" (their prime luminary). His motto was "*Nec Pluribus Impar,*" not least—hence first—among many. Louis was pleased to manifest his majesty in dancing. Something of his conscious courtesy has always clung to the classic style. Coming of age, gentlemen put on full-bottomed wigs, a property of the antique actor. Dancers were always masked; court manners, in fact, were masks of politeness. The self was hollow; princes chose their archetypes. It was easier for the king to see himself as Alexander, Rinaldo, or Apollo than Louis of France, fourteenth of that name. Hercules, the beneficial strong man, had been appropriated by Charles V, Holy Roman Emperor. He was hero, not god; he never danced or incarnated divine grace in action, but only superhuman energy. Hercules (with Jason) was also claimed by Italian princelings; he became a fixed French symbol with Henri IV ("Hercule Gaulois"), and then with Louis XIII. when *condottieri* in quest of power were replaced by a king who inherited it. France was not an empire; its aim was not limitless expansion but strength within natural frontiers. Louis XIV served as master image for many "apes of the king" in Saxony, Sweden, Poland, and Russia. In 1656, he took the Sun as his sign. In his reflected rays, ballet behavior spread over Europe.

Plot or Pretext:
In four "vigils," with forty-three entries, the ballet symbolically spanned twelve hours, three in each scene. An abbreviated outline follows:

I. Six to nine o'clock. Night, at-

tended by twelve Hours. "What ordinarily happened" within this time in town and country. Sun sets; Night follows on an owl-drawn car. Characters include hunters, bandits, shepherds, gypsies, knife-grinders, lamp-lighters, and dancers dressed as lamps. The scene shifts to a *cour des miracles;* beggars, vagabonds, false cripples cast off crutches for a grotesque serenade. This scene showed a Paris square into which police dared not go; it boasted its own lawless king. Three years later it was razed; Victor Hugo used it in *Notre Dame de Paris,* as did Jules Perrot, who turned his book into the ballet *Esmeralda* (1844).

II. Nine to midnight, time for fetes and ballets. Three ballets-within-the-ballet: *Les Noces de Thétis* (heroic myth); a masquerade with characters from *Orlando Furioso;* and *Amphitrion,* a *comédie-muette,* or dumb show (in the style of the *commedia dell'arte*). Three Fates, Gloom, and Old Age are powers of Darkness; Venus floats down with Comus, the Happy Spirit, accompanied by Smiles and Games.

III. Midnight to three A.M. The Moon loves Endymion. The astrologers Ptolemy of Egypt and Zoroaster the Persian, with telescopes, are amazed by the eclipsed Moon. Corybantes try to bring her back; a witches' sabbath. Thieves try to loot a burning house; half-naked sleepers carrying children, cats, and monkeys flee the flames; the thieves, though they pretend to be fire-fighters, are caught.

IV. Three A.M. to sunrise. Sleep, silence. Demons (Four Elements and Four Temperaments) are present. Counterfeiters quit their den; smiths fire their forge. The day-star shines. Aurora (dawn) appears with her twelve Hours, and Rising Sun (the king), accompanied by Happy Spirits, is praised by Honor, Grace, Love, Riches, Victory, Fame, and Peace.

Production:
The connecting theme was logical, continuous alternation of diverse elements—poetic, grotesque, picturesque, and satirical—combined with magic and allegory. There was metamorphosis in individuals as well as scene shiftings: Thétis became an animal, a rock, a fire. Jupiter turned into Amphitrion. Transformations of persons and places were Ovidian metaphors of unlimited power; magical changes promised unlimited political possibility. Halfway through the century we find in one spectacle, representing the developments of seventy-five years, social dances theatricalized, pure theater invention, realistic observation, and expressive mimicry borrowed from the Italian comedians, all still in combination with recitation and sung words. Professionalism in performance was not as advanced as engineering or design. The king, being the focus, guaranteed resources large enough to secure all available talent.

As for dancing, in Part II there was a deliberate introduction of (then) old-fashioned forms (courantes and branles) for the over-familiar characters from Ariosto, to contrast with others in the latest vogue. Here, already, is revivalism. A saraband by four small girls and a boy costumed as Spaniards introduced an exotic national note, and the vocabulary now included many accents: native, foreign, fantastic, grotesque, court, and country, with extension by step and gesture. Unlike many court shows, this was such a success, due in part to the scenic display (probably by Torelli), that it was repeated six times. There were over a hundred costumes. Jean Baptiste Lully, who had come from Italy, aged nine, and who was to dominate French music and dance for the rest of the century, may have appeared with the king, his future collaborator in ballet-opera. The Dukes of York and Buckingham danced with their French hosts.

61.

143.

131.

132.

133.

131. Street pageant. England, 1533.

132. Apollo (Louis XIV), 1651.

133. *Le Roi Soleil,* 1653.

134.

135.

136.

134. Money coiners. France, 1632.

135. Apollo (Louis XIV), 1653.

136. Night. Paris, 1653.

92.

137.

LES NOPCES DE PELÉE ET DE THÉTIS
(The Marriage of Peleus and Thetis)
April 14, 1654
Paris
Salle du Petit Bourbon, Louvre

Priority:
Although described as an "Italian comedy," *Les Nopces* was rather an opera plus dances. Ballets were interpolated after each act, referring directly or indirectly to subjects just sung. Opera was the basis, but dance took up the most time and best pleased the Paris public. The danced interludes of *La Finta Pazza* were unconnected with the story; here ballet was not incidental or accidental, but integrated—a parallel to the operatic action. This is one of the best-documented works in the century, since we have the original drawings, before they were made rigid by their engraver, Israel Silvestre.

Precedent:
The theme, drawn from ancient texts, is typical of those considered appropriate by court pedants; here it is taken from Euripides, Catullus, and Apollonius of Rhodes. Thétis (from *tithenai*, "to order") is another name for Aphrodite as Creatrix. Foam-born, like

all life, Love emerged from the sea; to Mediterraneans, seafood is aphrodisiac. Needing a wife who would be at home at the bottom of the ocean, Neptune (here confused or identified with Jupiter) covets Thétis, a Nereid, but it was foretold that any son born to her would surpass his father, so she marries Peleus, a mortal. There was an interlude on the same pretext in *Le Ballet de la Nuit* of the year before, resembling the Venetian entertainments designed by Torelli before he came to Paris.

Politics:
Spoken verse boasted the defeat of the Fronde, daring Spain, a possible new threat, to risk war. Mazarin, prime minister of Italian origin, was determined to make Italian opera succeed in France. The king wished to dance; he was finding a mind of his own, so it was decided to insert ballets between sung acts. Again as Apollo he appeared in six entries before the royal guests, Charles II of England and Henriette de France. The lavish spectacle made a huge impression, and the libretto was widely published. Embodying the state of Franco-Italian culture, it also manifested the skill and active presence of the young sov-

ereign. DuBois, a court chronicler, wrote on May 2, 1651: "The king danced a ballet before a great crowd. He amuses himself by dancing and watching others dance. . . . He studies in the morning after saying his prayers, then he takes dancing lessons, does exercises with weapons, breaks a lance (from the saddle), then takes lunch, usually with his ten violins playing very prettily." The stance for fencing and ballet were similar.

Plot or Pretext:
A series of scenes. 1. Parnassus. Apollo (Louis), surrounded by nine Muses, is seen on a mount that is pierced to form a triumphal arch. The chorus begs him to bless Peleus' suit of the sea nymph Thétis. The mount is lowered to the stage floor; Apollo descends and dances with his Muses. 2. A vast cave. Magicians bring Peleus to the Caucasus mountains. 3. A seascape. Neptune and Thétis ride in on huge cockleshells, and he declares his love. Dance of pearlfishers. The sea god blows up a storm. 4. Jupiter (again the king) appears from a cloud and makes love to Thétis. His wife Juno, in a jealous rage, summons her Furies. Jupiter rides off on an eagle. Torch dance

6.

131.

142.

137. Sirens. Paris, 1581.

of Furies. 5. The Caucasus. Prometheus is chained to a rock. Seven savages with clubs dance a "light and bizarre" figure. 6. Jupiter's palace. Tree dryads dance for joy; these earth spirits are envious of Thétis, a sea nymph. 7. Under the statue of Mars, there is armed combat. Peleus arrives. Military exercises are performed—a ballet-battle with officers, pages, drummers, heralds, judges, dwarfs, and troops. 8. The palace of Thétis. Chiron, the sage centaur, persuades Peleus to make a last attempt to win Thétis. Chiron's pupils are dressed as Indians in feathers with painted skins. He mounts a camel. Dance of monkey and parrot (here the king performed as a monkey; although usually cast as a god, he preferred less formal dances). 9. Entry of seven Useful and seven Liberal Arts. Cloud-machines. Dance of joy. 10. Olympus: a grand finale. The classical writers told that "their wedding was celebrated outside Chiron's cave on Mount Pelion. The Olympians attended, seated on twelve thrones. Hera herself raised the bridal torch, and Zeus (Neptune-Poseidon), now reconciled to his defeat, gave Thétis away. The Fates and Muses sang; Ganymede poured nectar, and the fifty Nereids performed a spiral dance on the white sands. Crowds of centaurs attended the ceremony, wearing chaplets of grass, brandishing darts of fire, and prophesying good fortune" (Robert Graves).

Production:

It lasted four hours. For the first time, ladies of the court appeared (as Arts and Muses), although they did not dance. Masked male courtiers took female parts. The ballet master was Beauchamps, with scenery and machines of great variety, complexity, and ingenuity by Torelli. The cave in which the centaur Chiron taught his pupils transformed itself into a seascape; Jupiter's palace was jeweled latticework, with twenty-three wings, revealing the depth of the vast stage. Scene 7 showed military exercises and a "combat at the barrier" set in a huge amphitheater. A toga-clad audience sat in three tiers. The scenery continued uninterruptedly the sight lines and architecture of the auditorium in a hybrid of classical, Renaissance, and Baroque ornament. Through the arch at the back could be seen three streets in accelerated perspective, as in the Olympian Theater in Vicenza by Palladio and Scamozzi. In the finale, cottony clouds on armatures in a counterweight system made a dance of their own in the air. There was a distinction between the dress of singers and dancers. The first wore a uniform styled on Roman armor, with leather cuirasses gilded to imitate metal. The dancers wore lighter and shorter versions of this, with sharper fantasy in detail and more freedom in cut.

At the start of the seventeenth century ballets were constantly danced on improvised stages. Even by 1650, few private mansions were large enough to be suitable. However, the palace of the Louvre, in its complex old and new, had five large-scaled halls where scenery and machines could be installed; the Grande Salle was some fifty by fifteen meters. Ballets were also given in the Palais Royal, the Tuileries, the Luxembourg, and at Vincennes, Fontainebleau, St. Germain-en-Laye, and Versailles.

75.

93.

138.

138. Sea creatures. Italy, c. 1540.

139.

140.

141.

139. Apollo (Louis XIV), 1654.

141. Marine cave. Paris, 1654.

140. Marine demigod. Paris, 1654.

142.

143.

142, 143. Palace of Thétis. Paris, 1654.

FRENCH COMEDY-BALLET

LES FÂCHEUX
(The Bores)
August 17, 1661
Vaux-le-Vicomte

Priority:
French poets responsible for court entertainment had previously been gentlemen-academicians. Now Molière, a professional actor and dramatist, injected rational sequence, satire on modern manners, and caricatural deformation of ordinary occupational gesture: he invented "comedy-ballet" —"a medley new to our theatre." Complaining of the shortness of time in which he had to write (two weeks), he apologized that his plot did not make more sense, an aim rarely striven for by earlier poets. In spite of this, his dance scenes were integrated into the action, carrying it forward. While influenced by the Italian comedians, Molière's style was peculiarly French. He had danced in ballets with Louis XIV since 1658; *Les Fâcheux* was prototype for *Le Mariage Forcé* (1664), in which the king also danced, *Georges Dandin* (1668), and *Le Bourgeois Gentilhomme* (1670), in which Molière played the principal role and Jean Baptiste Lully danced the Turkish *mufti*, to his own music.

Precedent:
Previous ballets were successions of entries, formal or fantastic in design, that decorated a general scheme, but barely linked loose narrative. Molière had been educated by the Jesuits, who had encouraged didactic theater. Allegory or mythology with capricious adornment had heretofore served as pretext for spectacle, but Molière suggested a contemporary comedy of manners with illustrative interludes.

Politics:
Fouquet, minister of finance, whose coat-of-arms sported a squirrel (a pun on his name), whose motto boasted of unlimit-

144.

ed heights he might attain, gave a magnificent two-day fete at Vaux-le-Vicomte, his country seat, under the supervision of Charles Le Brun, the king's painter, Torelli, his engineer, Lully, his musician, and Beauchamps, his dancing master. The show was of such proportions that the king abruptly sensed malfeasance and dangerous ambition in his treasurer and disgraced him, retaining the collaborators for his own even more lavish use at Versailles. This same year (1661), Louis founded an Academy of Dance, "to restore the dance to its perfection." There had been an Academy of Music and Poetry since 1570; an Academy of Inscriptions had ruled on subjects for legitimate shows, correct classical aesthetic, and the allegory of flattery, establishing orders of precedence in exits and entrances at court functions. This was possible in the hierarchy of aristocracy, where amateurs were the only performers, but it had a bad effect on efficiency in dancing. The foundation of the Academy of Dance was at first little more than a formality which, gathering thirteen of the foremost professionals, exempted them from taxes and guar-

144. Louis XIV, c. 1675.

anteed their children's right to work as the sole legitimate dancing masters. The Royal Academy of Music would be founded in 1669, with Lully, and in 1672, under it, the Academy of Dance finally became a working institution. The status of the dancer, mutating from amateur to professional, was being improved. Later, when Molière's Monsieur Jourdain wishes to emerge from his low bourgeois background, he hires himself masters of fencing, philosophy, music, and dancing. The *gentilhomme* becomes a master of skills, a comic hero here, but also, almost, an artist. The academies do not instruct for mere amusement; legitimate artistic disciplines are supposed also to improve morals. The entertainer is no longer unschooled; his profession is on its way to honor.

Plot or Pretext:
Eraste, a young dandy, loves Orphise, a languorous flirt. A variety of tiresome individuals manage to frustrate his suit. One displays dubious talents as a dancer, another complains of loss at cards, another boasts of wisdom, another of good business sense—all boring or irritating. The dancing master is a particular bore; here Molière and Lully, both interested in the establishment of their professions, were drawing attention to the lack of trained dancers and need for a school. Finally, the Swiss Guard (palace police) is called to disperse the tribe of bores. The wedding is arranged.

Production:
La Fontaine gives a vivid picture of Fouquet's green park theater in the open air, over whose proscenium the king's cipher was set. Torelli erected a stage that held a garden pavilion adorned with herms and jets of water, spaced between trees, through whose branches long alleys lay in deceptive perspective. The prologue began with a rockery that opened,

out of which a naiad issued on a seashell to flatter the king as young, wise, valiant, august, victorious, and as severe as he was sweet (which Fouquet, his host, was shortly to discover). Statues, forming pillars to the pavilion, started to move; La Fontaine admitted he could not tell how this was contrived. A ballet of fauns and bacchants commenced; the principal action followed. Due to the small number of well-trained dancers available, each entry was separated by prose portions, during which performers appearing in the next entry changed costume. Choreography borrowed familiar movements from the game of bowls, cobblers at work, card playing, battledore, and shuttlecock. Swiss guards with halberds scattered the bores in orderly confusion. The final dance called for shepherds and shepherdesses. It had grown dark; the ballet terminated with fireworks. Louis XIV, leaving the first performance, pointed out to Molière Monsieur de Soyecourt, a notoriously boring huntsman, wryly remarking, "There's one type you've not taken." Molière promptly added a seventh scene to include the tedious hunter when *Les Fâcheux* was performed at Fontainebleau six days later.

Lully, an accomplished man of the theater, collaborated closely with Beauchamps, the choreographer. The composer "remade entries, imagined expressive steps that enhanced the subject; when needed, himself danced before his dancers to make them sooner understand his ideas." Lully was accused of catering to his audience; his music was simple, clear, sensible, and useful; he disliked preciosity. A popular composer, he made ballet more than a court art, establishing its French dominance both by practice and political maneuver. The dance increased in expressivity when it became liberated from symmetricality—the formal regu-

larity of the court forms deriving from ballroom limits. Rejecting Italianate rhetorical decoration, Lully cultivated a characteristically French rhythmic precision. An accomplished comic dancer, excellent violinist, good administrator, and subtle courtier, his influence stayed long after his death. The ablest conductor of his time and a strict rehearsalist, he propelled the combined craft of music and dance into professionalism. His music was vigorous and clear cut, suitable to the ordered epoch he brilliantly served.

145.

145. *Les Fâcheux*, c. 1765–70.

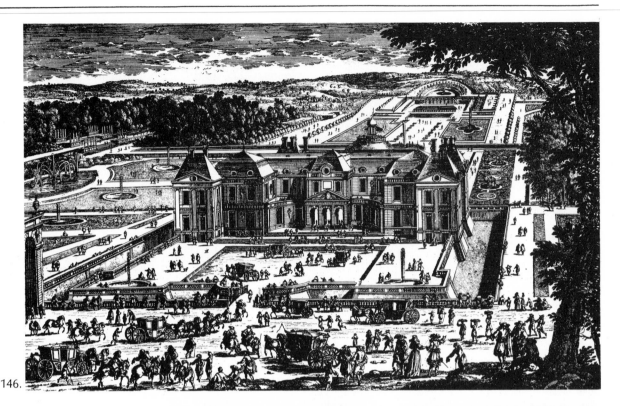

146.

147. 148.

146. Park theater. France, c. 1660.

147. *Les Fâcheux*, 1682.

148. The comedians exiled, 1697.

149. 150.

151. 152.

149. Molière: Debauchery, 1651.

150. Molière: Sganarelle, c. 1665–70.

151. Dubreil: Scaramouche, c. 1665.

152. Masked male dancer. France, c. 1680.

END OF THE AMATEUR

LES AMANTS MAGNIFIQUES
(The Magnificent Lovers)
February 4, 1670
St. Germain-en-Laye

Priority:

This *divertissement royal* by Molière possibly marked the last of Louis XIV as performing artist. He had appeared since he was thirteen in some twenty-seven ballets. Loving to dance and well equipped for such exercise, he even designed his own variations. Due in no small part to his active interest, the art assumed such importance that it became increasingly clear it could no longer be entrusted to amateurs, however devoted. Courtly dilettantes would be replaced by professionals, first male, soon female, whose aim was augmented virtuosity. The language of the dance could develop simultaneously with greater freedom and variety in music and painting. A middle-class audience for Parisian theater replaced the nobility of Versailles. In the brief list of ballet patrons down to Diaghilev in our own day, Louis XIV was the most intimately identified, endowing ballet with a magic its grand manner has never lost. Le Cerf de Vieville, Seigneur de Freneuse, in 1705 defended French art against Italian, citing his king as the ultimate authority (quoting Racine's *Britannicus*), "I should, madame, acclaim another name, knew I one mightier." Freneuse declared: "I am no courtier; put aside from the king's person all splendor which rank and reign bestow; consider him a mere subject in his realm. The huge number of ballets in which he has performed, of operas expressly composed for him or by his patronage, the honor he has conferred on Lully and so many others allowing them to approach him, testifies to his deep love of music."

Precedent:

As a rule, fetes were arranged for Carnival, and the great palace team—Lully, Molière, Beauchamps the dancing master, and Vigarini the machinist—prepared this one in six weeks. The king again appeared as Apollo. The dancing in the final scene recalls the combat from *Les Nopces de Pelée et de Thétis* (1654).

Politics:

The king was thirty-one, grown heavier. According to gossip, his retirement from ballet was prompted by a hint from Racine's tragedy *Britannicus*, Act IV, scene 4, which suggested it ill behooved the sovereign (Nero, *le monstre naissant*) to further vaunt public exhibition of his person:

> "To vaunt himself to Romans
> as a show
> And waste his life upon the
> theater."

However, it is possible the king did not actually perform; a libretto lists him, but this was printed in advance. He may have already seen the play, or read Tacitus' *Annals*, which served Racine.* Louis was surely too secure to worry about imputations of vanity.

Courtiers, from princes of the blood and royal bastards to *petite noblesse*, were delighted to dance beside him in a strict hierarchy of assigned roles. Members of the *parlement* were honored to be termed "dancers in ordinary" to such a monarch, who said: "People love spectacles; by these we hold their minds and hearts more often perhaps than by rewards or benefits."

The position of the king had changed. Formerly, he held the balance of power between parliaments, which were judicial rather than legislative assemblies. Now the king-judge was evolving into king-hero or king-god. A collective aristocratic condition became a unique monarchical one. By demonstration and insistence on divine right, the sovereign stood apart from simple historical process; he was permanent, continuous, immortal. "*Le roi est mort; vive le roi!*" But the king was also a mortal to whom many had access;† the quality of his dignity must be purified, elevated, and maintained as he matured. His status as performer might draw comparison with another Caesar: Nero. It was better to assign shows to unequivocal professionals. Molière announced in his published *avant-propos*: "The king, who desires the extraordinary alone in all he undertakes, proposes to give his court a divertissement which should be composed of all that theater might offer; to encompass so vast a diversity of elements, His Majesty has chosen as subject two rival princes, who in a rural sojourn in the Vale of Tempe, where are celebrated the Pythian games, regale a young princess and her mother with all possible gallantry." 144. 154.

Plot or Pretext:

Molière's piece called for danced and mimed scenes linked by song. The final *grand ballet* was a ritual sacrifice as for the Pythian games. Six athletes show their aplomb vaulting on wooden horses borne by slaves. There followed a dance of warriors; four soldiers liberate twelve slaves, who dance for joy. Men and women *à l'antique* form warlike groups. Trumpets announce Apollo (the king) entering through a main portal, preceded by youths with laurel-bound wands. Trophies are presented to six priests. Led by Apollo, a formal figure is executed in suggestion of an ancient religious celebration, a metaphorical homage to the god-king. 5. 100. 99. 133.

Production:

This single divertissement in an extended spectacle was one incident in the familiar mélange of song, mimicry, martial exercise, and dance, the last perhaps dominant. In other numbers there were: dances by children (fauns and dry-

---

*The tragedy had been a failure at its première, December 13, 1669. The house was empty, the town having flocked to see the execution of a Huguenot marquis. The king, hearing of the play or seeing it at subsequent performance, declared he much admired it, saving Racine's immediate reputation.

†"He was magical, but not mysterious; he rose and set like the sun . . . [dwelling in] Versailles, temple of the sun [with] . . . its silver furniture, the profusion of gilt bronzes, the gold of the hangings, the gold of the curtains, the gold of a thousand everyday objects, the gold of the tubs for the orange-trees, the gold of the roofings, the leads, the statues, the foun-

ads); a torch dance in which eight "statues" descended from pedestals, each holding two flambeaux. Venus appeared on clouds from which cupids peeped; "after several flights, with amazing speed, the machine closed and was flown off." After the king stopped dancing, the ballet was repeated, a noble assuming his role.

Invocation of the "antique" was the method of poets and artists for the king's glorification. At Versailles, the king's painter, Le Brun, saw Louis as Alexander the Great on ceilings swollen with overcharged ornament. Ostentation was the aim, rather than accurate revival of classical models.‡

In Rome, Nicolas Poussin was far closer to antiquity; his serene, frozen figures might well have served ballet masters restricted by the weight of intractable brocades and yards of symmetrical scenery. But much freedom of movement was hardly desirable. At Versailles, the nude or semi-nude would have seemed less provocative than poverty-stricken. The king's pleasure was to astound by sheer material splendor; it was state policy. Similarly with Lully: his music embodied majesty. The grand march in *Thésée* (1675) celebrates less the triumph of Theseus than the conquest of Alsace by the king's great general Turenne. Dance, in opera-ballet, to a degree it has not enjoyed since, was the vivid expression of its epoch, due in great part to Lully.

As for choreography, we have slight record of what was actually danced. Planimetric patterns, legible on ballroom floors of the sixteenth and early seventeenth centuries, were replaced by stereometric design; perspective scenery within a proscenium frame focused action that was primarily symmetrical and central. Human dynamism moved off the floor, defying gravity, in spite of the weight of stuffs. The province of air was increasingly

explored. Emphatic turn-out of the legs and feet served "pure" dance. "Turn-in" characterized burlesque, grotesque, or looser movement. Positions of the arms were regularized, the feet fixed. There were attempts toward greater lightness—*ballon* ("bounce")—and controlled multiple turns, although shoes had heels—poor fulcrums. Expression was typed rather than specified: Demons always jumped; Smiles and Laughter hopped. Costumes were more uniforms or armor than dresses for dancers. Masks ritualized the fete and added impersonal mystery, reducing human appeal. Until about 1700, there was tension between formal conservatism and the inevitable progressive exploration of dance movement, which, from now on, would benefit from a systematic training of male and particularly female professionals. With the end of the Sun King (1715), ballet as we think of it begins. Before this, to great extent, everything remains mysterious. Afterward, to some degree, everything seems recognizable.

154.

153.

LES AMANS MAGNIFIQUES.

LES AMANTS MAGNIFIQUES.

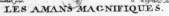

155.

tains, the carriages, the embroideries on the brilliant-colored costumes." (Philippe Erlanger, *The Age of Courts and Kings*.)

‡ In Joyce's *Ulysses*, there is a conversation on the "real" Rome. Professor

MacHugh avers, "We think of Rome, imperial, imperious, imperative, while on the other hand the Roman really said: 'It is meet to be here. Let us construct a watercloset.'"

153. *Les Amans Magnifiques*, c. 1770–75.

154. Roman soldier, c. 1725.

155. *Les Amants Magnifiques*, c. 1780.

156.

157. 158.

LES AMANS
MAGNIFIQUES

156. Royal ballet. France, c. 1660.

158. Classical drama. France, c. 1670.

157. *Les Amans Magnifiques,* c. 1680.

159. 160.

161. 162.

159. Bacchant. France, 1651.

160. Bacchante. France, c. 1675.

161. Masked male dancer. France, c. 1675.

162. Ballerina with mask. France, c. 1680.

FRENCH PANTOMIME

LES HORACES
(The Horatii)
December, 1714
Le Château de Sceaux

Priority:

Act IV, scene 5, from Pierre Corneille's famous tragedy *Horace* (1640), was transposed from spoken verse to formal dumb show, measured by music composed for the occasion. Without specific dance steps, it was mimed by two of the best opera dancers—Jean Ballon, whose lightness became a byword, and Françoise Prévôt, an excellent teacher and performer. This particular fragment—fourteenth in a series of *Grandes Nuits* of charades, parlor games, and improvisations ennobled by wit—focused attention on narrative mimicry through expressive manual and bodily gesture. It would be considered precursor of the *ballet d'action* and *passi d'azione*, pantomimic dance spectacles developed by subsequent choreographers—De Hesse, Hilferding, Noverre, Angiolini—over the next half century. Here was experiment outside official areas. It is too often assumed that the Opéra plus the Comédie Française stand for the whole story of French theater; this eliminates important factors beyond and in spite of government-controlled institutions. *Les Horaces* was performed on a country estate independent both of the city of Paris and the palace of Versailles. Its audience was an intellectual elite, its executants the best professionals available. Its guiding aesthetic was an early example of the anti-academic avant-garde manifesto. The awesome presence of the king, the scale of his parks and palaces, accommodated spectacles that, rarely novelties, were mainly decorative. At Sceaux, in a grand but smaller frame, entertainment was an elegant pastime for house parties devoted more to ideas than ostentation. The mimed scene of *Les Horaces* presupposed a dialogue between audience and actors that Versailles seldom permitted. Just as

the improvisatory, acrobatic Italian comedy of skill influenced official theater although rejected by it, so the taste of amateurs governed by erudite abbés and professional academicians enriched the tradition of French and thereafter of international theater practice without really being a part of it.

The *Ars Poetica* of Horace, a strong influence on policy at the official Comédie, forbade the actual showing of violence (butchering Medea's children; murder and suicide of Horatian brother and sister) on stage. The principle of decorum, of what was *convenable*—"suitable"—led from Aristotle's "imitation of nature" into severely conventional limits. Ethical censorship, in effect, determined what was fitting, appropriate, or inappropriate. Hence, the direct presentation of murder and suicide in *Les Horaces* would be revolutionary, a daring precedent for enlarged romantic or protoexpressionist realism. In Corneille's tragedy, the violence was described, not enacted.

As for style of performance, the formula of the Alexandrine couplet, with its metric encapsulated by final rhymed syllables, was so insistent a device that perhaps the pantomime attempted to measure itself by some sort of echoing plastic imitation. Racine's heroic style commanded a *récitatif majestueux* in verbal delivery, an operatic, chanted tone that was not considered incompatible with that *beau naturel*, or "perfect naturalism," that we today could hardly call realistic.

Precedent:

Imperial Roman models from Augustan drama, embodied in the discourse of Lucian of Samosata, *On Pantomime*, were invoked by the bluestockings of Sceaux. There were well-known English, German, and Dutch alphabets of gesture; the Jesuits, active in theater, provided a rationale for legible manual signals and expressive profiling

of the whole body in ordered sequence. Attempts were made to pass beyond rhetorical and mechanical conventions used by professional actors and singers. Molière's actors, imitating Italian comedians, initiated a more naturalistic style, in which gesture depended on psychological observation, increased fragmentation of movement. Much of this was found useful by dancing masters. The minuet, with its abstract movement of hands, elbows, and inclination of the body, turned into a dramatic duet with all the subtleties of a mating dance; slight accented hesitation, release and onward action, promised the expressive duet of later ballets' dramatic *pas de deux*.

Politics:

Anne-Louise Bénédicte, Mademoiselle de Charolais, Duchesse du Maine, married an illegitimate son of Louis XIV. She was an energetic, spoiled, clever, tyrannical, extravagant dwarf; her great house at Sceaux, later rebuilt by Perrault, had belonged to Colbert; Le Nôtre laid out its vast gardens, with Puget and Girardon designing its garden figures. Saint-Simon, hating the recently legitimized royal bastards, considered her behavior a scandal.

A pint-sized Versailles, Sceaux exactly suited its imaginative midget mistress. Madame la Duchesse suffered from insomnia; while the duke in his tower occupied himself with amateur astronomy, his wife planned a series of elaborate nocturnal distractions with the help of Nicholas De Malézieux, an erudite scientist and littérateur. *Les Grandes Nuits*, commencing in 1714, included political lotteries, the duchess herself enacting *Athalie*, symposia on Copernicus, solar theories, debates between Euripides (Medea's earliest dramatist) and Corneille (her latest). Among some seventeen *soirées*, starting with Night's gratitude to the duchess for preferring her to Day, was a dialogue between Archimedes and Descartes (who, in 1646, had

150.

28.

171.

167.

226.

---

* "Sceaux had become the scene of the ever wilder follies of the Duchesse du Maine, to the shame, embarrassment, and ruin of her husband, who was obliged to pay for her monstrous extravagance. Her house was a perpetual source of amuse-

written the libretto of a ballet on *Peace* for Queen Christina of Sweden). The gatherings at Sceaux may be situated between those of Versailles, the former unique solar center, and later dispersed salons of Encyclopedist pre-Revolutionary Paris. The breakdown of a rigid caste system can almost be said to have begun at Sceaux, *"une cour de gaie science,"* where men of ideas and erudition mixed freely with men of birth and fortune.*

Plot or Pretext:

Horatius, a patrician, has led Rome victorious against the Curiati, enemies of the state. In his hand he grasps as prize of war a Curiatian sword. But his sister, Camilla, in love with the leader of their enemy, and in spite of two older brothers slain, reproaches Horatius with the murder of Curiatius. Denouncing Rome as barbarous, she arouses his wrath to such pitch, that with her lover's (and his enemy's) bare weapon drawn, he drives her off-stage. Camilla (in Corneille's original tragedy, but not in the dumb show from it) expires behind the scenery. Horatius, his deed done, re-enters to pronounce:

*"... Ainsi reçoive un chastiment
soudain
Quiconque ose pleurer un enemy
Romain."*

"... So suffer immediate punish-
ment
Whoever dares to mourn a foe
of Rome."

Production:

Sceaux had a private playhouse. The fourteenth of the *Grandes Nuits* had Apollo and the Muses offering a "ballet," in the second interlude of which the god presents for Madame du Maine a *danse caractérisée*—or dramatic *pas de deux*—for Camilla and Horatius. The score was by the Abbé Jean Joseph Mouret, academician and follower of Lully, who composed the dumb show as for an operatic duet, but with the vocal parts

163.

omitted. The dancers, Ballon and Prévôt, seem to have adapted their action to musical dynamics. "These two artists, full of warmth and soul, though novices in the mimic art, caused the public to dissolve in tears." Was this conventional flattery or the personal sensibility of Madame du Maine's friends? When Ballon and Prévôt appeared in London, 1712, Addison and Steele's *Spectator* found them artificial, inexpressive, merely graceful, their display only "modulated mo-

164.

tion ... without reference to the imitation of the manners and passions of mankind." Ballon had made his début before the Dauphin at Chantilly as a faun in 1688. His father and grandfather were dancing masters, his father one of the original thirteen chosen to form Louis XIV's first Royal Academy. Ballon danced at the Opéra, succeeding Beauchamps as *maître de ballet* in 1719. The composer Rameau spoke of his "infinite taste and prodigious lightness"; yet the English master dancer Weaver found him inexpressive and dull. Françoise Prévôt was one of the first performers famous for her elevation. A renowned teacher, she trained the ballerinas Camargo and Sallé. She was also musically oriented and designed dances based on the structure of instrumentation, rather than stringing together effective ready-made steps.

172.

173.

183.

165.

166.

ment for Parisian society and the courtiers, who went there in vast numbers, and much despised her. She spent entire nights with lotteries, feasts, gambling and fireworks. ... She played *Athalie* several times a week in a company of profes-

sional actors and actresses." (Duc de Saint-Simon, *Historical Memoirs*, II [1710–15], trans. Lucy Norton [London, 1968], p. 366.)

163. Heroic tragedian. France, *c.* 1765.

164. Tragic gesture. England, 1822.

165, 166. Pantomimic action. Germany, 1780.

167.

168. 169.

Ch. Eisen inv.   *E. De Ghendt Sculp.*

167. Versailles in miniature. Sceaux, c. 1710.

168. Spirit of Dance. France, 1766.

169. Spirit of Tragedy. France, 1766.

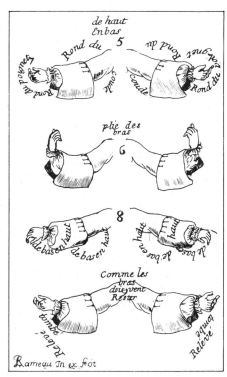

170. 171.

172. 173.

170. "The Hand in Rhetoric." England, 1644.

171. Movements of wrists, elbows, shoulders. France, 1725.

172. Ballon, c. 1700.

173. Prévôt, c. 1723.

**THE LOVES OF MARS
AND VENUS
March 2, 1717
London
Theatre Royal, Drury Lane**

Priority:

This "Dramatick Entertainment of Dancing Attempted in Imitation of the Pantomimes of the Ancient Greeks and Romans" is described by its author, John Weaver, as "the first trial of this nature that has been made since the reign of Trajan." Weaver, perhaps the most important British dance theorist, son of a dancing master, was himself an excellent performer and mime. The British have long had a predilection for narrative gesture, strongly influenced by the skill of Italian popular comedians—or, rather, British adaptions of French versions of *commedia dell'arte*. Weaver has been called father of what in the nineteenth century would be known as "pantomime," a musical extravaganza, hybrid of comic opera and ballet. He made early important distinctions between stage and social dancing. *The Loves of Mars and Venus* was, according to Colley Cibber, "a collected presentation of dances in character, wherein the Passions were so happily expressed, and the whole story so intelligently told by the mute narration of gesture only, that even thinking Spectators allowed it both a pleasing and rational entertainment." Academic dance steps suited to each character were tied by explicit manual and bodily movement to two types of music, describing either individual action or larger group numbers. Mars, Vulcan, and Venus were not heroic types but specific individuals; their dancing was not simply ornamental, but furthered dramatic action.

Precedent:

Weaver had translated the basic French social dance manual of his time (Feuillet's *Chorégraphie*, 1706) and knew the Paris dancing Academy, the fair-ground comedians, classical sculpture, and Baroque painting, at least as seen in engravings. A famous Italian mime was court favorite in England (1673–77), although he could not appear in public. Such artists brought from Italy through France passacaglia and chaconne, important group figures for ballet. Weaver had appeared in harlequinades—pantomimes with *commedia* characters—since 1703. In *Gorboduc* (1562), the first formal English tragedy, dumb shows before each act demonstrated events impossible to explain verbally under academic rules. These prefigured the melodramatic use of pantomime in *Hamlet* (Act III, scene 2, 1594). In Ben Jonson's *Masque of Love's Triumph Through Callipolis* (1631), "after the manner of the old *Pantomimi*, they dance over a distracted Comedy of Love." David Garrick (1717–79), the greatest English actor of his time, appeared as Harlequin in his apprenticeship (c. 1740); he was to have considerable effect on Noverre and the *ballet d'action*, the century's progressive genre of narrative ballet.

Politics:

This was a professional assertion of English expression, a production to please a general public, not only king and court. Weaver was overall producer-director, using the best British and French talent available. Under Cromwell, public theater had almost stopped; dancing under the Puritans persisted in schools. In 1651, John Playford's *The English Dancing Master*, a collection of native country dances, was published. In exile, Charles II had seen French court ballet. After his restoration (1660), stage dancing was confined to divertissement in plays and operas, although London saw professional performers before the Paris Opéra. Ballroom dancing developed, and stage dancing declined: the king liked to dance but did not wish to compete publicly with his uncle Louis XIV. The Duke of Monmouth, influenced by court ballet under Lully, imitated it in England with French and British ballet masters working side by side. Weaver considered French dancing too "genteel," Italian too "grotesque"; he preferred "scenical" forms, that is, his own native genre of narrative pantomime.

Plot or Pretext:

A martial overture leads into a Pyrrhic dance of Mars and his warriors. A passacaglia to a "symphony" of flutes introduces Venus and her Graces. She is revealed in her dressing room. Vulcan, smith of the gods, enters to a "wild rough air." Vulcan's forge. He delivers wires for the net in which the Cyclops, his slaves, will capture Mars and Venus. Feverish activity. A love scene reveals Mars and Venus in danced conversation, strength against softness. In the finale Mars and Venus are snared, surprised, and confused. There was only a single set of variations for the finale.

Production:

This ballet was on the same program with Beaumont and Fletcher's *A Maid's Tragedy*. An early English ballerina, Hester Santlow, was Venus; the great Louis Dupré, from Paris, Mars, while Weaver himself danced Vulcan; the musicians were Symonds, who composed the "symphonies," and Mr. Firbank, author of the "dancing airs." Weaver made a careful analysis of action; there were some fourteen separate gestures used by Venus to repulse Vulcan. Of the *pas de deux* of Venus and Vulcan he wrote: "This last Dance being altogether of the *Pantomimic* kind, it is necessary that the Spectator should know some of the most particular Gestures made use of therein; and what Passions or Affections they discover, represent, or express." To denote Vulcan's astonishment: "Both hands are thrown upwards towards the skies; the Eyes also lifted up and the body cast backwards"; anger: "The Left Hand struck suddenly with the Right; and sometimes against the Breast";

168.

60.

174.

5.

55.

power: "The Arm, with impetuous Agitation, directed forwards to the Person, with an awful Look." In the final scene, when Vulcan has ensnared Mars and Venus, they express entreaty: "The stretching out of the Hands moves downwards towards the Knees"; grief: "Hanging down the Head; wringing the Hands; and striking the Breast."

Weaver based his dances on French models and his anatomical studies on English surgeons. *The Life of Mr. Thomas Betterton* (1710) details the methods for mime of this famous actor, which Weaver may have read, applying it to dancing. Gesture, inspired by or illustrative of spoken verse, developed parallel to movement propelled by music. From *Betterton*: "The arm extended and lifted up signifies the Power of doing and accomplishing something; and is the gesture of Authority, Vigour and Victory. On the contrary, the holding your Arms close is a sign of Bashfulness, Modesty, or Diffidence." Weaver made an analysis of certain gestures at the end of his libretto: "*Triumphing*: To shake the Hand open, rais'd above our Head, is an exaulting expression of *Triumph, &c. Entreaty*: The stretching of the Hands towards the Knees is an action of *Entreaty*, and *suing* for *Mercy*. *Grief* is expressed by hanging down the Head; wringing the Hands and striking the Breast. *Resignation*: To hold out both Hands join'd together is a natural Expression of *Submission* and *Resignation*. *Forgiveness*: To extend and offer out the Right Hand is a gesture of *Pitty*, and Intention of *Forgiveness*. *Shame*: The covering of the Face with the Hand is a Sign of *Shame. Reconciliation*: To shake the given Hand, or embrace the Body, is an Expression of *Friendship, Reconciliation*, and the like." These gestures seem timeless and supranational. Modern definition seems largely to have derived from Italy, and Naples in particular. "The gesture to signify love, employed

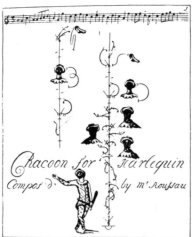

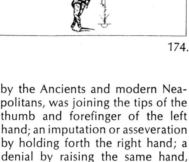

174.

175.

by the Ancients and modern Neapolitans, was joining the tips of the thumb and forefinger of the left hand; an imputation or asseveration by holding forth the right hand; a denial by raising the same hand, extending the fingers."*

The next year Weaver produced *The Fable of Orpheus and Eurydice*; the libretto was loaded with quotations from John Dryden's version of Virgil. It was a tragedy. ". . . the actions of Orpheus express the violence of his Grief." There was a bacchanal; when Orpheus forswears his vow to gaze on Eurydice, Music shifts to a rough, horrid Movement . . . Orpheus by his Actions expresses the utmost Rage and Despair." A rustic dance is set as contrast before the final catastrophe. In vain the farmers try to save Orpheus from the Bacchae. In 1733 Weaver produced a *Judgment of Paris*, but after that the comic pantomimes of John Rich (1692–1761), who performed Harlequin under the name of Lun and produced *The Beggar's Opera* (1728), seem finally to have removed Weaver from the scene. Rich produced his own elaborate version of the Orphic myth (1739). Of him, the greatest Harlequin of his time, Garrick, wrote:

"When Lun appeared with matchless art and whim,
He gave the power of speech to every limb;
Though masked and mute conveyed his quick intent,
And told in frolic's gestures all he meant."

61.

* R. J. Broadbent, *A History of Pantomime* (1901).

174, 175. Harlequin's movements. England, 1733.

176.   177.

178.

176. Harlequin. France, 1651.

177. Garrick: Harlequin. England, c. 1740.

178. Mars and Venus. Netherlands, 1585.

179.

180.

179. Orpheus and Eurydice. England, 1718.

180. Danced finale. England, 1711.

ROCOCO VARIETY

LES CARACTÈRES DE LA DANSE
(Types of the Dance)
May 5, 1726
Paris
Opéra

Priority:

This divertissement offered opera-house treatment of various forms taken over from folk and ballroom. Its subject was the structure of dance itself, and it displayed individual performers for whom music had been specially written to express a piquant variety of contrasting moods. Advertised as showing "all the movements of the dance," its aim was to demonstrate the grammar of theatrical dancing, as so far developed, on the threshold of an academic tradition. The choreography was established on instrumentation in the orchestra rather than available or habitual steps. The composer, Jean Fery Rebel (1666–1747), one of the twenty-four violins of the king, also led the orchestra at the Opéra; his score was descriptive, characterizing dancers by assigning them recognizable melodic themes or "leading motives," a device greatly developed in *Giselle* a century later.

Precedent:

It was usual to present a *pot-pourri* of song and dance on gala evenings at the Opéra or for artists' benefits. In 1720, Mlle. Prévôt, the ranking ballerina, had translated a capriccio by Rebel into purely plotless choreographic terms. Pretexts for dance numbers in the spirit of the *fête galante* and *fête champêtre* (elegant aristocratic gatherings in park or countryside) echoed a presumed Age of Gold under the Regency of Louis XV (1715–23). In the Rococo aesthetic, artless rusticity was thought quaint and charming; god and goddess became shepherd and shepherdess, and bucolic atmosphere, derived from the late antique, framed manners and fashions of modish gentry. Atmosphere was contemporary; Arcadian ideals of pastoral

181.

peace, innocent bliss, and virgin lovers displayed domesticated gallantry as a game; love was no passion but tame compulsion. Ballet was a perfect metaphor for erotic sport. Happiness and ennui were matched as in battledore and shuttlecock; fictive freedom among immaculate milkmaids far from the tedious town intrigued an ostensibly sated public. Rococo taste was not royal, as was the Baroque; while still aristocratic, its frivolity, nervousness, intimacy, and caprice tickled a middle class taking over from *la noblesse de l'épée* and *la noblesse de robe*.

Politics:

Court ballet as an innovative or progressive genre was dead; when amateurs stopped dancing in public, around 1670, few professionals were ready, and twenty years elapsed before the recently established (1661) official school produced technicians in significant number or quality. After his death (1687), Lully was canonized by an outworn tradition of spectacle lasting well into the next century.

Between 1700 and 1725 there was a revival of simple divertissement without expressive mimicry to connect a story. Dances were inserted into opera as a relief from singing but with no particular meaning of their own. Ballet became a competitive exercise for dancers, with dress, décor, and dance design habitually stylized. Dances, like scenery, were interchangeable in repertory. A set number of ballet entries were assigned according to an artist's rank in the operatic hierarchy. In 1713 the Opéra staff included twelve male and ten female dancers; a ballet master who taught class; a choreographer who arranged numbers; a designer; and a master tailor.

The upper ranks of urban society, enamored of the pastoral convention, proposed ballets as *tableaux vivants* of country life—gentleman farming is still today a metaphor for freedom—but these were no true portraits of a peasantry overtaxed and subject to *levée en masse*. The city audience thus indulged itself in vapid pastorals

186.

187.

181. Social dance choreography. England, 1720.

that progressive artists would soon try to replace by elevated ethical subjects in *ballets d'action*. Reforms in theater were danger signals, but for the rest of the century those paying for opera-house tickets would irresponsibly ignore them.

Plot or Pretext:
Among many numbers, these are representative:

Courante: A French dance of Italian origin, originally in duple time, named for its lively "running" steps. In the orchestral dance suite it changed to 3/2 or 3/4. An old gallant, in love with a young beauty who mocks him, begs Amor tell him if his love is returned. The slow tempo befits a creaky old (and old-fashioned) gentleman.

Menuet: A stately dance of French rustic origin in triple time (introduced to theater by Lully, c. 1650) A twelve-year-old girl, already prey "to a thousand confused movements," prays Amor to put her mother to sleep, since she awaits her lover.

Bourrée: In two sections, each repeated in 2/2 time. Its name would be given to a much-used continuous small running step (later on toe-point) in the academy. A shepherdess, in love, begs Amor to open the eyes of her shepherd lover, who barely notices her.

Sarabande: Of Spanish (or Oriental) origin, from the sixteenth century, which early earned a lascivious reputation. It was a slow and serious dance in triple time. A deceived lover complains of his fate and begs Amor's advice.

Gigue: A gay dance of English (jig) or Italian origin, associated with the early fiddle (from 1600). It is in two sections, each repeated, the second an inversion of the first. A giddy young thing, breaking all hearts, begs Amor for an amiable shepherd who is not slow to dance.

Rigaudon: From Provence or Languedoc, in 2/4 or 4/4 time, consisting of three or four repeated sections of unequal length. It is a country dance grown dignified at court. A fool assures Amor that, with his own cash, he can always find partners to choose from.

Also included were *Passepied,* originally a Breton sailor's dance; *Gavotte; Loure;* and *Musette* (a shepherd's bagpipe)—all French forms.

Production:
Rebel wrote his various numbers for first-dancers as he might have concerti for virtuoso violinists. While forms of transposed folk or social dances were basic, there was embroidery by characteristic gesture. The female first-dancer of the Opéra, Mlle. Subligny, had retired in 1705; her successor, Françoise Prévôt, probably arranged *Les Caractères de la Danse.* Credited with being the first French ballerina with notable elevation, Prévôt appeared as Terpsichore, incarnation of the Dance, in *Les Fêtes Grecques et Romaines.* Her star pupils, Camargo and Sallé, were both in *Les Caractères.* Their rivalry marked that contrast, which exists to this day, between virtuosity, brilliance of execution, and expressive spirituality.

Marie Anne Cupis de Camargo (1710–70), half Italian, half Spanish, having observed the male dancers Blondi and Dumoulin, aspired to greater freedom. Possessed of speed and drive, she is credited as inventor of new steps, or developer of old ones. In spite of Rule XXIII of the Opéra (1714)—"artists are obliged to sing and dance in clothes assigned"—she shortened her full skirt a few inches, by which reform feet and ankles could be seen, the body released from the floor. She was famed for a "frictionless" *entrechat-quatre* and extreme turn-out, superior to her teacher's; a wide base for the feet gave the greatest stability.

Marie Sallé (1705–56) learned expressive pantomime from Franco-Italian comedians at street fairs. Her father was a tumbler; in London she learned mime from the Harlequin John Rich. Although she "never cut an *entrechat* nor turned a *pirouette*," without leaps and bounds she delighted by grace of movement. She contributed to costume reform by appearing in *Pigmalion* in a muslin tunic, in London, 1734, the same year in which Handel composed *Terpsichore* for her.

183.

66.

67.

61.

37.

195.

182.

182. Peasant dance. France, c. 1712.

183.

184.

185.

183. Camargo, c. 1730.

184, 185. Gallant peasant; village belle. France, c. 1750.

186. Opera-ballet. France, c. 1735.

187. Peasant dancers. France, c. 1735.

188.

LA GUINGUETTE
(The Suburban Garden Tavern)
August 8, 1750
Paris
Théâtre Italien

Priority:
The Théâtre Italien of Paris was a vital link between humanizing traditions of gestural, acrobatic comedy and academic ballet at the royal Opéra. Luigi Riccoboni, actor and theater manager, had backed Marie Sallé's *Pigmalion* (1734), an innovation both in style and in that it was produced at the Italien, accustomed to light repertory rather than serious dramatic dancing. The Théâtre Italien and the Opéra Comique were lively counterbalance to the official Opéra, admitting novelties unseemly in the senior house. Jean-Baptiste de Hesse (also spelled Dehesse or Deshayes), an actor-dancer from The Hague, appeared in a *Pygmalion*, joining the company of the Italians that same year. He staged works such as *La Guinguette* with *commedia dell'arte*

types and comic divertissements, including an *Opérateur Chinois* (1749).

Holland had considerable theatrical dancing. De Hesse's pantomimic dance-dramas on mythological themes seem to have anticipated Noverre's *ballets d'action*. Since the Dutchman was a prolific contributor to the Paris stage, and since Noverre completely ignores him in his famous *Letters*, it is likely that he was party to the tacit conspiracy that excluded Noverre from the French capital for so long. Using his own strict methods, De Hesse trained his *corps* in expressive gesture beyond basic steps. Influenced by Dutch genre painting, notably that of Teniers, he exploited rural and village themes, which had had no part in heroic ballet, and he found new movement patterns, adapted from peasant games and folk festivals.

De Hesse was welcomed for "painterly" qualities in his composition; he translated the earthy heartiness of a Teniers or Jan Steen

into French—closer to the refinement of Pater or Lancret, but not entirely emasculated by Rococo fussiness. Diderot, the Encyclopedist, an important philosopher of theater, felt Teniers a far finer artist than Watteau. These were all steps in the gradual refutation of the Rococo of the Regency; a greater naturalism pointed toward reform or revolution, political and aesthetic. The so-called Dutch minor masters had no Versailles to decorate or king to deify. While their pictures showed domestic happiness, peace, skating, and village wedding feasts, the Netherlands had been devastated in savage battles for national existence. The paintings were a relaxation from tension; their climate would be borrowed by the French in their own prerevolutionary atmosphere.

193.

Precedent:
Guinguette, a word of obscure origin, possibly means an ordinary wine *(petit vin:* "guinguet"); thus it may have signified taverns or cabarets where such was sold. In 1724, Fuzelier, librettist for Rameau's *Les Indes Galantes*, provided *Les Dieux à la Guinguette*, an opera with dances. In 1729, English pantomime appeared in a show called *The Tavern* at the Opéra Comique. In 1731 came a Frenchified version—*La Guinguette Anglaise, Divertissement Muet Figuré en Ballet*. The subjects were love, intrigue, and jealousy amid low surroundings, components of comedy burlesque. English ballad-opera, leading up to *The Beggar's Opera* (1728), had made low life popular. Diderot restated the ancient dictum that social background was more important than personality; rank (as prince or peasant) more significant than individuality.

192.

53.

Politics:
In 1747, Madame de Pompadour, mistress of Louis XV, herself an able performer, set up her Théâtre des Petits Appartements at Versailles. For ballet master she chose

190.

188. "Comedians of skill," c. 1715.

De Hesse rather than a member of the Opéra, demonstrating her informed, independent taste. Subsidy enabled him to train some twenty children, aged nine to twelve, among whom emerged several talented future soloists of the Italian Theater and the Opéra. (One, Mlle. Puvignée, followed Sallé in *Pigmalion*). De Hesse also taught court ladies and gentlemen, who were still pleased to perform under professional direction. At first, the tiny theater seated but fourteen. It aroused such interest, due to the Pompadour's high standards, that the next year a larger hall was constructed. It could be quickly taken down and set up, as its site (the well of the Ambassadors Staircase) was needed twice a year for diplomatic functions.

Plot or Pretext:
The scene is a garden tavern or cabaret on the outskirts of Paris In the right corner, in profile, a man drinks, bottoms-up. Characters from various levels of middle- and lower-class society—*petits bourgeois,* lackeys, a soldier, an abbé, an ancient dandy chasing a girl with his umbrella—dance what might be some country figure or quadrille, suggesting an intrigue of four pairs of types, male and female, older and younger, richer and poorer.

Production:
Gabriel de St. Aubin's painting of *La Guinguette* (or rather the engraving from it) suggests an intimate stage rather than one with a big proscenium. Scenery is realistic; a pierced hedge at the back frames a distant windmill, familiar landmark of suburban Paris. Costumes are barely theatricalized class uniforms from ordinary civil dress. Light voluminous skirts allow easy movement, freer but less elegant than previously seen on stage. Robust accents are fixed in the rather ferocious silhouette of a common soldier, who has not troubled to discard his sword, and in the

Teniers-Steen-type toper. Remote provinces of France contributed a rich vein of local folk dance and song, which, exported to Paris, became the rage, serving ballroom and opera house in various transformations. Infusions of vitality from provincial or peasant sources, at first outside court theater, but shortly absorbed into it, gave new life to the central academy, always in danger of paralysis from inertia, habit, and tenure.

St. Aubin's companion painting to *La Guinguette, Le Carnéval du Parnasse* (c.1752), echoes it. Here we have three principal theaters personified. The Comédie Française is represented by an actor as Momus, with cap and bells, in classic plumes and *tonnelet.* The Théâtre Italien is impersonated by *commedia dell'arte* figures—Mezzetin, Pantalon, Colombine. In the center are dancers (and singers?) from the Opéra, where *Le Carnéval* was given on September 23, 1749, with music by Jean Joseph Mondonville. Court protection insured its success. Camargo appeared in it toward the end of her career. Having shortened her skirts early, by some important inches, she was a performer who enlarged the dance idiom by personal innovation. She wore "precautionary

camiknickers" *(caleçons de précaution)* under her skirts to ensure modesty; with this safety device, the path was open for less constricted movement, which, in fact, the peasantry had long practiced. Its label as *"ballet héroïque"* is ironic. *Le Carnéval,* as depicted by St. Aubin, suggests an open-air country dance; a glorified shepherdess watches from the left. By the middle of the eighteenth century, when this was presented, elements from Italian and English pantomime, together with national folk forms, reinforced choreography. *Ballet d'action,* dramatically oriented dancing in several individual styles, was seen all over Europe. Absolute priority among De Hesse, Noverre, Hilferding, or Angiolini in the development of a new genre is impossible to allocate. Most agree that Sallé's *Pigmalion,* which the ballerina herself arranged, was important as an example of self-presentation, the role suited to the expressive capacities of the ballerina. After that, each choreographer claims some innovations. In any case, activity between 1750 and 1770 is rich in variety; it is a period that, neither in Paris, Stuttgart, nor Vienna, has been investigated with the attention it deserves.

194.

61.

189.

189. Carnival street dance. Venice, 1756.

190.

191.

192.

190. *Acis et Galatée*, c. 1750.

191. Pompadour and de Rohan, c. 1750.

192. *La Guinguette*.

193.

194.

193. Peasant festivities. Netherlands, 1663.

194. *Le Carnéval du Parnasse, c.* 1752.

195.

PYGMALION
1752–53
Vienna
Theater am Kärntnertor

Priority:

Our chief illustration for this work may indeed not refer to some specific *Pygmalion*, of which there were several, but rather to an anonymous ballet listed as *La Statue et les Jardinières*, eight performances of which were given, October–November, 1753, both at Burgtheater and Schönbrunn. But this drawing, misattributed to a Bibiena, once in the collection of Count Durazzo (present whereabouts unknown), is one of the clearest documents of this type of ballet, of which representations are rare. In spirit it could be close to a famous *Pygmalion* of Franz Anton Hilferding van Wewen, an influential master. Trained at the Austrian court ballet school, he was sent to Paris to study under Michel Blondi (1675–1737), eminent teacher and dancer, favorite

partner of Mlle. Prévôt and lover of Camargo. Embracing the Encyclopedist philosophy, Hilferding wished to reform outworn modes and "imitate nature." He led a revolt against the tyranny of classical models, while still working within tradition, as seen in his staging of Racine's *Britannicus* as pantomime (similar to *Les Horaces* at Sceaux). He devised comic ballets, replacing *commedia dell'arte* stereotypes with characters from Austrian country life. Noverre in Stuttgart and Angiolini in Vienna came under his influence. In 1758 he was called to St. Petersburg as the first important foreign ballet master to help determine a national Russian school. The librettist Metastasio said that Hilferding "trained his dancers to insinuate themselves into the hearts of their audience by the expression of emotion." Hilferding has perhaps more right to be credited with the formulation of *ballet d'action* than Noverre, who claimed its inception. As for the theme of *Pygmalion*—a statue coming to life— there were to be several similar nineteenth-century ballets, notably *The Marble Maiden* (1845), *Alma* (1862), and, as a variant, *Coppélia* (1870). A statue, doll, puppet, automaton, given a soul and volition, is as metaphorically perfect a subject for dancing as a birdcatcher, a golden cockerel, a nightingale, or two cats in love are for singing opera.* Prometheus molded men out of inert matter to make them move. Pygmalion is no demi-god, but an artist, endowed with personal genius. As Professor Gombrich sees him:

"When Pygmalion blocked out a figure from his marble he did not at first represent a 'generalized' human form, and then gradually a particular woman. For as he chipped away and made it more lifelike the block was not turned into a portrait—not even in the unlikely case that he used a live model. So when his prayers were heard and the statue came to life

she was Galatea and no one else. . . ."

A hundred years before the ballet, she might have been the idealized portrait of a princess who paid for the fete.

The figure of Pygmalion is an early statement of the artist as hero. Apollo, lord of technique and craft, was divine and all-powerful; hence his artifacts or miracles were hardly supranormal for a god, merely supernatural for a man. Pygmalion is human; his gift may be god-given, but we are surprised by his genius or potential, which, while mortal, results in sculpture that, born from inert matter, survives his death, an object created within metaphors of miracle and immortality. Humane art now becomes an heroic subject; art itself, the creation of masterpieces rather than praise of princes. In time, plots will concern themselves no longer with the acts of artists, sculptors, or dancing masters, but rather with the grammar itself— charted movement designed by artist-choreographers who themselves never appear. Increasingly ballet will be about dancing.

198.

430.

Precedent:

In London, 1734, Marie Sallé appeared in *Pigmalion*, her own arrangement. In a thin shift, she was hardly naked, but only divested of customary pannniered skirt, and wigless. (Oddly enough, this radical outfit had little immediate sequence as a revolutionary step in costume reform.) By simple but telling pantomime, with only a partner and eight dancers, Sallé enjoyed an historic success. *Le Mercure de France* for April, 1734, wrote:

". . . the statue, little by little, becomes conscious, showing wonder at her changed existence and all around her. Amazed and entranced, Pigmalion takes her hand, leading her down from the pedestal. Step by step she feels her way gradually assuming the most grace-

---

195. *Pygmalion*. France, c. 1750.

* Mozart, Rimsky-Korsakov, Stravinsky, Ravel.

ful poses a sculptor could possibly desire, with steps ranging from the simplest to the most complex."[*] In 1745, Barbera Campanini (1721–99), known as La Barberina, *maîtresse en titre* to Frederick the Great, appeared in Berlin in a pantomime of *Pygmalion* as an opera-interlude. She is immortalized in panels by Antoine Pesne, painted for the music room of Sans Souci, Potsdam, Frederick's imitation of Versailles. In the panels she is shown nude, which on stage she was not. The ballet master De Hesse danced in a Paris version; Noverre may have appeared in it in Berlin. In the last scene of Rameau's ballet *Pygmalion* (1748), in addition to *danse simple* and *danse d'action*, there was indication for a *danse pantomime*. Plate 24, Part II, of Lambranzi's *New and Curious School of Theatrical Dancing* (1716) shows:

". . . a wooden statue which has been covered with pieces of stone, made to adhere by means of plaster, so that it appears shapeless. It is set upon the stage. Then enter two sculptors who chisel the statue as they dance, so that the pieces of stone fall off and the mass is transformed into a statue. . . ."[†]

Pygmalion, according to one legend, was king of Cyprus, Aphrodite's favorite isle. He is disgusted by local girls who deny her divinity. She punishes them; losing their modesty, they offer themselves to all comers. For this they are turned to rocks. Pygmalion was happy only among stones like those he carved, toward perfection. Devotion to the goddess crowned his masterpiece with life.

Politics:

It is sometimes forgotten that, along with its opera activities, Vienna was important as a ballet center from the seventeenth century. Count Giacomo Durazzo (1717–94), of an ancient Genoese family, Intendant of the Imperial Theaters under Maria Theresa, was a gifted musical amateur, patron of Gluck and of the ballet masters Hilferding, Angiolini, and Noverre. An administrator who encouraged progressive innovation, a diplomat, courtier, and promoter of theatrical creation, he was also a friend of Francesco Algarotti (1712–64), whose widely read lecture on opera (1755) established a rationale that Noverre applied (without thanks) in his own *Letters on the Dance* (1760). Durazzo was the Diaghilev of his day, employing the finest Italian stage-designers, the foremost international dancers and ballet masters.

Plot or Pretext:

Pygmalion, the sculptor, enters his open-air studio, accompanied by assistants and apprentices. In the ensuing dance they brandish mallets and chisels. The yard is filled with plaster models and works in progress. Pygmalion admires his most recent handiwork, a woman poised on a pedestal: she is in hooped skirts; he in the uniform of a court dancer, plumed. He caresses his statue, adorns it with jewels, embraces it, and prays to Venus to turn stone to flesh. Three rays of light descend and bring the statue to life. To general amazement, the figure starts slowly to move. It breathes; it tests arms and legs. It expresses astonishment at each new object that greets its eyes. With his aid the living maiden descends from her block to feel the ground and her new freedom. Pygmalion, sculptor (as dancing master), indicates at first simple, then more complicated steps and poses, which she follows. Their *pas de deux* is blessed by Venus and Cupid from the clouds. There is general rejoicing.

Production:

Hilferding's production was on the big stage of the Kärntnertor Theater, far larger than that which Sallé had at her disposal. Count Durazzo had been made *Generalspektakel-* *direktor* at about this time, with considerable resources available to him. Music was by Josef Starzer (c. 1726–87), a fine violinist and ballet-composer who would later work with Noverre along the same lines. Scenery was probably by Giuseppe Galli Bibiena (1696–1757), one of the eight members of the famous Italian dynasty of stage architects who set the style of the late Baroque for European theater. The scene did not immediately correspond to one of the ten canonical types of stage set: it showed an exterior landscape with monumental elements, but also a particular rather than general site, more realistic than ideal. Giuseppe had made innovations in stage-lighting and in 1748 had built the opera house in Bayreuth, which still exists. While the chief dancers wore traditional dancing dress, workmen turned grindstones and fired their forge in aprons and civil costume. There was a combination of realism and opera-house magic—real ropes and pulleys to lift Pygmalion's marble, and (invisible) ropes and counterweights to bring Venus on her cloud. Throughout the seventeenth century, the use of everyday occupational gesture and ordinary familiar atmosphere had been possible only as satire; it was deemed unworthy of the heroic style. Halfway through the eighteenth century, there was a new impulse toward the human scale, expressed on one hand by a theatricalization of daily life, on the other by borrowings from exotic lands and people. It is hard to realize that ordinary everyday reference could be exotic, but on stage, contrasted with the petrification of opera-house practice, it was.

78.

199.

53.

207.

---

[*] Stanley W. E. Vinve, "Marie Sallé, 1707–56," *Theatre Notebook*, XII, no. 1 (Autumn, 1957).

[†] Trans. Derra De Moroda, ed. Cyril Beaumont (1928).

196.

197.

198.

196. Sculptor's studio. Germany, 1716.

197. La Barberina: Galatea. Prussia, 1745.

198. *Pygmalion et Galatée*. France, c. 1760.

199.

200.

201.

199. *La Statue et les Jardinières*. Vienna, 1752.

200. Ballerina's costume. Prussia, c. 1745.

201. Mrs. David Garrick, c. 1749.

202.

LES FÊTES CHINOISES
(The Chinese Festivals)
July 1, 1754
Paris
Opéra Comique

Priority:

This ballet was the first large success of Jean Georges Noverre, most literate of ballet masters, whose *Letters* (1760) provide a philosophical background for reform in stage dancing along with vivid pictures of dancers in his time. As distinct from dancing produced at the official Grand Opéra, *Les Fêtes Chinoises* issued from the Opéra Comique, a privately managed house, in the manner of the fairs of St. Germain and St. Laurent, which had traditionally sheltered the popular improvising comedians. Noverre had a European career outside Paris. An extremely energetic ballet master, he was highly influential and established his own style of heroic action parallel to the work of Hilferding and Angiolini. In 1807 he said: "I made a revolution in the dance as striking and as durable as Gluck achieved in music." However, Mozart complained of his musical insensitivity. Noverre was a good academic dancer, trained by Jean (*le Petit*) and Louis (*le Grand*) Dupré. As for *Les Fêtes Chinoises*, for which Rameau may have written music (Noverre did not credit a composer,

and, disliking the ballet in later life, omitted it from his published librettos), coming from a ballet master whose reputation was chiefly made in the provinces, it astonished Parisians by splendid décor, ingenuity of its round dances, and the schooling of an amplified *corps de ballet*, superior to almost anything seen before. In quasi-realistic style, it consisted of danced pictures with little plot, incorporating elements of the real and ideal, including the exotic China of travelers and explorers and the fantastic Cathay of the Rococo *chinoiserie* designers.

Precedent:

There had been contact with China since Marco Polo in the thirteenth century; in the eighteenth, missionary Jesuit fathers made imitations of French gardens in Peking. The painter François Boucher may actually have depicted Noverre's theatrical China in his cartoons for a set of Chinese tapestries now at Besançon. Tapestries, ceramics, and lacquer in Chinese taste were extremely popular throughout Europe. By 1601 there had been a ballet of Chinese princes "dressed in feathers, mirrors, in black and white —who preferred inconstancy."* In 1723 *Arlequin Pagode et Médecin* was given with a backdrop showing the Imperial Palace, Peking.

In 1751 the French Academy in Rome gave a magnificent procession in Chinese style to honor Madame de Pompadour's brother, as it had in 1735, to please Saint Aignan, the Ambassador. In 1755, Voltaire wrote *L'Orphelin de la Chine*, a dramatization "of the morals of Confucius." Noverre had produced earlier versions of his *fêtes* at Stuttgart, Marseilles, and Lyons.

Politics:

Jean Monnet, a leading impresario, exercised the license for the Opéra Comique, competing with the Opéra. He organized able teams of talent and proved himself an innovator in design and management, making the Comique a far livelier house. It was he who replaced candles by oil lamps. The great English actor David Garrick held the license for Drury Lane; needing novelty, he negotiated with Monnet for Noverre's ballet with new machines and decorations. Threat of imminent war between France and Britain and the violent antagonism of London's audience to French dancers led to riots in which the production was destroyed—a great loss to Garrick. In his youth, Garrick, who was half French and half Irish, portrayed Harlequin; as a Shakespearean actor, he greatly impressed Noverre, who continually invoked his ex-

230.

177.

---

202. Chinoiserie, c. 1750.

* Saint-Simon records that, in 1700, at Versailles, at a ball given by Madame de Pontchartrain, "there were different rooms provided for a full-evening-dress ball, masks, a splendid supper, and booths

for the merchants of various countries— China, Japan, etc.—offering vast quantities of objects of beauty and *vertu*. . . ."

ample. His wife, Mlle. Violette (Weigel), had been a pupil of Hilferding in Vienna; Garrick appreciated ballet, and himself made radical reforms in theater practice that also influenced dance.

Plot or Pretext:
From an eye-witness:

". . . a public square decorated for a festival with, in the background, an amphitheater on which are seated sixteen Chinese, [and] thirty-two are seen on the *gradins* (stepped tiers) going through a pantomime. As the first group descends, sixteen further Chinese, both mandarins and slaves, come out of their habitations. . . . All these form eight rows of dancers who, rising and dipping in succession, imitate fairly well the billows of a stormy sea. All the Chinese, having descended, begin a character march. There are a mandarin, borne in a rich palanquin by six white slaves, whilst two negroes draw a chariot on which a young Chinese woman is seated. They are preceded and followed by a host of Chinese playing various musical instruments. . . . This march concluded, the ballet begins

and leaves nothing to be desired either in the diversity or in the neatness of the figures. It ends in a contredanse of thirty-two persons [in London augmented to forty-eight], whose movements trace a prodigious number of new and perfectly designed attitudes, which form and dissolve with the greatest of ease. At the end . . . the Chinese return to their place on the amphitheater, which is transformed into a china cabinet [or porcelain factory]. Thirty-two vases, which rise up, conceal . . . the thirty-two Chinese one saw before."

Production:
In London, where the ballet was given under the title *Les Métamorphoses Chinoises* (November 8, 1755):

"The sets were superb and the costumes magnificent. Ninety persons appeared in the march. The palanquin and the cars were richly decorated. All the wings were embellished with balconies filled with Chinese men and women spectators of the fete. The *corps de ballet* were well composed and well grouped, the individual *pas* agreeably varied, and the contre-

danse was executed with a precision and neatness unusual in *grands ballets*. . . ."

The costumes, designed by Louis-Simon Boquet, were not transpositions of classic ballet uniform—versions of Roman armor with incidental bits of applied "Chinese" ornament. Boquet used documents straightforwardly, which enhanced their novelty.

Instead of presenting a *suite de danses* or miscellaneous divertissements, Noverre was consistent in locale and atmosphere, focusing on a single rich style with little dramatic action, which struck his audience as something arresting and new. At the beginning of his career, Noverre felt all types, nationalities, and conditions of men were fit to depict, although by its end, he wrote that only nobly born heroes and heroines (mostly from the antique) were suited to the dignity of stage dancing.

209.

203.

203. Chinese procession. London, 1772.

204.

205.

204. "Chinese" ballet, c. 1770.

205. "Chinese" scenery, c. 1750.

112

206. 207.

208. 209.

206. "Chinese" dancer, c. 1750.

209. "Chinese" dancer, c. 1760.

207. "Chinese" ballerina, c. 1750.

208. "Chinese" pantomime, 1700.

210.

LE TURC GÉNÉREUX (DER GROSSMUTIGE TÜRKE)
(The Generous Turk, from Les Indes Galantes)
April 26, 1758
Vienna
Theater am Kärntnertor

Priority:

First given as part of *Les Indes Galantes* (1735), *Le Turc* was often revived in various versions up to the French Revolution. It marks the arrival of Jean-Philippe Rameau, the first innovator of dance music after Lully, who had served manfully, but invented less. Himself a dancer, Lully was bound by lack of professionals, restricted movement, and court forms. Rameau was no dancer, but he understood how to characterize dances to explain action. "Each character and passion have their particular movement; but this depends more on taste than on rules." He was an innovator with a symphonic imagination; choreographic structure was ingeniously suggested and it impelled movement. In spite of Lully's *airs de vitesse* ("quick tunes"), dances in his opera-ballets were earthbound, horizontal, regulated promenades. Around 1730, the *danse haute* (off the floor) tended to generally replace the old *danse basse*, or *terre à terre* (on the ground). Design became more ample and vertical, filling not alone the plane surface, but

the stage air. Lullists were horrified: "Before, they danced. Now, they jump." Elevation, for both male and female, increased, with the goal of professional virtuosity becoming part of academic training. Animation saved the *danse d'école* and the *danse noble et héroïque* from rigidity and monotony.

Precedent:

Les Indes Galantes displayed fastidious gallantry, a French specialty (*galer*, "to be gay"). *La Galanterie du Temps,* a masquerade of Lully (1656), equally exemplified the gallant manner, as did the *fêtes galantes* of *Les Plaisirs de l'Île Enchantée* by Molière and Lully at Versailles (1664).

In addition to gallantry at home, there was great fascination with exotic and far away places. The four quarters of the world (Europe, Asia, Africa, America) were popular themes in decorative art, and there was, in particular, a craze for things Turkish. In 1596, there had been a ballet for "*une troupe de Turcs Armez.*" In 1735 *Les Indes Galantes* was seen in prologue and four acts: Turkish, Peruvian, Persian, American. And in 1697 *L'Europe Galante* (De la Motte-Campra) had four entries: French, Spanish (*à sarabande*), Italian (*à la Scarlatti*), and Turkish. Since the late Crusades, Western interpretations of Turk or Saracen oscillated between Cruel Turk (Bluebeard) and generous Turk (Saladin), depending on war or peace between East and West. Harems, coffee, alchemy, tulips, bazaars, pirates, and dervish dancers decorated literature and spectacle. Turks were defeated in equestrian and marine shows. Molière performed a grand Turkish ceremony in *Le Bourgeois Gentilhomme* (1670). The tradition continues through the nineteenth century with *La Révolte au Sérail* (F. Taglioni, 1833) and down to our own day with Fokine's Turko-Persian *Schéhérazade* (1910).

36.

61.

213.

106.

368.

210. Moroccans at the Opéra. France, c. 1680.

Politics:
In the prologue of the first *Indes Galantes* (1735), the youth of four allies (France, Spain, Italy, Poland) are trained for war by the goddess Bellona. Instructed further by Hebe (Youth) and Amor, they quit sweet peace to seek fortune in foreign parts, an increasing knowledge of which was popularized by trade, exploration, conquest.

There had been numerous embassies to the West. In 1721, Mehmet Effendi, Turkish ambassador, was received by a splendid Paris procession. On April 17, 1758, the Emperor of Austria met Resmi Achmed Effendi, who notified him of the accession of Mustafa III, the new sultan. Count Durazzo seems to have ordered Hilferding to revive Rameau's first act, which he had probably known from Paris.

Plot or Pretext:
Fuzelier, author of the libretto, compressed each act to use but a single set. The first act of *Les Indes Galantes* tells of Osman, Pasha of a Turkish isle in the Indian Ocean, who loves his Provençal slave, Émilie. She has been captured by corsairs from Valéry, her fiancé, a French naval officer. Tempest-tossed, then cast ashore, Valéry also finds himself captive of Osman. After a show of feigned cruelty, Osman magnanimously renounces his own passion, awarding Émilie to Valéry. The act ends with combined rejoicings of Osman's African slaves and reunited sailors of Valéry's flotilla.

Production:
The final act of the Viennese version (1758) exists vividly in a superb engraving by Bernardo Belotto, nephew of Canaletto and painter of townscapes of Vienna, London, and Warsaw. This artist may have designed the ballet scenery as well. Ladies of the ensemble run in from their harem, at the left; French sailors dash on from the right; in the center, statuesquely heroic, are the principals.

211.

Count Durazzo supervised. Hilferding was called to Russia later during the year, his place taken by Angiolini, who would follow him to Petersburg. Noverre's ballet *Les Fêtes du Sérail* ("The Seraglio Festival") was produced in Lyons, September 21, 1758, stemming from common sources. In citing model ballets, Noverre drew particular attention to *Le Turc Généreux*, either designed or performed by Marie Sallé (1735), who arranged her own entry for the Rose Queen (of Persia). She alone stood erect in spite of tempests blown up by Boreas, god of winds, until gentle Zephyr wafted in to resuscitate broken blossoms (*corps de ballet*).

The enormously successful revival of the entire spectacle at the Paris Opéra (1952) gave ideas of the original, in which a Peruvian volcano erupts on stage; a congress of all-Asian odalisques gathers for a flower festival; a ceremony of the Pipe of Peace is performed by American Indians under their Grand Calumet.

Ballet, once a subsidiary part of opera, became a principal attraction around 1740; Rameau was even accused of reducing drama in favor of divertissement. Distinction was drawn between *la danse simple*—decorative entries without specific program to enrich stage atmosphere: an animated cortège; *la danse d'action*—narrative, dramatic, and climactic pantomime; and *la danse figurée*, in which pattern was the point—a large dance for its own sake without reference to plot.

Scenery had changed considerably. The solemn grandeur of the seventeenth century, its symmetrical inflexibility and central focus, had been replaced by scenes set on the angle, which enlarged the apparent space; architectural and garden elements were combined. More intimate realism and attention to local color in asymmetrical composition provided backgrounds that enhanced the dances rather than merely framing them.

186.

26.

79.

216.

212.

---

211. Persian. France, c. 1740.

212. "Mascarade orientale." France, c. 1730.

213.

214.

215.

213. Turkish Embassy, Paris, 1721.

215. Indian Prince. France, c. 1685.

214. *Amorous Turk*. France, c. 1740.

216.

217. 218. 219.

EUROPEENS. GREQUE. FATIME AFRICAINE.

216. *Le Turc Généreux*, Vienna, 1758.

217. European lover. France, c. 1770.

218. Greek maiden. France, c. 1770.

219. Fatima the African. France, c. 1770.

220.

**DON JUAN ou LE FESTIN
DE PIERRE**
*(Don Juan, or the
Stone Guest's Banquet)*
October 17, 1761
Vienna
Theater am Kärntnertor

Priority:
The score by Gluck is perhaps the most considerable written for dance in the eighteenth century. His comprehension of the possibilities of theatrical dancing as an autonomous form, beyond association with opera, enabled him to write without conventional rhetoric or ornament, which even Rameau had hardly done. Gluck's dramatic directness, his analysis of structure building toward exciting climax, marks another powerful partnership between dance and music on the highest expressive level. *Don Juan's* choreographer, Gasparo Angiolini, may have been as inventive as Noverre; his dominant influence seems to have been in Austria, Italy, and Russia, while Noverre affected Germany, England, and France. Noverre, in Stuttgart, attempted to build ballet on heroic gesture, suggested, in part, by Garrick's plastique for Shakespeare. Angiolini's *passi d'azione* (or *pas d'action*) in Vienna, prompted by Hilferding and Gluck,

seems to have accented dancing itself. In the preface to *Don Juan* (libretto by Raniero Calzabigi): "If we can stir up every passion by a mute play, why should we be forbidden to attempt this? If the public does not wish to deprive itself of the greatest beauties of our art, it must accustom itself to being moved by our ballet and brought to tears." One is not so reduced by virtuoso divertissement. Diderot and apologists for the *ballet d'action* believed they wished to make drama direct, intimate, and touching. Spectators had sat on the stage ever since theaters were built in France; it was a noble's privilege. Not only did this impede action, it made it more artificial. Diderot wished to remove "the fourth wall," so that players performed as if there were no audience at all. What led to naturalistic acting—ultimately to the self-hypnosis of Stanislavsky's method—in ballet led only to a shift in emphasis. Realism in ballet is associated with mimicry, not dancing. The *ballet d'action* as unified artwork was always an anomaly.

Precedent:
The Gluck-Calzabigi ballet, based on Molière's *Dom Juan, ou le Festin de Pierre* (1665), in turn influenced Mozart's *Il Dissoluto Punito ossia Don Giovanni* (1787). Angiolini, invoking Lucian of Samosata, asserted his own *ballo pantomimo* was the first "true revival" of Roman mime; similar claims were made for mimo-drama at Sceaux, Weaver's London pantomimes, and Hilferding's treatment of Racine. Insistence on mimicry, as opposed to "pure dance," was already a progressive theory when French pedants produced antique justification. *Les Amants Magnifiques* (1670) demonstrated academic categories of mimicry. Gluck used variants on a main characterizing theme, as in the old dance suites with theme and variations, but here he produced heightened emphasis and unity. Don Juan—lover, libertine, professional indulger in one-

night stands—developed from the Zeus who became a swan or golden shower to ravish innocent beauties. Molière's immediate prototype was Don Juan Tenorio, anti-hero of Tirso de Molina's play (c. 1630), based on a work of Lope de Vega, which was embroidered from a medieval *romancero*. Molière had not read the Spanish, but he saw adaptations by *commedia dell'arte* players in Paris from 1658. Don Juan may have been a historical personage from Seville, a Christian sinner, at death repentant, begging absolution. Molière made him a courtier at Versailles, a sadistic atheist fearing neither God, man, nor devil, on good terms with such as the Grand Condé and Princess Palatine, who burned a bit of the True Cross, the Duc de Nevers, who baptized a pig, and the libertine who, bored at his fatuous banquet, laid bets on who could blaspheme best.* A fastidious hypocrite, free of morality, professor of *actes gratuits,* which suspend human causality, Juan plays God. "Who am I?" he asks through Tirso de Molina. "A man without a name," but a man with a long list of those he'd loved—once. The endocrinologist Dr. Marañon was perhaps the first to claim Juan had no title, only sex, and that his obsession proved him impotent or invert. Juan is an existentialist; the Stone Guest is not Jahveh, Judah's judge, but Juan himself, whose promiscuity petrifies appetite before flesh is putrid. His nature makes him kin in paradox to Don Quixote, fool and saint, and Hamlet, philosopher and prince-politico. Since the lapse of classical, Biblical, and medieval myth, these three have become secular archetypes. It is by no accident they are incarnated for world reference in masterworks.

Politics:
Ideas of general reform of academic ballet by infusions from drama were widespread. Despite the famous quarrel between Angiolini and Noverre (1772), both

224

220. Grotesque musician. France, c. 1680.

* André Castelot, preface to Esther van Loo, *Le Vrai Don Juan,* 1950.

shared similar aesthetics, inspired by rational "realism." Both wished "to imitate nature"; they differed in method. Noverre provided descriptive programs. Angiolini considered this deceptive, since it is impossible to detail movement in a program. Noverre ignored Aristotelian unities of time, place, and action, supporting the heresy that while it was well to have learned five academic basic positions, it was better to forget them. Angiolini defended the priority of his master Hilferding, attacked Noverre's padding, and proclaimed his own superior musicality.

Plot or Pretext:
Angiolini wrote that Gluck "fully grasped terrific elements in the plot and tried to express passion as well as horror. *In a pantomime, music is the main thing . . .* which speaks; we dancers only make movements like actors in old tragedies and comedies (who had stanzas recited by others) and only gesture."

The overture is a short sonata symphony, in which is first heard the recurring motif of threatening trumpets.

I. The Commander's house in Madrid; a balcony. Don Juan with his servant and friends serenades Donna Elvira with a *siciliano;* guitars are simulated by plucked strings. The Commander, sword drawn, protects his daughter. In the ensuing duel Juan wounds him; he rallies, attacks, then faints and dies.

II. Don Juan's banquet. Gavotte, contredanse, country minuet; dinner music (fandango). There are knocks at the door followed by the comic fearful coming and going of his servant to answer. Glass in hand, Juan courteously answers the door. Enter the marble statue of the dead Commander. Toasting him, Juan invites him to dinner. There is terror among the guests, who escape. The Commander refuses the invitation and departs (noble minuet), first inviting Juan to dine at his tomb.

III. Graveyard. Juan rushes in to orchestral shivers. The Commander steps from his tomb (solemn minuet) and scolds Juan (echo of the dinner invitation). Juan displays vanity, frivolity, bravery. Cli-

max. Irrevocable judgment. Final passacaglia. Ominous horns and viols. Graves fly open. Flames. Orchestral horror. Juan sinks to hell.

Production:
Count Durazzo supervised the production. Gluck set each act in a different key, relying on emotional sense in every dramatic situation for dynamics and phrasing. The score presupposes a close collaboration and analytical agreement in depth between composer and choreographer. The vigorous danced duel in Act I suggests broad leaps and turns; in Act II, the knocks at the door are separated for a rising accumulation of tentative responses and refusals. In Act III, the symphonic description of a graveyard atmosphere—a combination of weird *pizzicati* in the bass, a sustained horn note, and repeats in the upper strings—mounts to an ominous expectant climax. Gluck's finale will become the great "Dance of the Furies" for his *Orfeo ed Euridice* (1762). The last dance of demons who come to seize Don Juan is in the traditional form of ballet finales, the chaconne, a dance of Spanish origin, in 3/4 time, with the accent on the second beat. Here it is a moderately slow series of variations on a ground bass. Gluck took given forms and developed them dramatically. He surpassed the conventional practice of Lully and his followers, projecting here a denouement of dark, melodramatic, particularized detail. Following him, Angiolini was attempting to render drama through dance rather than gestural pantomime, without divertissement or rhetorical display. Action is concentrated and concise, with the initial impulse seeming to come from the music, whose noble severity gives hardly any occasion for mere virtuosity. Michel Fokine, a reformer in our time of the line of eighteenth-century apologists for a *ballet d'action,* revived the score with his own dances (London, 1936).

221. Lully and Rameau meet Orpheus. France, 1774.

222.

223.

222. Count Durazzo, c. 1755.

223. Gluck, c. 1755.

LE FESTIN DE PIERRE.

224.

225.

224. *Dom Juan,* 1682.

225. *Don Juan,* 1780.

226.

JASON ET MEDÉE
(Jason and Medea)
February 11, 1763
Stuttgart
Grand Ducal Theater

Priority:
Noverre's treatment of this Greek legend was one of his greatest successes, constantly revived with or without acknowledgment or his supervision from Paris to Petersburg into the first decade of the next century, providing important vehicles for famous dancers. It is particularly identified with Gaetano Vestris. *Jason et Medée* is the heroic type of *ballet d'action*, as distinct from comic, exotic, or fantastic. Here ballet was seen almost as a department of spoken drama, but "a step, a gesture, a movement and an attitude express what no words can say." Stylized as it

might seem to us, in its own time it pointed toward psychological definition—realism divested of rhetoric. Even in spoken drama and opera Diderot favored the substitution of natural gesture and mimicry for the automatic proliferation of Alexandrine couplets. As a bourgeois, he preferred a direct, domestic human scale. Noverre's heroic use of dumb show was closer to actuality than traditional practice.

Precedent:
In 1736 Marie Sallé, a dancer much admired by Noverre, danced *Medée et Jason*; the story was familiar from many treatments in classic drama, starting with Corneille's version of Euripides (1635). As early as 1454 it was used for a dumb show in Lille. At a banquet in Milan, 1489, the dancing master,

Bergonzio di Botta of Tortona, made a ballet for Jason and his Argonauts that became a model for subsequent danced entries to be treated in a variety of styles and tastes. Horace's *Ars Poetica*, a manual of aesthetics much invoked since the Renaissance, warned poet and painter against depicting aberrations of nature, monstrous or fantastic, citing as an example Medea butchering her children. Problems of decorum, what was suitable, *aimable*, or *convenable*, had their effect on Noverre, who while resistive to conservative convention, gave lip service to an antiquity largely of his own interpretation. In his early career his work seems not too different from the academic but he would push it increasingly toward a picturesquely vivid and plastic pantomime. Noverre's stylistic ideal was that of David Garrick, as described by Baron Grimm:

"We saw him play the dagger scene in 'Macbeth' in a room in his ordinary dress, without any stage illusion; and, as he followed with his eye the air-drawn dagger, he became so grand that the assembly broke into a cry of general admiration. Who would believe that this same man, after a moment, counterfeited with equal perfection, a pastry-cook's boy...."

Politics:
Karl Eugene, Duke of Württemberg, provided six thousand troops for France in return for a subsidy; he dismissed his prime minister, divorced his wife, and then felt free to spend taxes on what he most loved—theater. The duke could afford the best in theatrical collaboration for opera: the Neapolitan, Jomelli (as conductor and composer); the engineer and scenic artist Servandoni; the costumier Boquet; as dancers, the brothers Vestris, Dauberval, and Le Picq; as ballet master, Noverre, who came to Stuttgart in 1760, and who, by 1764, headed a company of seven first-dancers, twenty-three men and twenty-one women, many trained

56.

23.

25.

79.

226. Jason and Medea. France, c. 1740.

by himself. For the celebration of the duke's birthday in 1763, Noverre composed *Jason*, to follow the first act of a new opera by Jomelli.

Plot or Pretext:

Jason, in order to obtain his throne, usurped by an uncle, sets out with his companion Argonauts to find the Golden Fleece. With the aid of Medea, a powerful sorceress, he conquers the dragon that guards it. By her he has two children. After ten years he deserts her for the nymph Creusa. Medea sends the girl as gift a poisoned mantle whose fire consumes her. Mad with jealousy, Medea slays the children. A Paris libretto of 1780 describes it as *"Ballet Terrible*, ornamented by dancing, suspicion, darkness, pleasure, horror, gaiety, treason, pleasantry, poison, tobacco, dagger, *salade* ['hotch-potch'], love, death, assassination, and fireworks."

Production:

Jomelli's opera of Dido abandoned by Aeneas was in some twenty acts; after the first came Noverre's ballet, echoing its drama. Complete in itself, it presented danced emotion and drama related to the previous singing. Ballet was no longer subsidiary; it supported and furthered operatic action, although dance music was by another hand. Medea was an English ballerina, Mlle. Nency, who, "apart from her amazing dancing talent, succeeded by showing in her acting ability all the soul and expression of that incomparable actor, the celebrated Garrick, in England where the dancer, trained by Mr. Noverre, was born." Gaetano and Angiolo Vestris were Jason and Creon. In addition to the principals, Fire (burning mantle), Steel (Medea's sword of vengeance), and Jealousy danced. It was reported from Stuttgart that when the Furies first appeared, with wild glances and streaming hair, some in the audience fainted, while others fled. This continued an honorable tradi-

tion; in fifth-century Greece, Aeschylus' *Eumenides* ("The Furies") caused ladies in the audience to miscarry. Gaetano Vestris (1729–1808), a pupil of Dupré, was the *dieu de la danse* of his era; he appropriated Noverre's ballet, adapting it freely all over Europe. In 1781 he appeared in London without mentioning the original author.

John Boydell's engraving of a Vestris performance (1782) is a savage caricature of heroic posturing in *ballet tragique*. While the orchestra tootles unconcernedly, Jason (Vestris), Medea (Simonet), and Creusa (Baccelli) wildly overact; no hint of realism or reform touches these preposterous poses, costumes, or headdresses. The postures read as parodies of academic operatic conventions. In Henry Siddon's English version (1822) of the German Engel's famous book on stage acting, the plate illustrating *Horror* is thus annotated:

"Whilst Medea, transported with rage, consults with herself on the way she may inflict the most sensible wound on the heart of the perfidious Jason, and distracted by the desire of vengeance, forms this wish, 'Ah, why has he not children by Creusa?,' or while she makes this still more terrible question, 'Is he not already a father?' Then, with averted face, she holds forth her hands and throws back her body, whilst revolted nature makes her breathe a sudden cry from the bottom of her heart."

In spite of working and writing for half a century, Noverre did not make much headway against conservatism. He was castigated for fussy pantomime, which may have been as over-elaborate as abuses in coloratura. In 1818, looking back on Noverre's past glory, M. J. Chénier wrote in his *Essai sur les Principes des Arts*:

"I do not wish to see Jason's children
Strangled, dancing—by their mother-dancer,

'Neath rhythmic blows, perish on the beat. . . .
Noverre, in the art he deemed a universal craft
Would have caused Joad, Phèdre and Misanthrope* to dance.
To limit pantomimes to *thèmes aimables.* . . .'"

Baron Grimm in 1771 made this distinction:

". . . in the ballets of Noverre [i.e., his later work], dancing and rhythmical walking are quite distinct. There is dancing but in the great movement of the passions, in the decisive movements, in the scenes, there is walking, in time it is true, but without dancing, and from the dance to the rhythmic walk, it is necessary in this spectacle as in the transition from recitative to song and song to recitative in opera, but dancing for the sake of dancing cannot occur until the danced play is over."

Which hardly indicates the integration of mime and dance of which Noverre, in theory, was such an ardent advocate.

Style, substance, and quality of the *ballet d'action* remain disputed, confused by puristic claims, and by the lack of balance actually achieved between mimicry, music, and dancing. Racine commented on Euripides' *Medea*, his source: "Music was invented for feasts in which there is already too much fun; no one has dreamed of making music to assuage grief." Strict academicians felt music had no place in tragedy, nor had dance, décor, or song. The chief glory of theater was language, in one idiom —French. Noverre wished a supranational dumb show, claiming for dancing what Racine had done for drama. Racine felt tragedy was interpretive rather than imitative art. Noverre, working in a nonverbal idiom, somehow hoped to improve on the prestige of the spoken tirade's metric and melodrama.

---

* Characters in Racine and Molière.

227.

228.

229.

227. Medea. France, c. 1750.

228. Fury. France, c. 1750.

229. *Jason and Medea*. London, 1782.

230. 231.

LA JALOUSIE.

LE POISON.

232. 233.

230. Heroic acting. London, 1775.

231. Heroic gesture. London, 1822.

232, 233. Heroic sentiment. France, 1763.

234.

235.

236.

LA FILLE MAL GARDÉE
(The Ill-guarded Girl)
July 1, 1789
Bordeaux
Grand-Théâtre

Priority:

It was not in Paris, which may have schooled the best professionals, but in such provincial centers as Lyons, Stuttgart, Vienna, and Bordeaux, freer from conservatism and power politics than the official Paris Opéra, where choreographic innovation might unobtrusively appear. Bordeaux, with its magnificent theater by Jean-Victor Louis (built 1780), and its gifted ballet master, Jean Dauberval (1742–1806), was no negligible institution. Dauberval, son of an actor, made his Paris Opéra début (1761), later benefiting from contact with Noverre at Stuttgart. *La Fille Mal Gardée* was a new type, based on a middle-class vision of peasant life. Although produced on the eve of the French Revolution, it was hardly a manifesto, since it still shared the late Rococo coyness of Marie Antoinette's picturesque dairy farm. Dauberval introduced a preponderance of character dancing, or that genre known as *demi-caractère*—an amalgam of folk dance and academic steps, adapted

to opera-house practice. In his light-hearted exploitation of peasant life, he was accused of giving up what remained of heroic style (left over from Louis XV) in favor of popular melodrama and facile charm. Dauberval seems to have developed the comic side of Noverre's narrative preoccupation. Apart from *Les Caprices de Cupidon*, produced by Galeotti (Copenhagen, 1786), which is unremarkable for choreographic innovation, *La Fille Mal Gardée* bears the oldest name in our repertory, due to constant revival, although now little music and less dancing from any original remains.

Its ballerina, a carelessly guarded virgin, proposed ideal proletarian innocence. An artless peasant lass, she was still a flirt with enough native French energy to dance steps characterizing a loyal peasantry. This was neither "realistic" nor did it herald revolutionary activity in Paris or the provinces. The Republican painter David's contribution to theatricality would be organized in open-air mass demonstrations rather than opera houses, but even as guillotines were sharpened, opera houses were full, as they are in most moments of national crisis. If lib-

ertinage was the badge of tyrants, and the *droit du seigneur* could provide *Le Mariage de Figaro* (1784) with Beaumarchais' pretext for Mozart's great lyric comedy of 1786 (of which Louis XVI said after reading it in 1782 that the play should under no circumstances be permitted production), *La Fille Mal Gardée* only faintly echoed progressive politics. Here peasants were picturesque, acquiescent, comic—quite under the thumb of those paternalistic liberals who ultimately precipitated the Terror.

184.

Precedent:

Country dances had long been performed at court; in 1631, the Cardinal Prince, Maurice of Savoy, introduced native music, costumes, and steps from his home province in a royal entertainment. Since codification of dance steps in the late Renaissance, a division had been established between the slow, grave, deliberate, noble *basse danse* for aristocratic use and the quick, gay, lively *haute danse*—off the earth, of country origin. Dauberval based his ballet on a well-known comic-opera libretto already produced in 1758; the audience was familiar with his plot. The music was a mishmash of folk dance and airs in vogue.

43.

88.

234. Colas. Russia, c. 1842.

235. Colas. Russia, c. 1890.

236. French genre, c. 1765.

Heroine and clown here recall Harlequin, Columbine, and Zany (numskull or clown) of the Italian popular comedy, transported to provincial France. Dauberval is supposed to have seen in a print shop window a "crude color-print showing a village youth escaping from a modest cottage, with a furious old beldame hurling his hat after him, while a peasant lass [her daughter?] wept." *Les Nopces de Village,* danced once in Vincennes by Louis XIV, 1663, had village characters: bailiff, police, six rich gentlemen, a midwife, bourgeois, etc. The king performed both village maid and gypsy fortune teller.

Politics:
Dauberval's picture of lower-class manners was more decorative than democratic, in the nature of *paysannerie*—picturesque peasantry—a lighthearted aspect of Rococo taste. With the times this attitude would develop into the *pastourelle républicaine* of Consulate and Empire, and, later, the *ballet-bourgeois* of Empire and Bourbon Restoration. A prototype was Jean-Jacques Rousseau's opera, *Le Devin du Village* ("The Village Soothsayer"), 1753. Rousseau's father was a dancing master (watchmaker and author). In his *Dictionary of Music* (1767), he complained of general nonsense in opera-ballet, pleading for worthy plots. The popular engraving that is supposed to have inspired Dauberval suggested the sentimental anecdotes of Greuze, an artist admired by Denis Diderot, who said that a single virtuous canvas contained the germ of an entire novel. Greuze canonized peasant life for the middle class; his didactic, sentimental morality anticipated the bloody revolution instigated by the very bourgeoisie who, in Bordeaux, applauded *La Fille Mal Gardée* as comforting novelty.

Plot or Pretext:
I. A village. At one side is the house of Widow Simone, a wealthy farmer (danced traditionally by a man *en travesti*). Dawn breaks; shepherds and farmers pass, bound for their fields. Lise, daughter of Simone, is in love with Colas, a poor but honest farmer lad. But the widow wishes her to marry Alain, a blessed simpleton, who is heir to fertile vineyards. Byplays at the dairy; then the churn and bowl of cream. Village harvest dance, a "composed" (or complex collective dance) number; sickles had been distributed as hand props; arm positions were borrowed from folk dance and were apparently more "realistic" than in the run of operas. The scene changes to one filled with harvesters. Noon. Colas commands a meal; country dances to a flageolet. Alain expresses his jealousy. A final divertissement, interrupted by a summer thunderstorm.

II. Inside the widow's house. There is a stair leading to attic room above. Byplay with spinning wheel; tambourine dance, during which the widow falls asleep. Lise spies Colas outside. The widow awakes, abruptly banging her tambourine. There is a dance of comic mother and charming daughter. Field hands bring in sheaves of wheat to get their pay. They want drink. The widow goes to the cellar, but locks Lise in as precaution. Colas emerges from a heap of sheaves; the ensuing *pas de deux* (Lise and Colas) displays their alarm, discretion, and love. Simone returns; Colas escapes upstairs. Mother, suspecting something, orders Lisa to her own room, where Colas already hides. Alain, the simpleton, arrives with papa and a village notary to sign marriage contract. However, notary, villagers, and field hands persuade the Widow Simone to consent to the love match rather than a mere marriage of convenience. A village festival forms the finale.

Production:
National dances characteristic of various people and places cannot be transposed to theater without compromise of authenticity. Folk dancing is more fun to do than to watch; making it both legible and entertaining to non-participants depends on tactful translation, in which a pure flavor, if not the form, of characteristic simplicity is retained. Arm positions, heeled shoes, kerchiefs, accompaniment by regional instruments (tambourine, flageolet) and folk-tunes are all outside the academic syntax, although a tradition of balleticized folk or character dancing grew up in opera houses, fully developed by mid-nineteenth century, with contributions from Spain, Central Europe, Italy, and Russian Poland (cachucha, polka, tarantella, polonaise). Increasingly, ethnic elements served as decorative detail on a base of school steps. Dauberval used positions that were "incorrect" from an academic viewpoint to realize his peasant steps; arms were akimbo, not rounded, and there was unclassical heel stamping, and deliberately rough accents. In Russia, this ballet was popular as *Vain Precautions,* latterly a vehicle for Anna Pavlova. Fanny Elssler danced it for her American farewell (1842). Enrico Cecchetti (1850–1928), the great Italo-Russian teacher and mime, was a famous Widow Simone. In 1960, Sir Frederick Ashton made a successful reconstitution for the Royal Ballet. Few echoes of Dauberval survive, except in the intention of the mime scenes following first libretto.

24.

315.

312.

46.

187.

237.

238.

239.

237. Peasant ballet. France, 1779.

238, 239. Village gallant; peasant belle. France, c. 1760.

240.

241.

242.

243.

240. Opera setting. Bordeaux, 1780–83.

241–43. Widow, Colas, Lise. Russia, 1882.

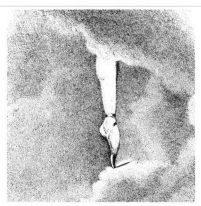

244.

FLORE ET ZÉPHYRE
(Flora and Zephyr)
July 7, 1796
London
King's Theater

Priority:
This ballet, by Charles Louis Didelot (1767–1836), is often held to be the first in which dancing on *pointes* —on toes—was highlighted. It is of the Anacreontic genre, in which classical themes were domesticated and prettified rather than inflated to operatic grandeur. Gods were no longer heroic, but frankly professional dancers with developed techniques, wearing abbreviated Greek- rather than Roman-inspired shifts and tunics. It was the most successful work of Didelot, a pupil of Auguste Vestris and Noverre, later called to Russia by Paul I (1800), where he determined the direction of the Imperial Academy in Petersburg for three decades.

Didelot is credited with an early use of flesh-colored tights (Paris Opéra, c. 1813). Called *maillot*, after their inventor, a hosier at the Opéra, tights soon replaced stockings, making a cleaner profile in movement. Didelot also advanced the development of *pas de deux*, emphasizing the polarity of masculine and feminine movements— male strength in support, lifts, and leaps; female quickness and lightness.

Precedent:
Anacreon of Teios, a Greek (active c. 521 B.C.), few of whose poems survive, praised love and wine. The tradition of this elegant if trifling poetry extended from Alexandria to Byzantium. During the Renaissance Anacreon was translated, adapted, and imitated all over Europe, in England by poets from Ben Jonson and Herrick to Shelley and Tennyson. Here is an Anacreontic fragment:

"When I find you among youth, the soul of youth is within me. I am old, yet winged for the dance. I leap madly about. Cybele cannot compete. . . . Like a youth I will dance with the young. Pass me God's liquor of life. Mark the might of an old man who may teach you to sing, drink, dance, with grace."

At the end of the eighteenth century Anacreontism was again fashionable, at a time when ponderous court antiquarianism of the preceding age had been exhausted, and when the persisting classic type and myth appeared on stages domesticated to a metropolitan scale, for a careless rather than erudite audience.

Politics:
The French Revolution did not transform ballet, but it licensed freedom in theme and costume. French dancers, formerly attached to the official theaters, crossed the Channel to dance in exile, and London for a time became the center of activity. London preferred its ballets shorter, more compact than Paris; it liked "dramatic" themes, full of busy action, without subplot or extra episodes.

While there had been dancing in Russia for a century, Didelot's assumption of the direction as *maître de ballet* in 1816 laid the groundwork for Russia's ultimate technical efficiency. A fine dancer, a great teacher, he used national themes for his ballets, borrowing some already rhymed by Pushkin, and trained native ballet masters.

He transmitted to Russia classical French elegance, based on the theories of Noverre, until he was retired in 1829 as the result of a quarrel with Prince Gagarin, Intendant of the Imperial Theaters. Similar incidents were to occur later on several occasions, including the forced resignation of Serge Diaghilev from the Imperial Theaters in 1901.

Plot or Pretext:
Greatly abbreviated, the libretto includes the following action: Zéphyre, the inconstant Breeze, descends from heaven with Cupid in his arms. The God of Love fosters Zéphyre's fickleness by finding Flore, a nymph, to replace his first love, but warns him he must repent. Zéphyre's new partner traces his shadow thrown on a temple wall (an allusion to the invention of the art of painting). Cupid warns Zéphyre that his first love is about to appear, at which the inconstant spirit abandons the new nymph and flies away. Later, to prove his constancy, he lets his wings be clipped; the nymph takes them for her own, and she flies up and out. In the end, Zéphyre recovers his wings, and all is well. Finale: Dance of shepherds and shepherdesses.

Production:
Called a ballet-divertissement in

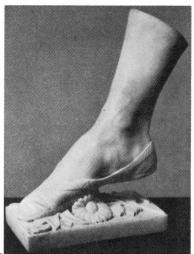

245.

244–47. The toe shoe, 1841–1914.

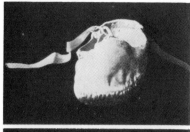

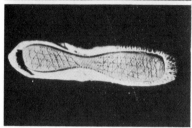

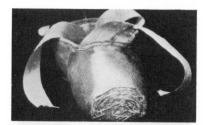

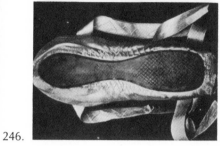

246.

247.

for instance, another Zéphyre bore Psyche to the Palace of Love and vanished with her amid the clouds. The machine was well devised and produced an excellent effect; but you see, or you imagine you see, the apparatus. Didelot's *Zéphyre* is much more wonderful: alone, apart, without any followers to distract the attention, he rises from the center of the stage by his own strength; with disdainful foot he spurns the earth he forsakes, soars for several minutes [*sic*] into space, grazes with the tips of his wings the greenish tops of the trees, and at last majestically disappears amid the azure vault. . . . Applause was prolonged far into the interval and broke out with redoubled vigor when Zéphyre, returning in the same way as he ascended, rose a second time bearing Flore in his arms."

248.

one act, *Flore* featured machinery by the engineer Liparotti. Dancers had appeared on cloud machines since the *nuvoli* of Renaissance religious and secular shows, but here Didelot's machinist used counterweighted wires to balance, support, and fly individual dancers. At first this was employed only for a few principals. Later there were whole aerial *corps de ballet,* whose members were paid extra for their hazard. In one production of *Alceste,* torch-bearing demons whizzed out into the auditorium itself, over the orchestra. Wires also enabled dancers to pose on the tips of their half-toes (*demi-pointe*), promising the eventual possibility of *pointe* work, when stitched, and later blocked, toe shoes gave enough support for the ballerina to move on toe-tips without other artificial aid. At the start, poses were only momentarily sustained, but once the principle was established, enormous development was possible both for ballerina and male dancer. She turned more bril-

liantly on *pointe;* he could turn her more rapidly; profiles in combination became more extended. Dance-slippers without heels promised the final blocked toe shoe (the exact moment of change from heel to heelless shoe is hard to pinpoint). Introduced after 1795, toe-dancing was already established by 1830, to be refined for decades after.

Flore et Zéphyre was continuously revived in various versions for half a century. In 1834, it was a vehicle for Jules Perrot and Marie Taglioni. The novelist Thackeray's caricatures show a production in long Romantic ballet skirts. Théophile Gautier, poet and ballet librettist, cited it as a type of outworn convention that Romanticism, his new dispensation, would replace. When Didelot's production was shown in Paris, 1815, it was a sensation:

"There have often been admirable flights at the Opéra. In *Psyche* (choreographed by Gardel, 1790),

248. Dancer. Italy, c. 1806–9.

131

249. 250.

251. 252.

249–50. Flora and Zephyr. France, c. 1750.

251–52. Amor and Zephyr. France, c. 1765.

253. 254.

255.
256.

253. Anacreontic ballet. France, 1806.

255–56. Flora and Zephyr. England, 1836.

254. Flora and Zephyr. Italy, 1828.

133

257.

257. Bacchic dance. Asia Minor, 100 B.C.

LA VESTALE
(*The Vestal Virgin*)
June, 9, 1818
Milan
La Scala

Priority:
Salvatore Viganò was renowned for his *choreodrammi*—his personal extension of the *ballet d'action*—in the line of Hilferding, Angiolini, and Noverre. He seems to have had a genius for manipulating masses and characterizing crowds, achieving a demechanization of the *corps de ballet*. Before him, uses of the *corps* tended toward symmetrical subservience, making it a unisonal background that occasionally performed in the spotlight to allow principal dancers to catch their breath. Viganò started with a large plastic group design, injecting into it fragmented detail.

The vast scale of his ballets at La Scala was matched in no European theater. The plasticity of his compositions derived from his close study of antique carving in the Vatican and other famous collections as well as his association with Antonio Canova, the most distinguished contemporary sculptor. His gestural expression was relatively free from opera-house tradition and more in harmony than usual with the music. As for dancing it-self, there seems to have been little enough, except in festive ceremonials required by librettos.

Viganò won a large following. Beethoven composed a ballet, *Creatures of Prometheus,* for him; the novelist Stendhal was an enthusiastic witness of his spectacles, one of which, *The Titans,* may have, in subject at least, given ideas to Richard Wagner for his epic *Ring of the Nibelungs.* He was greatly aided by his scenic-designer, Alessandro Sanquirico, whose large plates are the best record we have of Viganò's general contention. *La Vestale* is important more as representative of Viganò's scale and style than as an expression of any particular originality. Also, the sequence of Sanquirico's illustrations provides a coherent idea of Viganò's work.

Precedent:
Dauberval, his master, took Viganò to London, where he saw Noverre's last ballets. These still displayed marked divisions—long pantomime numbers, separate dances. In his own work Viganò tried to fuse movements into fluid sequential action, although he was hampered by the use of bits and pieces of available music. *La Vestale* was based on Spontini's opera, premièred in Paris, 1807. Archeological revival and research, the aesthetics of Winckelmann, the engravings of Piranesi, and the philosophy of the French Revolution and Napoleon's Empire in taking Roman manners and architecture as universal models provided the climate for Viganò's dance-dramas. If one is to credit Stendhal's descriptions, he may well have accomplished what Noverre and his colleagues proposed but only partially achieved: an archeological correctness in costume and decoration, and performance by actor-dancers rather than dancer-acrobats, with both qualities enhanced by a stupendous physical apparatus.

Politics:
La Scala, built in 1778, was a private institution controlled by boxholders and subscribers and aided by the city. It had resources dwarfing those of London or Paris. Viganò could rehearse indefinitely with ninety dancers and a token orchestra instead of a single fiddler or a rehearsal pianist. But his huge ballets did not remain long in repertory, nor survive his passing. With scheduled seasons subscribed and boxholders satisfied with one view of novelty, there was little reason to repeat works already given. The Milanese always preferred novelty. Before Viganò, there had been no dominant ballet master, nor would he be followed by one. After Viganò, Italy faded as a source of progressive choreography. Its schools continued to flourish, however, and the pupils of the outstanding teacher Carlo Blasis (1803–78) would enrich European opera houses for the rest of the century, establishing new criteria of virtuosity and pedagogy.

Plot or Pretext:
I. Circus Maximus, Rome. Anticipating *Ben Hur* and cinema spectaculars, the arena is packed with toga'd citizens, consuls, and priests. At the back, a chariot race is in progress, with horses on treadmills. Enter the procession of Ves-

13.

tal Virgins, bearing crowns for victors in the games, among whom is Decius. Receiving his trophy, he notices Emilia, a Vestal. The finale takes the form of a sacred bacchanal. (A pedantic critic noted that Decius, son of a consul, would not have been allowed to compete in the arena.)

II. A feast. Lovelorn Decius despairs while watching a *pas de deux* of Greek slaves. To a friend he confesses his guilty passion for the Vestal, for whom he is contemplating suicide. The friend knows of a secret passage to the virgin's convent. (Critics complained that the slave *pas de deux* was inserted as concession to Milanese taste and that a scene in which one friend seduced another to an evil act was not truly "Roman.")

III. Temple of Vesta. Emilia, in love and anguish, allows the sacred flame on her altar to go out. The Vestal Virgins, horrified to find Decius and his friend profaning their sanctuary, cannot save Emilia from judgment.

IV. A hill overlooking a sacred wood. Emilia's trial. Decius pleads with his father, the consul, to save her. A high priest condemns her to death, tears off her sacred amulet, and drapes her with a black veil. Witnesses are in tears; the consul is shamed by his son's conduct. Vestals and high priest move off in one direction, consular suites in another.

V. The execution ground. A procession and prayers to the gods expiating sacrilege. Emilia is entombed alive. Decius rushes in with armed friends and remonstrates with the cruel high priest. He is cut down and dies on his Vestal's grave.

Production:
It was assumed that the audience knew the tunes of Spontini's opera. On substructures of poses derived

258.

from Pompeian painting or Neoclassical sculpture, Viganò's actor-dancers used extravagant facial expression, rolling eyes, and heaving bosoms. We are aware of the exact moment when Emilia "changes expression" to signify love, terror, and hope for mercy, recalling silent-film pantomime. Vestals entered to a rhythm of "appealing gravity," with plastique taken from figures on Roman triumphal arches. Rossini complained of too much pantomime and not enough dancing. Viganò was accused of betraying the academic dance, altering honored legends, and of being uninterested in individual star dancers. This was one more clash in the constant battle between "pure" dance and "expressive" gesture, fought on another level between followers of Lully and Rameau, Gluck and Piccini. Viganò, like his predecessors, Hilferding, Angiolini, and Noverre, believed he achieved a true synthesis, which seems to have been more of scale than innovation. A devotee of Shakespeare and the choreographer of a huge *Otello*, he was,

like Noverre, favorably compared to the Bard. A good musician, a tactful.editor of musical fragments, Viganò attempted to describe his characters as persons, not types, and to re-create in detail the atmosphere of their historic epoch.

258. Neoclassic ballet. Russia, 1838.

259.

260.

261.

262.

259–60. Roman pantomime. Netherlands, 1827.

261–62. The Viganòs, c. 1790.

263. *La Vestale*. Act III.

264. *La Vestale*. Act IV.

LA SOMNAMBULE ou L'ARRIVÉE D'UN NOUVEAU SEIGNEUR
(The Sleepwalker, or The Arrival of the New Lord)
September 19, 1827
Paris
Opéra

Priority:
While this ballet has few claims to choreographic originality, it focuses several elements, representing a transition between eighteenth-century tradition in desuetude, and nineteenth-century renovation, on the verge of a Romantic repertory. Jean Aumer (1776-1833), pupil of Dauberval at Bordeaux, was an excellent dancer, but, too tall to perform, he became a choreographer, achieving considerable success. He made his reputation at the Porte St. Martin, one of the most important boulevard theaters, where he started his career by remounting ballets by Dauberval. The boulevard theaters were for common people, as opposed to the élite audience at the Opéra, and in them innovations were projected far in advance of the bureaucratic habits

of the official house.

Ballets had often borrowed plots from drama and opera, and audience familiarity with existing music and story ensured almost certain acceptance, compensating for lack of novelty. But novelty is always desirable. Aumer found a collaborator in Eugène Scribe (1791–1861), the most prolific popular playwright of his period; at thirty-five, he had already a hundred and thirty comedies and fifteen comic operas produced. A skillful craftsman, he dramatized the domestic manners of his own bourgeois society without recourse to stock types, myth, or allegory—the usual devices on operatic stages. In the eighteenth century most choreographers supplied their own plots with pretexts for dancing contrived more perfunctorily than ingeniously. Much of the dancing was for opera interludes. Noverre's mimodramas borrowed famous legends but he arranged the sequence. With Scribe came definite literary involvement (although at first he remained anonymous), which later strengthened dramatic structure in dancing.

The ballerina as sleepwalker afforded a psychological extension of histrionics at once realistic and Romantic. Somnambulism was hardly madness, nor was it hysteria, yet it tapped mysteries of the unconscious. Animal magnetism, phrenology, hypnosis, demi-sciences manipulated by Dr. Mesmer, Lavater, Count Cagliostro, and others, were implements for charlatans, which, nevertheless, had at their root elements that would later fascinate Charcot, Mantegazza, and Freud. The display of some factor of extrasensory perception, while vaguely sexual, was long licensed. Lady Macbeth showed guilt; *La Somnambule* innocence. It was hardly shocking for parents to watch a sleepwalker tremble on a mill wheel's brink, since their children often skirted tricky cornices or dangerous stairs and went back to bed, safe and sound. In this ballet, somnambulism was also a metaphor for freedom, not as pathology, but in the instinctive purity of virginal (although temporarily suspect) innocence, natural as a baby's sleep. A pure heart mastered an impure (or rather, unhealthy) bodily aber-

265. Ballroom dance. France, c. 1815.

267.

ration, possibly deriving from nothing worse than indigestion. Galatea, the ivory hunk, was freed by Pygmalion's chisel, and, through the grace of love for his Muse, his craft, and his created object, she took on life of her own; moving and dancing by a miracle of faith. Thérèse in her nightdress, naked as Galatea, is animated (sur pointe) by dark psychic powers operative only after dark, where nightmares dispute sovereignty with maidenheads. The ambiguity of the virgin's blind desire, a love that hardly senses its object (the free-wheeling libido), expressed by the perils of roof-walking and its stylization in movement on toe-point (even to the limited extent to which it had then advanced), capped by the ultimate proof of pristine maidenhood, provided that comestible *frisson* which titillated a bourgeois public.

Precedent:
Usually, ballet borrowed from opera. In the case of *La Somnambule*, Bellini's beautiful work followed Aumer's ballet (1831). Scribe had written a comedy of the same name (1819), but it had slight connection with this ballet. The famous mime of the boulevards, Deburau, had played *Pierrot Somnambule*, 1823. George Balanchine's *Night Shadow* (1946), known also as *Sonnambula*, employs a similar subject, set to a Vittorio Rieti score of themes derived from Bellini. *La Somnambule* might be considered a daughter of *La Fille Mal Gardée*, which Aumer restaged at the Porte St. Martin in 1804, although the level of society depicted is different and the theme is dramatic rather than comic.

Politics:
The prestige of ballet had considerably declined in the serious theater. Able performers there continued to be, but few ideas for narrative action were available beyond those transposed from drama or opera. There were no passionate polemics, no philosophers aiming to establish a rationale, like

Noverre or Vigano. Situations were preformulated. Scribe provided a chain of events leading up to a flashy climax, set in a quaint though not unfamiliar climate that, in performance, seemed to have piquancy, pathos, and the hint of pornography. Supposedly, he took on the task as a joke but he read his libretto to distinguished members of the Institut de France; the press claimed much good might come of collaboration in the twin skills of literature and dance.

Plot or Pretext:
I. Provence; the Camargue. At a village crossroad signs point to Arles and Tarascon. On one side, gates lead to a farm; on the other an inn. Haymakers lounge and dance. Edmond, a wealthy farmer, intends to marry Thérèse, an orphan who has been brought up by a rich miller's widow. She has a savage rival in Gertrude, who keeps the village inn. Edmond attempts to accommodate the two ladies in a *pas de trois*. The new lord of the nearby hereditary domains arrives with his servant, incognito. He is invited to spend the night in Edmond's farm but prefers to sleep at the inn. The scene ends with village games, including blind-man's buff.

II. The Inn; an upstairs room. Night. Gertrude waits on the new lord, whose identity has been betrayed. He attempts to seduce her, but on hearing a sound at the dormer window, she escapes, leaving her shawl. Thérèse, in only her nightdress, enters by the window carrying a lantern. Realizing she is a sleepwalker, the lord tries to help her from stumbling. Villagers arrive to pay their respects to their new master. Edmond, horrified to find Thérèse en *déshabille*, renounces her.

III. A Provençal landscape showing a mill with turning wheel. Edmond refuses to believe the truth; he will marry Gertrude, instead, but she, too, is compromised; her shawl was found in the lord's bed-

room. The stepmother of Thérèse comes out of the mill to denounce her daughter's rival. The lord points toward the mill, where Thérèse is seen walking on the brink of the roof, toward the turning wheel. All kneel, praying that catastrophe may be averted. Thérèse in her dreams imagines she hears the bells for her lover's wedding. She safely descends the crumbling wall, and Edmond realizes his error. All is well.

Production:
The curtain rose on a village round already in progress, a pleasing innovation, since an act usually concluded with such. Viganò, in *Otello* (1818), commenced his ballet with a *furlana*, which was successful for the same reason. It is hard to realize how rigid was theatrical habit and how gratefully violations of it were received. Ferdinand Hérold, Aumer's composer, tried to write a descriptive background to each episode rather than to edit a patchwork of familiar tunes.

The effect of the sleepwalker's first appearance was marred by poor lighting; her face was too dim. At the second performance, in her nightgown, with one foot bare, the audience felt "a sensation of alarm." "The attic window through which the sleeping girl emerges is now placed in the middle of the roof instead of at the side, and it is toward the edge . . . that she makes her way toward a dreadful death. A precipitous drop lies before her. It is at the very instant of putting out her foot and holding it suspended over the abyss that Thérèse imagines she hears the church bells, turns and descends by the ruins, . . . passing over the mill wheel. . . . This moment sends a chill of fear running down the spine of the least impressionable spectator."

266.

267.

266. *La Somnambule*. Scene 2. Vienna, c. 1830.

267. *La Somnambule*. Scene 3. Vienna, c. 1830.

268.

269.

268. Thérèse. Paris, c. 1828.

269. Thérèse. Berlin, c. 1829.

ROBERT LE DIABLE
(Count Robert the Devil; Act III,
"Ballet of the Nuns")
November 22, 1831
Paris
Opéra

Priority:
The third and fourth acts of Giacomo Meyerbeer's opera, to a libretto by Scribe, framed this veritable novelty. Instead of the normal
mythological subject, Duponchel,
charged with visual aspects at the
Opéra, wished to demonstrate
newly installed gaslighting, whose
reflectors cast a stronger, more
controlled light. Ciceri, the scenic-
designer, inspired by the cloister
of Saint-Trophime, Arles, imagined
its carved colonnade by moonlight. The hero of this opera, a
wicked knight in search of a talisman to aid him win his princess,
comes to this graveyard, where
lapsed nuns lie buried. The theme
is passion and death, love beyond
the grave—strivings toward mysterious unattainables. The scene is
night rather than day, Gothic
rather than antique. After a century rooted in the rational—the
"imitation of nature" and the revival of classical models—there
was a new taste for the miraculous, vague, mysterious, doomed,
instinctive.

The Romantic movement was a
revolution in feeling. Romantic ballet replaced more or less logical
narrative procedure with intensity
in atmosphere and sentiment. It
was incarnate in a new archetype,
the Romantic ballerina, who, whatever role she assumed, was first
of all a dancer, and then mistress of
the superreal, ethereal, or impossible. In the "Ballet of Nuns" the
abbess Helena was danced by Marie
Taglioni (1804–84), with choreography by her father, Filippo Taglioni (1778–1871). As her teacher
and dance-designer, he analyzed
the "faults" of her physique, dis-
guising her long arms with new
arrangements; he said he would
curse her if he ever *heard* her

dance. Light, with elevation and
ballon, no showy technician, she
transformed toe-dancing, which
had become increasingly popular
over the preceding quarter-century,
from an acrobatic device to a new
lateral extension of almost imperceptible movement. The antithesis
of flirt or coquette, she embodied
a "Christian" spirit. Though her
nun's white habit was soon exchanged for layers of pale tulle in
La Sylphide, there would always
remain a virginal paleness, sweet
suffering, soulful abnegation—
qualities inherited in our time by
Anna Pavlova (1881–1931).

Roman history and Greek myth
were exhausted; exotic India was
still to be sounded. There remained
an unexploited epoch—the Gothic
—once called "barbarous," now
"picturesque." Novels by Sir Walter
Scott and "Monk" Lewis and
English plasterwork Gothick provided another decorative continent, a newfound land stranger than
Cathay, Turkey, or the Americas.

Precedent:
The "Ballet of Nuns" was almost unprecedented. Unthinkable before
the French Revolution disqualified
Christian theology, it would have
been equally improbable in the era
of Anacreontics. Elements of *ballet
romantique* had been present in
popular theaters on the boulevards
for twenty years, where since 1810
traps on English models had been
installed, effecting miraculous entrances or exits; since 1817 gaslighting had been tried in London.
But the introduction of such innovations at the official Opéra gave
them solid prestige. While dancers
as courtesans had won international renown, Taglioni was the
first to enjoy a reputation as priestess, elevated to a higher moral
level than that of mere performer.
She established the ballerina's uniform, her silhouette, hair-do, and
dedication, for a world audience.
A mixture of Swedish and Italian,
with French training, above all im-

mediately provocative sex appeal,
modest, well brought up, without
affectation or strain, Taglioni was
a star phenomenon. As for remote
precedent, a ballet of *Robert le
Diable* was danced in Paris, before
Her Highness Mlle. de Longueville,
in 1652.

Politics:
Administration of the Opéra had
just been reformed; the Ministry
of Interior, under which it oper-
ated, awarded it as private enter-
prise to Dr. Louis Véron, an inventor of patent medicines, clever
journalist, gourmet, ugly bachelor,
who became a brilliant impresario.
Disregarding considerations of tenure, nationality, hierarchy, or custom, he elevated his new star to
an unprecedented position: Marie
Taglioni received 30,000 francs an-
nually and her father was named
ballet master with a three-year
contract. Véron realized that the
Opéra was, after all, an official conservative house, but he was aware
of what the boulevards had pioneered. His daring was rewarded
by Taglioni's success. The Bourbon
Restoration of 1818 had been
more favorable to secondary theatrical ventures; it did not extend
unique patronage to the Opéra,
which in the future would be
forced to protect its prestige past
official security.

Plot or Pretext:
In the ancient medieval cloister of
"Sainte-Rosalie," Bertram, cloaked
in black, summons ghosts of nuns
who violated their vows from individual graves, commanding them
to seduce Robert, known as "the
Devil," into accepting a fatal talisman. Helena, their abbess (Taglioni), bids them waltz, and, in
spite of their sacred oaths, deliver
themselves to voluptuous pleasure.
Robert appears; the nuns hide, but
later return to prevent his escape
when he finds himself, terrified,
before the tomb of a saint. The
dancing abbess lures him toward
the talisman; he seizes it from the

278.

270.   271.

272.

saint's carved hands while surrounded by dancing nuns, their
white habits swirling like huge
night moths. The nuns then sink
into their opening graves, and
slabs slide back to cover them. A
choir of demons continues the
action of the opera into Act IV.

Production:
The première was marred by a gas-
light falling and a trap that failed
to close. When a piece of scenery
fell, almost hitting Taglioni lying
on her grave, Véron lowered the
curtain. But the ballerina composed
herself, and the evening ended in
triumph for Meyerbeer, Taglioni,
and the new manager. Between
1831 and 1876, the opera was given
some six hundred times. Degas
painted it in several versions (1871–
76). Taglioni only appeared in it
some dozen times (by contract),
but her role became a grateful
vehicle for a succession of dancers.
The poet Longfellow's future wife
would write:

"The diabolical music and the
dead rising from their tombs and
the terrible darkness and the
strange dance unite to form a stage
effect almost unrivalled. The famous witch's dance [Miss Apple-
ton was confused between nuns
and witches] in the freezing moonlight in the ruined abbey, was as
impressive as I expected, though
there was no Taglioni to lead the
troop. They drop in like flakes of
snow and are certainly very charming witches with their jaunty Parisian figures and most refined pirouettes!"

André Levinson, critic and historian
of Romantic ballet, said: "The academic dance had been an agreeable
exercise to watch. Now, it clarified
matters of the soul. Ballet was a
divertissement. It became a mystery."

275.

270. Dancer prepares. Paris, c. 1845.

271. Ballerina corrected. Paris, c. 1845.

272. *Robert le Diable*. Paris, 1836.

143

273.

274.

273. "Ballet of the Nuns." Vienna, c. 1840.

274. *Robert le Diable*. Paris, c. 1832.

275.

276.

275. ''Ballet of the Nuns.'' Paris, 1832.

276. ''Ballet of the Nuns,'' 1872.

277.

LA SYLPHIDE
(The Sylph of the Highlands)
March 12, 1832
Paris
Opéra

Priority:
The libretto was based on a fanciful Scottish tale by Charles Nodier. Full length (two acts) rather than an opera-interlude, it became the prototype of Romantic ballet, wherein flesh-and-blood ballerinas were translated into otherworldly sprites —whose habitat was sky, sea, magic lake, or haunted glen. A supernatural female enchants an earthbound male. A hearty peasantry exults in folk dance; as contrast, a floating aerial sisterhood in gossamer tarlatans performs evanescent nocturnal rites. In one aspect this was the latest definition of *la basse danse*—movement rooted on the province of earth—and *la danse haute*—aspiring toward air—as originally analyzed by early dance masters. *La Sylphide's* heirs would include *Giselle* (1841), *La Peri* (1843), and, later, *Swan Lake* (1877–95), finding an ultimate abstraction in Fokine's *Les Sylphides* (1909).

Long, full skirts of layered tulle became a virginal uniform, at first skimpier than the crinoline silhouette of the Second Empire. By this time toe-dancing was mandatory; later, blocked shoes eased the weight of whole bodies, increasing the vocabulary enormously. Imperceptible movement on toe *(pas de bourrée)* further etherealized performers whose voluntary discipline framed them in the provocative atmosphere of a lay order. Woman conquered by her seeming abdication of the flesh; emphasis on star personalities ended equality or polarity of male and female, and after relegation to mere support or body-bearer *(porteur)*, the former *danseur noble* reached his nadir when he became, briefly, a girl, *en travesti,* supporting the ballerina.

La Sylphide established the mystique of the Ballerina. Famous dancers, from Dupré to Vestris, were Gods of the Dance; no ballerina had been hailed as Priestess, and Taglioni now assumed this title. A new criterion was established by analysis of individual temperament and physique; Filippo Taglioni's corrective *ports de bras* for his long-armed daughter became part of canonical instruction. The sylph, an aerial creature, seems once to have been a role for the male principal, commanding a train of

"Transparent Forms, too fine for
mortal Sight
Their fluid bodies half dissolved
in Light."*

The sylph(ide) became dominantly feminine, a symbol of lightness, who conquered air and space, and gained freedom from the tyranny of the down-to-earth; she was a metaphor of evanescence, transparency, floating, the essence of ballet as an ideal concept.

Precedent:
Greek *silphes* were beetles who became butterflies. In medieval iconology, sylphs were intermediaries between their world and ours. By the eighteenth century they were graceful young women; by the nineteenth aerial spirits, male or female. In his introduction to *The Rape of the Lock* (1712), Alexander Pope wrote that the Rosicrucians imagine gnomes or earth demons delight in mischief. ". . . the *Sylphs,* whose Habitation is Air, are the best-considered Creatures imaginable. . . . Mortals may enjoy their company easily . . . with an inviolate Preservation of Chastity."

The romances of Sir Walter Scott were widely translated in the nineteenth century. The *écossaise* and *schottische,* adaptations or variants on country dances, were popular ballroom forms, used by Schubert and Beethoven; their "Scottish" authenticity was on a par with theatrical mythology. Dancers were becoming accustomed to wings. In eighteenth-century productions of Shakespeare's *Macbeth,* doubles for the witches were flown. Sylphs in Didelot's *Flore et Zéphyre* (1796) flew. The swirling white habits of the lapsed nuns in *Robert le Diable* (1831) prefigured *La Sylphide's* light vestments. We shall meet the motif of the scarf again.

278.

254.

274.

Politics:
Dr. Véron, director of the Opéra, justified in producing his expensive discovery, Marie Taglioni, as a nun, was eager to cap this by complete canonization. Presented as an incarnation of decent mystery, she acquired an enormous vogue; her name entered common parlance. From lithographic documentation, her characterization has been studiously imitated by dancers of our day from Anna Pavlova to Alicia Markova.

The appellation "Romantic ballet" is confusing. It connotes neither a new school, an addition to the idiom, nor a revolutionary genre. Principally, it applies to ballerinas and pretexts for their dancing between 1830 and 1870. Romanticism

277. "La Sylphide." c. 1835.

* Alexander Pope, *The Rape of the Lock.*

146

shared a passion for the wild, savage, untamed; but there was something anomalous and soon ludicrous in the Romantic ballerina typed as irrational, since every step she took depended on rigid analytical training and severe discipline. (However, as a metaphor for wildness, or at least oddness, a synthetic Scotland—or Spain, as in the famous *Cachuca* of Fanny Elssler —seemed satisfactorily exotic.) Hysteria, madness, and magic represented mindless freedom from causality, which, however, was only legible to a mass audience through rational techniques, as in *bel canto* or ballet. Both survived social eruption with aplomb. 1789, 1848, 1870, 1917—years that shook worlds— had slight effect on virtuoso expression. Where Rousseau's noble savage had been the guide of bourgeois revolt, where antiquity had been idealized as less complex or more innocent than a corrupt present, and where a future had been imagined as recovering natural grace, Romantic philosophy proposed no return to a previous existence but, rather, projected what immanent man might become through industry or socialism. While music and painting had long assumed some propulsive modernity, ballet did not identify with progressive ideas until the twentieth century. Elsewhere a sense of class replaced a sense of tradition; in ballet there was only one class under one condition: the unclassed artist, performing. Ballet has revived the past by echoing lost styles and manners; it reflects the present by borrowing from popular sources. It has little to do with a future that never existed.

It has been claimed that Romanticism in ballet, by emphasizing the female ideal, led to an extreme development in the aerial province —specifically, higher jumps and toe-work. By the promotion of the ballerina to priesthood, male dancers were demoted to the servility of support. Impulse toward elevation had existed since ballet

was born; by inherent muscular potential, it is primarily a male realm, but this was encouraged to lapse after about 1840. Toe-work seems to have been presupposed by 1830. New steps and positions were regularly introduced, season to season, in every epoch. The Romantic ballet skirt substituted one waistline for another, but the body was less corseted between 1790 and 1815 than it would be again until Isadora Duncan. Romanticism left a sticky inheritance in which girls became ghosts and boys neuters. The prestige of personalities was commercially popular; the dancer, not the dance, was the residue of Romanticism.

Plot or Pretext:
I. Dawn. A farmhouse interior with a fireplace and, at the rear, a large window. James, a young Highlander, dreams of a sylph. Dreams come true; she hovers about him, but as he wakes, she disappears up the chimney. He is shortly to be married, but the vision of the sylph troubles him. Old Madge, a hideous witch, enters and offends him with dour prophecies and threats. The sylph reappears, in despair that James is to marry an earthly maid. She siezes the wedding ring as he offers it to Effie at the start of the betrothal ceremony. James leaves the room in confusion. Villagers pour in, with his fiancée. A rival of James reports that he has been seen flying up toward the highlands, with a young woman, or—a sylph! There is sympathy for the fiancée and general indignation.

II. Night in a forest. A cavern. Madge the witch casts spells. Witches dance around their cauldron. James enters with the sylph, who presents him to her sister spirits, with whom he must dance. He is confused; each one seems a replica of another. Has he lost the lass he truly loves? As he is exhausted, his sylph manifests herself, then vanishes. Has he abandoned his fiancée for a vague sprite? Madge gives him a magic

scarf; if a sylph but wears it her wings fall off. James traps the sylph; she fades, and her companions bear her away. James marries happily. The sound of wedding bells is heard and a bridal procession is seen in the background.

Production:
More than a dozen brave girls received a small bonus for risking flight on wires. Apart from Taglioni's impersonation, there were few choreographic surprises. Her envelope of fairy remoteness and chaste flirtation fitted her role to perfection. She repeated her Paris triumph all over Europe, and was later accused of dancing the sylph no matter what ballet was assigned to her. The ballet survived many versions, of which the most lasting was produced by Auguste Bournonville for his seventeen-year-old pupil Lucile Grahn (Copenhagen, 1836). A strong, prolific teacher and choreographer who established a national Danish style, he had new music written for his production and placed more emphasis on James, who has been admirably performed for our time by Erik Bruhn. As for Taglioni: "The *danse noble* is as foreign to Taglioni's style as natural dancing is to that of her rivals. . . . Notice the absence of *pirouettes*, *entrechats* and other technical difficulties! . . . She has completely reformed the ballet of her time." By *danse noble* was meant eighteenth-century heroic behavior, the dead hand of opera-house convention. An artificial style, licensed by inertia, it was replaced by the *style romantique*, which, though equally artificial in its impersonation of the mysterious and in dispensing with heroism or realism, produced a new sense of theatrical superreality.

22.

288.

229.

147

278.

279.

280.

278. *La Sylphide*. New York, 1839.

279. ''La Sylphide,'' 1845.

280. *La Sylphide*. Act I. 1845.

281. *La Sylphide*. Act I. Denmark, c. 1915.

282. *La Sylphide*. Act II. Denmark, 1882.

283.

GISELLE ou LES WILIS
(Giselle, or The Wilis)
June 28, 1841
Paris
Opéra

Priority:

While precedents and parallels to *Giselle* exist, its popularity, preeminence as a type, and persistence in repertory depend on sturdy elements: talent in collaboration, literary and choreographic strength; particularly the music of Adolphe Adam (1803–56), which is of a dramatic authority and logic superior to nearly any ballet before Tchaikovsky's *Swan Lake* (1877). Anticipating Richard Wagner by twenty-eight years, Adam used some five leitmotivs, each characterizing a mood for dancing. These serve as accumulative reminders of individuals in shifting situations. Orchestral themes are matched by recurring gestures and linked steps. Giselle, in her sim-

plicity, loves to dance, expressing her naive innocence (theme 1). She loves to dance with Albrecht, a duke incognito (theme 2). "He loves me; he loves me not" in Act I (theme 3) is echoed by the same "flower motif" in Act II, when Giselle, now a wraith, tosses him the lilies he has brought to her grave; in her "mad scene" the theme also reappears. First heard in the overture, a menacing motive of fear repeats in her mother's admonition and later in the dance of the Wilis, one of whom, despite warning, Giselle has become (theme 4). A hunting call sounds at certain dramatic crises, not to support action, but to accent abrupt contrast, as in the entry of Albrecht's high-born fiancée; the betrayal of his own aristocratic identity; and his confrontation with Giselle (theme 5). There is a symphonic density in the score superior to almost any danced drama before it; in its own terms, it still convinces and continues to provide roles for soloists and *corps* transcending period or genre. While individual characters had been introduced by signal themes in ballets and operas by Rameau, Gluck, and others, Adam's use of leading melodies is more emphatically descriptive and more psychologically effective. In their mounting recurrence, they not only recognize reappearances of the same dancer, but provide the choreographer with a musical pulse and impulse toward increased depth in motivation and movement.

In Germany, since the mid-eighteenth century, a separation from society, politics, and "daily life" had been felt by men of imagination. The exceptional man—artist, poet, genius, or actor-dancer—expressed individual virtuosity, and by his traditional craft was seen apart from the stolid values of middle-class dullness. The red waistcoat that Théophile Gautier had the (bad/good) taste to sport at the première of Hugo's *Hernani* (1830) was echoed by Grisi's

284.

white skirt in *Giselle*. Apollo, the god, had been lord of poesy. Now poetry, not as manifesto of divinity, but as art for its own sake, was to serve as subject. The means would become the end. Gautier said: "God, perhaps, is merely the greatest poet in the world. . . . Glowing words, luminous words, filled with music and rhythm—there's your poetry." Neither sentiment nor instruction was to rule, but aesthetic virtuoso autonomy. And *Giselle*, whose pretext is dancing itself, is a milestone in establishing choreography as autonomous speech.

After classical myth had been exhausted, long before the French Revolution, plots for ballets shifted from the heroic to the fantastic. The romantic current in the Baroque had its escape into Antiquity, in the nineteenth century into the medieval or "Gothic." Both shared a vague nostalgia for far-away times or places. Themes, wherever they were borrowed, were largely decorative. The serious factor—the chance for ingenuity—was in the frames offered for academic dancing. Very occasionally, as in the neurasthenia, sadness, inevitable doomed loss, and *Weltschmerz* of Giselle, an idea embodied its epoch. Danced hysteria, marvelously presentable by mounting physical exuberance (in which seeming excesses of unrestrained emotion are in fact supported by

292.

289.

disciplined acrobatic display), corresponded to operatic arias of revenge or madness. Variations of the ballerina were like *cabalettas*, ending in the collapse of the exhausted dancer—a fictive death on-stage. Such was a metaphor for insanity, suicide, and the despair of individuals in the face of indifferent Great Nature. The cross on Giselle's grave was simply decorative, since the collaborators were entirely cynical. The divine symbol was now simply picturesque. It marked the death of youth, hope, aspirations of an unlucky low-born virgin-artist-saint; an end to that (Roman) Catholic faith no longer redeemed by royalty on earth or gods in heaven. The ballerina's performance, her wildly applauded nightly ritual suicide, became an indulgence in emotion for its own sake, which, in less than extraordinary hands, became a sentimental parody of itself. The ballerina at once canonized and restricted classical dancing after 1845, for she might only behave in a single, given, "Romantic" style. Much of her potential expression withered, or was salvaged only by technical display.

Precedent:
Giselle, a daughter once removed of the abbess in *Robert le Diable*, is also cousin to Ophelia and La Sylphide; *Giselle* has been called the *Hamlet* of ballet. Its first act recalls numerous pastoral or village fetes, here with Germanic overtones. The music includes a quotation from a "Huntsman's Chorus" of Carl Maria von Weber; the waltzes were favorably compared to the elder Strauss. There had been balletic mad scenes from *La Finta Pazza* (1645) to *Nina, ou La Folle par l'Amour* (1813). The pervasive atmosphere was beholden to poets, specifically to Victor Hugo, Heinrich Heine, and Théophile Gautier, who was also a great ballet critic. The professional librettist for *Giselle*, Vernoy de St. Georges, had first been attracted by one of Hugo's *Orientales*, with its evoca-

tion of a ballroom where dancers were condemned to dance all night; Heine's *De l'Allemagne* proposed the notion of Wilis, Slavonic will-o'-the-wisps who lured young men to death by dancing, perhaps a memory of dancing mania, the St. Vitus' dance of the Middle Ages. The second acts of *La Sylphide* and *Giselle* are related in mood, although the former is a fantasy with a happy ending, while the latter is drama, darker and more tragic.

Politics:
Taglioni was nearing forty; her rival, Fanny Elssler (1810–84), a star of more febrile excitement and physicality, was no longer a sensation; the Opéra needed a new name. Carlotta Grisi (1819–99), a Viennese with Italian schooling, was twenty. Gautier wrote: "Carlotta danced with a perfection, lightness, boldness, and a chaste and refined seductiveness, which place her in the front rank between Elssler and Taglioni; as for pantomime, she exceeded all expectations; not a single conventional gesture, not one false movement; she was nature and artlessness personified." Jules Perrot (1810–92)—"Perrot the aerial, Perrot the sylph, Perrot the male Taglioni"—gifted as performer, ballet master, and teacher, became Grisi's lover, supervising her brilliant career. But he was not officially attached to the Opéra and received no credit for that choreography for which he was probably responsible: Grisi's solo variations and *pas de deux* and those portions when she appeared with the whole company. In the program Jean Coralli, the incumbent ballet master, was given overall credit.

Plot or Pretext:
I. An imaginary Rhineland (Gautier said "on the coast of Bohemia"): vineyard country. At the left stands Giselle's cottage; behind, a castle on a crag. Giselle, a peasant lass who "loved the dance over-much and was to pay with her life," does

not know that Albrecht, the youth she adores, is a disguised duke. A jealous game-keeper, noticing his rich cape and sword, surmises this truth. The ducal hunting party sweeps in, including the noble lady who is Albrecht's intended bride, and the game-keeper reveals the duke's identity. Giselle seizes his sword and goes mad; she slays herself.

II. Midnight in a forest glade, showing Giselle's cross-marked tomb; beyond, a lake. The Queen of the Wilis imperiously summons her ghostly subjects; Giselle rises from a new grave. The Wilis entice the wicked game-keeper to drown himself. The Queen would have Giselle condemn her Albrecht to a like fate, but Giselle protects him until dawn, when magic fades.

Production:
Act II is of interest in whichever of several surviving versions for the balance and blocking of the *corps de ballet*, its linear and angular patterns, its force as a collective identity. Its maneuvers, commanded by the Queen as by a colonel, two Wili officers, and a regiment of fairies, maintain a military order, but their structure is not simply symmetrical; balance is ingeniously subdivided, deployed, reunited. Characterizations of soloists—their self-descriptive variations and by-play—retain a solid design that time has dented but not denied. Present performance takes on the aspect of ceremony; ballerinas are judged as thoroughbred on their interpretation of Giselle. Absolute "accuracy" in revival is relative; dramatic logic rather than adherence to documents is preferred. Finally, we realize that Romantic ballet is not a school opposed to classical, but a stylistic exposition of a subject matter. *Giselle* underlines the contribution of participatory rather than decorative *corps de ballet*, whose movement is constant, more expressive and legible than that of a conventional chorus.

290.

29.

285. 286.

287. 288.

285. Myrtha. London, 1843.

286. Giselle. Paris, c. 1850.

287. Grisi: Giselle, 1845.

288. Grahn: Giselle, c. 1850.

289. *Giselle*. Finale, Act I. 1845.

290. *Giselle*. Act II, c. 1849.

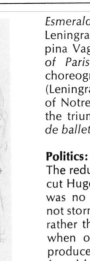

291.

LA ESMERALDA
March 9, 1844
London
Her Majesty's Theatre

Priority:

This was the longest lived work of Jules Perrot, whose precise contribution to *Giselle* is disputed. The more one studies him, the more he emerges as rival if not equal to Marius Petipa and Lev Ivanov, key figures in the Franco-Russian tradition. In repertory (in Russia) within memory, *Esmeralda* represents a broadening of psychological realism in characterizing individuals, and in individuation within the *corps de ballet*.

The son of a stage-carpenter, Perrot early imitated the acrobatic dancer-mime Mazurier, who had spent three years playing a clown, two as a monkey. Training in popular theater taught Perrot virtuosity in mimicry. He became the finest male dancer between Auguste Vestris (1760–1842), his master, and Vaslav Nijinsky. Taglioni was jealous, since he upheld the male position despite the tyranny of Romantic ballerinas. After Didelot, Perrot reinforced French elegance in Petersburg,

291. Street dancer. Paris, c. 1845.

establishing a repertory and method in designing dances that was inherited by Petipa, Ivanov, and, finally, by Fokine. The heroine of *Esmeralda* was still first a Ballerina, but both she and subsidiary characters were delineated through an approach to more realistic mimicry.

Precedent:

The story was roughly based on Victor Hugo's medieval panorama, *Notre Dame de Paris* (1831). Following Viganò, a choreodrama on this subject was produced in Milan (1839), with the main parts undertaken by mimes, and only Fanny Cerrito (1817–1909), third of the great Romantic stars, actually dancing. The subject was suggested to Perrot by the clever impresario Benjamin Lumley, who had Carlotta Grisi under contract. The archeological restoration of Gothic cathedrals and castles under Viollet-le-Duc replaced earlier preoccupation with Greek or Roman archeology. Notre Dame and La Sainte Chapelle were being refurbished. In *Le Ballet de la Nuit* (1653), Louis XIV's dancers were already in the original Court of Miracles, which had just been cleared of its derelict and destitute population.

Esmeralda was restaged by the Leningrad dancer-teacher Agrippina Vaganova (1935). *The Flames of Paris*, a "heroic" work with choreography by Vasily Vainonen (Leningrad, 1932), used the towers of Notre Dame as background for the triumph of a proletarian *corps de ballet*.

297.

Politics:

The reduced and simplified libretto cut Hugo's more lurid pages; there was no torture; Notre Dame was not stormed, and there was a happy rather than tragic finale. However, when on January 2, 1849, Perrot produced the ballet in Russia, he found himself in trouble. Saburov, Intendant of the Imperial Theaters, objected to a police officer playing the villain, a priest ruining an innocent girl, and the mob (*le peuple*) depicted as heroic demonstrators against feckless aristocracy.*

Did Perrot deliberately bait the authorities by his democratic tendencies? In 1859 he was forced to resign. Individualizing obscure members of the *corps de ballet*, he had more success in Moscow than Petersburg. Later in life, returning to Paris as an eminent teacher, he was portrayed by Degas (c. 1871) in a glorious picture that typifies the dignity of a dancer in useful, healthy old age, intent as a surgeon upon the bodies of young aspirants—gardener of budding ballerinas in their forcing shed. Great teachers exert dictatorial powers. Those dominant are first-dancers as well as ballet masters. Few have been both. No one can teach choreography, but potential choreographers have learned from academicians such as Perrot, Petipa, Fokine, and Balanchine.

3.

Plot or Pretext:

I. Sunset at the Court of Miracles, Paris. Brigands, thieves, and gypsies dice, fight, and dance. Gringoire, a poet, pursued by outlaw beggars, finds himself in forbidden territory. The beggar king condemns him to death since he has no ransom save

* *The New York Times* (March 2, 1969) reported that "a new play whose villain is a Stalinist army officer has created the latest stir." Because of its anti-Stalinist overtones, the piece became controversial. The critic N. Leikin devoted a full page to it in *Literaturnya Rosiya*, express-

his poems. He can be reprieved only if a beggarwoman will marry him. Esmeralda, a street dancer, with her goat and tambourine, pities his plight and agrees to marry him. "*Valse du Vieux Paris*" by the *corps*, followed by a *pas de deux* (Grisi and Perrot) showing her amusement and compassion, but not her love. A Bacchanal develops, stopped by curfew bells. Esmeralda notes the sinister interest of Frollo, an evil priest, who tries to bribe the beggar king to obtain her. Esmeralda, aided by Quasimodo, the hunchbacked bell-ringer, is abducted but rescued by a night patrol, whose captain, Phoebus, falls in love with her. She begs for the hunchback's release; Phoebus offers his scarf for a kiss; she refuses, escaping into the night.

II. 1. Esmeralda's hovel. She explains to her poet that she married him from pity; he can accompany her street dances, but that is all. Frollo and Quasimodo try to kidnap her, but she escapes through a secret passage. 2. Garden of a mansion, scene of preparation for Phoebus' marriage. Esmeralda entertains the haughty guests, and it is clear the guard captain loves her, not his fiancée. There is indignation among his guests; protected by her poet, she flees.

III. 1. Seine-side cabaret. The beggar king and evil priest enter and hide. Phoebus and Esmeralda enter and perform a duet in which love is questioned. How can he possess both her and his fiancée? The priest now springs forth, apparently kills the captain, and escapes. Esmeralda is arrested. 2. Towers of Notre Dame above Paris roofs; Esmeralda, escorted by archers, is led to her doom. Gringoire tries to stir up the mob to save her. Procession of the Feast of Fools, with Quasimodo as mock-Pope. The priest will save her if she marries him, but Phoebus has not been killed. Maddened, the priest tries to stab her, but Quasimodo slays him. Esmeralda is freed. General rejoicing.

292.

Production:
Perrot's processions and crowds were not mere display; they furthered narration. Individual vignettes framed linking incident. Long intervals were avoided, as some scenes were danced before drop curtains that hid scene shifts. Perrot used simultaneous action: the Feast of Fools proceeds upstage while Esmeralda enacts her tense climax in front. The massive Bacchanal (Act I) was new and striking: ". . . Some crosses are formed . . . bisected by moving lines at right angles very ingeniously. . . ." Perrot seems to have suggested complex psychological intention purely through dancing—by char-

acteristic body movement. He fragmented gesture and with it built individual characters. Compared to previous ballets, here was intense realism, analogous in picturesque violence to the large historical compositions of Eugène Delacroix. When entirely restaged by the Russian dancer and choreographer Alexander Gorsky (1871–1924) in Moscow, 1902, it was attacked as being under the influence of Stanislavsky's Art Theater and emulating dangerous realism, particularly in the mob.

296.

ing current conservative dogma—condemning Stalin's excesses while savaging the playwright. "He said he agreed with the officers in the play (*The Night of the Nightingales*, by Valentin Yezhov, winner of a Lenin Drama Prize), that the lieutenant was wrong to bring political charges

against the soldier, but chastised the author for making heroes out of men who flouted military discipline."

292. *La Esmeralda*. Russia, c. 1848.

155

293.

294.

295.

293. Elssler: Esmeralda. Vienna, c. 1845.

294. Grisi and Perrot. London, 1844.

295. "Feast of Fools." London, 1844.

296. *La Esmeralda*. Moscow, 1902.

297. *The Flames of Paris*. Leningrad, 1932.

298.

LE PAS DE QUATRE
(The Grand Quartet)
July 12, 1845
London
Her Majesty's Theatre

Priority:
This divertissement presented the talents of four outstanding first-dancers of their epoch, flattering individual gifts and uniting them in the competitive climate of a sporting event. A ritual celebration of achievements in academic classic ballet as developed over two and a half centuries, it exposed a virtuoso language as brilliant in itself as the extraordinary range and flexibility of *bel canto* singing or the manual dexterity of great pianists and violinists. There was no pretense that the participants were nymphs or sylphs: they were stage dancers. Their proclaimed art licensed and justified them in acrobatic or expressive display. While advertised as a spectacular to attract a popular audience, *Le Pas de Quatre* was perhaps the first delib-

erately "abstract" ballet whose subject was the *danse d'école* itself, without apology, autonomous and absolute.

Precedent:
It was the age of ballerina personalities. In 1841, *The Judgment of Paris,* in which Taglioni, Elssler, and Cerrito were to appear, was announced but never given. In 1843, Benjamin Lumley, the astute manager, succeeded in bringing Elssler and Cerrito together in a *grand pas de deux.* Two years later Taglioni, Cerrito, and Grisi were promised, and then the recent brilliant appearance of the young Dane, Lucile Grahn, caused her name to be added to the final roster. Solo numbers in which the reigning queens of the dance were set off in jeweled splendor were no novelty, but never before had there been such a concentration of fame and talent, governed by the analytical intelligence of a ballet master who made each shine and none suffer.

Politics:
Lumley was credited with supreme diplomatic tact. His four stars could not have loved one another; each was exigent and willful. Lucile Grahn, the youngest, "possesses a genius for diplomacy in its most subtle, intangible, and ethereal form. She is Metternich and Talleyrand in one; she is the whole Congress of Vienna in petticoats." Perrot, the ballet master, had a task comparable to making lions and tigers waltz in the same cage. Lumley ordered the senior dancer to take precedence; no one wanted to be thought oldest, so Perrot settled his sequences as he wished.

Plot or Pretext:
The quartet commenced with an equally balanced ensemble for the four, who had entered together simply, hand in hand. They then assumed posed groupings with Taglioni centered, as if paid homage by her juniors. "A quick traverse movement" led to a brisk solo by

288.

298.

298. *Le Pas de Quatre.* London, 1845.

Grahn, followed by a *pas de deux* for Cerrito and Grisi, then a series of broad leaps all across the stage by Taglioni (her specialty). Each tour de force was greeted by rising applause, acknowledged by the individual dancer's curtsy. Grahn, in a brief allegro, turned on point "with dainty semi-circular hops." An andante for Grisi was all coquetry and spice. This contrasted with the ensuing andantino for Taglioni and Grahn in a slower, more Romantic vein, which was interrupted by a brilliant series of turns, bounds, and balances by Cerrito. Taglioni followed in an allegro. The coda was a four-cornered contest. At the curtain call, Cerrito crowned Taglioni with a wreath of white roses while the public deluged the stage with bouquets.

Production:
The ballet took place in a brightly lit landscape—"the well-known divertissement bower." All four wore pale pink with roses in their hair and on their bodices. They only appeared four times in this vehicle (Queen Victoria and Prince Albert saw the third performance), of which a lady correspondent wrote: "There are more than ten ballets of the calibre of *La Esmeralda* in this new effort of Perrot's." Distilled, refined, concentrated—it was like chamber music on a symphonic scale, at once exercise and portraiture.

Taglioni was forty. La Sylphide still danced admirably and held her public; maturity and reputation made up for the pristine freshness that had passed. Fanny Cerrito, twenty-eight, was a product of the ballet school of the San Carlo Theater, Naples. She appeared at La Scala, 1838–40, and benefited by training with Perrot. Carlotta Grisi, twenty-six, an Austrian, was a star of the Scala school at ten; touring Italy, she met Perrot in Naples. In 1840, she appeared in Paris in a series of character dances— Bohemian, Italian, German; *Giselle*

299.

marked the beginning of her alliance with Théophile Gautier. Lucile Grahn, twenty-six, was taken by her master, Auguste Bournonville, from Copenhagen to Paris in 1834, where she saw Taglioni in *La Sylphide*, in which she appeared later at home in a new arrangement by Bournonville. Perrot carefully anatomized his four given bodies: Taglioni exuded a secure authority, possessing a gracious mystery accented by her ability to suggest repose in movement; Cerrito shone in firmness, vigor, a staccato attack; Grisi's strongest qualities were brilliance and rapidity; Grahn had freshness and power.

The solo variation, the *pas de deux, pas de trois,* and *pas de quatre* are the acid test of a choreographer. Stripped of rhetorical gesture, divested of obvious novelty by strict adherence to the medium, unadorned in sequences of familiar movement, Perrot's choreography offered the eye nothing new save dancing tailored to personal capacity. Perrot exploited differences in age, style, and technique; he made star turns for each dancer, but what was glorified was not alone the Dancer, but the Dance. Profile and plasticity, lightness in air, sureness on the floor; rapidity in turns, secu-

rity on poised *pointes;* suppleness, extension; firmness and softness— the accumulated lore of two centuries of slow growth and varied practice—were manipulated by Perrot in a synthesis of the European schools, Italian, French, Danish, and Austrian. The pale uniform of the ballerina no longer need be associated with a single Romantic genre. The dance itself, without recourse to sewn-on wings, would be seen as dramatic in the act of its own execution. Independent of mimicry, plot or pretext, it became exciting in and of itself, by virtue of its flexible, infinitely extensible vocabulary.

18.

16.

300.

299. Star supports. Paris, 1838.

300. *Les Graces*, 1850.

301.

302, 303. The rivalry continued.

304.

304. The young Petipa, c. 1832.

LA FILLE DU PHARAON
(Daughter of the Pharaoh)
January 18/30, 1862
St. Petersburg
Marinsky Theater

Priority:

Marius Petipa (1822–1910), due in great part to three ballets with music by Tchaikovsky (*Swan Lake,* 1877; *The Sleeping Beauty,* 1890; *The Nutcracker,* 1892)—even though he was not completely responsible for their choreography—remains the best known dance-designer of the nineteenth century. Born in Marseilles to a theatrical dynasty, trained in Bordeaux, he made his début in 1831, toured the United States and Spain, danced in Paris, and finally came to Russia in 1847 as first-dancer of the Marinsky Theater, St. Petersburg. At Jules Perrot's dismissal in 1862, he became a ballet master in the Imperial Theaters, remaining for forty years. *La Fille du Pharaon,* his first big success, makes heavy use of formulas he would reiterate in some forty-six subsequent works—each act having its *pas d'action,* its variations for principals, its *pas de deux,* and a final *ballabile* for the whole company. While the pattern was rigid, Petipa's abstract design was personal, captivating, efficient, and ingenious. Today, Perrot and Lev Ivanov are recognized as his equals, but Petipa's contribution stacks larger in history. He distilled the procedures of Perrot and Saint-Léon, another prolific ballet master in St. Petersburg, into his own. A masterful bureaucrat, he assigned the composition of male variations and such parts as did not interest him to subordinates (Ivanov; Christian Johannsen; Nicolas Legat). His ability to cope with pressures in a court theater spared him little time for aesthetics or real novelty, but Petipa bequeathed an operative mechanism and viable repertory to successors. He must be understood as a reflection of the peculiar isolation of the Romanov regime in its long decline.

3.

331.

325.

Precedent:

Egypt had been a nominal source for opera and tragedy since translations of the Bible, Plutarch, and Shakespeare. Napoleon's Egyptian campaign (1799) precipitated scientific archeology, collection, and publication by the great European museums. In 1808 Aumer staged *Les Amours d'Antoine et Cléopâtre.* Impressive scenery by Alessandro Sanquirico and his followers, of considerable archeological accuracy, dressed the Scala, Milan, for *Psamos, King of Egypt,* by Salvatore Viganò (1817); *Ramses or The Arabs in Egypt,* by Alessandro Fabbri (1819); and *Sesostris,* again by Viganò (1824). Théophile Gautier, poet and ballet librettist, had written a tale, *Le Pied d'une Momie,* which Petipa asked Vernoy de St.Georges (collaborator on *Giselle*) to adapt as a *ballet à grand spectacle.*

263.

Politics:

Saburov, Intendant of the Imperial Theaters, protected Carolina Rosati (1826–1905), an excellent Bolognese dancer and pupil of the great teacher Carlo Blasis. A work was needed in which she could

13.

* Prince Kropotkin wrote in his *Memoirs* of the atmosphere in 1866: "The very tastes of society sunk lower and lower. The Italian opera, formerly a forum for radical demonstrations, was now deserted; the Russian opera, timidly assert-

star, but Rosati, now thirty-six and about to retire, was told there were no funds. However, her contract specified she must have a new ballet, and Petipa, knowing lack of money was never a valid excuse, produced this complex spectacle in six weeks. Budgets were covered by the tsar's privy purse, which, by 1890, was two million gold rubles a year (about a million dollars); Imperial Russian ballet never depended on a commercial audience.

During the period 1862 to 1866, the policy of Alexander II assumed a reactionary character.* An imminent return of manorial justice and serfdom was expected in spite of token liberation. Ballet existed in a vacuum. A return to the horrors of the reign of Nicolas I was awaited with apathy by the court. Considering the close attachment of ballet to the throne and the appalling guilt the monarchy was piling up for itself, it is amazing that ballet as an institution survived the inevitable revolution. It was the inherent strength of the virtuoso art, and its promulgation later by Diaghilev as a national resource for exportation, that preserved it.

Plot or Pretext:
Prologue: 1. The desert. An English party—Lord Wilson, his servant, and John Bull—are entertained by Armenian merchants. In the ensuing sandstorm, they take refuge in a pyramid. 2. Interior of a pyramid showing a stone pharaoh and, center, a mummy case. The English smoke opium to relive the past. Aspicia, daughter of the Pharaoh, comes to life.

I. Lord Wilson, transformed, becomes Ta-Hor; he saves Aspicia from a wild lion. Pharaoh, at first jealous, is grateful. They form a procession toward his palace. Grotesque importance of the ex-English servant. The palace at Thebes. A rivalry for Aspicia de-

velops between Ta-Hor and the Nubian king. Dancing, processions, slaves, children fill the halls. A maid helps Aspicia and Ta-Hor, now lovers, escape; they are pursued by camels, monkeys, saber-dancers.

II. A fisherman's hut. Three peasants crave shelter (Aspicia, Ta-Hor, servant), followed by a Nubian king, also disguised. After a melodramatic confrontation, she casts herself into the Nile. Beneath the Nile. The king of this River summons Guadalquivir, Thames, Rhine, Congo, Tiber, and Neva, who engage in national dances. A vision of the lovers appears.

III. After religious ceremonies, the prisoners are condemned, but pardoned. Death by snake bite? No. Aspicia is saved. Festival.

Epilogue: The pyramid opens, revealing Isis, Osiris, and lesser deities. The Englishmen awake wondering where they are.

Production:
The first performance took four hours and involved nearly four hundred dancers and supernumeraries. Rosati's dancing was disappointing though her mimicry was praised, and the part of Aspicia became a favorite with imperial ballerinas into the new century. In Petipa's ballets there was slight thought of reality, psychological justification, or poetic logic. Action arbitrarily set first-dancers as jewels. Sequences of national dances and pantomimic fragments (Aspicia terrified by the lion) massed unisonal numbers for a big *corps*. Fast build-ups to bring down the curtain, plus scenic effects in which guardsmen from the palace regiments were detailed to move, under painted canvas, like waves of the sea, framed solo numbers. Petipa would be accused of "lacing ballet in a woman's corset," and of caring little for male dancers. In a court theater, the imperial family wished to be amused, not elevated; tragic end-

ings were unfortunate reminders of life itself. Boxes were subscribed by the court, by hussars, horse guards, the English, and yacht clubs. Audiences were passive or blasé. Creatively, ballet withered. Few painters or musicians of quality were attached to the theater. Need to accommodate mistresses of officials and the retardative taste of intendants (frequently, retired army officers) left Petipa small leeway for innovation. When the Danish master Bournonville visited Russia in 1874, he accused Petipa of "divertissementation." Petipa agreed, but was powerless to alter the pattern. Staff musicians, designers, tailors, choreographers, operating under a system that was effectively censorship (militating particularly against native Russian talent), produced few surprises. Tchaikovsky would barely be a success in his lifetime. Russia, with Dargomyzhsky, Glinka, Balakirev, Moussorgsky, Rimsky-Korsakov, had fine composers, but they would wait. Scenic artists were never easel-painters of talent until Muscovite theaters found them at the end of the century. What dignified Petipa was tact and ingenuity, at court and on stage.

313.

22.

332.

305.

305. Mathilde Kschessinska, 1899.

ing the rights of its great composers, was frequented by a few enthusiasts only. Both were found 'tedious' and the cream of St. Petersburg society crowded to a vulgar theater where the second-rate stars of the Paris small theaters won easy

laurels from their Horse Guard admirers . . . Offenbach's music reigned supreme." (Prince Peter Kropotkin, *Memoirs*, Horizon Press, New York, 1968.)

163

306.

307.

308.

306. Egyptian mural.

307. *La Fille du Pharaon*. St. Petersburg, 1890.

308. Kschessinska, 1899.

309.

310.

311.

309. *La Fille du Pharaon*. Moscow, 1905–6.

310. Egyptian slaves. Moscow, 1905–6.

311. Lord Wilson and John Bull. Moscow, 1905–6.

KONIOK GORBUNOK
(The Humpbacked Horse)
December 3/15, 1864
St. Petersburg
Bolshoi Theater

Priority:

The Frenchman Arthur Saint-Léon (c. 1815/17–70) was an efficient working ballet master, although never a great performer, due to an unfavorable body. However, he attained the rank of first-dancer and was a teacher in Paris and a fine violinist. He invented a system of dance notation and married the ballerina Cerrito. In 1859 he went to Petersburg, ballet capital of Russia, where his compliance with the administration and prolific output were appreciated. He claimed *The Humpbacked Horse* was the first "national" ballet; it was, however not even the first Franco-Russian ballet, but it remained in repertory in various versions for a century. His cast was entirely Russian; the ballerina, Muravieva, danced on toe. Saint-Léon taught Petipa formulas for transforming folk dancing into theater. Any authenticity they achieved derived from native performers rather than from choreography, or from music by the staff hack, Cesare Pugni (1802–70), who, on schedule, composed some three hundred ballets.

Precedent:

Both Didelot (who was in Russia, off and on, from 1801 to 1836) and his favorite pupil, Adam Glouzkovsky, used native Russian themes, Didelot in *The Prisoner of the Caucasus* (1823), his student in *Russlan and Ludmilla* (1821), both based on Pushkin. Didelot arranged Persian and Tartar dances for Cavos' opera, *The Fire Bird* (1815). Earlier Russian-born ballet masters adapted folk steps and arm positions from the provinces—from Christmas or Shrovetide peasant festivals—for use in serf and court theaters. Between 1812 and 1814, Didelot produced Russian divertissements in London in the wake of the anti-Napoleonic alliance. Ivanushka, hero of the tale on which this ballet is based, may be read as a local variant of Pedrolino, a character from *commedia dell'arte*, as well as ancestor of the agonized puppet-clown-hero of *Petrouchka* (Stravinsky - Fokine - Benois, 1911). Perrot had restaged *La Fille Mal Gardée* (1848), contrasting country dances with academic composition. The classic vocabulary of posture and movement based on turn-out of the feet was reversed and augmented by jumps and kicks, heel-taps, and hand claps, in boots and peasant dress.

Politics:

Perrot, though greatly gifted, independent, and original, failed as politician and diplomat. Saint-Léon, on the other hand, was an excellent linguist, businessman, and agile courtier. He would be accused of flattering the emperor in this adaptation of Ershov's folk tale, already a children's favorite, particularly for changing a lazy tsar to a fat oriental khan (similar to Rimsky-Korsakov's hidden political caricature, *The Golden Cockerel*), thus suppressing any implied satire. Saint-Léon was superficially instructed in folklore, but he took advantage of growing nationalist feelings. A French-speaking Petersburg public considered itself cosmopolitan, in contrast with provincial Moscow, but even at the Petersburg court there was a new sense of Russia's indigenous culture. However, balletomanes' demands that the legend be treated by a native choreographer and composer carried no weight. Saint-Léon ignored his critics, insisting that not only would the ballerina dance *sur pointe* but that she was the heroine of the piece as well, although many Russians felt that Ivanushka Douratchok—"little Ivan [John], the simple soul," a traditional folk hero, was focus for the fable.

The ballet audience was assigned seats in rigid hierarchy: high nobility was located on the floor nearest the proscenium; foreign bankers occupied the fourth-row armchairs; local merchants assumed the fifth and sixth-row places. None had more than a token interest in the imaginative life of recently liberated serfs but Saint-Léon sensed he could please by evoking the patriotic as the picturesque. Unlike native artists, as a foreigner he was free to handle native themes as exotic novelties, and it was more the folk-toy aspect of the Russian past than chauvinism that he exploited. *Koniok Gorbunok* represented "Russian" ballet before it became known as *ballet russe* (although later Muscovite productions turned *The Humpbacked Horse* into a more authentically Russian ballet). Nicholas II, last of the Romanovs, an ardent nationalist, maintained its popularity as his favorite into the next century.

Plot or Pretext:

I. A country bazaar. Ivanushka, youngest son, village innocent, despite birth and misfortune, always wins in the end. The luckless boy works in the fields. His father is without money in the market; his wheat has been hoof-trampled. He tells his three sons to find the culprit. Ivanushka, searching the field, finds a mare; she begs him to let her go, promising him two gold-maned horses and a humpbacked colt. However, his older brothers rob him of his prize.

II. The Khan's court. The brothers bring their mounts to the Great Khan. Ivanushka claims them as his own, and the Khan buys them, making him the groom. The humpbacked colt gives the boy a magic whip; if he cracks it, all wishes will be granted. A young slave nearby tells of a dream in which beautiful girls, like those on oriental carpets, danced for him. Ivanushka cracks his whip, producing a dance of "Persian" houris. The Khan dreams also. Ivanushka shows

317.

314.

312.

him pictures of sample beauties. The Khan chooses one, the Tsar Maiden who lives on the Mermaid's Isle. The humpbacked horse makes fountains rise around her so she can be captured.

III. Ivanushka brings the Tsar Maiden to the Khan's court. She begs to be free. The Khan vows her rich gifts and his favorite wife dances. Ivanushka's brothers try to play on a pipe, but cannot; Ivanushka plays and the Tsar Maiden dances. The Khan, entranced, wishes to marry her. She agrees, provided she is given a ring from the depths of the sea. The Khan sends Ivanushka for it.

IV. Search for the ring. The humpbacked horse sends an eel for the ring.

V. The Tsar Maiden has been sent to prison because she will not marry. Ivanushka returns with the ring, but she still refuses, telling the Khan her husband must be as

young and beautiful as herself, which he can effect by plunging himself into a boiling cauldron. The Khan tests this on brave Ivanushka, who emerges a shining prince. The Khan follows and is boiled alive. The Tsar Maiden marries the prince, and the ballet concludes with a grand divertissement of Ukrainian, Ural, Lettish, and Georgian national dances.

Production:
Pugni had difficulty finding enough native material for his score, and saw no harm in using a bit of a Rossini overture. He based a mazurka in Act IV on a Russian children's song, "Granny Had a Little Goat." Lacking more than a naive ethnic musical substructure, this ballet was less Russian than a variant of the French form, with mimed scenes, *pas d'action*, divertissements varied by scenic transformation, voyages through the air, fire, and water—all serving as pretext for dancing soloist or massed *corps*.

312. Polish dance, c. 1865.

167

313.

314.

313. Opera setting. St. Petersburg, c. 1860.

314. Tsar Maiden's entourage. St. Petersburg, c. 1870

316.

317.

318.

315. Ukrainian dance, 1857.

316. Lev Ivanov and partner. St. Petersburg, 1864.

317. Ivanushka. St. Petersburg, 1864.

318. Latvian dance. St. Petersburg, 1864.

COPPÉLIA ou LA FILLE AUX YEUX D'ÉMAIL
(Coppelia, or The Girl with Enamel Eyes)
May 25, 1870
Paris
Opéra

Priority:

Léo Delibes composed a sprightly score, the most durable since Adam's *Giselle* (1841). Dance music had become a miserable servant, and although the superior gifts of Delibes and Tchaikovsky dignified repertory, neither precipitated reformation in dance design. Delibes provided color, fuller rhythmic variety, and richer orchestration. Borrowing directly from Polish and Hungarian sources, propelling a new authenticity from folk forms, he gave Saint-Léon impetus for his final work. The *Coppélia* score became a criterion for a new generation; Tchaikovsky and later Stravinsky would be in Delibes' debt. He also aided the Swiss musical theorist and educator Jaques-Dalcroze, who would affect Nijinsky.

The concept of a doll that danced symbolized what had happened to the French classic academic tradition. From the impersonation of kings as gods, through the descent of professionals as heroes, aerial sprites, peasants, or Orientals, the mythological, picturesque, or exotic were now equally threadbare. Male dancers had disappeared; the ballerina was here dehumanized into a doll, partnered by a girl in pants. Swanilda, the real focus of the dancing, was a typical dancer's role. But Coppélia was at once a ballerina, a female, and a puppet. The dancer seemed a mere toy in a cold, heartless form—*chair à plaisir*, "flesh to fool with"—an object, hardly a person.

La Mettrie, French philosopher and physician, proposed man as machine, formulating one of the key ideas of the Enlightenment. His *L'Homme-machine* (1748) followed mechanistic theories from Bacon to Spinoza and Descartes. Leibniz saw man as a plant; when does he become an animal? The machine-man will be fearful and anxious, a rival to "natural" man. Are machines also a part of nature? If so, who determines mechanism? Man no longer controls matter; the machine (industrial society) usurps him. At the end of the century, the French philosopher and physician Cabanis saw the mind as a machine that manufactures thought. Is Frankenstein then a Romantic father of cybernetics and computers? These problems underlie philosophies of movement and metric today, involving the future of music. But Freud had to abandon psychology based purely on physics; mechanics have to admit indeterminacy. In the evolution of science, metaphysics, poetry, and art still function.

Precedent:

Prometheus, thief and trickster, who stole fire from heaven, made man out of earth and water (his own tears). Lucian (190 A.D.) told of a sorcerer's apprentice who could not control forces he released. This served Goethe for a ballad, *Triumph of Sensibility* (1778), prompting Paul Dukas' tone poem (1897), of which Fokine made a ballet (1916). In Goethe's work a prince prefers a doll to a queen—art winning over reality. In the story of Pygmalion, which served Sallé (1734), a statue, without interior mechanism, comes alive through divine intercession. Don Juan's stone guest, though briefly animated, was still a statue. In *Coppélia* the miracle is domesticated; a self-deceived charlatan or an artist deluded by curiosity is, as Cyril Beaumont wrote, "half mechanic, half necromancer." Mechanical toys, long known in the East, appeared in Europe around 1600; some from Nuremberg, city of toys, amused Louis XIII. Automatic musicians, letter-writers, geese, or chess-players were faintly sinister contrivances exploited by showmen through the nineteenth century.

Automata are metaphors for unguessed possibility in raw material, whether metal machine or flesh-and-blood ballerina. A choreographer of mannequins (the magician Coppélius) is archetype of ballet masters. Charles Nuitter's libretto derived from E.T.A. Hoffmann's *Der Sandmann* (1815), a nocturnal fantasy that inspired operas by Spontini (*Olimpie*, 1819); Adolphe Adam (*The Nuremberg Doll*, 1852); and Offenbach (Act I, *Tales of Hoffmann*, 1881); as well as a play by Barbier and Carré (1851). Hoffmann (1776-1822), poet, critic, theater-manager, draftsman, composer, would provide pretexts for many lyric works; his sensibility was admired by Beethoven, Weber, Schumann, Tchaikovsky, Busoni, Hindemith, and Stravinsky. At the climax of the original tale, comedy turns to catastrophe. The doll's china eyes fall out when she is torn between her rival inventors, quarreling over which feature each created.

In succeeding versions of the story, sinister elements became diluted. The essential subject—the artist responsible for creating work with independent or eternal life—remained. Delibes' final divertissement recalls the theme of the Triumph of Time, met in *Le Ballet de la Nuit* (1653) and again in *Le Pavillon d'Armide* (1909).

136.

343.

Politics:

During three years of protracted preparation, search was made for some new Russian or Italian star. The choice finally fell on Giuseppina Bozacchi, a sixteen-year-old Milanese, who died soon after her huge success in the ballet during the siege of Paris, following the disastrous Franco-Prussian War, which France was to precipitate six months after the première. Attending *Coppélia*, Napoleon III sat in his old imperial box a last time; Prussian soldiers would later use

319.

the magnificent uncomplete opera house designed by Charles Garnier as a stable.

Since *Coppélia* France has rarely provided international standards in dance instruction or choreography. Already the opera and ballet had gained renown as a brothel maintained for the élite Jockey Club, whose members enthusiastically contributed to the public disaster of *Tannhäuser* (1861) upon Wagner's refusal to insert his opening bacchanal later, in the opera, so they might finish their wine and cigars. Charles Baudelaire, greatest of poet-critics, an early Wagnerite, wrote: "Keep your harem; conserve its traditions religiously; but let us have a theater where those who think otherwise can find pleasure better suited to their tastes." The local custom was preserved, however; that "other theater" lay in Petersburg, not Paris.

Plot or Pretext:
I. A border town in Galicia. Swanilda, a village maid, is jealous of a large china doll in the window of Coppélius, the toy-maker. Is this a puppet or the toy-maker's daughter? Franz, her fiancé, flirts with Coppélia. Swanilda catches him at it and breaks with him. A crowd gathers; the local lord has given a bell to the town that will strike the hour for a marriage festival the next day. A Hungarian national dance, the *czardas*, is performed (for the first time in the West). Swanilda, obtaining keys to the toy shop, enters secretly with her friends. Franz, with a ladder, tries to gain access through the window, but is surprised by Coppélius in the act of breaking in and flees.

II. Coppélius' upstairs work room filled with life-size wind-up toys in various stages of construction, including a white-bearded Persian magician with his book; a black-amoor with raised scimitar; a cymbalist seated on his cushion; a Chinaman with a dulcimer. Swanilda realizes that the object of her

jealousy is only one more toy. Her friends wind up the mechanical figures, who begin to dance. Coppélius enters, furious, and all escape save Swanilda, who hides. Franz enters by the window. Coppélius, knowing he is in love with his "daughter," plies him with wine. The boy sleeps. Swanilda dresses herself in Coppélia's clothes. Coppélius invokes magic, now more Faust than fraud. He seems to draw strength from the sleeping Franz to infuse his other creatures with real life. To his delight, Coppélia seems to waltz, but instead of responding as a well-behaved puppet, to his commands, she is a naughty child, capricious and ill mannered, and ignores his wishes. She runs for the wine, kicks his books, runs the Moor through with his own sword. Franz awakes and escapes by the window, soon followed by Swanilda. In the alcove where Coppélia is kept, Coppélius finds only her naked armature and realizes he has been tricked.

III. Village festival. The great new bell is blessed; the bell-ringer animates the hours of the day, posed on its car. Divertissements: Waltz of the Hours; dances for Day, Night, Peace and War. The procession and finale include a joyous *pas de deux* for Swanilda and Franz.

Production:
Bozacchi, at sixteen, was greeted as successor to Carlotta Grisi. She was a product of the "pure" French school, as opposed to the more "gymnastic" Italian; despite her origin she had been trained in Paris since the age of ten. Her toe-work was quick, her attack marked; she was steady and musical, lacking only a bit of elevation and bounce. Particularly admired were her hands "that thrill, quiver and do not fall lifeless amid the folds of muslin [of her skirt], but play an active and intelligent part in the dialogue of her mimicry."

The longevity of *Coppélia* is due

more to its music and the chances given to a ballerina for "doll" pantomime (stiff legs, angular hands) than to any definitive choreography. In Russia, versions were attributed to Petipa or Ivanov (1881–83). A German variant, known as *Die Puppenfee* (Josef Bayer, 1888), vaguely foreshadowed Diaghilev's *Boutique Fantasque* (Rossini-Respighi-Massine-Derain, 1919). The East European national dances performed by companies unfamiliar with their character make dreary theater. But the piece persists (some 800 performances in Paris alone) —school exercise or stylistic echo —as a trifle presumed especially appealing to children.

319.

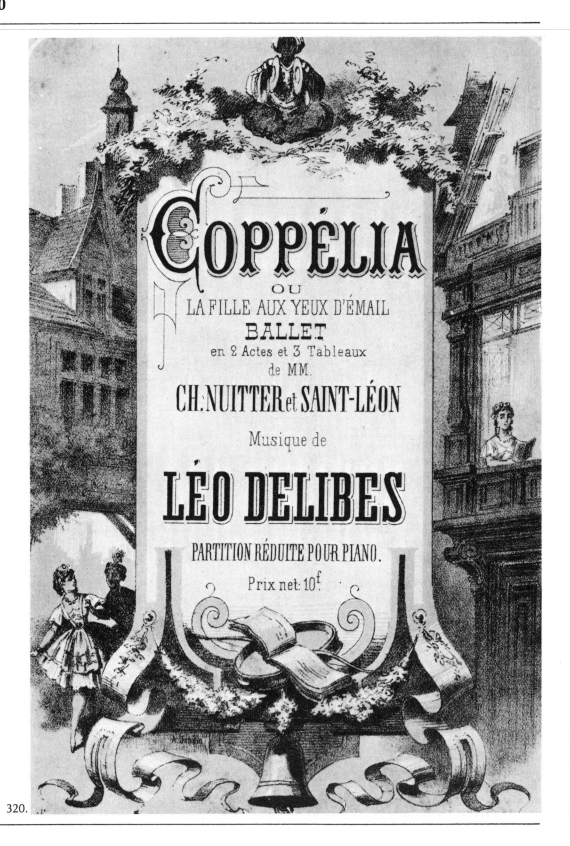

320.

320. Piano score, 1870.

321.

322.

323.

324.

321. Opera setting. Paris, c. 1868.

322–24. Czardas dancers; Dawn. Paris, 1870.

ROMANOV BALLET DE COUR

325.

LA BELLE AU BOIS DORMANT
(The Sleeping Beauty)
January 3/15, 1890
St. Petersburg
Marinsky Theater

Priority:
This was a final definition of tsarist spectacle (although versions seen today derive from Diaghilev's London revival [Sergeyev, 1921]). Petipa, in four decades of service, had attained superior proficiency, unmixed with new music or ideas. But Tchaikovsky's score, the scale of production, the presence of native and Italian personnel inspired him, and, more importantly, the young men who would form Diaghilev's team twenty years later. They saw in it a statement of ballet as major art. Serge Diaghilev, a provincial aristocrat attached to the Imperial Theaters, would reproduce the work as an act of piety; a commercial failure, his production nevertheless was a milestone that inspired the English with an ultimate goal of the Royal Ballet. This work's constant revival has framed England's best dancers; it remains academy, ritual, and reminder. While today the complete ballet may seem overextended, individual numbers resist erosion; it has become an anthology of exercises in the developed idiom.

Last and greatest of court ballets, apart from music, it seems an early eighteenth- or late seventeenth-century piece, skipping the nineteenth. It still manages to evoke an "historic" style, representing the structures of ballet as some vestigial survival, petrified like Noh or Kabuki. But there are serious stylistic confusions that emanate from its origin; unlike true court ballet, the *Sleeping Beauty* is more an academic than an aristocratic formulation. Even though, spiritually, it aimed at royal homage, its initial technical determinant was canonical legibility.

The silhouettes of ballet positions are neither habitual nor natural; they are established for largeness, clarity, flow, command of space, and illusions of aerial conquest. Movement is centrifugal, opening rather than enclosing. The ballet vocabulary was framed by noble sponsors, but divinity and divine right were increasingly identified with humanism rather than kingship.

In the twentieth century, attempts have been made to replace *la danse d'école* with simple inversion based on a balletic fallacy. Centripetal movement from the lower gut, turned-in stance, is thought of as at once more sincere, decent, and appropriate as an expression of People. At its inception, fifty years ago, what is still called modern dance was further burdened by its identity with the machine. Biomechanics of the human body were a metaphor for industrial man; *corps de ballets* could represent steel mills. Action from the solar plexus—somatic spasms—were more honest than movements of revelation, apparition, or openness. The idiosyncratic proposals of Dalcroze, Laban, Wigman, and their epigones enlarged theatrical language and rid it of much dryness, while imposing their own inevitable artificiality. But, generally, the inversion and critical opposition also moved to revitalize academic tradi-

tion, which nevertheless remained essentially, grandly Baroque.

Precedent:
London first saw a *Sleeping Beauty* as a show with speech and music about 1805; an opera by Carafa (1825) and a ballet (1829), based on the Perrault tale, were produced in Paris. The ballet had a book by Scribe, choreography by Aumer, music by Hérold.

Persephone's return from the underworld and other revival myths are part of Western cultural inheritance. Charles Perrault, a writer of fairy tales, allegedly recalled country customs from the High Pyrenees in which the Green Man (the year) was on each May Day kissed alive by his dancing fiancée. The novelist Turgenev translated Perrault into Russian in 1864.

In a sense this ballet can be considered as an end to Baroque tradition, whose style it attempted to imitate or revive. It was as ostentatious or extravagant as seventeenth-century ballet had been; its aim was still to instruct, delight, and move. Expression and metaphor were prime persuaders in the policy of kingship. *La Belle au Bois Dormant* officially reinforced the illusion that the Romanov court was a stable inheritance, that nothing had changed in the world since a courtier of Louis XIV wrote his fairy tale, and nothing need ever change.

143.

Politics:
A. I. Vsevolozhsky (1835–1909) was named Intendant of the Imperial Theaters in 1881, a post he held for eighteen years. A skilled courtier and man of taste—rare qualities in an Intendant—he was also a talented amateur who designed the *Sleeping Beauty* costumes after Gustave Doré's illustrations for Perrault (1862). He encouraged Tchaikovsky even after the initial failure of *Swan Lake* (1877).

326.

325. Marius Petipa, c. 1895.

The Tsar was personal patron of the ballet, and his annual subventions exceeded a million gold rubles. The imperial family attended rehearsals, distributed graduation prizes, and took mistresses from the companies. Ballet was diversion, hardly the place for allusion to an undesirable change, novelty, experiment or unrest. However, the implied comparison of the Romanov to the Sun King's court, on the heels of a Franco-Russian alliance was not unpleasing. In 1889, the Tsar, grateful for a French loan, permitted the *Marseillaise* to be played before him for the first time. But all Tsar Alexander uttered on Tchaikovsky's magnificent music was: "Very nice." Cantalbutte, pompous Grand Master of Ceremonies in the ballet, caricatured a well-known court servant; this "in" joke was appreciated. Both Tsarevitch Nicholas and the boy Stravinsky, whose father was a basso in the Imperial Opera, attended preparations. In 1921 Stravinsky reorchestrated portions of and additions to the original for Diaghilev's orchestra of less than imperial proportions.

Plot or Pretext:
I. Baptism of Aurora, the dawn princess. Fairies bring gifts, including the language of flowers, and song and speech from the twittering Canary Fairy. A Bread Crumb Fairy was added by Petipa, alluding to the Russian custom of breaking a loaf over cradles. All good fairies were invited to the festivity; only Carabosse, a wicked humpbacked demon, was omitted. In the midst of the ceremony she appears to threaten revenge; the princess will die on her sixteenth birthday. The Lilac Fairy (Wisdom), who has not yet presented her gift, mitigates the curse; the babe will not die, but fall into endless sleep.

II. The palace garden; Aurora's coming of age. Suitors have traveled from four corners of the world; she dances with each in the "Rose Adagio" (ballerina supported by four cavaliers). Maids of honor dance. Disguised as a beggar, the evil Carabosse intrigues the princess with a spindle. She pricks herself and faints. Soon the entire royal court is overcome by sleep. Under the spell of the Lilac Fairy, a forest grows to hide them for a hundred years.

III. A century later; a forest glade; sunset. A royal hunting party picnics and starts a game of blindman's buff. The Lilac Fairy reveals a vision of the sleeping princess to Prince Charming, and, following her, against a moving panorama, he approaches the castle in its thicket.

IV. 1. Huge spider webs shroud the hall. Aurora awakens with the Prince's kiss; the palace slowly revives. 2. Attending the festival celebrating the marriage of Aurora and Prince Charming are Red Riding Hood, Puss in Boots, Bluebeard, and two dazzling bluebirds. The dances culminate in a *grand pas de deux* for the bridal couple; a final tableau evokes royal majesty.

Production:
Vsevolozhsky intended to contrast the High Baroque of Louis XIV with the high Rococo of Louis XV. The ballet was produced with enormous luxury but little taste. Watteau, Lancret, and Pater provided models, but the sets were vulgarly designed by staff hacks. Thin décor lacked the massive grandeur of the Bérain or Bibiena, which Léon Bakst superbly restored for Diaghilev. Carlotta Brianza (1867–1930), a pupil of Carlo Blasis, one of a generation of Italians who revived the Milanese tradition, was the first Aurora, a role incarnated in our time by Margot Fonteyn. Paul Gerdt (1844–1917), the greatest Russian male dancer before Nijinsky, who, incredibly, performed from 1860 to 1916, was Prince Charming. Petipa, aged sixty-eight, was set in his ways in service to the tsar—whoever reigned at the moment—and to his ballerina; he let men set their own variations.

Together with *Swan Lake,* this ballet has now taken on an atmosphere of ritual, ostensibly ennobling the company that performs it, in whatever adaptation. In spite of weak links and trite numbers, music often manages to support dancing, lending propulsion to over-familiar steps. No longer a criterion, enough remains for it to be a standard of efficiency in academic execution.

326.

327.

326, 327. Fairies and pages. St. Petersburg, 1890.

328.

328. Composite action. Russia, 1890.

329.

330.

329. Aurora's christening. St. Petersburg, 1890.

330. Aurora's wedding. London, 1921.

331.

290.

331. Lev Ivanov, c. 1890.

LE LAC DES CYGNES
(Swan Lake)
March 1/12, 1894 (Act II);
February 15/27, 1895 (complete)
St. Petersburg
Marinsky Theater

Priority:
The second (and fourth) acts established Lev Ivanov (1834–1901) as a choreographer in the first rank. Working as under-ballet master (1885–95), his passive nature under bureaucracy robbed him of his due. Unlike Petipa, he was musically oriented, a brilliant pianist. While Petipa skillfully constructed separate numbers, Ivanov moved his whole *corps* as a many-voiced instrument. Graduating in 1852, disliked (because he was Russian) by Perrot, his personality made him a "silent shadow," although, historically, his choral dances for Borodin's opera *Prince Igor* (1890) and his own successful *Nutcracker* (1892) place him as chief link between mid-nineteenth and early twentieth centuries.

Tchaikovsky's score, one of the richest ever written for dancing, was first considered too "Wagnerian," and several numbers were pronounced undanceable, since their depth and resonance in orchestration allegedly did not permit individual steps, and its symphonic form was felt too dense for pantomime. The ballet had been a failure; it remained for Ivanov to provide its present skeleton. Tchaikovsky's apprehensive melancholy found a perfect counterpart in Ivanov's moody dances.

Precedent:
Tchaikovsky saved an *adage* from his unsuccessful and unperformed opera on La Motte Fouqué's *Undine* (1870), most of which he destroyed. On holiday (1871), he wrote a small ballet for his sister's children, calling it *The Lake of Swans*. He had been impressed by the texture of Delibes' and Bizet's dance music for Paris.

The second act of *Giselle* and acts II and IV of *Swan Lake* are sisters. Swans are cousins to Wilis; the Wilis' Queen is counterpart to the dark side of the Swan Princess. Act IV of Petipa's *La Bayadère* (1877), with its extended entrance for veiled ghosts of Indian temple dancers, promises beginnings for Act II of *Swan Lake*. Perrot had created *Ondine* for Cerrito (London, 1834), inventing a creature who was mistress of water and air.

Politics:
Beguichev, Intendant of the Moscow Theaters, where ballet was somnolent but less rigid than in Petersburg, persuaded Tchaikovsky to undertake this libretto, though the composer preferred to imagine a *Cinderella*. The première of *Swan Lake* (1877) had scant success; another attempt in 1880 little more. But the scores for the *Sleeping Beauty* (1890) and the *Nutcracker* (1892) made Petipa reconsider *Swan Lake* when Tchaikovsky died (1893) and the administration wished a memorial. Act II was to be given; Petipa assigned it to Ivanov. A year later, when produced complete, he kept acts I and III for himself; they were less distinguished than Ivanov's. Petipa fell ill, Ivanov pieced the ballet to-

gether, after which he lapsed into subservience and drink. Ivanov was Russian, neither Swedish, French, nor Italian; hence his initial passing over.

Pierina Legnani (1863–1923), a strong technician, was the first Swan Queen. Only in 1895 was Mathilde Kschessinska, a Russian, established as principal ballerina, a position due as much to court connections as her undoubted merit.

Plot or Pretext:
I. Prince Siegfried's coming of age. He attends a village festival. His mother arrives and reproaches him for low company. She demands he marry. She departs; dancing continues; a *pas de trois* and variations. The prince's tutor thinks such dancing is poor and clumsily corrects it. Overhead—a flight of swans. A hunt is proposed.

II. A lake. A magician tends swans, who, at midnight, become enchanted maidens. Siegfried and his companions are about to shoot, when Odette the Swan Queen, now in human form, pleads for her flock. Siegfried, smitten, invites her to his espousal ball. But she is under a magic spell and can never be his bride. The prince nevertheless swears fidelity. At dawn the magician reclaims his swans.

III. The ball. Guests arrive in suites. Siegfried and his mother inspect possible wives. Six dance; none please. The royal company is entertained by national dances. Trumpets announce the magician and his daughter Odile, whom he has made seem the image of the Swan Queen. After a virtuoso *pas de deux*, Siegfried declares his love for her, breaking his vow to the true swan, who, in a vision, tries vainly to warn him. Too late he sees his pleading Odette. The hall is plunged into darkness, echoing with the magician's mocking laughter.

IV. The lake: night. Siegfried seeks his betrayed Swan Queen; she forgives him, realizing he has been tricked. The magician raises a storm to drown the swans, and Siegfried carries Odette to a hill, ready to perish with her. His love and sacrifice break the spell; the lovers are united. Dawn.

Production:
Ivanov borrowed preening, fluttering, quivering gestures from birds, translating wings into feathery arm movements. Petipa's first act is conventional prologue; Ivanov's second a series of large symphonic designs, building, in artfully constructed climaxes, to a huge danced denouement, swelling with big melodies into large melodrama. Tchaikovsky supplied an impetus, whether in group or solo numbers, pantomime or *pas de deux*, characterizing tenderness, fright, loss, and grief in fluent movement, never fragmented by mimicry, always coherent, mounting in continuous motion. The role of Swan Queen, doubling as the daughter of the magician, has been called (by Cyril Beaumont) the Jekyll and Hyde of ballet. Originally composed for two dancers, it is often danced by one, covered by another for the apparition (Act III). Dual impersonation of good and evil is a prime vehicle for exploitable personalities, although even more interesting choreography exists in the concerted designs for the entire *corps*. A brilliant *pas de deux* (Act III) framed the ballerina's famous thirty-two *fouettés en tournant* (whipping turns), originally introduced by Legnani in Petipa's and Ivanov's *Cinderella* (1893). The combination of orchestral score and symphonic choreography would have no equal until *The Firebird* (Stravinsky-Fokine, 1910). *Swan Lake* is the most popular of ballets, existing in many versions. In 1951 Balanchine distilled Act II as his own homage to Ivanov. Full-length versions now in repertory often derive from choreography by Nicholas Sergeyev (1876–1951), a former regisseur in

Petersburg who revived *Swan Lake* in London, 1934.

332.

333.

334.

335.

333. *Le Lac des Cygnes*. Moscow, 1877.

334. *The Swans' Lake*. London, 1884.

335. *Le Lac des Cygnes*. St. Petersburg, 1895.

336.

337.

336. *Swan Lake*. New York, 1951.

337. *Swan Lake*. Moscow, 1960.

133.

431.

338.

339.

340.

341.

LE PAVILLON D'ARMIDE
(The Pavilion of Armida)
May 19, 1909
Paris
Théâtre du Châtelet

Priority:
This was presented at the opening of Diaghilev's first season in Western Europe, an event altering dance history. A collaboration between the designer, Alexandre Benois (1870–1960), the composer, Nicholas Tcherepnine (1873–1945), and the choreographer, Michel Fokine, *Armide* compressed the full-length *ballet à grand spectacle* into one act, a novel concentration. In bringing combined stars of the Petersburg and Moscow theaters to Paris, Diaghilev overwhelmed an international public by the unexpected and heretofore unseen resources of Russian ballet, the native treasure of a culture that had been considered provincial if not barbarian. Talent, execution, and taste made a thunderclap announcing Diaghilev's domination of dancing for two decades.

The choice of French subject was tactful, if daring. Russia was returning to France the dance she herself had almost forgotten. Baroque and Rococo were restored in a robust aristocratic frame, recreating a style that at home had declined to insipidity and middle-class dilution.

Precedent:
Armida, the enchantress, had been a favorite protagonist since the seventeenth century. *Armide* as a single scene was produced for the graduating class of the Petersburg Imperial Academy, 1907. In 1900, Benois read Théophile Gautier's *Omphale*, from which he derived an ideal libretto, influenced also by *Coppélia* (1870), the tales of Hoffmann, and an intensification on a visual level of the *Sleeping Beauty* (which, while a monument, lacked a worthy collaboration). But the Marinsky administration to which it was offered was unenthusiastic. Benois, grandson of a French *émigré*, had profound insight into the epochs of Versailles and was master of strong forms and colors in advance of usual opera-house decorators.

Of all non-dancers in the history of ballet, Diaghilev is greatest; he birthed an era more important to us than the *ballet de cour* (1570–1680), *ballet d'action* (1740–80), or *ballet romantique* (1830–70); he was responsible for *ballets russes* which flourished—embodied by his company—from 1909 until his death in 1929, and which has survived as a genre, in one form or another, for forty years longer. A character of Tolstoian or Dostoevskian complexity, he was aware of his capacities, writing to his stepmother in 1895:

"I am: 1. a charlatan, moreover with lots of dash. 2. a great charmer. 3. an insolent [dandy].* 4. a man with plenty of logic and few scruples. 5. one in torment seeming likely to be without talent. Besides, I believe I've found my true vocation: artistic patronage. For that I have everything needful, except money—and that will come!"

Louis XIV was first-dancer and prince-patron. Diaghilev was a courtier, a gifted musical amateur, and a catalyst of genius. His moral energy in bringing his ballet into being and maintaining it in spite of loss of base was heroic. He spans history. He marked the end of one epoch and named another; what he managed remains our model.

132.

387.

Politics:
The circle of young artists flanking Diaghilev had a passion for the then avant-garde (*fin de siècle* art, modern Russian painting and music), with ambitions to raise ballet to its high potential, as they had already indicated fragmentarily but not yet as a coherent whole.

So influential and complex an event as Diaghilev's triumph in Europe must be understood in context. Apart from conflicts within the administration of the Imperial Theaters, to which Diaghilev

338–41. Fokine: Viscount. Paris, 1909.

* "A gentleman is one who is never rude unintentionally." George Bernard Shaw.

had been attached, tension in international events was responsible for motivating his venture, in which he persisted despite last-minute withdrawal of foreign-office support. The Franco-Russian alliance (against Germany) was announced in 1891. Japan defeated the Russian navy in 1905. Diaghilev on his own had organized exhibitions and concerts of Russian painting and music in Paris before 1908, the year he presented Chaliapin in *Boris Godunov*. Denied official subvention, he ·nevertheless gathered private guarantees to ensure a season at the Théâtre du Châtelet, a popular municipal house, less chic but far larger than the Opéra.

Diaghilev was not alone in wishing to take Russian art and the evidence of its renaissance to the West. Grand Duke Alexander, cousin of Nicholas II, describing the first decade of a new reign, tells how this young sovereign was tormented by four giant uncles. "Uncle Serge and Uncle Vladimir developed equally efficient methods of intimidation. . . . They all had their favorite generals and admirals, . . . their ballerinas desirous of organizing a 'Russian' season in Paris, their wonderful preachers anxious to redeem the Emperor's soul. . . ." His soul had been shared by Mathilde Kschessinska, the ballerina, whom he met in the spring of 1890 when she was seventeen, graduating first in her class. The imperial family attended graduation supper and performance. Alexander III demanded: "Where is Kschessinska?" He pressed her hand and issued her ukase: "Be thou glory and adornment of our ballet." When, four years later, Nicholas married Alix of Hesse-Darmstadt, Kschessinska was heartbroken. Marius Petipa, whose Princess Aurora and Sugar Plum Fairy she danced, consoled her: "Suffering for love is good for art." She was also comforted by Grand Duke Andrei, by whom,

in 1902, she had a son, and whom, in 1921, she married.

Plot or Pretext:

I. Armida's pavilion; Louis XIV architecture, with two huge windows and above each, an *oeil de boeuf* ("bull's eye"). In the center stands a huge bronze clock before a Gobelin tapestry. A young Viscount traveling toward his fiancée, overtaken by storm, seeks refuge. The room is owned by a Marquis-magician, while the tapestry shows a former owner—Armida, the enchantress. Midnight: Time, a figure supporting the clock, reverses his hourglass. Love banishes Time; twelve Hours (small boys) dance. Figures in the Gobelin glow mysteriously and are animated.

II. Palace gardens (now in the style of Peterhof—the epoch of Catherine the Great—rather than Versailles), with topiary hedges and real fountains. Armida enters with her suite, including her slave (Nijinsky). The Marquis-magician transforms Armida into the Viscount's lover. A festival. Ballet interludes: abduction of *almées* from a harem; comical pasha with scimitar; devils; masked monsters; buffoons. Armida gives the Viscount her gold embroidered scarf. A bacchanal. At dawn visions disappear.

III. Sunrise; the pavilion. Shepherd and shepherdess (with real sheep) pass by the windows. The Viscount tries to recall his dream. The Marquis-magician shows him Armida's scarf draped across the clock's face; in the tapestry, behind, Armida no longer wears it. The Viscount is overcome; is magic truth? Pantomimic finale—an innovation replacing usual group dances—for Magician and Viscount alone.

Production:
Russian machinists at the Théâtre du Châtelet improved on the Petersburg production by including real fountains. Diaghilev used first-dancers from both imperial ballet companies. On the opening 342.

night Pavlova and Fokine danced the Viscount and Armida. Vaslav Nijinsky, greatest dancer of his time, appeared as her slave; the French would compare him to the first Vestris (1729–1808). The program included a divertissement to show off the company, comprising typical numbers by Petipa, as well as the last act of Borodin's *Prince Igor*, with Fokine's Polovtsian dances, a *coup de grâce* of violent and savage "Tartar" action, contrasting with the deliberate classicism of the academic dance.

346.

Diaghilev always dealt in assaults on accepted taste. In *Armide* he infused the vapid Rococo (epitomized by Massenet in *Manon*), a property of high bourgeois culture, with a bold dose of the Baroque; the Viscount was presented in Louis XIV's costume as The Sun.

133.

Official French scene-designers had hardly taken advantage of their native Post-Impressionist painters; but Diaghilev's designer for *Prince Igor*, Nicholas Roerich, had seen early Gauguins, already in great Muscovite collections, and his broad handling glowed in huge, heavily brushed backcloths. Treatment of both old and new styles was a revelation to the West.

342. Nijinsky: Slave. Paris, 1909.

183

343.

344.

343. Russian palace gardens. Paris, 1909.

344. *Armide* in performance. Paris, 1909.

345. 346.

348.

347.

345. Armida. Paris, 1909.

347–48. Nijinsky. Paris, 1909.

346. Pavlova and Nijinsky. St. Petersburg, 1908.

185

349.

LES SYLPHIDES
(The Sylphs)
June 2, 1909
Paris
Théâtre du Châtelet

Priority:
This dance-suite to variously orchestrated piano pieces by Chopin distilled nineteenth-century Romantic ballet as *Le Pavillon d'Armide* had eighteenth. Its technical demands as such are not pressing, but it takes skillful artists to maintain a gentle aura of tender, urgent lyricism. Subtly balanced for contrast in evanescent action, its subject is a style of movement attached to a particular period, of which the type is Taglioni. (Fanny Kemble, the English actress, noted [1882] that "Chopin said he had more than once received his inspiration from Taglioni's dancing.") The easy flow and formal structure were rooted in the school vocabulary, but the ballet's insistence on pure movement and its novel adoption of a familiar pianistic climate were almost unprecedented. Diaghilev had slight part in its creation, but it remained his fa-

vorite. The English dancer Lydia Sokolova would recall that when she joined the troupe in 1913, new members had to be in the company six months before being permitted to perform it.

Precedent:
Fokine's ballet was first produced in Russia, 1908, with the title *Chopiniana,* as a series of scenes based on idealized incidents in the composer's life: at a ruined monastery (Valdemosa) with his muse; Polish wedding; ballroom polonaise; Neapolitan tarantella. In the later version, premièred in Paris as *Les Sylphides,* he omitted all character dancing and program notes, dressing his new conception in the uniform of the *ballet blanc*. Petipa had perhaps furnished a prototype with his revision of Filippo Taglioni's *La Sylphide* (1892), which critics dismissed as old-fashioned. In 1901 the Muscovite ballet master Alexander Gorsky had mounted Glinka's *Valse Fantaisie* as a purely musical work, without literary or narrative pretext.

Isadora Duncan, American crusader for a free dance, appeared in Petersburg (1905) and is considered to have influenced Fokine by her plastic use of arms—outside the academic discipline—and her unprecedented action on the floor to project her body at full length, as well as by her choice of important music. Arm movements may also have been suggested to him by a "ballet of hands" performed by Siamese court dancers in Russia around 1900.

Nijinsky's behavior as the poet presupposed the roles of James in *La Sylphide* (1832) and Albrecht in *Giselle* (1841), but added an important new concept. Male dancers had been gods, princes, peasants. Here, the epicene poet, Chopin's genius or daemon, took on new identity—the dancer as performer, whose manner is determined solely by music, whose sole history is the time it takes him to move.

Politics:
Nijinsky was presented by Diaghilev as a phenomenon: a male dancer on a par with ballerina. In 1909, for this performer of Polish extraction and unstable temperament, with supreme physical appeal and technical mastery, the future in the Imperial Theaters was obscure. Diaghilev engineered his protégé's abdication from Russia in 1911, focusing the triumph of his own great venture—the establishment of a permanent ballet company with no connection to the Imperial Theaters—on a unique personality. Nijinsky personified the male principle, which had been lost since the young Perrot. Anna Pavlova quit the company forthwith.

Plot or Pretext:
The participants: three groups of four dancers, plus four soloists, symmetrically composed. The divertissements: Nocturne; Waltz (Karsavina); Mazurka (Pavlova); another Mazurka (Nijinsky); a Prelude; Valse; *Pas de deux* (Pavlova and Nijinsky); and final *Grande Valse Brillante* for the company. Through a cat's cradle of choreography, academic classicism, divested of bravura, virtuoso decoration, or rhetorical pantomime was demonstrated as an instrument in itself. Adopting the essence of an historic style in revival, choreography surpassed archeology to become something new toward an extension of a language.

Production:
Nijinsky, the single male dancer, was costumed by Benois in a rather improbable "troubadour" tunic, long blonde wig, and white tights. The sylphs were those seen in the lithographs of the eighteen-forties. The original backdrop was a vaguely ruined chapel in a forest glade derived from *Giselle,* Act II, which, in later productions, gave way to a woodland scene of Corot-inspired fuzziness. Having long familiarity with the music, Fokine was able to compose his dances

347.

353.

354.

in three days. During his lifetime there were fairly satisfactory revivals, although lacking the original cast. Recent productions have been more distinguished by piety than perfection; the ballet is now a kind of diploma piece. It still has its historic appeal but its seductive simplicity is hard to manage so that the whole keeps much meaning, considering what has happened in dance over the last fifty years. The best key to the intentions of the original is found in Fokine's *Memoirs of a Ballet Master* (1961, p. 130) in which he analyzes individual dancers. His book is an absorbing professional document, like an architect's plan for a building or a surgeon's description of an operation. Pavlova gave him the impression of flying, not leaping. Karsavina, neither as slim nor as light, grasped the heart of Romantic expression in the exquisite positioning of shoulders and torso. Preobrajenska, the third ballerina in the original Russian production, had exceptional balance in motion; her freezing on *pointe* was a monumental accent. She danced the Prelude as choreographed, then for an encore, repeated it in an entirely different improvisation. Such behavior was quite usual in Petipa divertissements, but Fokine was furious, for he had pivoted within a frame by Chopin his model of a Platonic ballet realm, in which parts echoed the whole in a delicate balance of music and motion. It was a moral ceremony, with individuals sometimes subordinate, sometimes the focus, but always components in sequences of disciplined action, which, on stage, seemed far more grandly scaled than the relatively small forces it numerically required. One could also·think of Chopin's piano, starting with the *corps de ballet* as notes in music. And there was implied drama— the hint of genius cut off in its prime, the evanescence of dreams, desire, melancholy—the mutability of existence.

396.

350.

423.

351.

352.

350, 351. Dalcroze dancers, *c.* 1910.

352. *Salammbô.* Moscow, 1910.

353.

354.

353. Nijinsky: Poet, 1913.

354, 355. *Les Sylphides*. Paris, 1909.

355.

356.

356. *Les Sylphides*. New York, 1916.

357.

SCHÉHÉRAZADE
June 4, 1910
Paris
Opéra

Priority:

This "choreographic drama" typifies Diaghilev's first Parisian period, with its fusion of overcharged décor, the aristocratic miming of Ida Rubinstein, Nijinsky's panther presence, in Fokine's shrewdly contrived orgy. Although later repudiated by Diaghilev, and now sharing the vulgarized nostalgia of early silent-films, *Schéhérazade*

meant "*ballets russes*" to world audiences for thirty-five years. The ballet's concentrated action eliminated divisions between divertissement and drama. Bakst's strident décor and harem trousers ·had wide influence on civil dress and decoration. Archeological borrowings and tight corsets of the ordinary wardrobe were set aside. His synthesis of Persian, Turkish, and Moghul miniatures, blown up to opera-house scale, combined with Rimsky-Korsakov's orchestration, which strongly propelled Fokine's violent dances, made a pro-

found impression, not alone on the general public, but on advance-guard artists, who, while smiling at such deluxe exoticism, were excited by Post-Impressionist principles applied to the stage and by the possibilities such spectacle might hold for easel-painters. (In Russia, important painters—Mikhail Vrubel, Korovin, Golovin —had long designed opera, raising the prestige of scenic presentation, in broad effects of splashed and running pigment; this was, however, new in the West. Russians painted on the floor, capitalizing on accident, while the French used a perpendicular canvas, more fussy and "correct.")

New visual freedom, a liberation of human bodies, dense orchestration—not written for ballet but ingeniously adapted to it—caused a revolution also in choreographic devices. The dancing was no *danse d'école,* but without that instruction, its performance would have been impossible.

Precedent:

Harem dancers, the *almées* of Egyptian pashas, Nubian slaves, and cruel or generous Turks had been familiar since the seventeenth century. In Paris, at the Porte St. Martin (1817), there was given a ballet-pantomime, *Haroun el Rashide et Zobéide, ou le Caliphe Généreux.* Filippo Taglioni produced *The Revolt in the Seraglio* for his daughter Marie, complete with black slave, eunuch, and bathing scene (1833). However, the immediate source of *Schéhérazade* was perhaps Fokine's own *Cléopâtre* (1909), the final novelty of Diaghilev's first Paris season. In *Cléopâtre*'s first version (called *Une Nuit d'Égypte,* Petersburg, 1908), Fokine borrowed the wardrobe from Petipa's *La Fille du Pharaon* (1862), calling his heroine—danced by Pavlova—Ta-Hor, the name of the hero in Gautier's tale. Léon Bakst (1866–1924), the designer, had looked at Delacroix's *Death of Sardanapalus* in the

80.

214.

305.

359.

357. Nijinsky and Diaghilev. Monte Carlo, 1912.

190

Louvre, the source of Shah Schariar's make-up and beard in an "Assyrian" style. And in the second scene of *Le Pavillon d'Armide* (1909), there was an entry of *almées*, abducted from their harem, with a comic pasha and his scimitar.

Politics:
Alexandre Benois, designer of *Armide* and *Les Sylphides*, chief catalyst in Diaghilev's early cabinet of all the talents, was responsible for the use of Rimsky-Korsakov's score, as well as for the over-all plan of action. Diaghilev gave him no credit in the program, precipitating the first of many scandals which peppered twenty years of personal intrigue, infighting, and reconciliation. Diaghilev was never slow to accuse others of disloyalty; he was envious or jealous of any progressive work outside his personal apparatus; his private sentiment became public policy; he was at once ruthless, tyrannical, capricious, and generous, quite ready to abandon any collaborator and as eager to welcome them back. In Paris, the sight of a white-skinned ballerina being fondled by a black man was hardly shocking, but in the United States (1916), the slave wore tan tights.

Plot or Pretext:
A huge emerald-green drapery swathes hanging lamps in the closed harem of Shah Schariar. To the left, center, three peacock-blue doors; at the far left, a stair leading up to a high divan. Cushions and rugs splash the red-orange floor. The Shah is morose, suspicious of his favorite wife, Zobéide. He pretends to prepare for a hunt, to the feigned sorrow of his harem. He is solemnly armed for the chase; he leaves. His delighted wives bribe the Chief Eunuch, in whose custody they are left, to release the male harem slaves. From the first door emerge rose-clad Negroes; from the second, those in green. Zobéide demands the third door be opened; the Eunuch

is loathe; she bribes him with her pearls. Four subalterns leave to warn the Shah. A Negro slave in gold (Nijinsky) is loosed into the hall. Slaves, *almées*, and fruit-bearing youths join in a huge wheeling dance. The harem writhes—a drunken amorous gang—culminating in an orgy, at the height of which appears the Shah. The bacchanal stops; all try to flee, but guards cut them down. Zobéide, seeing her slave slain, kills herself. The Shah is disconsolate. Slow curtain.

Production:
Nijinsky's death was electrifying: "a fish tossed onto the sand," his wife wrote. S. L. Grigoriev, Diaghilev's stage manager for twenty years, recalls:

"The 'orgy' in the middle was especially striking. By means of intricate evolutions for the various groups of dancers woven in with a number of individual moves, Fokine contrived to endow this dance with such rich variety that its climax was tremendous. The strongest choreographic moment came when, having combined all the choreographic groups into one, he used a pause in the music suddenly to halt them, and then, while accelerating the pace still more, as it were to unravel this human tangle. The effect was overwhelming: the audience roared its applause. . . ."

358.

358. "The Sultan's Favorite," 1915.

191

359.

360.

361.

362.
363.

359. Prototype: The Shah. 1826.

360–66. *Schéhérazade by Segonzac, 1910.*

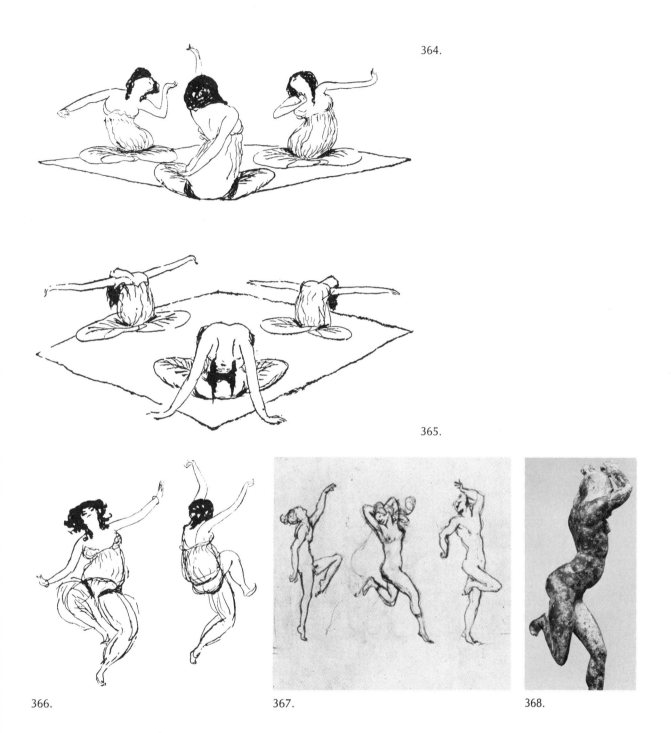

364.

365.

366.

367.

368.

367. *Narcisse*. Paris, 1910.

368. Hellenistic dancer, c. A.D. 260.

BALLET RUSSE: Music and Magic

369.   370.

PETROUCHKA
June 13, 1911
Paris
Théâtre du Châtelet

Priority:

Stravinsky's stunning score, following *Firebird* (1910), marked him as the era's composer, the seminal influence on progressive choreography. Throughout his career, he has made music, not to serve dance, but to control it. *Petrouchka* was the climax of Diaghilev's first period, incorporating revivalism, the exotic, and the picturesque. The culmination of Fokine's gifts, combining the scale of *ballet à grand spectacle* with surprising intimacy, it looked back to Perrot and Saint-Léon, yet Fokine's mosaic vignettes of a bustling holiday crowd were the antithesis of the geometric symmetry in the traditional subordinated *corps de ballet*. Such quasi-accidental genre sketches had been suggested before, but here it was augmented by a commanding presence: the orchestra with its new role in organizing accident and suggesting incident.

Fokine's choreography for Nijinsky as a puppet set patterns for that mesmeric dancer's future, bringing him a heady taste of world fame. Much later the chore-

ographer wrote: "My devil of a Petrouchka has been responsible for any number of natural children . . . jerky movements have been introduced everywhere. . . . It has become a habit. It is easy to imitate Petrouchka's mechanical gestures."

When Pygmalion sculptured Galatea, he was blessed by Aphrodite; but who helped Frankenstein? Were Coppélius' toys dolls or dancers? Automata are self-movers by definition—machines assuming functions of man—with chances of being both more and less mechanical. Automation remains material for fascinating metaphorical use. Fokine's movements for *Petrouchka* were by no means dehumanized, but hinted at the reduction of persons into objects. Stravinsky's hero is shown surviving his dolldom by the triumph of his essence, which can be read as humanist or nationalistic metaphor.

Ten years later, in Weimar, Oskar Schlemmer produced his *Triadic Ballet*, in which the dancers became impersonal as chessmen. Later, ballet elected movement itself as subject, independent of the pretext of poetry or decoration. Dance emerged as autonomous,

measured by sound or silence alone. The kinetic structure of human anatomy was plot or pretext enough. Quality of movement, descriptive or abstract, would be the dance's organic material in the new century.

Precedent:

The characters are old friends: Ballerina is cousin to Columbine and Coppélia; Moor, a medieval wild man, an instinctive, savage bully, is descendant of the cruel or generous Turk; Showman derives from the charlatan doctor familiar from Italian comedy; Petrouchka is at once Little Ivan the serf, Pierrot, and Pedrolino. A fifth character is collective—the bustling crowd, here more particular and contemporary than in Perrot's *Esmeralda* (1844).

Stravinsky had seen the *Sleeping Beauty* prepared; at sixteen he played *Coppélia* four-hands on the piano. For *Petrouchka* he embroidered a quilt of folk tunes, street songs, peddlar's cries, French music-hall fragments, and Viennese waltzes turned on hand-organs. The idea for the ballet was his. While Benois, the designer, set his Admiralty Square in his grandfather's youth, he was thinking of his own, bidding farewell to Romanov Russia on the brink of dissolution.

Politics:

After two smashing Paris seasons, Diaghilev could form his own troupe, independent of tsarist theater and its dancers. At last he could plan. Before, repertory was haphazard, and music, except for *Firebird,* less consequential than other elements.

Diaghilev's initial use and prompt abandonment of Fokine, later of Nijinsky, illuminate risks taken by a highly educated instinct: he was super impresario, at once generalissimo, father, lover, slave driver, and friend. Stravinsky wrote: "The success of *Petrouchka*

320.

214.

317.

292.

373.

369, 370. Nijinsky: Petrouchka. London, 1911.

194

was good for me in that it gave me the absolute conviction of my ear, just as I was about to begin."

Plot or Pretext:

I. "Butter-week" in Petersburg, 1830; a street fair. A show booth; behind, the Admiralty's needle spire. A crowd of peasants, police, street dancers, gypsies, with a hurdy-gurdy fills the street. A bearded old Showman steps through curtains of his booth; when drawn, they reveal puppets, sprawled on armatures: Blackamoor, Ballerina, and Petrouchka. The Showman (danced by the great teacher Enrico Cecchetti, who had personified the Chief Eunuch in *Schéhérazade*) makes his dolls budge, then dance. A drum-roll (*tambour de Provence*) is heard.

II. Petrouchka's dark den, exuding a cold northern climate, stencilled with icy stars. He is kicked inside by the Showman and tries to escape. Ballerina enters stiffly on toe—a silly puppet, but beautiful to him. His japes and tricks do not impress her, and she leaves, ignoring his love. Abandoned, he pounds the paper walls.

III. The Moor's room, warm south —rich, red, painted with palms. He sprawls on his divan, juggling a coconut. His scimitar can't crack it; it must be a god. He worships it. The Ballerina struts in, blowing her tin trumpet. The Moor loves her. Petrouchka enters; the lovers spring apart. The Moor chases Petrouchka, boots him out, and sets the Ballerina on his lap again.

IV. The street fair; night. The busy crowd includes coachmen, nursemaids, a dancing bear, ribbon venders, masked revelers; commotion from the show booth. The Ballerina in pursuit, Petrouchka, chased by the Moor's scimitar, is struck down. Blood on the snow. When police arrive, the Showman can point only to his doll's sawdust stuffing. The crowd disperses. Suddenly, above the booth, Petrouchka is seen alive, jiggling and quivering. The charlatan is amazed and terrified. His risen doll is immortal. Snow falls.

Production:

Fokine, an experienced academic dancer, had studied national forms from Ukraine to Caucasus; here he used them not as divertissement but as descriptive miniatures, focusing individual fragments in a crowd. For the Ballerina, he accented pizzicato points. The Moor was turned out (*en dehors*); Petrouchka turned in (*en dedans*). By limiting movement and gesture to a flat and rigid single plane, he proposed mechanical, semi-automatic regularity, in contrast to the semi-accidental haphazard naturalism in his conglomerate vignetted *corps*. Small, clear mimic detail demonstrated the Moor's naive pride, the Ballerina's silly narcissism, Petrouchka's pitiful jealousy and helplessness, all ordinary enough in the tradition of mime, but transformed in performance by the brilliance of Orlov, Karsavina, and Nijinsky.

Fokine complained his crowd was never sufficiently rehearsed; Nijinsky that its movement was largely improvised and never really designed; Benois that Diaghilev stinted miserably on the totality of desired effects. Revived since, the work means little. Revivals lack life. Music survives to tempt future ballet masters, when comparisons with a lost original are meaningless. The metaphor of manipulated automata remains poetically powerful, now haloed in the nostalgia of many period memoirs. Did Benois see Diaghilev as a charlatan Showman? Was Nijinsky typecast as Petrouchka?

371. Nijinsky by Rodin, 1912.

372. Diaghilev and Nijinsky, Paris, 1913.

373.

374.

373. Street fair, St. Petersburg, 1803.

374. Street fair, St. Petersburg. Paris, 1911.

375.

376. 377. 378.

375. Moor, Ballerina, Petrouchka. Paris, 1911.

376. Russian peasant woman. Paris, 1911.

377. Nijinsky's costume. Paris, 1911.

378. Karsavina's costume. Paris, 1911.

197

L'APRÈS-MIDI D'UN FAUNE
(The Afternoon of a Faun)
May 29, 1912
Paris
Théâtre du Châtelet

Priority:

This "choreographic tableau in one act," Nijinsky's first composition, marks a break absolute with classic tradition, the first of such impact in four centuries. Nothing was retained from the academy save disciplined dancers. Debussy's shimmering score offered no obvious divisions to aid a metrical structure. Nijinsky conceived a strict two-dimensional limitation; his dancers moved as in a slot, with abrupt profiled turns. Poses recalled sixth-century Greek vases and stone reliefs; the girls wore clinging pleated shifts reminiscent of *korai*, the standing sculptures of draped maidens deriving from Egypt or Phoenicia. The subject—a recognition through auto-eroticism of adolescent sex—and its treatment both seemed extreme. While Nijinsky ostensibly borrowed a "Greek" manner, it was his personal stylization, shaped by an archaic epoch Bakst chose and by the choreographic discipline he set himself. He was bound by no previous vision, neither Fokine's nor Isadora Duncan's more amply heroic Hellenistic plasticity. He analyzed motion and its arrest. Returning instinctively to the sacral birth of theater, he anticipated further uncharted development—dance in itself, no longer diverting, but ritualized.

Faune was also Diaghilev's public début in manipulating his shock technique. His first two Paris seasons had been astonishing, surprising, revelatory—but not yet brutal. When he required of Cocteau: "*Étonne moi*," did he command "Astound me" or "Shock me"? Diaghilev was an exemplar of Anglo-French *dandysme*. In Petersburg he belonged to "The Pickwickians"; the young Dickens considered himself midway between Byron, Brummel, and D'Orsay. Diaghilev added as his exemplars Baudelaire, Wilde, and Beardsley. Barbey d'Aurevilly gave the classical definition: "The dandy is an historical androgyne, a double or multiple nature of indecisive intellectual sexuality whose grace derives from strength; whose strength gains from grace." Beau Brummel was stoic innovator and chose to shock. His laconic simplicity amounted to rudeness. This was new; now, patrons—prince or public—were not courted but systematically insulted. It was an aristocratic morality, flamboyant, revolutionary. The dandy amateur became the professional Bohemian. Dandies had been horsemen and swordsmen; they would now be artists. Dandyism was a cult of self pitched against inchoate vulgarity—narcissistic but athletic. Nijinsky became epitome of dandy as first-dancer, Diaghilev's honed instrument to torment, attract, and conquer a mindless but susceptible public. Through *Faune*, Nijinsky evolved in his own person a modern archetype, an artist canonized in the tragedy of his unique craft and gift, like Rimbaud, Van Gogh, or T. E. Lawrence.

Such an eminent witness as Stravinsky said that Bakst created *Faune*, not alone supplying decoration but inventing everything else, "... *c'est lui encore qui indiquait le moindre geste de la chorégraphie.*"* With due respect, this was not true. Stravinsky's preoccupation with sonority often makes him a dubious critic of the visual. Léonide Massine, dancer and ballet master, wrote in his memoirs (1968), "Watching [Nijinsky] rehearse the girls in *L'Après Midi d'un Faune* and show them in the most meticulous way the characterization of each small detail of his work, I was astonished by his innate ability and by his instinctive feeling for choreography."

Precedent:
Fokine had composed "Greek" numbers since *Eunice* (1906), based on Sienkiewicz' novel *Quo Vadis*: "a dance of three Egyptian girls in which I employed for the first time profile positions and angular lines borrowed from paintings and bas-reliefs of ancient Egypt." Viganò used Hellenistic sculpture, Petipa Egyptian in *La Fille du Pharaon*. Closer in planar movement were the three dancing puppets of *Petrouchka*, echoing *Coppélia*. More important was Nijinsky's knowledge at one remove of Émile Jaques-Dalcroze, the Swiss musicologist, to whose school, near Dresden, Diaghilev had been drawn by Prince Volkonsky, Intendant of the Imperial Theaters. Marie Rambert (1888–1982), a gifted student, later instructed Nijinsky in Dalcroze's dynamics, or Eurythmics, musically motivated body action. As for the famous scarf, have we not seen it before in *Le Pavillon d'Armide*, draped across a clock? In Marivaux's first comedy, *Arlequin poli par l'amour* (1720), Harlequin, managing to steal Sylvia's kerchief, hides it in his jacket; then rolls on it in ecstasy upon the stage.

Through the nineteenth century "Greek" art usually meant Hellenistic or Roman sculpture, or more popularly the carving of Canova and Thorwaldsen, with a glance at Pompeiian wall-painting. It was a Neoclassic version from white marbles or plaster casts that had shed their polychromy, until German archeologists restored color. In 1877, fourteen *korai*, with their archaic smiles, inscrutable as Leonardo's ambiguous *Gioconda*, were unearthed near the Erechtheion. These were as atypical of what was taken to be Greek as if they had been Chinese or Aztec. Bakst had sketched in Crete and Attica as an informed amateur archeologist. He had painted a huge easel composition, *Terror Antiquus*, suggesting the mystery of Attica's remote and unfamiliar past. Nijinsky applied a vision of archaistic innocence to real life.

306.

350.

396.

423.

16.

368.

430.

389.

---

* "... and further, it was he [Bakst] who specified the least gesture of the choreography." (*Chroniques de Ma Vie* [1935].)

Stephane Mallarmé's eclogue (1876) was originally a recitation for the elder Coquelin, a great French actor. Debussy planned a "Prelude, Interlude, and Final Paraphrase," of which only the Prelude was completed (1892–94). Musically, his piece was never a transcription of the whole poem, which expressed the frustration of a half-bestial creature rejected by beauty. For Mallarmé, it was metaphor of the poet's incapacity to compose an absolute or perfect construct. Whether or not Nijinsky read or understood this is unimportant. Mallarmé's method, borrowed by Debussy, was defined in his *Magie* (1893): "To evoke the unmentioned object in a deliberate shadow, by allusive, never direct words, that all amount equally to expressions of silence, is to attempt something that comes close to an act of creation."*

Nijinsky took the subject—the creative act—for sex itself; the shock lay in that "the unmentioned object" had been heretofore unmentionable. Convention canonized copulation; masturbation was heresy. Mallarmé wished to depict, not the object, but the effect it produced. In obscure verse this was safe; in danced action obscene. Nijinsky was no simple narcissist. He was an artist and a naive philosopher with ultimate aspirations toward sainthood. In three ballets, he paralleled Freud's chart of man's developing psyche: in *Faune*, adolescent self-discovery and gratification; in *Jeux*, homosexual discovery of another self or selves; in *Le Sacre du Printemps*, fertility and renewal of the race.

Politics:
Diaghilev was ambitious for Nijinsky as an extension of himself. Nijinsky at nineteen knew his own merit. This first work was both a coming of age and declaration of independence. To Diaghilev, Fokine was already old-fashioned. All futures lay with Nijinsky, both as first-dancer and ballet master.

He was fascinated by the boy, as was Nijinsky by himself, who wrote: "The Faun is me." He required some hundred and twenty rehearsals for an eight-minute work. He was no simple Slavic soul, but experienced, educated, and a careful pianist. A keen observer, his diary reveals uncanny psychological insight. The Faun's final act, thrusting his body into the nymph's scarf, caused a scandal, which the press whipped up into a *cause célèbre*. The sculptor Rodin defended Nijinsky; the Russian embassy was horrified; Diaghilev delighted.

Plot or Pretext:
" 'A faun sleeps: nymphs trick him. A forgotten scarf satisfies his dream. The curtain falls so the poem may continue in every memory. S. M.' It is not 'The Afternoon of a Faun' by Stephane Mallarmé; it is the musical prelude to this panic episode, a short scene which precedes it." Thus the program note. A faun lolls on a hillock, fingers extended imitating Panpipes. Seven nymphs in chain step shuffle past. Curious, the Faun descends to watch. Curious, then alarmed, they flee, to return shyly. The Faun tries to play with them, but they are frightened by this half-boy, half-beast. The least shy, for a second, returns; they link arms. Contact frightens her; she escapes, dropping her scarf. For one moment she is eager to stay, but the creature seems too threatening. Leaping onto his rock, he carries her scarf, a sad substitute. Arching his body, he thrusts his length into it.

Production:
Bakst wished to show Nijinsky Greek galleries in the Louvre; the dancer insisted on stopping in the Egyptian. His movements would be angular, while Bakst's curtain was blurred, Post-Impressionistic, fluid—like the music. Costumes of the girls were pleated, clinging, pliant, contrasting with movement that was abrupt, nervous, rectilin-

ear. The nymphs, sandaled, not in toe shoes, moved with feet raised three-quarters off the floor, as if by definite rules. They turned in place, palms extended, always flat to the front. They wore close wigs of gilded cord. Tension between curve and angle, flow and sharpness, profile and plasticity—focused on Nijinsky's astonishing physical magnetism, caught in the firm net of restricted action—suggested an unfulfilled promise of rape. His shameless innocence and heavy animal charm was provocative and beautiful. Laconic mimicry was scanned to his intimate measure; gestures while logical were legible in a cursive short hand. Here was a mind dominating bodies in an intense interrogation of the roots of movement. A specialist anatomized the body of ballet. Nijinsky transcended any historic or theatrical Greece. Decoration was lushly present, but choreography dominated. Effectively, both faun and nymphs were costumed in transparent movement. Accustomed to an artificial grammar which had been contrived over three centuries for extreme legibility needed in opera houses, Nijinsky now concentrated on both its reversal and extension. Only a trained dancer could find such a flexible springboard to launch him into new dimensions. Duncan danced, explored space, new music, and the floor, but left no immediate issue. The Faun deliberately walked; walking took the place of legato movement. Was walking dancing? It was also dancing. Stage-dancing, already revitalized by steps borrowed from the folk, was now seen to be capable of visual extension past virtuosity. But only virtuosos could penetrate its implications.

382.

379.

* Trans. George Wooley.

379.

380.

381.

379, 380. Precedents. Greece, c. 500 B.C.   381. Faun. Paris, 1912.

382–84. *Faune*. New York, 1916.

MODERNITY: Sex as Sport

385.

386.

JEUX
(The Tennis Game)
May 15, 1913
Paris
Théâtre des Champs Elysées

Priority:
Jeux was the first ballet in our time to capitalize on a contemporary theme—visually, musically, and in its narrative pretext. While sport was its ostensible subject, tennis was but a metaphor for psychological patterns in modern manners. *"La vie moderne,"* which Baudelaire had defined in dandyism as moral elegance seventy-five years before, had never attracted ballet, although it had been a staple of lyric theater, drama, and boulevard comedy. Nijinsky, the choreographer, was handed sport as a springboard; his invented incident derived from his life with Diaghilev. It was not love poeticized, made satirical or fantastic, but a *ménage à trois* charted. Few dancers before had translated private tension into public parable.

Since the Renaissance, gallantry of the gods had done duty for constant comment on *l'amour*. In *Jeux* the map of give and take in a love-set was designed for a threesome

rather than mixed doubles. Nijinsky established an immediacy close to Post-Impressionist painting. His plastic profiles were not "beautiful," as ballet was supposed to be, so his formal reversal seemed harsh or "ugly." He was attracted by Gauguin, not to the South Sea dreams, but to his structure of formal solidity and contained gesture; Bakst imagined the décor as a private park in the intimist style of Bonnard or Vuillard. With *Jeux*, which in 1913 Diaghilev wished to date "as of 1930," theatrical dancing drove deep into the twentieth century.

Precedent:
Motives from athletics had been used by Luigi Manzotti (1835–1905) for *Sport* (1897), one of a series of huge Milanese dance spectacles; the music-hall stage introduced numbers based on horse racing, yachting, etc. Children's and adult games—blindman's buff, hide-and-seek—provided skeletons for composition in masquerades and early ballets, while contests of the Roman arena had figured in ballets by Viganò and much earlier masters. Although athletic, these had a martial rather than a sportive air. Plate 32 in Part Two of Lam-

branzi's *New and Curious School of Theatrical Dancing* (1716) shows a danced tennis game.

Politics:
Diaghilev asked Jacques-Émile Blanche, a shrewd society painter and social historian, to suggest a frame for presenting Nijinsky as Modern Man. Proposals, aesthetic and political, involving implications of a mechanized industrial future, were in the air. Futurism, glorifying the machine, war, and the dynamism of objects, was an advance-guard movement with which Cubism and all progressive plastic research was confused. Nijinsky censored the Machine; it was man's psychological possibility he pioneered, even into realms of the polymorphous perverse. He did not feel industrial society (although he adored automobiles) the way he knew high life in Petersburg and Paris, his domestic relationship to Diaghilev, and classic dancing. Marcel Proust and Colette wrote parallels in prose. The revival of Olympic Games by Baron Pierre de Coubertin (Athens, 1896; Stockholm, 1912) gave a new image of international sport as the virtuoso province of an amateur élite. Ballet as advance-guard art, the dancer as athlete, love as a triangular tennis match gave Diaghilev a satisfactorily provocative succession to the scandal of *Faune*.

Jeux also marked the opening of Auguste Perret's Théâtre des Champs Elysées, a keystone of modern architecture, the most important auditorium since Garnier's Opéra (1873). It was decorated by the painter Maurice Denis and the sculptor Antoine Bourdelle with themes inspired by Isadora Duncan* and the Russian ballet. Diaghilev's troupe, after four years, was enshrined. Ballet seemed secure for the first time as an autonomous art, independent of opera houses, in full equality with music and theater.

69.

---

385. Nijinsky as student. St. Petersburg, 1907.

386. Nijinsky as tennis player. Paris, 1913.

* Bourdelle's bas-relief was based on Isadora's body; different heads for the nine muses appeared on the same Junoesque torso.

Plot or Pretext:

Dusk in a private park off the Bois de Boulogne. Shadowy chestnuts. A ball bounds on stage; Nijinsky, in a red tie, white tennis clothes, with racquet, bounds after it. Too dark for a game, he is bored. Two girls in sport dress follow. Their three-sided flirtation is no imitation of a game with rules, but an extension of it into modern gallantry —a triangular design; acid, brittle, cynical. Combinations in choreography include the boy alone, two girls, girls and boy; finally, boy alone. There is a pervading atmosphere of leisure-class ennui, of post-adolescent love and self-love. It was *Design for Living* as a *pas de trois*, a high comedy of manners in motion, a modern Marivaux twenty years before Noel Coward.

Production:

First planned in London, June, 1912, the work was completed that fall in Venice. Debussy accepted Diaghilev's commission of ten thousand gold francs. The dancers called

387.

the rehearsals "arithmetic" classes; with no tunes to follow, they were forced to count. Bakst's first idea for Nijinsky's costume, denoting more soccer than tennis, was rejected for one suggested by the practice uniform of the imperial ballet school. Before anything else, this champion was a dancer. Tamara Karsavina and Ludmilla Shollar, both exceptional dancers, were his partners. Karsavina was the most stylish, intelligent, and proficient of Diaghilev's ballerinas. Her cool elegance as doll or princess was here transformed into the air of a young *grande dame*, already an experienced flirt. There was little "real" dancing; Nijinsky crossed the stage at first in two huge leaps, but relied more on posturing in abrupt snatches of fluid pantomimic gesture. A projection beyond *Faune*, not as schematic or restricted, seemingly more playful and spontaneous, the tiff between the two girls, their badinage and reconciliation, was compared to cinema.

On the dancer as athlete Jacques Blanche quoted the great tennis player Suzanne Lenglen:

"Daily exercises introduced me to Greek sculpture, whose grandiose beauty is due to the essential rhythm of arms, torso, and lower members, stretched and ordered by athletics, whether bow, javelin, or discus. Tennis-players follow this almost automatically. Having gained the Davis Cup, if I am professional today, I owe it to my hours spent in the Louvre. There are no two ways of serving and receiving a ball in flight."

While musicians (like Debussy) had contempt for Dalcroze as a second-rank composer, and stage producers (like Gordon Craig) saw he had slight interest in theater, it is probable that his method of Eurythmics, or what Nijinsky used of it, helped him analyze his music relative to motion measured. Dalcroze offered a logical structure on which he improvised, altered,

and built without reference to the traditional academy.

350.
423.

388.

389.

387. Diaghilev, *c.* 1914.

388. Nijinsky as soccer player. Paris, 1913.

389. Bakst by Picasso, *c.* 1917.

203

390.

391.

392.

390. Shollar, Nijinsky, Karsavina. Paris, 1913.

391, 392. Nijinsky. Paris, 1913.

393.

394.

395.

393, 394. Shollar, Nijinsky, Karsavina. Paris, 1913.

395. *Le Train Bleu*. Paris, 1924.

RUSSIAN BALLET: Rite and Revolution

LE SACRE DU PRINTEMPS
(The Rite of Spring)
May 29, 1913
Paris
Théâtre des Champs Élysées

Priority:

Nijinsky's two previous works, *Faune* for eight, *Jeux* for three dancers (all soloists) framing him, were preparatory. Now he used the full company without himself. For music, he was assigned Stravinsky's stupendous score, surpassing sonorities and rhythms hitherto imagined. This colossal fanfare, ostensibly an evocation of prehistory, formally announced our twentieth century in its compulsive accelerating tensions and explosions. The music survives, our era's criterion of innovative genius; the ballet as first produced was lost after six performances. Subsequent revivals have never found choreography to equal the score. As interpreted by the composer, from 1930 to 1967, Nijinsky got no credit for the overwhelming visio-aural impact of its première. In 1967, due to Stravinsky's rediscovery of notes guiding the choreographer, after half a century, we find he then considered Nijinsky as an efficient, and powerful collaborator. Due to circumstance that always obliterates much important choreography —in this case, Nijinsky's break with Diaghilev—small justice has been accorded the dancing, except in brilliant essays by Jacques Rivière,* and now, in Robert Craft's fine publication of documents (New York, 1969).

Giving a first impression of "gymnastics" rather than "choreography" (the former "mechanical" *per se*, the latter "beautiful"), Nijinsky's work again violated previous aesthetics, forcing new notions of what was proper or possible. As Stravinsky wrote, "A method is replaced; a tradition is carried forward to produce something new." Listing precedents in four centuries, we realize how unique is true novelty. Dance elements in *Le Sacre*

stemming from past practice are nothing in comparison to its tremendous newness, its correspondance to the need for expressing a new era by the evocation of weather, tribe, race, and sex. Nijinsky invoked controlled hysteria. His discontinuous confrontations were asymmetric, knock-kneed, spasmic. Rivière wrote, "An absolutely pure work, harsh, bitter, . . . complete, brutal, . . . all raw, . . . undigested; . . . frank, limpid and coarse . . . a sociological ballet; we are present when man's movements are not individualized."

The score, though proposing a folk climate, was more universal than ethnic; early critics associated broken rhythm and jagged harmony with Cubism, announced by Picasso's *Demoiselles d'Avignon* (1907). Cubist theory or images had no real part, but the aura of Cubist revolt, strangeness, assertion, separation from past metaphysic had an echo. Beauty was disengaged from habit. Stravinsky's sound was split from former hearing.

The shock, which cannot be recovered, lay neither in Nijinsky's sensuality (more impersonal than in *Faune*), nor in exoticism (more unfamiliar and provocative than *Schéhérazade*), but in its serious charmlessness. *Le Sacre* was seriously ugly, a manifesto against tyrannical symmetry or timid dislocation that had governed ballet since its beginning. Massing bodies as collective forms of focal importance rather than insistence on individual soloists appeared as unprecedented reversal. Style was *en dedans* rather than *en dehors* (turned in, not out). Pagan Russia was a metaphor for unconscious mind; a fictive prehistory permitted tradition to be wiped out. At the same time, this appeared as another Futurist program, akin to those in other directions that Italian or Russian painters and poets were pursuing. For a future, blind energy, rather than man, was proposed as self-willed, merciless,

mindless, unloving, impersonal, mechanical, superhuman, triumphant. Nijinsky's mute mob of throbbing bipeds responding to the seasons alone denied four centuries of humane art. Nuclear fission in miniature, his hero was nature, without aim or romance save in muscular action.

Precedent:

Possibly Gorsky's or Fokine's† choral dances for Borodin's opera *Prince Igor* were suggestive, but Nijinsky took no steps from ethnic sources; he invented an idiom. In 1911, the painter-explorer Nicholas Roerich was with Stravinsky at the house of Princess Tenisheva at Talankino, near Smolensk. She had opened a school for peasant handicraft, including song, patterned after William Morris and Tolstoi. Her collections of folk art had prompted progressive stage-designers, chiefly for Muscovite private (as opposed to state-supported) opera. Stravinsky's *Firebird* (1910) ended with a wedding combining church and folk ritual. Finishing it, he imagined "a solemn pagan rite; wise elders seated in a circle watching a young girl dance herself to death. They were sacrificing her to propitiate the god of spring." Nijinsky diabolically informed a London reporter "the whole spectacle had been designed with the most reverent reliance on existing records of Muscovite life in the fourth century before Christ," of which there were none. The importance of Marie Rambert, who was now clarifying Dalcroze's plastic musical method for Nijinsky, has never been fully acknowledged. Her guidance, based on Stravinsky's detailed chart of his score's metric, provided the dancer with means to harness movement to music. Roerich's synthetic ethnography— the guiding mode for his scenic designs derived from Gauguin's sophisticated primitivism—invoked Yarilo (Erilo, possibly Eros?), Slavonic god of spring and first sowings, ithyphallic and uncontrolled. The Orthodox Church for-

396.

423.

---

* *Nouvelles Études* (Paris, 1947), pp. 69–97.

† Fokine was Diaghilev's first choice for the ballet early called "The Great Sacrifice." He refused; the price was not right. Diaghilev then considered Gorsky.

bade his "satanic games." The virgin chosen as his bride is surrounded by a *khorovod* (possibly derived from Greek *choros*). Yarilo makes grain grow; in summer, his straw image was burned at sunset with drink and dance.

Politics:

Five years before the October Revolution, Diaghilev glorified popular rather than imperial aspects of Russian power, daemonic, undeniable, in a collaboration that would never have been permitted in any tsarist opera house, which would be heard in Russia only some thirty years after 1917.

Not since the battle for Romanticism at the debut of Hugo's *Hernani* (February 25, 1830) had theater seen such spontaneous violence. The scandal, which Diaghilev's permanent advance-guard always aspired to repeat, was *not* granted London, where a lecture was offered before the performance. Not only Philistines were shocked; Gordon Craig, lover of Isadora, prophet of a "new theater," complained the dancing was too material, projecting too much sweaty over-stimulation.

Le Sacre was a watershed. Its primitivistic, self-intoxicated spasms magnetized Germans and Central Europeans. Duncan had been an anti-academic apostle of sweetness and light, promising unlimited optimism. Nijinsky and Stravinsky plumbed darker sources in the psyche. One school of Freudian- (or rather Jungian-) oriented dancers, led by Mary Wigman (b. 1886), herself a Dalcroze pupil, began to present themselves as a priesthood, improvising an idiosyncratic grammar. Others, led by Rudolph von Laban (1879–1958), Wigman's teacher, pursuing the "mechanistic" aspect in Nijinsky's (and Dalcroze's) movement, attempted to mold a basic body mechanics (eukinetics); absorbed in biomorphic research, they abandoned traditional virtuosity and theatrical ex-

citement for individual expressionism. From these emerged the self-styled modern (concert) dance, which never embodied a central technical system, nor a repertory capable of transmission. But *Le Sacre* and, almost as importantly, *Les Noces* (1923) revealed limitless resources within a revitalized academy, when propelled by Diaghilev's catalysis of earth-shaking music and dance.

Plot or Pretext:

Stravinsky corrects the usual title to "The *Coronation* of Spring: (a picture of pagan Russia in two acts)." It details the rebirth of life after winter sleep, also a metaphor of deep changes in adolescent sexuality. Apotheosis of the volcanic crack of winter ice in old Russia's April, Stravinsky recalled it from his childhood.

I. Lush green hillside: Nature's awakening ("scratching, gnawing, wiggling of birds and beasts"). Auguries of spring. Boys enact a mock abduction ritual. Girls join in a round dance. Games of rival clans. Procession of the Wise Elder. Earth worship.

II. Barren steppes with sacred stones; three poles topped by ox skulls. Mystic circle of virgins. Choice and dedication of a chosen maiden. Summoning of tribal ancestors. Sacrificial dance; the virgin's self-immolation.

Production:

In 1967, Stravinsky recapitulated his method: "The score records most of my original plan of choreographic movement, and in this plan an unfamiliar analysis of rhythmic structure. As a record of a composer's conception of choreography it must be one of the most explicit in existence if only for the reason that the composer was attempting to translate his music into a language the choreographer could understand. My method of translation was to mark the principal choreographic accents and phrase units, which were seldom coterminous with the accents and phrases of the music.

In addition, I canceled the metrical units of the music on the assumption that to count beats instead of measures of irregular lengths would approximate ballet routine; but on this point, and after re-examining the score, I have changed my mind: I consider now that it would have been easier to follow the prosody and meters of the music."

Nothing was comfortable in performance; dancers in heavy peasant flannels were drenched in sweat. Elders in long beards, flaxen wigs, and conical hats huddled together, shaking, quivering. General paroxysms; the Shaman, repository of tribal secrets, was spread-eagled over earth, lowered to kiss it. An ancient woman instructed adolescents. "Scarlet groups would constantly dominate the stage in certain passages for horns and trumpets, while violins or flutes carried the sense of white on grey, or orderly ritual or wavering uncertainty" (W. A. Propert). The entranced victim is dedicated to the sun. Her ecstatic self-sacrifice: "A mad innocent dance, of an insect, of a kid fascinated by a boa constrictor, a dance of the assembly-line" (Cocteau). Her rigid corpse, raised high to the rising sun, is run off-stage. In group dances "terrified women [were] thrown as if by centrifugal force, out of the turning, swarming crowd, lashed by the orchestra's whips, snapped up by the instrumental cyclone" (Émile Vuillermoz).

405.

396.

396. Marie Rambert, *c.* 1930.

207

397.

398. 399. 400. 401.

397. Russian tribal maidens. Paris, 1913.

398–401. Russian tribal elders and maidens. Paris, 1913.

402. "Nijinsky's choreography." Paris, 1913.

403. Stravinsky by Cocteau, 1913.

404, 405. *Sacre* by Barcet. Paris, 1913.

406.

PARADE
"Realistic Ballet in One Act"
May 18, 1917
Paris
Théâtre du Châtelet

Priority:
Parade was a modernist manifesto in ballet terms. Book, music, and décor outweighed Léonide Massine's choreography, which was almost deliberately secondary. The aim and effect were to plunge a public used to the lushness of Diaghilev's pre-World War I spectacles into totally unfamiliar areas. Cocteau called it "realistic" (as against *Schéhérazade*); Apollinaire "superreal," promising Surrealism a decade before its formulation was official. Cocteau as poet-philosopher, Satie as sound-furnisher, Picasso as decorator, Massine as dance-arranger mixed magic from the ordinary, "to rehabilitate the commonplace." Propelled by Cubism's analysis, in a society deranged by the 1914–16 military debacles, improvisation was elevated into method.

Apart from Stravinsky and Nijin-

sky, Diaghilev's first seasons had hardly taken advantage of an advance-guard. Now he combined a team of its standard-bearers, transforming his apparatus from a Russian into an international institution, whose base was no longer Petersburg but Paris. *L'âme slave,* the Slavic soul—alien, quasi-barbaric, mystical—was replaced by *l'originalité outrancière,* outrageous, unprecedented novelty. *Parade*'s originality also lay in its reduced, domestic, anti-opera-house scale. As pure choreography, its virtues lay in Massine's wit, his borrowing from music hall or film, and his quasi-cinematic editing. *Parade* was also the first European concert treatment of American jazz; bands did not appear in Paris until a year later, after the Armistice. Its fragmentation prophesied a new era, the Jazz age of the 'twenties.

In his *Success and Failure of Picasso* (1965), John Berger places *Parade* as no revolutionary program, but, rather, as a bourgeois palliative. "The objective social function which *Parade* performed was to console the bourgeoisie which it shocked." He sets its conscious triviality against the Battle of the Aisne, fought a month before, in which 120,000 Frenchmen died, followed by open mutinies partly inspired by the Russian Revolution. Berger ignores the fact that both Cocteau and Apollinaire had been at war, that the audience was unaware of the scale of loss, that the ballet was an anti-German demonstration on an aesthetic level. "Why *Parade* . . . can be . . . finally dismissed is not because it ignored the war, but because it pretended to be realistic. As a result . . . it shocked in such a way as to distract people from the truth. The audience who shouted *'sales boches'* ['lousy Krauts'] felt, at the end of their evening, more patriotic than ever. . . . A performance of *Les Sylphides* would not have had the same effect." However, what Cocteau and his

collaborators were supporting was the survival of art in terms of a present, despite the madness of men at war. They proclaimed that art was indestructible. The secret in Massine's imperturbable Chinese Conjuror was a metaphor for the creative spirit.

411.

Precedent:
A *parade* is not a showy procession, but a free come-on to attract paying customers before the side show starts. Older than the seventh-century fairs of St. Germain and St. Laurent, where comedians, acrobats, and charlatans performed, it was later immortalized by Daumier and Seurat. As for effects, theaters on the grand boulevards in the early nineteenth century showed elaborate ballet-pantomimes, using as aural accompaniment clashing swords, artillery, cries of the wounded, street noises—ancestors of our sound track. Cocteau had his first idea for *Parade* at the première of *Le Sacre du Printemps.* Identified with Diaghilev since his first Paris season, he wrote, designed posters, and collaborated on an ineffectual Hindu ballet, *Le Dieu Bleu* (Reynaldo Hahn-Fokine-Bakst, 1912), for Nijinsky. His long association with ballet recalls Gautier's the century before. In 1913, he proposed a subject to Stravinsky: a modern fair ground on which an acrobat parades. A clown's megaphone hails mighty David, urging the crowd to go inside and watch him whip Goliath. Diaghilev (perhaps wishing no echo of *Petrouchka*) vetoed it. But Cubism (along with Futurism in Italy, with which Diaghilev was already involved) could not be long denied. Automatic writing, chance, the unconscious, the vernacular mosaic of *papiers collés* presented new structures. Cocteau employed ballet as a "machine to produce a poem."

407.

403.

374.

One sketch for the Parisian Manager's costume-construction by Picasso (rejected) had *"merde"* sten-

---

406. Cocteau by Bakst, c. 1914.

cilled across it. *"Merde"* was the *mot d'ordre* of Alfred Jarry's *Ubu Roi,* first manifesto of the Theater of the Absurd. Jarry addressed his début audience on December 10, 1896, in a curtain speech that might have served *Parade* thirty years later: "It was very important that, if the actors were to be as much like marionettes as possible, we should have fairground music scored for brass and gongs and megaphones. . . ." *Jeux* was a gallant, almost Rococo comedy, updated from Marivaux or de Laclos. *Parade* was mechanized and automated for a megalopolitan audience wholly of the twentieth century.

Politics:

The collaboration, the exact proportions of which are still partisan concern, is a prime example of artistic politics. Douglas Cooper's majestic study of Picasso's theater (1968) assigns him overwhelming priority, heretofore claimed by Cocteau. Massine's memoirs (1968) add little. Documents leave Diaghilev a neutral catalyst (who thought the use of the human voice was going too far). Only Satie's music (with Picasso's front curtain) still exists.

Cocteau, in 1962, recalled that Picasso's colleagues hated him to work with Diaghilev. "The hand of dictatorship lay heavy on Montparnasse and Montmartre then, and Cubism was going through a period of austerity. . . . To do décor for theater, above all for the Ballets Russes, was a crime." Advance-guard artists felt themselves free agents, not yet the property of dealers, museums, or impresarios. Ballet was the sink of bad taste. Diaghilev's ritual premières (according to Cocteau) had their audience in stalls and boxes "playing their appropriate roles. . . . They rebelled, they hooted, they catcalled . . . where a thousand gradations of snobbery, super-snobbery and anti-snobbery, could be seen." Thus, *Parade* was also a

satire against that Paris public which always mistook the free show outside—*hors d'oeuvre*—for the real feast within, for which they were loath to pay or appreciate. It was a polemic against Goliath, the Philistine audience, which never saw below the surface of a new work or movement, in favor of the advance-guard David.

The 1914 war had forced Diaghilev to retreat. Paris and London were besieged. American tours were financial disasters. Nijinsky was gone, nor could Russia provide new dancers. His new team was violently anti-German. (Stravinsky hated Wagner since hearing *Parsifal* in Bayreuth, 1912.) Satie crusaded against overblown orchestral symphonism, preferring to play pianos in cabarets. Cocteau said Satie discovered an unknown dimension, in which one is simultaneously aware of *parade* and essential spectacle. American ragtime pounded on player pianos. Manhattan's skyscrapers loomed, a new exotic version of the Indies. Lacking stars, Diaghilev made poetry, paint, sound, and shock perform. Cocteau felt scandal was desirable; Diaghilev knew it as necessity. The première was only a shade less violent than *Le Sacre*'s. Patriotism as expressed by the light-hearted Gallic wit against heavy Wagnerian symphonism—French against German culture—was involved. Satie was threatened with a lawsuit. The event was a success.

Plot or Pretext:

Picasso's act-drop was a version of Watteau's exiled comedians, as if by a sentimental Sunday painter. It rose to reveal an inner stage crowned by Apollo's lyre. Behind: windows of a city block. A Cubist construction, eight feet high, worn as a costume by the Paris Manager (top hat, pipe, canvas) paces up and down. Whistle. A card reads "Number 1," as in vaudeville. A Chinese Conjuror produces an egg from his shoe, swallows it, breath-

ing fire. Enter the New York Manager, also eight feet tall, built of skyscrapers and wearing red shirt and cowboy boots. The Paris Manager complains his Chinaman was not appreciated. The American announces "Number 2," a small girl in middy blouse who imitates Charlie Chaplin and *The Perils of Pauline,* cranks an auto, takes dictation, drowns on the "Titanic," and plays on the sand. She makes no impression. Enter a comic dummy horse, then two acrobats (whom Proust said were like Castor and Pollux, the heavenly twins). General despair. Finale: If you will only enter our show—inside it is marvelous. The little American girl weeps. The Managers are worn out. The horse collapses. The Chinese magician is philosophical.

409.

410.

412.

411.

Production:

Cocteau managed to have clicking typewriters, but the full range of desired sound effects proved difficult in practice. "It was then that we substituted for the voices the rhythms of footsteps in the silence. . . . Our mannikins quickly resembled those insects whose ferocious habits are exposed on films. Their dance was an organized accident, false steps which were prolonged and interchanged with the strictness of a fugue." Satie, a French master in the line of Rameau—elegant, clear, rational, unpretentious—made a manifesto of his *"musique d'ameublement,"* house-furnishing, to serve, not to star. It would satisfy "useful needs. Art has no part in such needs. Furniture-music creates a vibration; it has no other goal; it fills the same role as light and heat—as comfort in every form." *Tout confort moderne;* Cocteau claimed Satie's contribution was the most audacious: to be simple.

Parade was the latest skirmish in an endless war between tradition and innovation fought once by colleagues of Noverre, later by Perrot, Fokine, Nijinsky. The contest continues.

211

407.

408.

407. Side show. Paris, 1887.

408. *Parade*. Paris, 1917.

409.

410.

411.

412.

409. New York Manager. Paris, 1917.

410. Parisian Manager. Paris, 1917.

411. Chinese Magician. Paris, 1917.

412. Little American Girl. Paris, 1917.

ABSTRACT BALLET: Costume as Décor

TRIADISCHES BALLET
(Triadic Ballet)
September 30, 1922
Stuttgart
Landestheater

Priority:

Termed "ballet"—in its original sense of "involving dancing"—this was, rather, an aesthetic demonstration reconsidering the entire spectrum of man as dancer *(Tänzermensch)*. Contribution by or to dance was nugatory, but the work is significant as a now familiar statement of dehumanization, with bankrupt choreography replaced by costume as décor. Dancers were pieces on a metaphysical board without personality or virtuosity. Movement resembled fluid geometrics. Performers were art students rather than trained dancers. The ballet entered no repertory and had no immediate issue. It was, however, memorable among experiments in circus and theater techniques extending from Italian Futurism to Russian Constructivism. Abstractionism had later echoes in Germany, subsequently in America.

Certain choreographers outside the classical tradition attempted to invent a new syntax. Some experiments were exciting, but, finally, since their movement was monotonous or naive, visual aspects became merely ingeniously repetitive. The philosophy of *Die Neue Sachlichkeit* ("New Objectivity"), new "reality" or functionalism to fit an industrial era—abstract, impersonal—led to anomalies. The *Triadic Ballet*, a presentation of essences, did not function as theater. As Rudolph Arnheim wrote:

". . . pure functionalism does not eliminate the need of stylistic choice. . . . Nor does a reduction to simplest shape produce pure functionality. In the furniture and implements designed at the Bauhaus, we discover by now a preference for elementary geometry, not derived from function but dictated by the character of its makers

and more directly expressed perhaps in Feininger's and Klee's Cubism or Schlemmer's 'Mechanical Ballet' [*sic*] of human robots."*

Precedent:

Oskar Schlemmer (1888–1943), painter, teacher, creator of the *Triadic Ballet*, acknowledged three predecessors in attempting to free man from the bondage of his body ". . . to heighten his freedom of movement beyond its native potential": E. T. A. Hoffmann, whose night fantasy *Der Sandmann* prompted *Coppélia*, with its dancer-automaton; Heinrich von Kleist, whose famous essay on marionettes speculated on superhuman potential; Gordon Craig, whom Schlemmer quoted: "The actor must go, and in his place comes the inanimate figure—the *Übermarionette* ('superdoll')." A contemporary Russian writer, Valery Bryusov, demanded that "we replace actors with mechanized dolls, into each of which a phonograph be built," recalling *Parade*, which, in Cubist terms, used mechanized sounds and shapes to project, not abstract universals, but concrete particulars of modern life. As for movement, he wrote:

"The laws of cubical space are the invisible linear network of planimetric and stereometric relationships. This mathematic corresponds to the inherent mathematics of the human body and creates its balance by means of movements, which by their very nature are determined mechanically and rationally. It is the geometry of calisthenics, eurythmics and gymnastics."

Hence, Schlemmer was aware of Dalcroze as well as Swedish gymnastics. His dances derived something from music hall or night club. The *Triadic Ballet* is relevant as a casuistic experiment attempting to surpass human functions by eliminating humanity. If our anatomy is mere machine, movement can be reduced to mechanics. Schlemmer imitated tidily what Bracelli's etchings, *Bizzarie de varie figure*

(1624), accomplished as fantastic caprice: however geometrical his figures, they still were anthropomorphic; hence their grotesquerie was the more sardonic.

Max Planck's quantum theory (1900), Einstein's essay on photoelectricity and relativity (1905) projected paths past Euclid, where time and space crossed. Over four centuries, ballet masters worked this area, using human anatomy as metaphorical measure. Schlemmer offered a Teutonic cerebration justifying a sentimental attitude towards the sacred future of the machine-soul which might proliferate into choreography: instant ballet by computerized dolls. Stark Young, ablest American theater critic of the 'thirties, wrote of Harald Kreutzberg and Mary Wigman: "What so often happens in the German dancers where there is not rarely a kind of false simplification [is that] German theory is often the patent application of sheer, not to say raw, psychology, . . . often overelaborate in spirit and in essence impure."

Parade was a bridge between Cubism and Surrealism. Neither it, nor the *Triadic Ballet*, had choreographic importance; both were polemics provoking inordinate exegesis. Schlemmer's work can also be read as a repudiation of Cubism. A colleague explained:

"He obviously knew—something we had all forgotten—that of all the visible shapes in nature, there is no such thing as the cube. We at the Bauhaus had placed ourselves under the sign of the right angle. The square was our favorite basic form. . . . Schlemmer placed himself under the sign of the arc, the curve and the circle. From these he formed the image of man, poised in harmonious movement."†

Germany has produced few first-rank dancers. It was not that Schlemmer fought academic classic dance; he borrowed its sym-

83.

409.

---

* Rudolph Arnheim, *Towards a Psychology of Art* (Berkeley, 1966).

† Quoted from Georg Munche, *Blinkpunkt*, in Eberhard Roters, *Painters of the Bauhaus* (New York, 1969), p. 74. See also Walter Gropius (ed.), *The Theater of the Bauhaus* (Middletown, Conn., 1961); Peter Gay, *Weimar Culture* (New York, 1968);

bolic silhouette of a ballerina's skirt. But he inherited no grammar, only inventing costumes whose plasticity provided a minimal idiom, licensing limited motion. Virtuosity lay in their manufacture rather than manipulation.

Politics:

In Moscow, 1825, Count Stroganov had founded a school of industrial art; crediting the independence and classlessness of genius, he encouraged home industry and folk craft (at this time) rather than machine art. Later, William Morris and others attempted to combine handicraft with industry.

During the First World War, the architect Walter Gropius, encouraged by the Grand Duke of Saxe-Weimar, planned "a consulting art center for industry and trades." Weimar had been home for poets —Herder, Wieland, Schiller; here Goethe administered drama. In 1918, a national convention created a German Republic. Gropius proposed that students would be taught both by artists and craftsmen. Combining the local craft school with the art academy under the name of *Staatliches Bauhaus Weimar*, Gropius summoned the painters Feininger, Kandinsky, Klee, and Moholy-Nagy for faculty positions. In 1921, Schlemmer, named "Master of Form," headed the sculpture studio, which developed into a theater workshop. He also danced, calling himself "Walter Schoppe," after a character in Jean Paul's *Titan*. Ideas, demonstrations, and artifacts from the Bauhaus— cut short by Hitler—had world influence and are still active in education, design, and craft.

Gropius, already a famous architect, did not teach. He appointed Johannes Itten, a student of Professor Hoelzel of Stuttgart, perhaps the first philosopher and grammarian of "modern art," to plan a basic program. Itten taught laws of contrast, proportion, and composition, using ancient and contempo-

rary examples. He was Schlemmer's master. In 1921, Itten's *Vorkurs* ("underlying basics") governed student work. In 1922, Paul Klee outlined in diagrammatic form the curriculum and philosophy: "A seven-pointed star is inscribed in a circular band; this band represents the preliminary training that encloses the several materials (glass, stone, wood) and the several courses (construction, colour, composition) and leads to the heart of the star, another circle, in which the double aim of the Bauhaus is proudly displayed: *Bau und Bühne* —building and stage."

While handicraft instruction was on a high level, however, Bauhaus ballet was hardly more than therapy for art students.

Germans, throughout their cultural history, reiterate what "Peter Gay" (Professor William R. Shepherd, Columbia University) calls in his clear study of *Weimar Culture* "the hunger for wholeness." All-embracing proposals confound in paradox; categories pointing to a universal rationale dissolve into vague generalization. In more sinister aspects, simple absolutes lead to some "final solution" to untidy social or political problems. Order has long excited the Teutonic imagination. Tyrannous abstraction, persuasively formulated by great artists from Wagner to Klee, has fortunately been repudiated in the superlative disorder of their masterwork. The Bauhaus, a "complete school for art and life," was impossible in Germany. Its program (except for theater) flourished in exile.

Plot or Pretext:

The intrinsic subject was "the metamorphosis of the human figure and its abstraction." In three parts, the work formed "a structure of stylized dance scenes, developing from humorous to serious." I. Lemon yellow: a gay burlesque. II. Pink: a solemn ceremony. III. Black: a mystical fantasy. "The twelve different dances in eighteen different

costumes are danced alternately by three persons, two male, one female. Costumes are partly of padded cloth, partly of stiff *papier-mâché* coated with metallic or colored paint."

414.

Production:

Schlemmer gives credit for the first tentative performance (1911) to "the dance-team Albert Burger and Elsa Hötzel . . . costumes executed by master craftsman Carl Schlemmer." As an art student in Stuttgart, Oskar Schlemmer received his first impulse toward theater at a concert of Arnold Schönberg's. Continual thinking developed this ballet, which was produced in part in 1916 and in entirety in 1922. In four diagrams Schlemmer reduced the human body to basics: 1. "Laws of surrounding cubical space"— torso sheathed in blocks (resembling Picasso's Managers in *Parade*). "Result: ambulant architecture." 2. "Functional laws of the human body in relationship to space"— typification of bodily forms: egghead; vase-torso (reminiscent of Rodin's *femme-vase*); arms and legs are clubs; joints are balls. "Result: the marionette." 3. "Laws of motion of the body in space"— various aspects of rotation, direction, intersection of space: spinning top, snail, spiral, disk. "Result: a technical organism." 4. "Metaphysical forms of expression: star-shape of the spread hand; the ∞ sign of folded arms; cross-shape of backbone and shoulders; the double head (Picasso's profile-plus-front face); multiple limbs; division and suppression of forms. Result: dematerialization." These, then, were possibilities for man as dancer, "transformed through costume moving in space."

410.

Hans M. Wingler, *The Bauhaus* (Cambridge, Mass., 1969).

413.

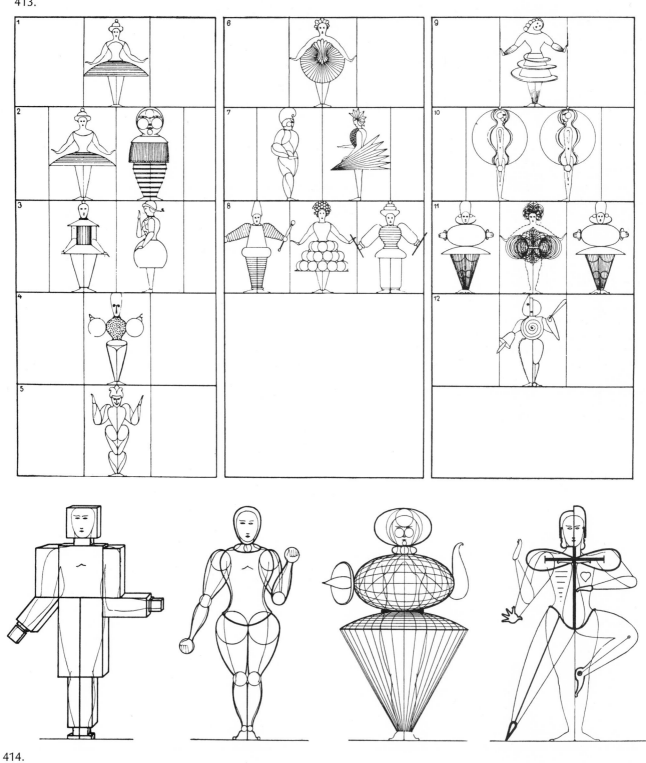

414.

413. *Triadic Ballet*. Concept. Weimar, 1922.

414. Bauhaus ballet: costumes. Weimar, 1922.

415. Photomontage. Weimar, 1921–23.

MOVEMENT AS MUSIC: Symphonism

TANZSYNFONIA
(Dance-Symphony)
March 7, 1923
Leningrad
Marinsky Theater

Priority:
This ballet, which a decade later might have been termed "symphonic" or "abstract," was given but one performance. It indicates paths Soviet classicism might have taken independent of, but parallel to, Diaghilev's new repertory in Western Europe. Feodor Lopoukhov (b. 1886), using Beethoven's Fourth Symphony, stated a formal aesthetic extending the traditional academy. Using the developed idiom, he embarked on an experiment that was immediately repudiated as being contrary to Bolshevik doctrine. Its schematic libretto and strict adherence to musical structure seemed to propose a bloodless purism unserviceable to a proletarian revolution and unintelligible to the masses. The next year, Lopoukhov choreographed *Red Whirlwind*, the first ballet with a Bolshevik pretext.

Already in 1916, he had attempted in private demonstration to synchronize movement with orchestral instrumentation, using dancers as strings, woodwind, percussion. In 1922 he revised Petipa's 1890 choreography for *The Sleeping Beauty*, utilizing an orchestral rather than a piano partition, which had been the practice of Petipa and previous choreographers. For Lopoukhov, orchestral sonority and dynamics were as important as melody and tempi. His own *Tanzsynfonia* had an elaborate libretto imposed on Beethoven's score. Scenery was eliminated, costume reduced to uniform.

In its cast was Georgei Balanchivadze, who had just graduated from the (now) State School, and was then studying piano, solfeggio, composition, counterpoint, and harmony at the Music Conservatory. In 1924, Diaghilev re-

named his final ballet master, aged twenty, Balanchine. *Tanzsynfonia* was prototype for work Balanchine produced in America twelve years later, notably *Serenade* (to Tchaikovsky's *Serenade for Strings*, 1935). *Tanzsynfonia* caused scandal; much of its movement was considered obscene by the erudite balletomane and critic, A. L. Volyinsky, who conducted a private academy along "philosophical" principles. The combination of insistent symphonism and presumed sexuality was shocking to public and professionals, who, cut off by war and revolution from Diaghilev's innovations, had seen little progressive choreography since Fokine's work before 1914. *Tanzsynfonia* was also censured as an impure manifesto by a decadent younger generation.

Precedent:
Perrot, Ivanov, and Fokine recognized the demands of the full orchestra as basis for choreography, rather than the thin profile of piano scores by staff hacks. Alexander Gorsky, some years before Fokine, pioneered in Moscow more individualized and enriched patterns for his *corps de ballet*, based on orchestral instrumentation. From her first appearance in Russia in 1905 to recitals after 1923, Isadora Duncan insisted on symphonic accompaniment. Lopoukhov (whose sister was a Diaghilev soloist), although staying in Russia, was aware of activity in Paris through scores and photographs. His credo, *Paths of the Ballet Master* (1916, unpublished until 1925), expounded his theories on symphonic choreography, including a project for *Tanzsynfonia*. The orchestra as basis for ballet had been rationalized by Dalcroze's method, introduced into Russia before 1914 by Prince Serge Volkonsky, penultimate Intendant of the Imperial Theaters. "Art for art's sake" and its corollaries— "music for the sake of sound," "ballet for the sake of dance"— rather than art as ethics, didactics, or therapeutics, had made consider-

able noise for thirty years. These were metaphysical rather than political premises, and Russia was, as always, however "revolutionary," a state whose policy was ultimately xenophobic and conservative.

Politics:
Russian modernism, experiment, and discovery were not new. Great Post-Impressionist paintings collected by Morosov and Shtukin had been seen early; Cubist painting was shown from 1910. Futurism, a revolutionary poetic movement, was in ferment. The end of the Romanov dynasty marked the liveliest flowering of Russian art since the great thirteenth-century icon painters and architects of Vladimir-Suzdal. Malevich, Larionov, Gontcharova, Kandinsky, Chagall, Burliuk, and others produced on the highest levels of an international advance-guard. But "Futurist" would soon be a libel meaning "traitor to the Revolution"; interest in pure aesthetic became treason. The Soviet system requires conformity, which defeats personal fantasy or unfamiliar plastic formulation. After the Revolution, the ballet, with its former status as an imperial household appanage, came under attack. However, Anatoli Lunacharsky, first Commissar of Education, persuaded Lenin to save the Bolshoi (1919), although Lenin then lacked means to support the simplest schools. But he said: "Theater is not needed as propaganda, but to relax tired workers after daily tasks. And it is still too early to stack archives with our inheritance from bourgeois culture."

Isadora Duncan returned to Moscow (1922), aged 44. Lunacharsky promised her a thousand children to train as instant dancers. Her own revolt was remembered, but now she was ineffectual. Lunacharsky invited Diaghilev to return and direct theater. This was not to be. Fokine was back briefly in 1921; after this, Russian contact with the West declined. Protletkult, a group of politically radical artists, attacked ballet as outworn, but Lunacharsky guaranteed it as a national resource. During the 'twenties there was thrilling activity in literature, architecture, cinema, and theater, with Mayakovsky, Tatlin, Eisenstein, Meyerhold, and Exter. *Tanzsynfonia*, officially unscheduled, was characteristic of this brilliant, short-lived activity.

After 1925, ballet survived with slight choreographic development, due to severe restrictions against international music, art and ideas. Ballet schools, state supported, maintained and increased traditional efficiency; but dance design was retarded. Two notable innovators were Kazian Goleizovsky (1892–1970), a student of Fokine, who in the early 'twenties experimented with acrobatics, and whose "Chamber Ballet" danced barefoot in Duncanesque tunics. Igor Moiseyev (b. 1906) in the late 'thirties and 'forties ingeniously adapted folk forms from city and countryside in a unique expression based on academic training.

The creative experiments of the 'twenties received their official epitaph from Yuri Slonimsky, one of Balanchine's earliest collaborators (1952): "In the 1920's Soviet Ballet went through all the phases of barefoot naturalism, strident constructivism, unnatural plastic expressionism, and erotic orientalism. But time and reality, as usual, exposed the fallacy of the then-prevailing conceptions." Thereafter massive somatic efficiency fills an imaginative vacuum; compare cinema activity of the 'twenties or 'thirties with that of our 'sixties. On February 22, 1969, three items from Moscow were quoted in the *New York Times:* an attack on young scientists for "skepticism, apolitical attitudes, nonclass interpretations of such concepts as democracy, personal freedom and humanism" (*Sovietskaya Rosia*); an attack on twentieth-century lyricism from Andrei Biely to the present (*Pravda*); an attack on radio programs for the armed forces "for presenting too many gloomy songs" (*Krasnaya Zvezda*). Lenin had also said: "Liberty is a bourgeois prejudice."

Plot or Pretext:
Subtitled "The Magnificence of the Universe," the ballet attempted to chart the entire cycle of life from its origins. I. Birth of light. II. Triumph of life over death. Growth of life (movement) out of preceding history. III. Nature's awakening in the spring sun. Grand adagio. IV. Joy of existence. Mirth of the

416.

Pithecanthropoi, or original inhabitants of our planet. Finale: "The Cosmogonic Spiral."

Production:
In Part I Andrei Lopoukhov, the choreographer's brother, strode toward the sun, his eyes dazzled by creation. A deep *plié* followed by a rise to *développé à la seconde* was used to express the "arousing of life." Part IV was realized with free movement, acrobatics, *demi-caractère* steps, and a plastic contrast of identical poses, seen front and back.

420.

422.

The ballet was composed for eighteen dancers; the girls, always on toe, wore white blouses and skirts, the boys black breeches and white shirts with black lapels. All wore black shoes to focus on feet and *pointes*. Emil Cooper, the conductor, worked with Lopoukhov for a year, instructing him in orchestration. Critics complained that Lopoukhov's plan had no contact with Beethoven, that its epic structure violated dancing on the scale of chamber music.

Yet, however naive his attempt, Lopoukhov's statement was important as a step toward autonomous choreography with music as governor, outlined in *Paths of the Ballet Master:* I. Choreographic themes should be worked out musically on parallel principles of competition, contrast, development, rather than by inherited formulas or casual steps; II. Music and movement are allied under the rule of rhythm; dance derives from music; III. The musical curve coincides with the dance curve; opposion of angular and curvilinear; IV. Relation of visual and musical tonalities: Major keys are open (*en dehors*); minor keys closed (*en dedans*). A ballet step, even *sur place*, can convey the quality of transient sonority. The placement of major and minor keys (a naive concept of "grace" and "ugliness"), i.e., major is suave and flowing, minor is abrupt and broken.

416. Space concept. Weimar, c. 1922.

219

417.

418.   419.   420.

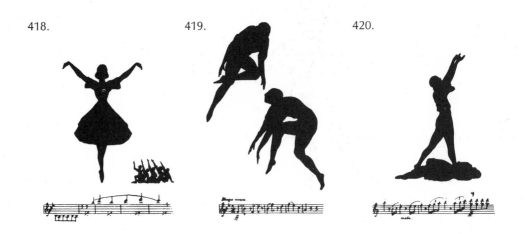

417. *Pas de Deux*. Leningrad, c. 1922.

418–20. *Tanzsynfonia*. Silhouettes. Leningrad, 1923.

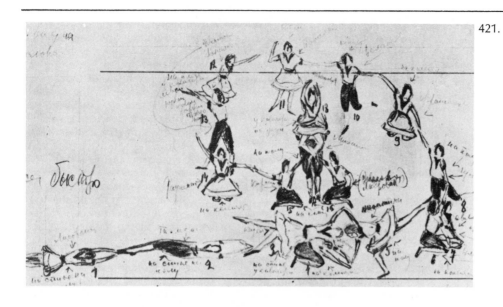

421. Finale, 1922.

422. Finale, 1923.

LES NOCES VILLAGEOISES
(The Village Wedding)
June 13, 1923
Paris
Théâtre Gaîté Lyrique

Priority:
Stravinsky's cantata on a peasant wedding supports the masterpiece of Bronislava Nijinska (b. 1891), Vaslav's younger sister. It was a step beyond *Le Sacre du Printemps*, in the same direction. *Le Sacre* with a larger format was more detailed and picturesque. The rituals celebrated were imagined reconstructions, realistically interpreted. *Les Noces* was a familiar celebration, highly stylized, deliberately monochrome. Drama was heightened by a chorus participating on the same level as dance. Stravinsky called it "a suite of lyrical wedding episodes told through quotations of typical talk (compared to a scene in Joyce's *Ulysses*) . . . in which the reader overhears scraps of conversation without a connecting thread." It was distinguished by unfamiliar sobriety, a concentration of varied but laconic action. It invented its own steps, suggestive of, not identical with, folk dance. Raw color, ethnic charm, signatures of early Diaghilev, were gone. A whole company performed, rather than soloists. Clear danced statements, driving toward essence rather than rhetoric, an area indicated by Nijinsky, were achieved in absolute synthesis by his sister. Timeless, pure, potent, now in an excellent revival by the Royal Ballet, it remains one of a half-dozen great ballets in repertory.

Precedent:
There had been interest in Russian folklore since the early nineteenth century on a level of systematic ethnography. Pushkin wrote ballads in popular idiom; foreign choreographers (Didelot, Saint-Léon, Petipa) as well as native (Glouzkovsky, Valberkh, Ivanov), used national themes and steps more or less authentically. Diag-hilev produced richly decorative ballets (*Firebird, Coq d'Or, Midnight Sun,* 1910–15) in styles ranging from brilliantly stenciled folk toys to angles and splinters in a Cubist idiom. *Les Noces,* while avoiding highly colored folk motifs or any trace of Cubism, presupposed them both in its intense distillation.

Politics:
The idea came to Stravinsky while composing *Le Sacre.* In 1915 Diaghilev proposed *La Liturgie,* planned with the Yugoslav sculptor Ivan Mestrović, to exploit gold-encrusted vestments, icons, and liturgy in the Greek Orthodox Mass. Stravinsky, a severe communicant, condemned such religious exploitation. Instead he turned to collections of folk verse and song. Nijinsky, who replaced Fokine, was in turn replaced by Léonide Massine, who after temporary defection, gave way to Bronislava Nijinska, an able pupil of Cecchetti, Fokine, and her brother, in 1923. Diaghilev's administration resembled the succession of cabinets in a government. Ballet masters, like prime ministers, were summoned, dismissed, recalled. Nijinska had returned to Russia at the outbreak of war and started her own choreographic career. She rejoined Diaghilev in London, 1921, contributing new numbers to his revival of *The Sleeping Beauty.* Influenced by her brother's innovation, she became a distinguished ballet mistress, the best of her sex, as well as an influential teacher.

The Russian ballet of tradition was in exile; it had once been an imperial agency. *Le Pavillon d'Armide* was an echo of Catherine the Great's homage to Peter the Great. *Prince Igor, Le Coq d'Or, Thamar,* and *Le Sacre du Printemps* glorified the race in terms of Russian history. *Les Noces* praised the strength and quality of the Slavic peoples for its permanence. It made no decorative reference to a colorful past; it was not nostalgic over the loss of tsardom. Diaghilev, who had been a courtier, was quick to hail the October Revolution, inserting a red flag in the finale of *Oiseau de Feu,* to the distress of the Russian Embassy; Stravinsky orchestrated *The Volga Boat Song* as a substitute for the imperial anthem. Diaghilev did not go back; the old order was over, the new one set. Ominous attacks against international advance-guard standards in art, the equation of Bolshevism with a lowest common denominator of taste at the moment he triumphed with the School of Paris, rendered his return unlikely, although he worked with Sergei Prokofiev (1891–1953), a loyal if suspect Soviet composer (*Le Pas d'Acier,* 1928; *Le Fils Prodigue,* 1929), until his death.

Plot or Pretext:
The ballet bears no detailed libretto; a few stage directions are indicated in the score.

I. 1. House of the Bride. She wears enormously long rope-like tresses, arranged in a variety of elaborate patterns by attendants. 2. House of the Bridegroom; he is prepared. 3. Departure of the Bride. "Everyone leaves the stage, accompanying her. The mothers of Bride and Groom enter from opposite sides of the stage." Lament. "Both mothers leave. The stage is empty."

II. The Wedding Feast. "The Bride's Mother leads her daughter to her son-in-law. . . . One of the guests chooses a man and his wife from among the friends and sends them to warm the bed for the bridal pair. . . . Bride and Groom embrace." Toward the close, the bed-warming couple return. The bridal pair is escorted to their room. The door is shut. Fathers- and mothers-in-law are seated before it; guests face them.

Production:
There were many stages before a noble starkness was fixed. Stravin-

81.

427.

sky first wished for an orchestra of some one hundred fifty pieces. By 1921, he essentialized a choir, underlined by percussion instruments with and without pitch, and four grand pianos, on stage. Nathalie Gontcharova's early costume sketches were in bright folk pattern. Later, she found perfect uniforms for girls and men—skirts, blouses, pants, in coarse brown-black linens. Scenery was reduced to essential platforms, suggesting timber cabins. "Though Bride and Groom are always present, the guests are able to talk about them as if they were not there—a stylization not unlike Kabuki theater."

Press and public were generally uncomprehending; there was no acrobacy, no exciting personalities. Music was harsh, unyielding. Nothing was pretty, nor yet was it overly exotic. Nijinska's firmly structured groups were undecorated in their strong human architecture. A poor rather than a rich style was proposed. Again Diaghilev provided an abrupt shift in taste for which a great part of his public was rarely prepared.

The School of Paris had established itself, thanks in great part to Picasso's décor for Massine's ballets: *Parade* (1917), *Le Tricorne* (1919), *Pulcinella* (1920). Massine made theatrical dances, impressive in his own and others' performance but seldom on a level of innovation. He efficiently suggested past forms or national character; he lacked training or authority in the classic academy. Nijinsky and Nijinska were legitimate heirs of three centuries of practice; they took a given language and transformed it. They attacked choreography as sculptors whose tools followed protuberances and hollows in music, its silence, and sonorities, without reference to fixed formulas. The frame was music, not painting; the means choreography, not mimicry or atmosphere. *Faune* and *Sacre* were visually sumptuous, but the décor for one was inconsistent,

the other suspect. *Jeux* was luxuriously neutral. *Les Noces* in its poverty, its negation of color, was a positive complement to choreographic impulse. Now, preoccupation was dance more than theater. New possibility for human anatomy in orchestrated structure was the material—the unique power of dance as measured movement, which the Nijinskys pushed to limits that within two decades would be the presupposed syntax for twentieth-century progressive tradition.

423.

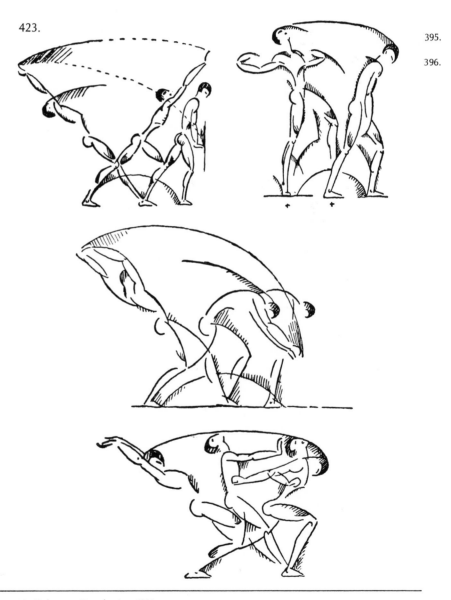

395.

396.

423. Dalcroze: Eurythmics, 1916.

424.

425.

424. Marriage feast. Russia, c. 1850.

425. *Les Noces*. Paris, 1923.

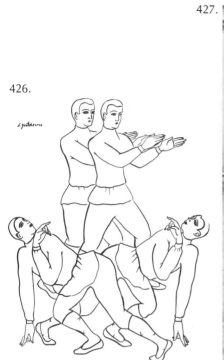

427.

428.

426. Groomsmen. Paris, 1923.

427, 428. Rehearsal. Monte Carlo, 1923.

APOLLON MUSAGÈTE
(Apollo, Leader of the Muses)
June 12, 1928
Paris
Théâtre Sarah Bernhardt

Priority:
Since Nijinsky's *Jeux* (1913), the classic academic traditional idiom enjoyed slight impetus forward. Diaghilev's revival of Petipa's *Sleeping Beauty* (1921) confirmed the vitality of an inheritance without extending it. Léonide Massine's best work (1915–23) depended on revivals of past styles or national motifs expressed in pantomime. With *Apollon*, George Balanchine, in the guise of inverted homage to *la danse d'école*, recapitulated three centuries of formal development while projecting an unlimited future. Supported by Stravinsky's reillumination of many of ballet's most articulate composers, *Apollon* is a synthesis of an academy transformed and launched toward twentieth-century classicism. Focusing on four first-dancers, one male virtuoso with his trio of ballerinas, Balanchine, in a cumulative succession of solo variations, duets, and supported adagio, introduced unfamiliar silhouettes and novel plasticity, renovating patterns assumed outworn by inventing sequences of an intimate and, at the time, outrageous originality. Newness caused laughter; deformation or inversion of classroom routines evoked dismay, providing Diaghilev with still another proof of his power to shock, and revitalize.

Son of a composer famed as the "Georgian Glinka" and a skillful classic dancer, Balanchine graduated from the State Ballet School, Leningrad, in 1921, and later studied at the Musical Conservatory. After leaving Russia in 1924, he abruptly became Diaghilev's final ballet master, despite his extreme youth. From the beginning, Balanchine had been closely associated with Stravinsky, with *Pulcinella* (in Russia, 1920) and *Le Chant du Rossignol* (for Diaghilev, 1925), and

the continuing association between choreographer and composer over fifty years has resulted in the dominant international repertory for the second half of the century.

Precedent:
Le Pas de Quatre (1845), canonizing four Romantic ballerinas, is a forerunner, with one important difference. Music had been tactful but unimportant; emphasis was on a capitalization of four exploitable personalities. In *Apollon*, transformed echoes of Lully, Handel, Rameau, Glinka, Delibes, and Tchaikovsky distilled, reversed, enlarged, and partnered designs grander than any single star dancer's requirements. *Apollon* emphasized dancing, not dancers, being no flashy divertissement, but a coherent extended composition. Its atmosphere was like that of some unhurried *ballet de cour*, from deliberate narrative prelude to crowning apotheosis. Stravinsky, fixed in the mind of the public as a Slavic nationalist, tried "to find a melodism free of folk lore." His subject suggested "not so much a plot as a style."

The year before, Jean Cocteau and Stravinsky had produced the nobly static oratorio *Oedipus Rex*, its text in Latin; Picasso's recent monumental paintings reminiscent of Pompeian murals and incised Greek mirror backs led to a Neoclassic revival. But allusions to antiquity in *Apollon* were less pictorial or decorative than metrical and rhythmic and lay ultimately in the serene ambience of its steps. A modern Parisian rather than a Hellenistic or Napoleonic vision of Parnassus, it invoked echoes of the Versailles of Louis XIV, who also danced the Sun.

Politics:
The Library of Congress, Washington, awarded Stravinsky the commission (1927), stipulating, due to its small stage, no more than six dancers. Adolph Bolm (1884–1951), a former important character

dancer for Diaghilev, then teaching in Chicago, made dances suitable for his own students. Diaghilev availed himself of the published score after the American première. His company, now in exile and separated from Soviet sources, was no longer strong in soloists, although he had recruited some excellent English dancers. With Balanchine came a handful of well-trained Russians from the Leningrad school, including Tamara Gevergeva and Alexandra Danilova. Serge Lifar (b. 1905), a pupil of Bronislava Nijinska in Kiev, interested Diaghilev, who wished to display him as a potential star. Balanchine took advantage of Lifar's brusque coltish athleticism with such insight that sometimes it was assumed Lifar was *Apollon's* choreographer as well as hero.

Diaghilev was pleased with his success, but claimed Balanchine's variation for Terpsichore was "too long" and temporarily cut it. The real reason was that he was enraged by Lord Rothermere, the press baron, who had paid for two seasons in London and was promising a third. He had demanded his protégée, Alicia Nikitina, be given a leading role, which was done, although Balanchine desired Alexandra Danilova for Terpsichore. When Rothermere unexpectedly withdrew his support, Diaghilev vented his fury on the dancer, eliminating her exquisite solo.

Plot or Pretext:
Stravinsky wrote: "The real subject of *Apollon* . . . is versification, which implies something arbitrary and artificial to most people, though to me art is arbitrary and must be artificial." Hence, its drama derives from an ordering in art.

I. Prologue: Night. Birth of Apollo: on a high rock, his mother, Leto, in birth pangs, delivers him. Bound in swaddling bands, he is freed by attendant nymphs, who bring him his divine lute. Tentatively he starts to move, from infantile hesitance to mature proficiency. The nymphs, setting his hand on a lyre, demonstrate music's power. The young god teaches himself to dance by measuring rhythm, tone, and accent.

II. Parnassus: Sunlight. Apollo, still boyish and angular, grows to full godhead. Calliope (poetics, metrics, rhythm), Polymnia (mimicry), finally, Terpsichore (gesture, dance) offer their symbols—scroll, mask, and lyre—and are recognized by his divine authority after each shows her special talents. Calliope's variation, with cello solo, was suggested by one of Pushkin's Alexandrine couplets. Polymnia's *allegro* scurries on toe points. Terpsichore's *allegretto* is climaxed by four huge sustained *attitudes*. The muses quit the stage for Apollo's grand variation: broad leaps, delicate beats, sweeping arms—a huge, complex definition of the modern male dancer as heroic athlete. The ensuing duet with Terpsichore, his chosen companion, leads logically from the final pose of Apollo's variation to an echo or "quotation" from Michelangelo's *Creation of Adam*, in which God's fingertip summons Adam to plastic life. Their *pas de deux*, punctuated by peculiar and ingenious supporting figures, also suggests flying and swimming.

In the lively coda, Apollo drives the Muses, harnessed *à la troika* for his chariot, to a brisk gallop. Then, in grave procession, the god ascends Parnassus. In the original, a horse-drawn quadriga descended from heaven.

Production:
Diaghilev, desiring to distinguish a reborn classicism from outworn versions of Greece formulated by such archeological painters as Alma-Tadema or Puvis de Chavannes, commanded scenery from a Sunday painter, André Bauchant, in the line of the Douanier Rousseau, but blander. In truth, Diag-

hilev had need of a contemporary Poussin, and such décor was finally provided by Pavel Tchelitchew for the Buenos Aires production of 1942. In 1928, however, fearful of identification with such "Greek" works as *Narcisse* (1911), *Daphnis and Chloe* (1912), or *Midas* (1914)—to say nothing of Nijinsky's *Faune*—Diaghilev wished a naive, or at least a new, eye on traditional antiquity. Bauchant provided equivalent to neither music nor dancing.

The costumes, after several compromises between full-length ballet skirts and modern sport dress, were designed by the great *couturière* Madame Chanel, who bound the Muses' bodices with men's cravats. Apollo, wigged in gold, wore a scarlet tunic. In recent revivals Balanchine eliminated all adornment, concentrating on naked structure, as generated by melodic and rhythmic plasticity in the music. He said: "A choreographer can't invent rhythms; he only reflects them in movement. The body is his medium and, unaided, the body will improvise for a short breath. But the organization of rhythm on a grand scale is a sustained process. It is a function of the musical mind."

The élite at the first Paris perform-

ance was shocked at both musical style and substance. Stravinsky used only strings. After *Le Sacre* and *Les Noces* with their full apparatus, this was taken for poverty. There were but four soloist dancers. Detection of echoes from three centuries was interpreted as an anthology of familiar quotations; homage to Delibes and Debussy was all but insulting. Educated by Stravinsky's cacophony, had we not got beyond revivalism? The score was dismissed as pastiche, the choreography as perverse. Diaghilev had tamed a hypersnobbish Parisian public, which followed fashion at one remove. It was the index of his daring that he led rather than listened to it.

In spite of this, *Apollon* enjoyed a *succès d'estime* among the cognoscenti whom Diaghilev always commanded. Stravinsky attributed the ultimate triumph and lasting power "to the beauty of Balanchine's choreography, especially to constructions such as the 'troika' in the coda, and the 'wheelbarrow' at the start, in which two girls support a third carrying Apollo's lute. . . . *Apollon* was my first attempt to compose a large-scale work in which contrasts of volumes replace contrasts of instrumental colors."

320.

390.

435.

429.

429. Balanchine and Stravinsky. New York, 1957.

430. 431.

432. 433.

430. Apollo. Greece, c. 320 B.C.

432, 433. "Greek" costumes, 1796 and 1900.

431. Apollo. France, c. 1750.

434.

435.

437.

436.

434–37. *Apollo*. New York, 1956–65.

438.

JARDIN AUX LILAS
(Lilac Garden)
January 26, 1936
London
Ballet Club

Priority:
This specifically English work established a new genre, reaffirming the British genius for narrative gesture. Avoiding virtuosity, its movement remained within the classical grammar, yet connective action told a legible tale, based on musical structure. Pantomime, consistently laconic, fused in dance; although relations between four main characters are complex, motivation is never in doubt. On the first level, the ballet is a miniature tragedy of love denied; on a second, psychological recovery of a past in the present; on a third, a picture of manners in a particular society in history. Its basic subject is the marriage of convenience, in which human emotion is reduced to negotiable commodity.

The cool tact of Antony Tudor's observation and the flow of his design to Ernest Chausson's opulent violin *Poème* construct a durable ballet, but one which, due to its delicacy and evanescence, requires

intensity in expert performance, which it seldom receives. In later work, Tudor strained psychological overtones toward melodramatic vehicles for dancers, but here, stoic irony and intense feeling have kept *Jardin* alive for more than three decades.

Precedent:
Tudor drew from three main sources: the philosophies of Marx, Freud, and Bergson (especially as seen through Proust).* The ballet's characters exist on a particular social level at a moment in time: middle-class England in the post-Victorian epoch. Materially favorable marriage improves family security. Romantic or sexual needs are secondary, however strong. All that is left of passion is memory, increasingly faint. The present is tinctured by a past fleetingly recollected, put in its impotent place by urbane necessity. For social comfort, the prevalent code of manners smothers intrusive, insistent emotion.

Jardin recalls short tales of de Maupassant, Henry James, Chekhov; plays by Pinero and Granville-Barker. Tudor commenced by taking a Finnish story in which a peasant couple in love, about to be married, submit to *le droit du seigneur*. The bride goes to the local lord, but with a dagger. Tudor completely transposed this plot, which recalls *ballets paysans et bourgeois* of the early nineteenth century. He was a pupil of Marie Rambert, the aid to Nijinsky who was herself a student both of Dalcroze and the classic teacher Enrico Cecchetti. Tudor had no chance to see Nijinsky's *Jeux* (1913), a comedy of upper-class manners also set in a park, nor is it likely he was affected by the German Kurt Jooss's *Ball in Old Vienna* (1932), in which the mood was persiflage and the characters types rather than persons. Joos (b. 1901) had broken with academic ballet, attempting to introduce a less artificial dynamism outside the

classic school, but he was restricted by limited apparatus. Tudor was not discontented with ballet, but, viewing Diaghilev's later repertory, made a personal departure, creating mood, character, and dramatic climax within the rich tradition of English pantomime. Tudor served an apprenticeship acting Shaw and Shakespeare in semi-professional companies before he came to ballet. His first work was based on *Twelfth Night*; subsequent choreography depends considerably on narrative structure and gesture.

Politics:
Marie Rambert, having left Diaghilev, opened her own school in London and later organized a small company whose performances as the Ballet Club (1930) provided a seedbed for developing British choreographers and dancers. Tudor, her pupil, became secretary of the Club. By 1931 he had started to compose ballets. In 1926 Madame Rambert introduced another important English dancer, Frederick Ashton, who became principal choreographer of the Ballet Club.

396.

Diaghilev died in 1929; the Russian succession was obscure. English dancers had been able to make their way in his troupe, but always with Russified names. With Diaghilev gone, there seemed slight chance in the Russian orbit. England fell back on her own resources; the next decade saw activity leading toward foundations for the Royal Ballet, its school, repertory, and audience under the inspired leadership of Ninette de Valois, a former Diaghilev dancer of Irish origin. In 1937, Tudor formed his own company. Later, in the United States, he established himself as a ballet master and teacher.

Plot or Pretext:
Moonlight in a garden hedged by lilacs. Ladies and gentlemen in Edwardian balldress. Caroline, the hostess, is about to be wed to a man she cannot love; she receives

442.

---

* Henri Bergson (1859–1941), particularly in his *Creative Evolution* (1907), stressed the role of duration in experience. With time's passage, an observer stores up accumulated experience that becomes a store for conceptual recall. Incidents or objects take on symbolic metaphorical importance, such as Proust's *madeleine* or Tudor's spray of white lilac.

her former lover for the last time. In a contrasting scene the man she will marry bids farewell to his mistress, whom he must abandon. Private feelings are submerged in the public decorum of social dancing, although spasms of true emotion momentarily betray tensions below a smooth surface. Conventional custom, the crushing presence of friends smother a show for natural sentiment. Separate members of the luckless quartet weave a cat's cradle of risk, frustration, vain regret. Always, in this over-scented garden, the exterior world looms—censorious, relentless. Past pales into present. A spray of white lilac is Caroline's sole souvenir of the man she might have married.

Production:

In presentation *Jardin* is less explicit than any verbal description. Packed with suggestive—never literal—detail, it builds a skein of jealous anxiety, guilt, apprehension, loss. At the end, Caroline bids farewell to each guest; by the extension of her hand in varied positions, she reveals her precise attitude to each. Each responds by bodily inclination according to his or her morality, worldly or compassionate. Tudor used leaps both metaphorically and realistically, **as** when, in a climax, the rejected mistress "throws herself" into her lover's waiting arms, risking imminent exposure from the re-entrance of other guests. Narrative short circuits—sequences of almost cinematic cutting—are juxtaposed. At the grand crisis, when Chausson's theme is most assertive, Tudor freezes his group; only Caroline moves, slowly, sideways, front and back, as if almost free to act against a choice already made. "Time has stopped; when it starts again, the lover relinquishes her right hand, which he was about to seize; the husband-to-be takes her left arm; and all know that the moment for rebellion has passed."*

439.

---

* John Percival, "Antony Tudor, Part I: The Years in England," *Dance Perspectives*, No. 17 (1963).

439. *Lilac Garden.* New York, 1950.

440.

441.

440, 441, 443. *Lilac Garden*. New York, 1950.

442. *Lilac Garden*. London, 1950.

442.

443.

FANCY FREE
April 18, 1944
New York
Metropolitan Opera House

Priority:

Fancy Free, the first ballet by Jerome Robbins and an immediate success by the most able native-born American ballet master, remains the sturdiest characteristic national work. Robbins had gained for himself a broad theatrical instruction as well as performing experience. In 1940, he joined Ballet Theater, benefiting by contact with Michel Fokine, whose roles he danced. Intimate with both popular and classical idioms, excellent dancer and sensitive musician, Robbins had been imagining elaborate full-length scenarios for some time. *Fancy Free* involves but six characters—three sailors, two girls, and a bartender—and is a model of construction. Against Leonard Bernstein's witty synthesis of jazz then in fashion and Oliver Smith's translation of musical-comedy décor to opera-house scale, Robbins' fusion of Broadway, Harlem, and Hollywood forms was set on a strong armature of academic ballet. Its journalistic topicality endeared it to a mass audience. Steeped in the popular vocabulary, Robbins deployed it with pert ingenuity and knowing innocence.

Precedent:

In earlier spectacles, such as *The Black Crook* (1866) and *The White Faun* (1868), Italian ballerinas appeared on Broadway in shows that were little more than pretexts for big dance numbers. Fokine, having left Diaghilev and Russia, made miniature ballets for Florenz Ziegfeld's *Follies* (1923). Later, George Balanchine, also a refugee from Russia and Diaghilev, produced ballets for the final *Follies* (1935). In a series of musicals by Lorenz Hart and Richard Rodgers for which he provided the dances (1936–38), the credits included, at Balanchine's insistence, the then-unfa-

miliar term "choreography by." In vaudeville, musical comedy, and films, a brilliant performing tradition in dance was maintained by George M. Cohan, Fred Astaire, Ginger Rogers, James Cagney, Bill "Bojangles" Robinson, Buddy Ebsen, Buster West, and Ray Bolger. Attempts to canonize American archetypes (gangster, cowboy, mechanic) within the framework of the classical ballet were marked by Lew Christensen's *Filling Station* (Thomson-Cadmus) and Eugene Loring's *Billy the Kid* (Copland-French), both 1938.

One of the characters in Léonide Massine's *Les Matelots* (Auric-Pruna, 1925), presented by Diaghilev, was an American sailor. In the 'twenties, U.S. fleets were frequent visitors to the Côte d'Azur, where Ballets Russes collaborators vacationed. In 1927, the first act of the Soviet patriotic ballet *Red Poppy* finished with *Ech Yablochko* ("little apple"), Reinhold Glière's famous sailor dance, with choreography by Lev Lashchilin. Based on a 1917 Civil War folk song, the tune went round the world. The American Gob had succeeded Britain's Jack Tar, when, in 1900, Admiral George Dewey's Great White Fleet circled the globe on a "goodwill" cruise, affirming the United States as a prime seapower.

In W. H. Auden's *The Enchafèd Flood* (1950), there is an extensive analysis of romantic iconography for the symbolic sailor as a young god from the sea. We have seen Neptune-Poseidon, with coral-crowned sea creatures in *Les Nopces de Pelée et Thétis* (1654). Except for popular tradition descending from American vaudeville dancing, Robbins was probably unaware of any of these precursors. However, he had seen paintings of New York life by Reginald Marsh (1898–1954) and Paul Cadmus (b. 1905), satirical comment involving sailors and floozies. Cadmus' *The Fleet's In* (1934), painted for the Public Works of Art project, cre-

ated a national scandal when the Navy objected to public funds being spent on a lampoon of its personnel in their private operations.

Politics:

Fancy Free was first seen when New York was a P.O.E. (Port of Embarkation) for the Western Front during World War II. Sailors in a bar were an appropriate metaphor for abrupt and unsettling contrasts in service and civilian life. Shore leave, when one could be irresponsible, yet subject to military orders, was anxious respite from tension and promised danger. The side-street bar as locus was fixed by W. H. Auden in *The Age of Anxiety* (1948), of which Bernstein, Robbins, and Smith later made a ballet (1950): "When the historical process breaks down and armies organize with their embossed debates the ensuing void which they can never consecrate, when necessity is associated with horror and freedom with boredom, then it looks good to the bar business."

By no accident, one of Auden's four types is a young naval officer. ". . . fully conscious of the attraction of his uniform to both sexes, he looked around him, slightly contemptuous when he caught an admiring glance, and slightly piqued when he did not."

Robbins' dances, undimmed by irony or tragedy, glorifying the sailor's camaraderie, energy, and lechery, corresponded to a need for making something comic, domestic, and lyrical out of a climate that, when considered in any depth, could only be bitter, anarchic, or sinister. In Ballet Theater, the company in which Robbins danced, there had been an influx of Russian themes and dancers of the post-Diaghilev persuasion, stemming from the company's inheritance from Mikhail Mordkin, its artistic founder. Robbins wished to assert a distinct American contrast and a

446.

contemporary flavor. In this he was encouraged by Oliver Smith, who was both director and designer for Ballet Theater.

Plot or Pretext:
Manhattan; inside-outside a side-street bar. Against the night sky, a street lamp; city lights; square patchwork of signs and windows. A bartender, alone and bored, smokes and spreads war news on his empty bar. In summer whites, three sailors race in and swing around the lamp post, a vaudeville trio. They order beer. Bartender: "Who pays?" As always, when these three cruise, one is tricked into treating his two buddies.

Nothing happens; the night is electric, awaiting ignition. The three share a pack of gum; who can flick its wrappings furthest? Abrupt boogie-woogie; a girl saunters past. No more sharing; each wants her for himself. The competition ends in a small battle. One sailor is floored; the others follow the girl out. Another floozie passes; the remaining sailor buys her a beer. *Pas de deux.* The others return. Three boys for two girls? Individual variations; more drinks; the same sailor pays. Then a fight, the girls lost in a shuffle. One last stick of gum is split three ways. A new babe waltzes by. "Second verse, same as the firs'."

Production:
Oliver Smith's décor was a huge, glowing, neutral space, pricked with night lights. Bernstein's driving score sounded like an overture to a Broadway hit. The sailors—Robbins himself, Harold Lang, John Kriza—flashy and magnetic character dancers, were partnered by Janet Reed and Muriel Bentley, excellent comediennes as well as classical ballerinas. Each understood the manners, atmosphere, and music of 1944 as an historic style, no less full of a special fragrance than 1844, 1744, or 1644. Robbins' own variation was based on the Latin-American *danzon;* he had observed

sailors improvising their own dances in saloons and dance halls from Fire Island to Forty-Second Street.

444.

445.

444. Sailor dance. Russia, 1939.

445. Sailors on leave. New York, 1944.

446.

447.

446. *The Fleet's In!*, 1934.

447. *Fancy Free*. New York, 1944.

448.

449. 450.

448. Bar scene, wartime. New York, 1944.

449. Sailor. New York, 1944.

450. Sailor and girl. New York, 1944.

451.

ORPHEUS
April 28, 1948
New York
City Center of Music and Drama

Priority:
This ballet, combining proven talents, marked the achievement of stability by George Balanchine, who, after fifteen years in America, working in commercial theater, opera, film, and ballet, founded a school and found patronage. By 1948 his company was capable of incorporating a national style for an international repertory. His education at the Russian Imperial and State Schools (1914–22) and his years with Diaghilev (1924–29) determined his program. After the Second World War, with Lincoln Kirstein he formed Ballet Society, a private subscription organization producing lyric theater. Commissions were awarded progressive composers, painters, and choreographers, the results of which would serve as substructure for an eventual company. Of these works, *Orpheus* (Stravinsky-Balanchine-Noguchi) and *Four Temperaments*

(Hindemith-Balanchine, 1946) were lasting. Stravinsky's tender score, Balanchine's ritual choreography, Noguchi's exquisite décor, costumes, and sculptured objects composed a work of sober elevation. Its impression was enduring rather than novel; its efficient professionalism affirmed a new and serious institution supporting tradition.

Precedent:
From 1936 to 1938, Balanchine's American Ballet, founded in 1935, served the Metropolitan Opera. On May 22, 1936, he produced Gluck's *Orfeo ed Euridice*, designed by the painter Pavel Tchelitchew (1898–1957). Due to the artists' insistence on a radical vision in a conservative opera house, the work was ill received; Balanchine subsequently withdrew. This event might have triumphed two decades later, but then was neither time nor place for novelty.

The legend of Orpheus, the eternal poet, remained in Balanchine's mind; he proposed it to Stravinsky as sequel to *Apollon Musagète* (1928). (Apollo appears in the

apotheosis to make Orpheus' lyre immortal.) Stravinsky insisted on an un-Greek frame. Tchelitchew had given Gluck an unadorned moonscape of bare craters, skeletal birches, and an unornamented surround in three dimensions, with Hell as a concentration camp and limbo as an ether-dream. Noguchi, the gifted Japanese-American sculptor, created for Stravinsky a stark, breathless set, accented by elegant carved lyres and gilded masks. Pluto was no customary devil, but recalled Kali, Hindu lord of Hell; the infernal regions were framed in huge modeled flames and bones. In 1933, for *Errante* (Schubert-Balanchine), Tchelitchew invented a vast china-silk cloud, which fell at the finale, engulfing the hero. For *Orpheus*, Noguchi hung an enormous china-silk curtain to separate the scenes. This had life of its own; blown by random currents of air, it enveloped and involved the dancers with its accidental movement.

Stravinsky's score re-echoed the Orphic legend from Monteverdi (1607) through Gluck (1762). In 1697, in Turin, Antonio Sartorio's opera *Orfeo* had the poet charm beasts by his voice; during the aria, an ape led a pantomime of other animals, playing tricks on them. In 1739, John Rich in London produced an elaborate opera-pantomime with comic scenes of *Orpheus and Euridice*, which cost two thousand pounds and was frequently revived. Among its attractions were a realistic serpent and a surprising growth of trees.

Balanchine saw Hermes-Mercury, messenger of the Gods, as the Dark Angel, intermediary between earth and underworld. Hermes Psychopompos, "guide of dead souls," leads them to Pluto, king of Hell, who controls the earth's crust and hence its fertility. In the Middle Ages, in Ovid *moralisé*, Mercury turns from messenger into demon. Balanchine took this aspect of the myth; his ballet is as much about

452.

179.

144.

451. Orpheus and the Dark Angel. New York, 1947.

Orpheus' relationship with the Dark Angel as that with his lost Eurydice. Orpheus, the Thracian son of Apollo and eloquent Calliope, was a hero, but poet rather than warrior. Concomitant with his genius, he was impulsive, impatient, imprudent. He maddened the furious bacchantes by his single-minded love for Eurydice; this disdain caused his death, but his dismembered body floated fragments down the streams of time.

Politics:

Balanchine came to America in 1933. (Following Diaghilev's death in 1929, he had been ballet master for the Royal Danish Ballet.) Aided by Edward M. M. Warburg and Lincoln Kirstein, he founded the School of American Ballet, New York City, bringing as his faculty Pierre Vladimirov, and later Anatole Obukhov, Muriel Stuart, Felia Doubrovska—dancers from Diaghilev, the Marinsky Theater, and Anna Pavlova. Shortly, Balanchine drew dancers from his school to form producing groups. In 1941, the State Department, under Nelson A. Rockefeller, sent Balanchine's American Ballet Caravan to Latin America on a cultural mission. In 1947, at the première of *Orpheus*, Morton Baum, an eminent tax lawyer and chairman of the Finance Committee of the City Center of Music and Drama in New York, was present. He asked Balanchine to form the New York City Ballet, and for the next twenty years supported it. Due to his sponsorship, grants were made by individuals and foundations. Baum, in funding Balanchine and Stravinsky, is the most recent in a line of non-dancers, from Count Durazzo, who backed Gluck's *Orfeo*, to Diaghilev, who served the dance. He offered a climate in which creation continued.

Plot or Pretext:

I. Lament for Eurydice. Orpheus is consoled by friends. Fauns, dryads, satyrs, and forest creatures* prance

in spite of his personal tragedy; nature continues despite death. The Dark Angel, with his black cord, binds Orpheus to him in an eternal alliance. A huge cloud descends. Orpheus, with his inseparable lyre, is lead to Hell.

II. The damned, gray prisoners bear huge boulders in feckless labor. The power of Orpheus' lyre persuades Pluto to release Eurydice, provided she does not look at him until earth is regained. The silk cloud falls. Near the end of the long upward journey she persuades him to embrace her. The lyre is snatched from Orpheus when he most needs it, and a hundred invisible hands drag Eurydice back to Hell.

III. Bacchantes, outraged at Orpheus' grieving disdain for all women, tear him to pieces. Out of his grave a laurel blooms; Apollo, leader of the Muses, gilds Orpheus' lyre with eternal light.

Production:

Noguchi's colors were pale dawn pink, gilt, azure, and black. At the moment Orpheus was given Eurydice by Pluto, a shaft of blue, pennon-like, dropped—a glimpse in Hell of sky above and outside. The extended *pas de deux*, first for Orpheus and the Dark Angel, then for Orpheus and Eurydice, were marvels of human interlace. The music, of quivering serenity, suggested limbos of suspended animation. There was a single brief, violent action backed by sonorous fury when bacchantes devoured Orpheus. Otherwise, grave plucked strings and thin resonances of harp as lyre measured movements as in a ceremony attached to no time or place. Tragedy was not abstract, but personalized by three young bodies in a serene synthesis of loss and transfiguration.

Balanchine did not receive a finished score, unlike *Apollon* (1928) and *Jeu de Cartes* (1937), but worked with the composer con-

tinuously; Stravinsky attended rehearsals; the work was true collaboration at every step. Each number was planned with stop-watch exactitude. The music throughout is as restrained as Monteverdi's *Orfeo*, except in the *pas d'action*. The composer says that even this Furies' music is "soft and constantly remains on the soft level." Stravinsky rendered Orpheus' lyre as a harp; song is translated into mimic terms to plucked strings, instrumentally rather than vocally. The singing harp moves Pluto to release Eurydice. In the apotheosis, the harp, for a last time, breaks into a fugue for two horns with two brief rippling bursts ("cut off with a pair of scissors"), re-echoing the song sung in Hell. Stravinsky wrote: "Here in the Epilogue it sounds like a kind of . . . compulsion, like something unable to stop . . . Orpheus is dead, the song is gone but the accompaniment goes on."

451.

452.

---

* Noguchi's costumes for these strongly recall Picasso's *Joie de Vivre*, both the painting and its sketches (1946).

452. *Orfeo ed Euridice*. New York, 1936.

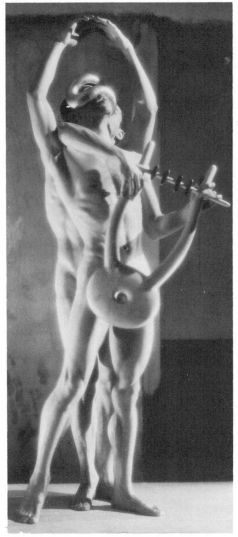

453.

454.

453, 454, 456. Orpheus and the Dark Angel. New York, 1947.

455. Underworld. New York, 1948.

455.

456.

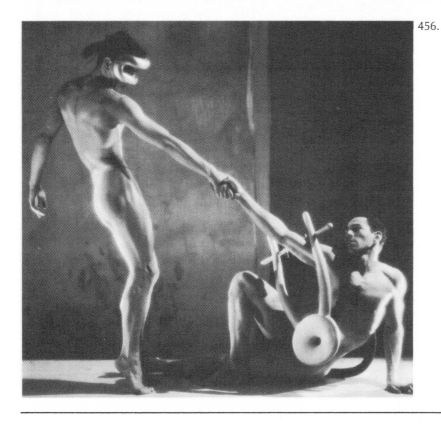

MASTERY BY MUSIC FOR MOVEMENT

AGON
(The Contest)
December 1, 1957
New York
City Center of Music and Drama

Priority:

Agon defines the developed classical dance as forged between Stravinsky and Balanchine. In its richness upon a severe structure, it pursues and fulfills the direction of *Apollon* (1928). (In decades between, composer and choreographer often collaborated.)

"Agon" is Greek for "contest"; the ballet presents unwinnable games for a dozen dancers and ceremonial competitions between them. With no literary pretext, it strives for plastic ennoblement within rules, projected particularly by the twelve-tone serial writings in its score. It is more impersonal, quirky, nervous, and compulsive than the melodic *Apollon,* and has been compared to Mondrian's balanced abstractions (though in no way rectilinear), or the soulless computations of systems analysis—an I.B.M. device, but one that thinks and smiles. Its syntax is the undeformed, uninverted grammar, with shades of courtly behavior and echoes of antique measure. Group numbers assume the well-oiled synchronism of electrical timekeepers, achieved by humane teamwork rather than mechanics in automata. Blocks of units in triads and quartets shift like chess pieces or players in musical chairs. Dancers are manipulated as irreplaceable spare parts, substituting or alternating on strict beats. Insertions of novel support and balance extend from *Apollon;* the male soloist supports from his back on the floor, handling the ballerina as if she were an articulated crane seeming to violate anatomy, but always elucidating or glorifying it. Impersonalization of arms and legs into geometrical arrows (all systems "go") accentuates dynamics in a field of force; dancers are magnetized by invisible commands according to logical but arcane formulas. Yet the aura is not mechanistic, but musical, disciplined, witty—offering the epoch's extreme statement of its craft. At a time when experiment had become a necessity for instant novelty, the innovation of *Agon* lay in its naked strength, bare authority, and self-discipline in constructs of stressed extreme movement. Behind its active physical presence there was inherent a philosophy; *Agon* was by no means "pure" ballet, "about" dancing only. It was an existential metaphor for tension and anxiety. In Renato Poggioli's *Theory of the Avant-Garde* (1962–68), there is a relevant chapter on Agonism and Futurism.

"If agonism meant no more than *agone,* it would be only a synonym for activism and would express only the modern cult of contest, sport, and game. . . . The agonistic attitude is not a passive state of mind, exclusively dominated by a sense of imminent catastrophe; on the contrary, it strives to transform the catastrophe into a miracle. By acting, and through its very failure, it tends towards a result justifying and transcending itself. Agonism means tension: the pathos of a Laocoön struggling in his ultimate spasm to make his own suffering immortal and fecund. In short, agonism means sacrifice and consecration: an hyperbolic passion, a bow bent towards the impossible, a paradoxical and positive form of spiritual defeatism."

Precedent:

Balanchine first presented *Apollon* in New York (1937) with *Jeu de Cartes,* the latter commissioned from Stravinsky by the American Ballet, then in the service of the Metropolitan Opera. Then *Orpheus* (1947) was ordered by Ballet Society. For 1957, the choreographer wished to add a third work, forming a related triptych. As completed, *Agon* was plotless, triggered by dance manuals of Mersenne (1636) and de Lauze (*Apologie de la Danse,* 1623). Stravinsky says there are traces of boogie-woogie in the *Bransles,* which originally belonged to the fifteenth-century *basse danse* and were characterized by a swaying step.

Politics:

By 1950, Balanchine had both a company supplied by his own School of American Ballet and a home at the New York City Center of Music and Drama, with Morton Baum, a worthy successor to Durazzo, Lumley, and Vsevolozhsky, as manager. *Agon* was paid for by the Division of Humanities, Rockefeller Foundation, revealing a new aspect of public patronage. Stravinsky started composing the score in 1953, stopped for other work, then continued and completed it in 1956. He recast numbers already written "to link them with a minimum of disturbance to the serial technique that by then was becoming his current idiom" (E. W. White). The grand *pas de deux,* one of Balanchine's most personal constructions, was designed for a white girl and a black boy (Diana Adams and Arthur Mitchell). When it was shown in Moscow (1962), attention was drawn to an imagined servility and pathos, as a metaphor of inequality in American society; previously, in the United States, the reaction had been the reverse. Balanchine, as always, took notice of the endowment of given dancers (as in *Apollon*), prising from unique bodies movement that enlarged a language.

Plot or Pretext:

A dodecaphonic composition, *Agon* employs twelve dancers, four men and eight girls, in a dozen sections, four parts of three dances each.

I. *Pas de quatre:* "four men aligned across the back of the stage, back to the public." Double *pas de quatre:* four men and four girls. Triple *pas de quatre:* four men and eight girls.

459.

434.

460.

242

II. First *pas de trois:* two girls and a man. *Sarabande:* two men (solo violin, xylophone, two bass trombones). *Galliard:* male solo (cannon for harp, mandolin, flute). *Coda:* girls and men.

III. Second *pas de trois:* two men and a girl. *Bransle simple:* two men (canon for two trumpets; blues). *Bransle gai:* girl's solo (woodwinds, castanets). *Bransle de Poitou:* girl and men (solo trumpet, unison violins).

IV. *Pas de deux.* Four duos. Four trios. The ballet ends as it began.

Production:
As in many Balanchine works to important modern music (Hindemith, Schönberg, Webern, Ives, Xenakis), costumes are black-and-white practice uniforms, near nudity. Here "production" consists of execution alone, determined by the austere complexity of music in the serial method, patterns of cellular structure involving a continuum of variations on a twelve-tone set. No dance work has been more highly organized or is so dense in movement in its bare twenty minutes. Clock time has no reference to visual duration; there is more concentrated movement in *Agon* than in most nineteenth-century full-length ballets. There are no interstitial gaps for parade or decoration. The choreography projects a steel skeleton clad in tightly knit action, lacing a membrane of movement over a transparent net of contrapuntal design, which in shifting concentration on separate dancers gives an impression of intense drama. It is the culmination of a revolution started by Stravinsky and Nijinsky in *Le Sacre du Printemps* (1913)—insistence on rhythm in asymmetrical balance. Symmetry, the basis of composition for centuries, focuses on stage center. The new asymmetry broke up the balance of right and left, distributing blocks into shifting cells employing stage periphery equally with a center. New attacks on temporal

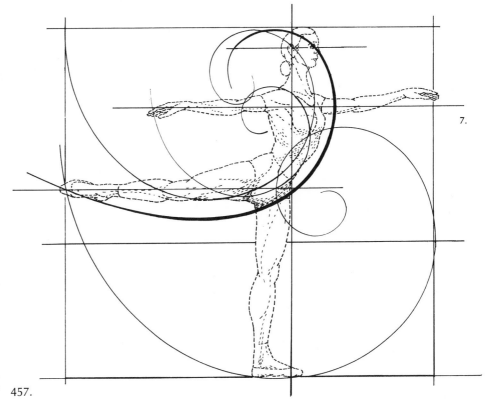

7.

457.

measure involved new conquest of space.

The mere use of a tonal series, however, does not insure legibility; one can listen to the score without comprehending it through the eyes. That *Agon* is visually and aurally legible is due to tenacious attachment to the academy, in its illuminated grammar and renewed plasticity. Aural geometry and visual counterpoint are the result of four centuries of practice by ballet masters who have, each for his own time and to his epoch's music, found means to fill space by new measuring. Balanchine wrote in his analysis of the ballet:

"As an organizer of rhythms, Stravinsky, I have always thought, has been more supple and various than any single creator in history. What holds me always is the vitality in the substance of each measure. Each measure has its complete, almost personal life; it is a living unit. There are no blind spots. A pause,

an empty space, is never empty space between indicated sounds. It is not just nothing. It acts as a carrying agent from the last sound to the next one. Life goes on within each silence. . . . As always in his ballet scores, the dance element of most force was the pulse."

429.

457. Arabesque.

459.

458.

460.

458–62. *Agon.* New York, 1957–63.

462.

THE COMPOSER AS FIRST-DANCER

ENIGMA VARIATIONS
October 25, 1968
London
Royal Opera House,
Covent Garden

Priority:

This balletic group portrait canonizes that hero who previously has been God, King, Prince, Peasant, Athlete, and Dancer. Here, the Musician triumphs through his score. The work's protagonist is a native artist in specific context. It is no updating of the myths of Apollo, leader of muses, or of Orpheus, divine poet; its action frames the recognition of Sir Edward Elgar (1857–1934) as national genius of international repute. The choreography by Sir Frederick Ashton also stands as metaphor for the success of British ballet, which has become, in his hands, the most stable national dance institution since the Russian Revolution of 1917. Elgar, greatest English composer since Purcell, commenced by composing quadrilles for a madhouse orchestra. After years without recognition, aged forty-one and fighting provincial insularity, he learns that his masterpiece—*Enigma Variations* —will be performed by Hans Richter, the era's symphonic dictator.

Elgar had said that if his *Variations* had been written by a Russian they would long ago have been a ballet. He saw the site as a banquet hall, with the "enigma" a veiled ballerina revealed at the finale. Ashton transformed them into a family conversation piece, as derived from plump Victorian photographic albums, plush covered and copper clasped. He portrayed the musician in a domestic rather than a tragic or romantic ambience. Love is present, not as passion, but blanketed by maturity and friendship. What might have been parochial proved, through the images Ashton found, a dance-drama recreating a special world, parallel to those evoked by Turgenev, James, or E. M. Forster, unthinkable in other backgrounds than their own, yet transcending them into a universality by intensity of emotion and human savor.

Precedent:

The Maker, Poet, Artist, Painter, Performer took something over a century and a half to turn from prototype into personage. Perhaps the start was Benvenuto Cellini's autobiography, which, although completed in 1566, was unpublished until 1728 and hardly current until translated for the German Romantics. In 1838, Hector Berlioz based his opera on the sculptor's story. Goethe had already written *Tasso;* Dumas the elder a tragedy based on the English actor Edmund Kean.

Creation myths utilizing Prometheus or Pygmalion had been popular for three centuries, but Fokine had taken the soul of a particular genius as pretext for *Chopiniana* (which was soon reworked into *Les Sylphides,* 1909). In 1934, Balanchine exploited Franz Lizst in *Transcendance;* Fokine used a similar scheme in *Paganini.* In 1944, Léonide Massine and Salvador Dali, in a Surrealist nightmare, related Richard Wagner to Sacher-Masoch and Ludwig of Bavaria. In 1950, Ashton created *Les Illuminations* (Britten-Beaton) for the New York City Ballet, based on the career of Arthur Rimbaud. Tableaux suggested by his poems projected in hallucinatory action his violently systematic dislocation of reality.

Starting in the 1930's, biographical films about painters from Rembrandt and Michelangelo to Gauguin, Van Gogh, and Lautrec were popular. Ken Russell, a gifted television producer for the British Broadcasting Corporation, made his prizewinning documentary of *Elgar* (1962), which he followed by those on Delius, Debussy, and Isadora Duncan.

Ashton had set dances to two librettos by Gertrude Stein, *Four Saints in Three Acts* (Thomson-Stettheimer, 1934) and *A Wedding Bouquet* (Lord Berners, both music and décor, 1937). Stein's influence on Ashton was capital. Her verbal formulas of repetitive short circuits, her reduction of behavior to the fabulously familiar in a domesticated mythology, were neatly equated by Ashton's kinetic descriptions of exceptional characters and events in their cosy atmosphere. In *Enigma Variations* Cocteau's working philosophy for rehabilitating the commonplace by rendering the ordinary magical *(Parade;* Massine-Satie-Picasso, 1917) was reversed. Here Ashton endowed genius with the homely pathos of its native vernacular.

408.

Politics:

Enigma Variations may also be read as commentary on the decline of an empire. Elgar's *Pomp and Circumstance* and other imperial marches gained him knighthood (1904), after which he composed the *Coronation Ode* for Edward VII. Made Master of the King's Musick (1924), he revived a lapsed tradition once distinguished by its great official composers: Byrd, Gibbons, Purcell. In the nineteenth century, British music was represented by Henry Bishop, now chiefly remembered for *Home, Sweet Home,* who was the first musician to be knighted (1842). Henry Irving (1895) was the first actor, Ashton the first male dancer (1962) to have been thus honored. Elgar had written music for the empire at its apogee, even as Kipling's *Recessional* and Housman's *Shropshire Lad* hinted that the sun which now never set on the Union Jack might one day dim. Ashton brilliantly captured the rural climate of middle-class security, sweetness, comfort, warmth, and faint menace. Chekhov's late Romanov Russia and Elgar's Edwardian England hold for us the allure of a *douceur de vie,* a vanished grace now remote as Versailles.

465.

Britain liquidated her world realm

246

and survived two world wars, emerging as a socialist monarchy with her culture a national concern, independent of royal or private patronage. The British Arts Council supports great companies for ballet and opera. To have made a national institution from nothing in three decades, as did Ninette de Valois and Frederick Ashton with the Royal Ballet, is the finest achievement in institutional theater since the death of Diaghilev. *A Wedding Bouquet* (1937), set in the bourgeois French family life of the provincial Jura, looked back to the 'twenties, reflecting on its parody of Parisian taste London's dependence on Paris of pre-World War II. *Enigma Variations* was a declaration of independence; English tradition was presented as comfy benefit and present patrimony.

Plot or Pretext:

There are fourteen variations on a theme (the "enigma"), each dedicated to an unnamed personal friend, "pictured within." Headed by C.A.E. (Elgar's wife), successive musical and choreographic portraits encapsulate each character: the crony with whom the composer plays chamber music, village children and gossips, maid and gardener, a son of Matthew Arnold, local gentry, his steadfast publisher—above all, repeatedly, his long-suffering, capable, adoring wife. Friends enter on bicycles and tricycles (1899 was a great cycling year); one exits *en arabesque* on a single pedal. As in paintings of people we recognize, but have never met, personal traits become familiar. There are japes, private jokes, and an encompassing air of suspended gravity. The end is masterfully constructed. An annunciatory telegram passes from hand to hand, up through a hierarchy of servants and familiars, a sacred screed, an oracle from Olympus. Elgar's piece will be played! Finally the message reaches Elgar, who presents it lovingly to his wife, to whom it may even

mean more. The village photographer captures a tableau celebrating an immemorial afternoon of art and empire. "Friendship has something to do with it, but it is more than that," wrote Andrew Porter.

"The dark theme . . . is the loneliness of the creative artist, the sense of desolation which not the sunlight of friends, not the moments of triumph, not even the shining steady ray of a loving helpmate, can dispel for long."*

Production:

Scenery and costumes of Julia Trevelyan Oman, member of a family of distinguished historians, were on a level with music and dancing. A skillful professional designer for film (*The Charge of the Light Brigade*), she made clothes that were hardly costumes, a site far more than scenery. Her tweed suits and muslin dresses looked as if they had always been worn by individuals who chose them with care. They might have seemed more suitable for cinema than choreography, except for their tact, accuracy, and rightness. The men were heavily characterized yet scarcely made-up; rather, the clip of hair, the twist of mustache, cufflinks, watch chain, gaiters, spectacles, bowler or stalking hat fused in a touching texture of verisimilitude that underscored nostalgic wizardry. The décor was at once garden and living room of a country house in its large landscape, paralleling the dancers' description of exterior mask and interior expression of personality and relationship. It is a British countryside, impossible of creation by anyone unfamiliar with Worcestershire. Garden gate, hammock, tea table, staircase leading to more intimate realms above assumed the immediate legibility of altars or sacred furnishings, serving a society of which they were the formal and familiar frame. Miss Oman used photographs, as Bakst and Benois borrowed from museum and library. Her documentation by

no means resulted in photographic realism; her color was muted from no kodachrome. The portraits were of persons; her palette was the haze of autumn afternoon. Here, the English genius for tailoring, pantomime, and lyric poetry achieved perfect partnership.

468.

463.

---

* *Financial Times* (London), October 28, 1968.

463. Sir Frederick Ashton, c. 1934.

464.

465.

466.

464, 466–68. *Enigma Variations*. London, 1968.

465. Sir Edward Elgar, 1927.

467.

468.

ACKNOWLEDGMENTS

Research for this book, an amateur's compilation using no primary sources, drew chiefly on the Dance Collection, Library and Museum of the Performing Arts, Lincoln Center (a branch of the New York Public Library), of which Miss Genevieve Oswald has long been Curator. Illustrations not otherwise credited come from that treasure house. I wish to thank colleagues at this great library who have lightened my labor: Miss Betty Budack, Miss Ruth Carr, Miss Barbara Goldberg, Mrs. Virginia Christ-Janer, and Paul La Paglia.

Miss Nancy Reynolds, editor at Praeger Publishers, herself a dancer, proposed this book; for three years she clarified, corrected, and reorganized; without her it could not have existed.

Mrs. Marian Eames, my former co-editor on *Dance Index* (1942–49), made more sense of prose and pictures. Madame Olivier Ziegel assiduously searched Paris libraries for documents and illustrations. Mrs. Henry T. Curtiss, my sister, suggested Count Francesco Algarotti's importance behind the *ballet d'action*.

Miss Felice Staempfle (Pierpont Morgan Library, New York), David Rust (National Gallery of Art, Washington, D.C.), and Miss Helen Willard (Harvard Theater Collection, Cambridge, Mass.) obtained illustrations from their collections, unique in America.

Sir Frederick Ashton, C.B.E., the late Anatole Bourman, the late Michel Fokine, Madame Alexandra Danilova, Madame Felia Doubrovska, the late Alexander Gavrilov, Madame Lydia Lopokova, the late Robert Edmond Jones, the late Anatole Obukhov, Madame Bronislava Nijinska, Jerome Robbins, Antony Tudor, the late Stark Young, the late Carl van Vechten, and Pierre Vladimirov supplied testimony to ballets they saw, danced, or invented. I am grateful to George Chaffee (and the late Richard Doubs) and to Walter Toscanini, whose accumulations of books, prints, and memorabilia are available at Lincoln Center or Harvard.

Many friends are no longer here to thank: James Agee, poet, first suggested American equivalents of classic archetypes. A. Everett Austin, formerly Director, Wadsworth Atheneum, Hartford, Conn., sponsored Balanchine's visa to America (1934) and acquired the Diaghilev-Lifar collection of scenery and costume sketches. Anatole Chujoy, critic, encyclopedist, balletomane, wrote on the New York City Ballet (1953) and was engaged on a sequel at his death (1969). Noah Greenberg, founder of Pro Musica (New York), enabled me to hear Lassus, Lully, Rameau, and earlier dance composers. Ifan Kyrle Fletcher, prince of book-sellers, found me needed rarities. The legacy of Lillian Moore, dancer and historian, to the Dance Collection at Lincoln Center, would, had she lived, have served us together on many projects connected with a sequence to this book.

For four decades, A. Hyatt Mayor, former Curator of Prints, Metropolitan Museum of Art, New York, historian of the Bibiena family, corrected my thoughts on theater. Sir Philip Hendy (in 1931, Director, Isabella Stewart Gardner Museum, Fenway Court, Boston), professors Denis de Rougemont, Rensselaer Lee, Meyer Schapiro, Jean Seznec, and Edgar Wind first taught me dimensions in metaphor expressed through iconography. Cyril Beaumont from 1924 first encouraged me to collect original material in books and prints. Eric Schroeder, Keeper of Islamic Art, Fogg Art Museum, Harvard, gave me Cocteau's description of Diaghilev, which started me writing ("The Diaghilev Period," *Hound & Horn*, 1930). Ivor Guest's massive treatment of nineteenth-century ballet in France and England is behind anyone's thought on this period and provides a model for an eventual treatment of the eighteenth and twentieth centuries everywhere else. The seventeenth century in France is served by two fine books: *L'Art du Ballet de Cour (1581–1643)*, by Margaret McGowan (Paris, 1964), and *Le Ballet de Cour de Louis XIV (1643–1672)*, by Marie-Françoise Christout (Paris, 1967). Their books and combined bibliographies subsume a comprehensive treatment of the seventeenth century outside France, which does not now exist. W. H. Auden's *Poets of the English Language* (1952), its prefaces and synoptic tables, suggested my unfulfilled scope. Quotations from Wystan Auden, and suggestions over three decades, are debts I cannot pay. Ezra Pound, thirty-five years ago, taught me to seek structure, here organized as "Priority," "Precedent," etc. T. S. Eliot's "Tradition and the Individual Talent" in *The Sacred Wood* (1920), read under the late Theodore Spencer at Harvard in 1926, triggered my respect for academic classicism.

George Balanchine has not read this book; but contact with him since 1933 makes me think. Igor Stravinsky has helped me since 1937. Since I cannot read a piano score, any "music appreciation" I have is due to Bob Craft, who tried to fill the gap. G. I. Gurdgieff's person and ideas, from 1926, deriving from Naqshbandi dervishes, and his support of Émile Jaques-Dalcroze, corroborated my notion of Vaslav Nijinsky, not as dancer, but as ballet *master*—possibly something more. S. Palmer Bovie, Professor of Classics, Rutgers University, translator of Virgil, Martial, Juvenal, Horace, and Lucretius, one-time companion-in-arms (1943–45), improved Latin quotations I could not decipher correctly.

Alexandra Schierman carefully typed and retyped the manuscript. James Devine, photographer, Library and Museum of the Performing Arts, solved photographic problems. Donn Matus, designer, is my virtual co-author; he tried to balance my words with the scale and placement of illustrations. Joel Weltman aided immeasurably in layout. Mrs. Eleanor Fardig categorized and compiled the index; considerations of space required her severe and cautious editorial elimination of secondary names and titles.

L.K.

NOTES TO ILLUSTRATIONS

Unless otherwise indicated, all illustrations derive from books, prints, or pictures in the Dance Collection, Library and Museum of the Performing Arts, Lincoln Center, a branch of the New York Public Library.

Frontispiece. Analysis of human movement, for the use of painters and sculptors. This manuscript (Codex Huygens, M.A. 1139) derives from materials available in the studio of Leonardo da Vinci, c. 1470, but was probably drawn by an anonymous Milanese artist a century later.

Pencil drawing on paper from the *Regole del Disegno*, Milan, c. 1579.
New York, Pierpont Morgan Library.

1. Ideal armed Renaissance noble youth, by a painter in Giorgione's circle, showing the Crusader as *condottiere*, a professional soldier hired by Italian princes who arranged great festivals. This pensive knight might be the hero of early opera-ballet (Rinaldo, Renaud; Godefroi, Godfrey of Boulogne) in repertory inspired by Tasso and Ariosto. Armor is carapace, not costume.

Oil on canvas, Venetian school, c. 1450.
London, National Gallery (reserve collection).

2. Ideal Renaissance acrobat-athlete. This boy in a handstand is modeled more from Florentine street games than from Athens or Olympia. There is no overdevelopment or muscular exaggeration. The exquisite casting and patina help suggest supple control in extreme tension.

Bronze by Domenico Poggini, c. 1550.
London, Wallace Collection.

3. Traditional ideal classic academic theatrical dancer. Jules Perrot is costumed for the "Gothic" role of Alain in *La Filleule des Fées (The Fairy's Godchild)* in tunic and tights, which hint at an historical epoch but do not obscure basic anatomy.

Lithograph by Alexandre Lacauchie from *La Galerie des Artistes Dramatiques,* Paris, 1849.

4. Male and female bodies furnish essential choreographic material. Degas, inspired by Plutarch's description of young Spartans daring each other to wrestle, transformed studio life-drawing by intimate observation of snub-nosed adolescents—types of eternal ballet students.

The Young Spartans by Hilaire Germain Edgar Degas, 1860. Oil on canvas.
London, National Gallery.

5. *Kouroi,* Hellenic youths come of age, dance to honor and protect the infant Dionysus. Later, in Rome, sword dances were performed as spectacle, imitating the Greek Pyrrhic, which was taught in 5th-century Attica as martial sport. The Roman version had single dancers in a weapons drill, duets as danced duels, and mimed combat maneuvers.

Roman marble relief, c. 150 B.C.
Rome, Vatican Museum.

6. In the school of arms, development of lighter blades paralleled codification of instruction. Strict profiles, as minimal exposed targets, along with geometry underlying economy, skill, and show, were based on a logic of necessity analogous to that governing academies of social and spectacular dancing.

Engraving by Crispin de Passe from *L'Académie de l'Espée,* Paris: G. Thibault, 1623.

7. Part of Hogarth's conceptual analysis of ideal visual structure (see p. 11).

Engraving by William Hogarth from his *Analysis of Beauty,* London, 1753.

8. The Greek *choros* was schooled for open-air movement. Costumes of wool and linen, light but voluminous, enhanced motion and served as models for costume reforms (soon lost in corseting) at the start of the 19th century, and then in the 20th, with Isadora Duncan and Léon Bakst.

Baked clay figurine, c. 150 B.C. Tanagra or Myrrha, Asia Minor.
Paris, Louvre.

9. In Renaissance Tuscany, dancing masters instructed on a musical metric both social dances and mimic action for festivals. Great painters designed décor and dresses based on figures from extant Roman triumphal arches and archeological discoveries.

The Birth of Venus (detail) by Sandro Botticelli, 1485–86. Oil and tempera.
Florence, Uffizi.

NOTES

10. By 1730, a stable academy forced professional dancers into uniforms of exaggerated silhouettes, thereby strait-jacketing epoch, class, character, and movement. Male *tonnelet* and female pannier of wire or willow-work derived from underquilting for armor and Spanish or Elizabethan farthingales. Monumental dignity enhanced heroic roles. Here, a conventional Fame with trumpet and laurel wreath demonstrates a target for Noverre's proposed reforms.
Watercolor on paper by Pierre Lior (att.), c. 1760.
London, Victoria and Albert Museum.

11. Vaslav Nijinsky in professional *déshabille*: the permanent ballet student as star. Such work clothes as tights—a metaphor of athletic nudity—the practice dress first proposed by Bakst for *Jeux* (see illus. 386), were adopted c. 1934 by George Balanchine as favorite formal costume for works in which choreographic pattern, rather than pageantry or pantomime, dominates.
Photograph White's Studio, New York, 1916.

12. Two centuries of analysis and codification by Italian and French masters established five absolute school positions, first for social, later for stage, dancing. Based on these unalterables, the idiom of academic dancing evolved from static to kinetic exercises. Extreme turn-out of legs from the hips enforces stability to start turns and jumps.
1st, 2nd, 5th positions
Engravings from *Le Maître à Danser* by Pierre Rameau, Paris, 1725.

13. A century of stage practice resulted in a vocabulary governed by concepts of correctness as formal as poetic or musical metric, but in ballet the language was based on human anatomy, solid geometry, and theatrical legibility. It was canonized by Blasis, a Milanese teacher and theorist. Linear clarity, which infused Neoclassic art, fixed a style that, for purity and logic, remains the ideal. There have been few innovations in the grammar since.
Engravings from *Traîté Élémentaire* by Carlo Blasis, Milan, 1820.

14, 15. Blasis studied his role as Mercury, god of speed and air, from the famous bronze by Giovanni da Bologna (1590). "I assumed the attitude . . . of the statue for my pirouettes. This lovely position is very hard to execute; unless one is naturally positioned, it is impossible to produce the pirouettes with real effect. The leg en *attitude* should be bent to complete the curve of the profile."
Bronze from the studio of Giovanni da Bologna, c. 1590.
London, Wallace Collection.
Engravings from *The Code of Terpsichore* by Carlo Blasis, London, 1830.

16. Antonio Canova, dominant sculptor of his era and favorite of Napoleon and his family, whose studio was open to the choreographer Blasis, left fine drawings and studies of dancers in plaster and marble (see illus. 248), documenting the plastic quality of taste and style in dancing from 1790 to 1825. When Romanticism replaced the Neoclassic ideal, Canova's genius was misprized, but he has recently emerged as far more than a wan revival of dead antiquity. Canova incarnated Blasis's plastic analysis in three dimensions.
Dancer by Antonio Canova, c. 1806–9. Marble.
Rome, Palazzo Corsini.

17. Dancers rose from the floor, first in heeled shoes, then in heelless slippers, to half-toe (*demi-pointe*) and later to three-quarters point by the last decade of the 18th century. It is difficult to say exactly how, when, or where they attained full point, but it was probably in Italy (see illus. 20, 21, 244–47).
Drawing of the Köbbler sisters by Johannes Jelgerhuis, October, 1812.
Amsterdam, Theater Collection.

18. Fanny Elssler, Viennese, was a Romantic ballerina, more fiery and folk-rooted than her rival Taglioni. Dissemination of cheap lithographs, later of *carte de visite* photographs, popularized ballet as mass entertainment. Elssler's layers of muslin are precedent for tarlatan skirts, long or short, that remain, with various modifications, uniforms for ballerinas.
La Volière by M. Gauci, lithograph (from a series) after a drawing by J. D. Francis, London-Paris, 1838.

19. From about 1850 on, toe shoes (or ballet slippers) had a reinforced blocked end, strengthened by stitching. Careful training insures control of the whole body on extended toes, which, while artificial, provides scope of movement otherwise impossible.
Bronze cast of Anna Pavlova's toe-point, c. 1916. Ex collection André Oliveroff.

20. Diagram of movement on toe-point, accompanied by balancing arm action, indicating imperceptible locomotion of the ballerina's body supported by the extended toe. Normal motion of one leg following another seems suspended; the body appears to float as though flying above the stage.
Pen drawing by Carlus Dyer from *The Classic Ballet* by Lincoln Kirstein and Muriel Stuart, New York, 1952.

252

21. The dancing teacher, also a music master, instructs young gentlemen in correct positions for social dancing. By 1600, dance manuals spelled out a universal system for ballroom use. Professional teachers served also as choreographers for spectacles.
Engraving by Crispin de Passe, Paris, c. 1620.

22. Auguste Bournonville, son of a ballet master, was responsible for much of the extant repertory of the Royal Danish Ballet. Teacher and theorist, here he holds his dancing master's fiddle, a descendant of the *pochette* (see illus. 22). He marks the measure of his own music, establishing rhythm and tempos for exercises and combined steps.
Cloth collage caricature of Bournonville, c. 1840.
Copenhagen, Theater Museum.

23. Madame Malvina Cavalazzi, retired ballerina, gives class for the Metropolitan Opera, New York. The exercise is 4th position *croisée, pointe tendue en arrière.* No boys; ballet at this time (c. 1916) was hardly a national asset. Nevertheless, Diaghilev's company was on stage five floors below, for a first time in the United States.
Metropolitan Opera Archives, New York.

24. Five out of fifteen figures describing the allemande, known as such even in Germany. These come from a German edition of a French pamphlet, which gave music and positions for the social dance that immediately preceded the waltz. Mozart's "German dances" promised an ultimate projection toward theatrical usage.
Engravings after Mme. Annereau (from drawings by Pasquier) from *Principes d'Allemande,* Berlin, 1768.

25. St. Aubin's magnificent plate shows an elaborately produced private ball with special costumes. The numbers were danced by courtiers rather than professionals, but they were choreographed and rehearsed.
Le Bal Paré (detail), engraving by Augustin de St. Aubin, 1763.
Washington, National Gallery (Widener Collection).

26. This drawing of a typical mid-18th century ballet, employing figures from the *commedia dell'arte,* shows linked arm positions borrowed from social dancing. Folk forms and social dances continue to affect theatrical use down to our own time.
Le Ballet des Fées Rivalles (detail), drawing by Gabriel de St. Aubin, c. 1780.
Paris, private collection.

27. Schematic indication of pattern of horse hoofs for shoulder-in, side-step, half-pass, hand changes, and turns, in the classical academic grammar of *haute école,* or dressage riding. Magnificently illustrated monographs on riding and fencing, dating from c. 1550, document the precision of these disciplines.
Engraving by Charles Parrocel from *L'École de Cavalerie* by François Robichon de la Guérinière, Paris, 1753.

28. Schematic indication of heel tracks in the minuet. The archetypal dance of the *ancien régime,* this was a basis for *pas de deux* of the academic theatrical idiom and remained popular even after the French Revolution until it gave way to the waltz, and later to polka, Bóston, two-step, and other styles or fads.
"Principal Figure in the Minuet," engraving from *Le Maître à Danser* by Pierre Rameau, Paris, 1725.

29–32. Choreographic diagrams for *Die verwandelten Weiber.* Based on *Le Diable à Quatre* (Adam-Mazilier-Ciceri, Paris, 1845), this was produced by Paul Taglioni (1808–84), brother of the famous ballerina. Asymmetrical alignments and subdivisions in the *corps de ballet* fixed patterns recapitulated in Fokine's *Les Sylphides* in 1909 (see illus. 354–56).
Watercolor drawings (from a series) by Paul Taglioni (?), c. 1860.
Berlin, Theater Museum.

33. In this renowned step, the two feet braid back and forth off the floor. *Capriuola intrecciata* means a jump during which the toes, stiffened straight, move back and forth in a twinkling flash. This illustration to a book of rhymed proverbs shows that the step was already popular by the start of the 17th century.
Engraving by Giuseppe Mitelli from *Proverbi* (No. 16), Rome, c. 1603.

34. This detail from a large engraving illustrating a Florentine fete, *Le Nozze degli Dei (The Marriage of the Gods),* shows theatrical use of an academic step whose execution becomes more brilliant from decade to decade, with the number of shifts of feet off the ground increasing from simple change to *entrechat deux, quatre, six.* The gain in virtuosity is shared by the whole idiom.
Engraving for the libretto by Stefano della Bella (after Alfonso Parigi), Florence, 1634.

35. A detail of an extraordinary illustrated manual of motions for stage dancing continues the documentation of the *entrechat.* At this point, there have been permanent theaters, with raked stages, for nearly a century. The proscenium

NOTES

frames dancers for an audience seated well below them. This step heightens a sense of elevation and the negation of gravity.

Engraving by Johann Georg Püschner from *New and Curious School of Theatrical Dancing* by Gregorio Lambranzi, Nuremberg, 1716.

36. Detail of frontispiece of a German dance manual. The conquest of air—the length and height of jumps—is the most exciting acrobatic effect of the male dancer. Its development can be compared to the increased efficiency of pole vaulters over the last two centuries due to the innovation of Fiberglas poles. (Heeled shoes for dancers were not discarded until c. 1775–80.)

Engraving (detail) from *Rechtschaffener Tanzmeister* by Gottfried Taubert, Leipzig, 1717.

37. This diagram from an influential manual incorporating technical information accumulated from 1600 to 1885 indicates an increased number of "beats" (shifts of feet). Male dancers in our time have been credited with eight; in the case of Nijinsky, with ten.

Drawing (detail) by Friederich-Albert Zorn from his *Grammatik der Tanzkunst,* Leipzig, 1887.

38. The three disciplines of gentlemanly education, codified in the 16th century, are still instructed in elite military academies. Riding, fencing, and dancing each have their criteria in syntax and correctness. The pattern or choreography of their movement, while based on varying necessities, is determined by similar moral, anatomical, and geometrical considerations.

Engraved frontispiece by BernisWerth (after drawing by B. Eheknecht) from *Der Ritter Lexicon,* 1742.
Paris, Collection M. Fernand Reyna.

39. The classic academy of *haute école* equestrian skill is maintained in several national military establishments, but notably in the *Hochreitschule* in Vienna, which supports a corps of riders for white Lippizan stallions that amounts to a company of trained dancers. Here they are seen in the cross-figure of a quadrille. The horse ballroom, or *manège,* a masterpiece by Joseph Emanuel Fischer von Erlach the Younger, was built in 1729.

40. Choreography for this equestrian ballet (or sham battle) was arranged by Cavaliere Tommaso Guidoni and performed at night before the Archduke Ferdinand and Archduchess of Tuscany in an arena next to the Grand Ducal Palace in Florence. Patterns were meant to be viewed from four sides; entrances were from cardinal directions.

Etching by Stefano della Bella (probably after a drawing by Alfonso Parigi), Florence, 1652.

41. This "danse générale et dernière" shows the start of the finale of *La Délivrance de Renaud* (see illus. 105–8). The V formation, with the king (Louis XIII) at its apex, indicates frontality determined by dancing within a fixed proscenium, rather than—as previously—with audience surrounding.

Engraving from the libretto, 1617. Paris, Bibliothèque Nationale.

42. Detail of illustration from *Le Nozze degli Dei* (see illus. 35) shows choreographic patterns forming the initials V and A, cipher of Princess Victoria of Urbino, in whose honor the show was given. The choreographer was Agniolo Ricci, a court servant who also designed equestrian ballets.

Etching by Stefano della Bella (after drawings by Alfonso Parigi), Florence, 1637.

43. Peasant dances throughout Northern Europe have a considerable iconography, including pictures by Pieter Brueghel, Albrecht Dürer, and other major painters. Folk forms were borrowed from field and village square for ballroom use and refined in the process. Such intrusions have enriched the academic idiom, down to present-day jazz and popular music.

Nasdansen vid Gumpelsbrun (detail) by Nikolaus Meldeman, c. 1500. Woodcut.
Stockholm, Royal Library.

44. Hogarth, in his influential *Analysis of Beauty,* used the minuet to demonstrate differences between linear and curvilinear pattern, the contrast of elegance and roughness in aristocratic or proletarian behavior, variations between sophisticated and naive manners. This epitome of the most characteristic 18th-century social dance, taken over on stage as *pas de deux,* can be read from left to right, high to low class.

"Social dance" (detail), engraving by William Hogarth from his *Analysis of Beauty,* London, 1753.

45. The ballerina Sofia Fuoco (1830–1916) performs the famous tarantella, a Neapolitan mimed dance that in its fury supposedly diffuses poison from a spider's bite. Many such ethnic forms were incorporated into stage dancing in the 19th century.

Lithograph (detail) by G. Sanesi, Paris-Florence, c. 1855.

46. A stage tarantella for *L'Étoile de Messine* shows an amplified "character dance" from a ballet at the Paris Opéra, utilizing Italianate local color, but with male support (now at its nadir) provided by girls *en travesti*. Folk dancing in ballet was conventional and perfunctory until invested with some authenticity by visiting Spanish and Oriental troupes appearing at world's fairs after 1850.

Lithograph (detail) by Jean Regnier (after painting by Morlon), from the series *Musée des Moeurs en Action: Scène de l'Opéra*, Paris, 1861.

47. The eminent choreographer Salvatore Viganò, here with his wife, Maria Medina, was observed in a series of fine drawings by the sculptor von Schadow. It is too early for toe shoes, which later rendered *pas de deux* a complex demonstration of extreme virtuosity, but the principle of male dancers' supporting partners to attain movement of far wider scope is already apparent (see illus. 261–62).

The Viganòs, pen drawing by Gottfried von Schadow, 1790. Berlin, Theater Museum.

48. The ballerina Amalia Brugnoli, supported by Jean Rozier in *Die Fee und der Ritter (Fairy and Knight),* shows an increase in spectacular acrobacy that toe shoes permit by extending possibilities for lightness and balance. Partnering becomes a skill to be learned as a special discipline, requiring not so much strength as consideration of the ballerina's particular needs.

Lithograph, signed "I.J.," Vienna, 1823.

49. This caricature of a *pas de deux* in *Giselle* (Act I) presupposes general acceptance of the form into the grammar of choreography. Already mannerisms and affectations of a new *style noble* have bred their professional deformation. When stars sacrifice all to personal projection, dancing becomes a circus act—or high or low camp.

Grise-Aile (Tipsy Wing), lithograph by Lorent Lorenz from *Le Musée Philipon,* Paris, 1841.

50. *Le saut périlleux,* the hazardous leap, was an innovating feature of *La Péri,* a ballet made popular by Carlotta Grisi and Lucien Petipa (1815–98). Its hero, Achmet, wakens from an ecstatic dream to receive the body, lighter than air, of a peri. Théophile Gautier followed his success as librettist for *Giselle* by this "thousand and second night's tale" from quasi-Oriental sources.

La Péri (detail), lithograph by Marie-Alexandre Alophe, Paris, 1843.

51. David Garrick and Mrs. Pritchard in *Macbeth.*

Mezzotint by V. Green (after a painting by Johann Joseph Zoffany), London, 1776.
Stratford, Conn., American Shakespeare Festival.

52. Dance steps, mimetic positions, and exercises had become codified by 1700, with some sophistication. The Jesuit system of education was influential in the establishment of an academy, recognizing as it did theatrical values for pulpit and didactic shows. Father Lang's study served as basis for further detailed analysis.

"A Classic Actor's Commanding Stance" and ". . . Entrance," engravings from *Dissertation on Scenic Action* by Franciscus Lang, S.J., Munich, 1727.

53. De Lairesse, friend and sitter to Rembrandt, compiled a lexicon of pictorial subjects from many sources. In a section on gesture useful to painters and sculptors, he cited famous works, among them Michelangelo's *Last Judgment.*

"Fright" and "Horror," engravings by Gérard de Lairesse from *Groot Schilderboek,* Amsterdam, 1707.

54. De Lairesse distinguishes habitual gestures of proletariat and bourgeoisie when eating and drinking. So-called Dutch minor masters (Jan Steen, Adriaen Brouwer, Adriaen van Ostade) depicted characteristic genre scenes that influenced mimetic practice through the 18th century. Gestural definition of class and quality increased the grammar of mimicry and movement.

Engravings by Gérard de Lairesse from *Groot Schilderboek,* Amsterdam, 1707.

55. Engel wrote specifically for theatrical rather than pictorial use. Basing observation more on nature than on plastic art, he looked carefully at social behavior determined by class distinction and, in a series of delicate illustrations, widely imitated, gave typical positions that are universally legible without verbal explanation.

"A workman gulps; a gentleman sips," engravings by Johann Jakob Engel from his *Ideen zu einer Mimik,* Berlin, 1785.

56, 57. Engel's *Thoughts on Mimicry* was popularized in England in Siddons's translation and adaptation. Heroic posturing useful for the tragic repertory of Corneille, Racine, and Voltaire, as well as Shakespeare, Dryden, Weiland, and Goethe, drew heavily on Neoclassic painting and the new archeology inspired by scientific excavation around Naples and Rome.

"Distraction" and "Persuasion," engravings by Johann Jakob Engel from his *Ideen zu einer Mimik,* Berlin, 1785.

NOTES

58. Anna Morgan, American student of elocutionary and gestural methods of François Delsarte, wrote one of many popularizations that served provincial autodidacts like Isadora Duncan in San Francisco, c. 1890 (see back endpaper F).

"Alas, Poor Soul! What Grief Is Thine!"—illustration by Rose Mueller Sprague from *An Hour with Delsarte: A Study of Expression* by Anna Morgan, New York, 1889.

59. Heirs of wandering dancer-tumblers who kept the tradition of performing skills alive after the destruction of Roman theater, professional entertainers at medieval shows possessed a vocabulary of grotesque gesture and movement that was inherited by the Italian comedians. Elements of this entered ballet idiom by way of Franco-Italian pantomime.

Der Schallesnarr (The Roguish Fool) by Erasmus Grasser, 1480. Carved and painted wood.
Munich, Altes Rathaus.

60. One of the earliest and still among the finest representations of the movement quality of the *commedia dell'arte* characters is this figure of Pantaloon by Callot, the great French graphic artist who observed the comedians in Italy.

Etching by Jacques Callot, 1616.
New York, Metropolitan Museum (Print Room).

61. Harlequin (Arlecchino, Arlequin), the most agile, mercurial, virtuosic of the *commedia dell'arte* figures, wore a tight provocative costume of stylized random patches, originally deriving from Middle Eastern Sufi sources. In England, he fathered a genre of mixed pantomime-dance-musical theater. Christmas pantomimes are presented in England still, with updated characters adapted from earlier harlequinades.

John Rich as Harlequin, 1753. Watercolor on paper.
London, The Garrick Club.

62. Jelgerhuis, a well-educated Dutch actor-mime, gave ten lectures on theater practice that were later issued in two volumes, one of which contains one hundred of his own clear drawings presenting the grammar of theatrical movement in its several genres as then taught and performed (see illus. 259–60).

Lithographic illustrations by Johannes Jelgerhuis from his *Lectures on Mimicry,* Amsterdam, 1827.

63. Faith bearing her pillar, Justice her scales, Charity her chalice, Prudence her wise serpent—these four personifications are heavily costumed, with full skirts and little freedom permitted (or needed) for movement, in spectacle in which choreography was subordinate to display.

Engraving by Jacques Patin from the libretto of the *Ballet-Comique de la Royne Louise,* Paris, 1581 (see illus. 90–96).

64. Castanet dancer wearing a well-cut theatrical dress permitting free movement. Shoes are heeled; the costume is fitted close to the body, defined with a fancy differentiating it from normal luxury of court uniform. The cut of French masculine tailoring, influenced by English military style, was a world standard until World War II.

Hand-colored engraving by Jean Bérain the Elder, c. 1680.
New York, Pierpont Morgan Library.

65. This splendid representation of Momus, god of banter, portrays a dancer of the Opéra in the uniform of his profession. The drawing may have been done as part of an uncompleted set of designs for private fancy dress, but it stands equally for the cumbersome silhouette of *tonnelet* and pannier that Noverre's reform proposals of 1760 castigated.

Red and black chalk drawing by Gabriel de St. Aubin, 1752.
New York, Pierpont Morgan Library.

66. A female Fury—in an idealized opera or ballet costume based on Medea's jealousy of Jason—shows incrustation of the huge official theatrical skirt, heavily embroidered with symbols of hatred, envy, and wrath (see illus. 227–28). Not until such overwhelming adornment was abandoned could freedom of movement be gained.

Engraving by Gaillard (after design by J-B. Martin), c. 1755.

67. The Revolution of 1789 precipitated violent changes in taste as well as politics. Appeal to the Plutarchian virtues also permitted reforms in theater, not the least of which affected costume; for the following quarter-century, at least, it approached nudity. Reaction, complete with corsets, set in after the Bourbon Restoration (1815), and not until Duncan's concerts, c. 1905, would dancers again be so lightly dressed (see illus. 69).

Marie Gardel as Psyche, colored stipple engraving by Jean Prudhon from *La Galerie Théâtrale,* Paris, 1790.

68. *Emma Livry as Le Papillon.* The great Romantic ballerina Marie Taglioni, marking her retirement, staged a ballet (to

256

music by Offenbach) in which her pupil, then eighteen, was presented as her potential successor. Two years later the girl was burned to death when her tarlatans caught fire from a gas jet. The silhouette of the full skirt, inherited from the 1830's, would be abbreviated by the end of the century to show more of the upper leg.

Lithograph by Bertaut (after a photograph by Disderi), Paris, 1860.

69. Isadora Duncan costumed for *La Marseillaise*, c. 1916, Paris, is uncorseted but scarcely nude. She realized, as did the Greeks, that the body in spectacular movement benefits by a covering of light drapery, easy to move in but generalizing or rendering monumental the accidents and particulars of a performer's body. By 1910, dancers began to abandon toe shoes for barefoot or sandaled "Greek" and "Oriental" choreographies, in great part due to Isadora.

70. Formal symmetry—authoritative grandeur swollen with overcharged massive detail—determined official opera-house scenery through the 17th century, with echoes well into the 19th. Fictive architecture for court shows, public festivals, and church ceremonies provided a frame of smothering richness that continued to overwhelm the dancing until it was rendered less ostentatiously symmetrical or lighter in form and color.

A Temple to Jupiter, stage design by Giuseppe Galli Bibiena, c. 1730.
New York, Pierpont Morgan Library.

71. Lord Clark defines "the system known as perspective, by which it was thought that with mathematical calculation one could render on a flat surface the precise position of a figure in space." Probably first thoroughly analyzed by the architect Brunelleschi in Florence, c. 1400, linear and then aerial perspective subsumed methods for creating imaginary spaces on vast ceilings and in the décor for opera houses.

Ideal Townscape by Luciano de Laurana, c. 1475. Tempera on panel.
Baltimore, Walters Art Gallery.

72. The establishment of single, and later of multiple, vanishing points by geometrical means determined the formulas by which painters and theatrical designers constructed a spatial ambiance within which actions transpired. Here, in this garden combined with architectural elements, landscape and foliage are imposed on a strict architectural structure.

A Villa Garden in the Veneto by Bonifazio de Pitati, c. 1540. Oil on panel.
London, ex collection Colnaghi.

73. Set pieces, often on rollers, built in three dimensions (here representing Circe's garden and palace), were arranged around the ballroom in which the first Renaissance court spectacles were performed (see illus. 95). Made of wood, cloth, metallic paper, and plaster, then painted, they were seen from at least three sides.

Engraving by Jacques Patin from the libretto of the *Ballet-Comique de la Royne Louise,* Paris, 1581.

74. "Circe's Magic Wood" for the *Ballet-Comique de la Royne Louise* shows careful construction of individual set pieces, made for a single occasion. There was no need to store or maintain scenery, since ballrooms were scarcely repertory houses; for every early fete, new scenery was designed and built.

Engraving by Jacques Patin from the libretto, Paris, 1581.

75. Cardinal Richelieu has as guests Louis XIII, Anne of Austria, and their small son (later Louis XIV) to view opera-ballet in his Palais Cardinal, designed for him by Jacques le Mercier. Later, this theater was used by Molière's troupe. The permanent facility, adaptable to repertory requirements, would use suites of generalized scenes for various sites: palace, garden, wild wood, encampment, heaven, etc.

Oil on canvas, 1641.
Paris, Musée des Arts Décoratifs.

76. Interlude from an important Florentine opera-ballet, showing the entire stage area, with ramps leading to the floor used for combined dances by performers and spectators at the end of the show. Focal point is the framed, elevated stage. By the end of the 17th century, this would develop into the opera-house auditorium as we know it (see illus. 101, 102).

First ballet interlude from *La Liberazione di Tirreno e d'Arnea,* engraving by Jacques Callot (after drawing by Giulio Parigi), Florence, 1616–17.
New York, Metropolitan Museum (Print Room).

77. Transformation scene, with breakaway stage effects. The palace of the enchantress Armida is set afire when she is spurned by the Christian hero, Rinaldo, who, convinced by his Crusader companions of her evil intent, quits her to save Jerusalem. In angry despair she flies off on a hippogriff, ostensibly to hell (see illus. 105).

Scene from the ballet-opera *Armide* (Lully-Quinault), Act V. Engraved frontispiece (detail) from the libretto, Paris, 1686.
Paris, Bibliothèque Nationale.

NOTES

78. Stage design for a palace scene in opera-ballet repertory, characteristic of the work of the Bibiena family, who worked for many princely theaters in Italy, Austria, and Central Europe. An impression of sumptuous atmosphere and limitless space provided an elegant but unobtrusive background for the rich mineral colors and grave movement of singers' and dancers' costumes.

A Palace Courtyard, drawing by Giovanni Galli Bibiena (?), c. 1725.
London, ex collection Christopher Powney.

79. Rigidly frontal symmetry in 17th-century stage sets shifted in the first quarter of the 18th, when focus was placed off-center, at an angle, suggesting deeper space and inviting the public into more intimate identification with performing areas. Servandoni worked for Noverre in Stuttgart.

Paper model by Jean Nicolas Servandoni, mid-18th century. Watercolor.
Paris, ex collection Mademoiselle de Castel Bajou.

80. Léon Bakst's tomato, malachite, sapphire, and gilt set for *Schéhérazade* represents the type of exotic vision introduced to Western Europe by Diaghilev in his first seasons. Bakst used the techniques of Post-Impressionist painting and the floor plans of the traditional Baroque designer; his knowledge of scale produced masterpieces.

Set for *Schéhérazade* by Léon Bakst, 1910. Watercolor on paper.
Paris, Musée des Arts Décoratifs.

81. Georges Rouault, an eminent master of the School of Paris, had been a favorite pupil of the fantastic "Orientalist" Gustave Moreau. Diaghilev took a characteristic watercolor in this painter's highly personal style and had it blown up by the great scene-painter Prince Schervachidze to stage proportions. This was initially shocking because of Rouault's seemingly naive approach to usual theater practice. By exaggerating a quality of freshness and innocence, Diaghilev rendered an intimate and interior art as perversely heroic—and a powerful complement to a major work of modern choreography.

Backdrop sketch for *Le Fils Prodigue* (Prokofiev-Balanchine), scene 2, by Georges Rouault, 1929. Watercolor on paper.
Hartford, Conn., Wadsworth Atheneum (Lifar Collection).

82. Teatro Farnese, Parma, designed by Giovanni Battista Aleotti, 1619 (now largely destroyed), shows a developed picture-frame proscenium, behind which stage machinery is hidden.

83. A series of fifty fantastic etchings by Bracelli suggests many metaphors of the human body moving in space in a wildly theatrical aura.

Etching by Giovanni Battista Bracelli from his *Bizzarie di varie figure,* Leghorn, 1624.

84. Henri III, King of France and Poland, had a medal struck, following custom for memorializing births, comings of age, victories, treaties, and deaths, which were also accompanied by solemn shows. Such miniature monuments, cast with exquisite artistry, were reminders of earthly glory and political power long after the initial occasion had been forgotten. Large plaques, painted and gilded, with appropriate Latin mottoes inscribed, were distributed at the end of festivals to princely participants and guests.

Bronze medallion of Henri III by Germaine Pilon (att.), 1575.
New York, collection David Daniels.

85. *Apollon* (leader of the Muses). Plaque awarded to the god's terrestrial representative at the end of the *Ballet-Comique de la Royne Louise.*

Engraving by Jacques Patin from the libretto, Paris, 1581.
New York Public Library (Music Division).

86. *La Volta,* a social dance in which ladies were whirled up and off the floor, considered an ancestor of the waltz.

Oil painting, c. 1582.
Rennes, Musée des Beaux-Arts.

87. *Le Ballet des Polonais.* Final figure: Deployment of the provinces of the French nation.

Wood engraving from the libretto, 1573.
Paris, Bibliothèque Nationale.

88. This represents the type of non-theatrical dancing enjoyed by the court of Henri III that followed a ballet performance but that, by virtue of its strict ordering and rich dress, held spectacular elements.

The Marriage Ball of Anne de Joyeuse and Margaret de Lorraine (detail) by Herman van der Most (att.), 1581. Oil.
Paris, Louvre.

89. Interior of a virginal cover, showing social dancers in the open air, accompanied by professional musicians.
Painted wood (detail) by Hans Reukers, 1581.
New York, Metropolitan Museum (Gift of B. H. Homan).

90. Plaque inscribed with a dolphin, given by the King to the Queen at the end of the *Ballet-Comique de la Royne Louise*.
Engraving by Jacques Patin from the libretto, Paris, 1581.
New York Public Library (Music Division).

91. The composer of *Le Ballet des Polonais* in the private music chapel of the dukes of Bavaria.
Miniature by Hans Mielich from Lassus's *Psalms of Penitence*, 1565.
Munich, Bavarian State Library.

92. Leonardo, like many Renaissance artists, delighted in designing festivities based on or adapted from antique motifs. These sea creatures, based on Greco-Roman precedent, may have served as models for many tritons through the 18th century.
Neptune Driven by Hippocamps by Leonardo da Vinci, 1504. Chalk drawing.
Windsor, Royal Collection.

93. *Ballet Comique de la Royne Louise*. Entry of music-making tritons (see illus. 137, 138).
Engraving by Jacques Patin from the libretto, Paris, 1581.
New York Public Library (Music Division).

94. *The Judgment of Paris. Tableau vivant* for the entry of Juana de Castille into Brussels, c. 1496. Paris and Mercury choose among Minerva, Juno, and Venus (see illus. 302).
Miniature, c. 1497–98.
Berlin, State Museum (Manuscript Section).

95. *Ballet Comique de la Royne Louise*. Entry of the Queen, the Princess of Lorraine, the Duchess of Guise.
Engraving by Jacques Patin from the libretto, Paris, 1581.
New York Public Library (Music Division.)

96. Fountain machine. Woodcut from *Practica di fabricar scene e machine* by Nicola Sabbatini, Venice, 1637–38.
New York, Metropolitan Museum (Print Room).

97. Wall fresco from the Triclinium Tomb, c. 490 B.C. Corneto-Tarquinio.

98. *The Mars of Todi,* 4th century B.C. Bronze.
Rome, Museo Etrusco Gregoriano (Vatican).

99. Armed dancers with flute player. Greek vase painting, c. 510 B.C.
Paris, Louvre.

100. Warriors keep time by clashing swords on shields.
Marble relief (detail), Hellenistic or Roman copy of 4th-century B.C. Greek original.
Rome, Vatican.

101, 102. *La Liberazione di Tirreno e d'Arnea*. Interlude II: Hell; finale: "The Court of Love Triumphant Over War."
Engravings by Jacques Callot (after drawings by Giulio Parigi), Florence, 1616–17.

103. Choreography with moralized patterns: "Powerful Love," "Ambitious Desire," "Virtuous Design," and "Immortal Fame" show naive floor plans for ballet figures.
Engravings from the libretto of *Le Ballet de Monsieur Vendosme,* 1610.
Paris, Bibliothèque Mazarine.

104. Tuscan river gods: Festival on the river Arno, a Florentine water spectacle designed for Cosimo de' Medici, based on the myth of Jason and the Argonauts (see illus. 226, 229).
Engraving by Giulio Parigi, 1608.
New Haven, Conn., Yale University (Theater Archives).

NOTES

105, 106, 108. *La Délivrance de Renaud.* "Armida summons to her aid demons who assume forms contrary to her design"; scene 2: Crusaders before a magic fountain (see illus. 95); sixth ballet entry: round dance.

Engravings from the libretto, Paris, 1617.
Paris, Bibliothèque Nationale.

107. *Round Dance for the Ring Prize,* a medieval social dance in which the winner seized a ring. Older folk forms were assimilated into choreographic designs for 17th-century ballet.

Engraving by Israhel van Meckenem, c. 1480.
New York, Metropolitan Museum (Print Room).

109. *Louis XIII Marries Anne of Austria* (1615), a combination of documentation and allegory.

Engraving by Picart from *Les Amours du Roy* by Puget de la Serre, 1624.
Paris, Bibliothèque Nationale.

110. "*Rinaldo with Armida*" (see illus. 346), illustration by Castello for Tasso's *Gerusalemme Liberata,* Genoa, c. 1590.
New York Public Library (Spencer Collection).

111. *Salmacida Spolia.* Costume design for a Fury and headdress. Pen sketches by Inigo Jones, 1640.

112. *Oberon: The Faery Prince.* Designs for two fays for Ben Jonson's masque. Pen sketch by Inigo Jones, 1611.

113. *Salmacida Spolia.* Costume designs for Furies. Pen sketches by Inigo Jones, 1640.

114. *Salmacida Spolia.* Costume design for Philogenes (played by Charles I). Pen sketch by Inigo Jones, 1640.

115. *Salmacida Spolia.* Décor for scene 5: "A Great City: In the Sky, Clouds with Deities."
Pen, ink, and wash drawing by Inigo Jones, 1640.

116. *Salmacida Spolia.* From anti-masque I: "Wolfgangus Vandergoose, Spagrick, Operator to the Invincible Lady, Styled the Magical Sister of the Rosicross."
Pen, ink, and wash drawing by Inigo Jones, 1640.

117. *Salmacida Spolia.* Costume designs for dancers in anti-masque. Doctor Tartaglia and the Pedant Francolin are figures borrowed from the roster of the Franco-Italian comedians of skill. Their abrupt, grotesque movements and mimicry contrasted with the noble heroics of allegorical action.
Pen sketches by Inigo Jones, 1640.

111–17 by permission of His Grace the Duke of Devonshire and the Trustees of the Chatsworth Settlement, Derbyshire.

118. Morisco dancer. The morris dance in England and on the Continent possibly derived from Moorish custom in Spain. Through the later Middle Ages a tradition of professional entertainer was maintained by the lively grotesque performers whose dress was adorned with small bells. (Inscription on balcony of inn: "Goldenen Dachl.")
Painted stone sculpture by Niklaus Türing, 1500. Innsbruck.

119. Frittelino, a type taken from the roster of the *commedia dell'arte*—here, a dandified dancer.

Engraved illustration from *Titulus Stultorum* by Bernard Picart, Amsterdam, 1696.

120–29. *La Finta Pazza.* Entries of ostriches, Indian savages, bears, parakeets.

Illustrations from the libretto, Paris, 1645.
Paris, Bibliothèque Nationale.

130. *Le Ballet du Roi,* 1651. Watercolor drawing, 1651.
Paris, Bibliothèque Nationale.

131. *Parnassus.* Arch for street pageant (with Henry VIII as Apollo) for Anne Boleyn's entry into London.

Pen and wash sketch by Hans Holbein, 1533.
Berlin, State Museum.

132. *Le Ballet du Roi.* Costume design for Louis XIV as Apollo.

Watercolor sketch, 1651.
Paris, Bibliothèque Nationale.

133. *Le Ballet de la Nuit.* Louis XIV as the Sun King.

Watercolor sketch by La Belle (?), 1653.
Paris, Bibliothèque Nationale.

134. *Le Ballet du Chasteau de Bicêtre,* 1632. Entry of money coiners.

Pen and watercolor sketch, 1632.
Paris, Bibliothèque Nationale.

135, 136. *Le Ballet de la Nuit.* Apollo (Louis XIV) as the Spirit of the Violin; the Spirit of Night on a Cloud.

Watercolor sketches, 1653.
Paris, Bibliothèque Nationale.

137. *Ballet-Comique de la Royne Louise.* Entry of sirens with mirrors.

Engraving by Jacques Patin from the libretto, Paris, 1581.
New York Public Library (Music Division).

138. Design for detail of curved ceiling for the Villa Adriana.

Pen and wash sketch by Cassiano del Pozzo Albani, c. 1540.
Windsor, Royal Collection.

139, 140. *Les Nopces de Pelée et de Thétis.* Costume for Apollo (Louis XIV); third entry: Monsieur le Comte de St. Aignan as a marine demigod. Watercolor sketches by Torelli (?), 1654.

141, 142. *Les Nopces de Pelée et de Thétis.* Third ballet entry: Marine cave with Neptune, Thétis, coral fishers; the centaur Chiron persuades Peleus. Pencil drawings by Torelli, 1654.

143. *Les Nopces de Pelée et de Thétis.* The palace of Thétis. Engraving by Israel Silvestre (after drawing of Francart, based on illus. 142).

139–43, Paris, Bibliothèque de l'Institut.

144. Louis XIV as triumphant Roman emperor. Coysevox served the Sun King as sculptor in much the same style as Lully. One of the most energetic and masterful of collaborators on the enrichment of Versailles, he here invests his lord with the triumph of Anthony and the benevolent patronage of Hadrian.

Marble overmantel by Antoine Coysevox, c. 1675.
Versailles, Palace Museum.

145. Molière's repertory became permanent in French theater as soon as it was printed. This illustration from the mid-18th century, a hundred years after *Les 'Fâcheux* was first presented, shows the work in then-contemporary terms.

Engraved frontispiece for *Les Fâcheux,* c. 1765–70.
Paris, Bibliothèque Nationale.

146. Vaux-le-Vicomte, general view of palace and park. Engraving by Perette, c. 1660.
Paris, Bibliothèque Nationale.

147. *Les Fâcheux.* Engraving by J. Sauné (after drawing by Pierre Brissart), 1682.
New York Public Library (Spencer Collection).

148. The company of Italian comedians exiled for lampooning Louis XIV's prudish mistress. Here the Doctor, Columbine, Pierrot, and Harlequin depart (see p. 22).

Engraving from *Le Théâtre Italien* by Evariste Gherardi, 1697.
New York Public Library (Spencer Collection).

149. "M. Molier": Molière is shown in this little-known portrait in the role of drunkard (Debauchery).

Watercolor costume sketch for *Le Ballet du Roi,* 1651.
Paris, Bibliothèque Nationale.

150. Molière as Sganarelle, tricky servant companion to his Dom Juan (see illus. 224, 225).

Engraving by Simonin, c. 1665–70.
Paris, Bibliothèque Nationale.

151. M. Dubreil as Scaramouche: a well-known French dancer in a role from Italian comedy.
Engraving, Paris, c. 1665.
New York, Pierpont Morgan Library.

152. Masked male dancer in the role of a peasant. Engraving for the publisher Mariette, c. 1680.
New York, Pierpont Morgan Library.

153. *Les Amans Magnifiques.* An 18th-century illustration to an edition of Molière. Engraved frontispiece, Paris, c. 1770–75.
New York Public Library (Spencer Collection).

154. The classic uniform of theatrical heroics established more than a century earlier and lasting well into the 18th century.
Pen and wash drawing by Giovanni Battista Tiepolo, c. 1780.
London, Victoria and Albert Museum.

155. *Les Amants Magnifiques.* Engraved frontispiece, c. 1780.
New York Public Library (Spencer Collection).

156. Ballet entry, possibly showing Louis XIV as first dancer. Drawing (detail) by Henry Gissey (?) c. 1660.
London, Victoria and Albert Museum.

157. *Les Amans Magnifiques.* Engraving, c. 1680.

158. *Britannicus.* Racine's tragedy presented at the Hôtel de Bourgogne. Engraving by F. Chaveau, c. 1670.

159. Costume sketch for *Le Ballet du Roi,* 1651.

157–59, Paris, Bibliothèque Nationale.

160, 161. Female opera dancer as a bacchante; masked male opera dancer with castanets. Engravings by Le Pautre, c. 1675.

162. Female opera dancer with mask in hand. At the start of the 17th century, dancers were male and masked. By the end, they included female professionals, and all masks were discarded. Engraving, France, c. 1690.
160–62, New York, Pierpont Morgan Library.

163. Tragic actor in repertory of the Comédie Française, showing posture and profile of the classic drama in official costume.
Gouache by Föch-Whirsker, c. 1765.
Paris, Musée de la Comédie Française.

164. "Jealous Rage" from the tragedy *Félix et Violante.*
Engraving from *Practical Illustrations of Rhetorical Gesture and Action* by Johann Jakob Engel, "adapted to the English drama" by Henry Siddons, London, 1822.

165., 166. Action studies. Engravings by J. F. von Göz for the poem *Lenardo und Blanchine* by Bürger, Berlin, 1780.
Reproduced in *Monodrama: Attitudes, Tableaux Vivants, 1770–1815* by K. G. Holmström, Stockholm, 1968.

167. Le Château de Sceaux. Engraving by Aveline, c. 1710.
Paris, Bibliothèque Nationale.

168, 169. Engravings (after drawings by Charles Eisen) for the poem *La Déclamation Théâtrale* by C. J. Dorat, Paris, 1766.

170. Engraving from *Chirologia* by John Bulwer, London, 1644.
London, British Museum Library.

171. Engraving from *Le Maître à Danser* by Pierre Rameau, Paris, 1725.

172. The dancer Ballon as a jester. Engraving by Le Pautre (after drawing by Jean Bérain the Elder), c. 1700.
New York, Pierpont Morgan Library.

173. Mademoiselle Prévôt as a bacchante (possibly in the title role of *Philomèle,* opera by Roy and Lacoste). Oil by Jean Raoux, *c.* 1723.
Tours, Musée des Beaux-Arts.

174, 175. *A Chacoon for Harlequin,* with indications of his movements. Engravings from the libretto-score by F. Le Rousseau, 1733.
London, British Museum Library.

176. Costume design for *Le Ballet du Roi,* Paris, 1651.
Paris, Bibliothèque Nationale.

177. *David Garrick as Harlequin.* Watercolor drawing, *c.* 1740.
Paris, Bibliothèque de l'Opéra.

178. *The Loves of Mars and Venus* (detail). Engraving by Hendrik Goltzius, 1585.
New York, Metropolitan Museum (Print Room).

179. *Orpheus and Eurydice.* Scene 2: Hell (see illus. 455). Engraving of pantomime by John Weaver, London, 1718.
Cambridge, Mass., Harvard Theater Collection.

180. *Wit at Several Weapons,* "a comedy of trickery" by Beaumont and Fletcher. Final Dance. Engraving, 1711.
London, British Museum Library.

181. Figures for a dance of two gentlemen, with choreographic floor patterns. Engraving by N. Fischer (after drawing by Kellom Tomlinson), London, 1720.

182. *Danse Paysanne* by Antoine Watteau, *c.* 1712. Oil.
Hartford, Conn., Wadsworth Atheneum.

183. *The Dancer Camargo,* engraving by L. Cars (after painting by Nicolas Lancret), *c.* 1730.

184, 185. Costumes for opera dancers as peasants. Engravings by J-B. Martin, *c.* 1750.

186. Idealized scene of opera-ballet. Painting by Nicolas Lancret, *c.* 1735–40.
Paris, ex collection Madame de Polés.

187. *The Great Fair at Bezons* (detail) by Jean-Baptiste Pater, *c.* 1735. Oil.
New York, Metropolitan Museum (Bache Collection).

188. *The Italian Comedians* by Antoine Watteau, *c.* 1715. Oil.
New York, Metropolitan Museum (Bache Collection).

189. *Minuet at a Venetian Carnival* by Giovanni Battista Tiepolo, 1756. Oil.
Barcelona, Catalonian Museum of Fine Arts.

190. Madame de Pompadour as Galatea; Monsieur le Prince de Rohan as Acis. Meissen porcelain figurines (after engraving by C. H. Cochin), *c.* 1750.
Hartford, Conn., Wadsworth Atheneum.

191. Pompadour and de Rohan performing *Acis et Galatée* in the Théâtre des Petits Appartements, Versailles. Drawing by C. N. Cochin, *c.* 1750.
Paris, Bibliothèque de l'Arsenal.

192. *La Guinguette, c.* 1753. Scene from the ballet. Engraving by F. Basan (after painting by Gabriel de St. Aubin), *c.* 1753.
Washington, National Gallery (Widener Collection).

193. *Peasant Celebration* by Jan Steen, 1663. Oil.
Washington, National Gallery (Widener Collection).

194. *Le Carnéval du Parnasse.* Engraving of scene from the ballet by F. Basan (after painting by Gabriel de St. Aubin), *c.* 1752.

195. Engraving by Charles Eisen (after drawing by E. de Ghent) illustrating Rousseau's mimo-drama, *c.* 1750.
New York Public Library (Spencer Collection).

196. Sculptor's studio as ballet setting. Engraving from *New and Curious School of Theatrical Dancing* by Gregorio Lambranzi (Plate 24, Part II), Nuremberg, 1716.

197. *La Barberina as Galatea,* painted panel by Antoine Pesne, 1745.
Potsdam, Palace (Music Room).

198. Engraved book illustration, France, c. 1780.

199. *La Statue et les Jardinières,* drawing falsely attributed to C. G. Bibiena, probable designer of *Pygmalion,* Vienna, 1752.
Ex collection Count Durazzo.

200. Watercolor costume design annotated by Frederick the Great, c. 1745.
Berlin, Theater Museum.

201. Eva Maria Violette (Weigl), wife of David Garrick and pupil of Hilferding. Painting by William Hogarth (att.), c. 1749.
New York, ex collection Victor Spark.

202. Chinoiserie figures (detail), red lacquer on wood, c. 1750.
Kansas City, William Rockhill Nelson Gallery.

203. "Procession of a Chinese Mandarin of the First Order," engraving from *Treatise on the Art of Dancing* by Giovanni-Andrea Gallini, London, 1772.

204. *A Chinese Ballet,* watercolor drawing by Louis-Simon Boquet, c. 1770.
Paris, Bibliothèque de l'Opéra.

205. *Le Temple de la Chine,* paper model for décor by Jean Nicolas Servandoni.
Château des Champs, Seine-et-Marne.

206. *A Chinese Dancer,* "which serves several divertissements, as in the ballet *Les Indes Galantes* and others."
Colored engraving by J-B. Martin, Paris, c. 1750.

207. *A Chinese Ballerina,* colored engraving by J-B. Martin, Paris, c. 1750.

208. *Les Chinois,* a "Chinese" number from the repertory of the Italian comedians, showing Mezzetin, the Doctor, and a "Pagod."
Engraving by M. Roquillard for *Le Théâtre Italien* by Evariste Gherardi, Paris, 1700.

209. Watercolor costume sketch by Louis-Simon Boquet, c. 1760.
Paris, Bibliothèque de l'Opéra.

210. *Ambassadors from Morocco in a Box at the Opéra,* engraving by Antoine Trouvain, Paris, c. 1680.

211. *A Seated Persian,* pencil drawing (after Antoine Watteau), c. 1740.

212. *Masquerade with Oriental Personages* (detail), pen and ink drawing by Claude Gillot, c. 1730.

211, 212 Boston, Museum of Fine Arts (Forsyth Wickes Collection).

213. *Entry of the Turkish Ambassadors.* Mehmet Effendi, Ambassador of Achmet, the Grand Turk, before the Tuileries. Engraving, 1721.
Paris, Bibliothèque Nationale.

214. Painting by Nicolas Lancret, c. 1740.
Paris, ex collection Madame la Princesse de Poix.

215. Engraving (after Jean Bérain the Elder) for *Le Triomphe de.l'Amour,* Paris, c. 1685.

216. *Der Grossmutige Turke.* Engraving of final act of the Vienna production (after Bernardo Belotto), 1758.

217–19. Costume designs by Louis-Simon Boquet for Noverre, c. 1770.
Warsaw, University Library.

220. Musician holding a *trompette marine* (one-stringed fiddle). Engraving from *Les Costumes Grotesques* by Nicolas Larmessian II, Paris, c. 1680 (see illus. 135).

221. *Lully and Rameau Welcomed by Orpheus to the Elysian Fields.* Engraving, Paris, 1774.

222. Engraving by Schmützer and Wagner (after painting by M. Mytens), c. 1755.
Vienna, National Library.

223. *Christophe Willibald Ritter von Gluck.* Bust by Jean-Antoine Houdon, c. 1755.
Paris, Musée de l'Opéra.

224. *Dom Juan ou le Festin de Pierre.* Engraving by Sauné (after drawing by Pierre Brissart) for an edition of Molière's plays, Paris, 1682.

225. *Don Juan.* Engraving by De Marc (after drawing by François Boucher) for an edition of Molière's plays, Paris, 1780.

226. *Jason et Medée* by Jean François de Troy, c. 1740. Oil.
London, National Gallery.

227, 228. Engravings by René Gaillard (from costume designs by J-B. Martin), Paris, c. 1750.

229. *Jason and Medea* with the dancers Bacelli, Vestris, Simonet. Engraving by John Boydell, London, 1782.

230. David Garrick as Macbeth. Copperplate engraving by C. White (after drawing by T. Parkinson), London, 1775.

231. "Horror." Engraving from Siddons's adaptation of Engel, London, 1822 (see illus. 164).

232, 233. *Jason et Medée.* Costume sketches by Louis-René Boquet for Jealousy and Poison, Stuttgart, 1763.
Warsaw, University Library.

234. I. N. Nikitin as Colas (later called Colin). Lithograph by Schmidt (from drawing by Trenzer), c. 1842.
Moscow, Bakhrushin Museum and Library.

235. S. Litavkin as Colas, Moscow-St. Petersburg, c. 1890.
Moscow, Bakhrushin Museum and Library.

236. *Une Jeune Fille Querellée par sa Mère.* Engraving by Pierre Philippe Chofart (after painting by Pierre-Antonine Baudoin), c. 1765. The inspiration for *La Fille Mal Gardée.*
Paris, Bibliothèque Nationale.

237. Peasant dance with Mademoiselle Guimard, Jean Dauberval, Marie Allard. Engraving by Pierre Leleu (after his drawing), 1779.

238, 239. Engravings of costume designs by J-B. Martin, c. 1760 (see illus. 184, 185).
New York, Pierpont Morgan Library.

240. Grand Opéra, Bordeaux, designed by Jean-Victor Louis, 1780–83.

241–43. *La Fille Mal Gardée,* St. Petersburg, 1882. Vasily Geltzer as Widow Simone; Pavel Gerdt as Colin; A. Prikhovnova as Lise.
Moscow, Bakhrushin Museum and Library.

244. Marie Taglioni's toe-point. Line and stipple engraving by Rait (after Lev Ivanovitch Kiel), St. Petersburg, c. 1841.

245. Fanny Elssler's foot. Marble by Félicie de Faveau, Florence, 1847.
Vienna, National Library.

246. Emma Livry's slipper, c. 1860.
Paris, Musée de l'Opéra.

247. Anna Pavlova's toe shoe, c. 1914 (see illus. 18, 20, 21).

246, 247 from *Ballet Design Past and Present* by Cyril Beaumont, London, 1946.

248. Pencil drawing by Antonio Canova, 1806–9 (?).

249, 250. Engravings after costume designs by J-B. Martin, c. 1750.
New York, Pierpont Morgan Library.

251, 252. Watercolor costume sketches by Louis-Simon Boquet (att.), c. 1765.
Paris, Bibliothèque de l'Opéra.

253. "The Vestriad." Engraving by J. Berchoux illustrating mock-heroic poem by Hans Busk, London, 1819 (Paris version, *Les Dieux de l'Opéra,* 1806).

254. *Zefiro e Flora,* Teatro della Pergola, Florence, 1828, with Adelaide Mersy and Giovanni Rousset. Lithograph by Salucci.

255, 256. *Réconciliation de Flore et Zéphyre; Jeux Innocents de Zéphyre et Flore.* Lithographs by Edward Morton after drawings by "Theophile Wagstaff" (William Makepeace Thackeray), London, 1836.

257. Terra cotta plaque, c. 100 B.C. Myrrha.
Paris, Louvre.

258. *The Aeolian Harp,* ballet by Fedor Tolstoi (1783–1873), a Neoclassic work based on Scandinavian themes and folklore. Tolstoi was an early native-born choreographer, a pupil of Charles-Louis Didelot, who profoundly affected the Petersburg academy and theater from the start of the 19th century.
Engraving (from a series) by Fedor Tolstoi (taken from his own pencil drawings), from *Didelot* by Yuri Slonimsky, Leningrad and Moscow, 1958.

259, 260. "Combat of Roman Warriors"; "Postures Suitable for the Death of a Roman Patrician." Lithographic illustrations by Johannes Jelgerhuis from his *Lectures on Mimicry,* Amsterdam, 1827 (see illus. 54).

261, 262. *Salvatore and Maria Medina Viganò.* Pen and watercolor drawings by Gottfried von Schadow, c. 1790 (see illus. 59).
Berlin, Theater Museum.

263, 264. *La Vestale.* Act III: Temple of Vesta; Act IV: The Sacred Grove. Engravings after designs by Alessandro Sanquirico, Milan, 1819.

265. *L'Été,* figure in a social dance (quadrille). Colored steel engraving by Lebas, Paris, c. 1815.

266, 267. *Die Nachtwandlerin* (Viennese version of *La Somnambule),* 1830. Scene II; scene III. Colored engravings by Zinke (after drawings by Schoeller), Vienna, c. 1830.

268. Pauline Montessu as the Sleepwalker. Stipple engraving by E. Rouargue (from drawing by Alexandre Lacauchie from *La Galerie Théâtrale),* Paris, c. 1828.

269. Desargue as the Sleepwalker. Lithograph by Sachse (after drawing by J. Scheppe), Berlin, c. 1829.

270. "A young shepherd prepares himself to go on stage with grace" (*Aux Foyer des Artistes).* Lithograph from *L'Opéra au 19ème siècle,* Paris, c. 1845.

271. "Here's an odd notion to invent a machine to maintain fourth position. My dear child, in order to succeed, first a dancer must break her legs" (*Aux Foyer des Artistes).* Lithograph from *L'Opéra au 19ème siècle,* Paris, c. 1845.

272. *Robert le Diable.* Act III, scene 2. Wood engraving from *Album des Théâtres,* Paris, 1836–37.

273. *Robert der Teufel.* Act II, "The Ballet of the Nuns," Viennese version of *Robert le Diable.* While Paris and, to a lesser degree, London were the original sources of the dominant Romantic repertory, Vienna remained an important ballet stronghold well into the 19th century.
Colored engraving by Andrei Geiger from *Theatralische Bilder, Galerie no. 2,* Vienna, c. 1840.

274. *Robert le Diable.* First performance, Paris, Opéra, 1831. Lithograph by J. Arnout, Paris, c. 1832.
Paris, Bibliothèque de l'Opéra.

275. Lithograph showing décor by Ciceri, Paris, 1832.

276. *Robert Le Diable, Ballet of the Nuns* (detail) by Hilaire Germain Edgar Degas, 1872. Oil on canvas.
New York, Metropolitan Museum (Bequest of Mrs. H. O. Havemeyer).

277. Marie Taglioni. Lithograph inspired by the statuette by Barre, c. 1835.

278. Paul and Amelia Taglioni in *La Sylphide,* Park Theater, New York, May 22, 1839. Lithograph by Sarony (after drawing by H. R. Robinson).

279. Marie Taglioni as La Sylphide. Steel engraving by W. H. Mote (after painting by Vidal) from *Les Beautés de l'Opéra et Ballet,* Paris-London, 1845.

280. *La Sylphide.* Marie Taglioni and Joseph Mazilier in "The Mountain Sylph." Lithograph by the Kellogs (after painting by G. Lepaulle), Hartford, Conn., 1845.

281. *La Sylphide.* Act I, Royal Danish Ballet, Copenhagen, c. 1915, with Karl Merrild as Madge, the witch.

282. *La Sylphide.* Act II, Royal Danish Ballet, Copenhagen, 1882, with Mademoiselle Tychsen and Hans Beck.

283. *Giselle.* Carlotta Grisi and Lucien Petipa. Lithographic music cover, c. 1842.

284. Théophile Gautier, poet, critic, librettist (1811–72). Lithograph from photograph, c. 1860.

285. *Giselle.* Adele Dumilâtre as Myrtha, Queen of the Wilis. Lithograph by Bouvier, London, 1843.

286. Hermine Blangy as Giselle. Lithograph by Charles Currier (after drawings by Francis Davignon and Joseph Volmering), Paris, c. 1850.

287. Carlotta Grisi as Giselle. Steel engraving by H. R. Robinson (after painting by A. E. Chalon) from *Les Beautés de l'Opéra et Ballet,* Paris-London, 1845.

288. Lucile Grahn as Giselle. *Carte de visite* photograph, Paris, c. 1850.

289. *Giselle.* Finale, Act I. Woodcut by Deschamps (after drawing by Jules Collington) from *Les Beautés de l'Opéra et Ballet,* Paris-London, 1845.

290. *Giselle.* Act II. American colored lithograph, c. 1849.
Cambridge, Mass.. Harvard Theater Collection.

291. *Esmeralda, the Street Dancer with Her Goat.* Lithograph, c. 1845.
Paris, Bibliothèque de l'Opéra.

292. *La Esmeralda.* Act III, scene 2. Elssler as Esmeralda; Goltz as Frollo; Perrot as Phoebus. Detail of watercolor by A. Charlemagne, c. 1848.
Moscow, Bakhrushin Museum and Library.

293. *Fanny Elssler as Esmeralda* (Act I). Oil painting by Paul Bürde, c. 1845.
Vienna, National Library.

294. Carlotta Grisi and Jules Perrot in *La Esmeralda.* Colored lithograph by Bouvier, London, 1844.

295. *La Esmeralda.* Act III, scene 2, "The Feast of Fools." Woodcut from *The Illustrated London News,* 1844.

296. *La Esmeralda,* Act I, revival by Alexander Gorsky, Moscow, 1902.
Annuals of the Imperial Theaters.

297. *The Flames of Paris* (choreography by Vasily Vainonen), Leningrad, 1932. Women from Marseilles advance on Notre Dame de Paris.

298. Taglioni, Cerrito, Grisi, Grahn. Woodcut from *The Illustrated London News,* July, 1845.

299. "La Claque en Action," lithograph by Bourdet from *Le Monde Dramatique,* Paris, 1838.

300. *Les Graces.* Marie Taglioni the Younger, Grisi, Amalia Ferraris. Watercolor by A. E. Chalon, 1850.
London, collection Minto Wilson.

301. Taglioni, Grisi, Cerrito, Grahn. Colored lithographic music cover by John Brandard, London, 1845.

302 *Le Jugement de Paris.* Saint-Léon as Paris; Perrot as Mercury; Cerrito, Taglioni, and Grahn as the rival goddesses. Woodcut from *The Illustrated London News,* 1850.

303. *Les Graces.* Taglioni the Younger, Grisi, Ferraris. Woodcut from *The Illustrated London News,* 1850.

304. Marius Petipa as a child. In the background, poster of the Royal Opera, Bordeaux, announces the ballet *La Danséomanie.*
Photograph of oil painting, Bordeaux (?), c. 1832.
Ex collection Lillian Moore.

305, 308. *La Fille du Pharaon,* revivial of October, 1899, St. Petersburg, with the ballerina Mathilde Kschessinska.

306. Flute player with funeral dancers. Wall painting for burial chamber, Egypt, 18th Dynasty.
London, British Museum.

307. *La Fille du Pharaon,* revival of December, 1890, St. Petersburg, with Marie Petipa and Serge Legat.

309. *La Fille du Pharaon.* Alexander Gorsky's elaborate revival of 1905–6 in Moscow typifies a certain grossness of style that Petersburg and the Marinsky Theater staff and audience held against the Muscovite Bolshoi. It also demonstrates the tight and "correct" archeological attitude against which Diaghilev and his designers revolted.

310. *La Fille du Pharaon.* Gorsky revival, Moscow, 1905–6. Procession of the Egyptian slaves.

311. *La Fille du Pharaon.* Gorsky revival, Moscow, 1905–6. Tikhomirov and Polivanov as Lord Wilson and John Bull.
309–11, *Annuals of the Imperial Theaters.*

312. Colored lithograph by H. Waldow, Jr., Berlin-New York, c. 1865.

313. Bolshoi Theater, St. Petersburg (destroyed), designed by Cavos. Watercolor by Sadovnikov, c. 1860.
Annuals of the Imperial Theaters.

314. *Koniok Gorbunok,* St. Petersburg, c. 1870. Tsar Maiden's entourage, with Lyubov Roslavleva.

315. Russian popular engraving, 1857.

316. *Koniok Gorbunok,* St. Petersburg, 1864. The ballet master Lev Ivanov and partner.

317. *Koniok Gorbunok,* St. Petersburg, 1864. Vasily Geltzer as Ivanushka.

318. *Koniok Gorbunok,* St. Petersburg, 1864. Latvian dance with G. I. Legat and M. S. Cranken.

319. Giuseppina Bozacchi (1853–70). *Carte de visite* photograph, c. 1870.

320. *Coppélia.* Lithographic music cover by Alfred Janin for the piano score by Léo Delibes, Paris, 1870.

321. The Paris Opéra (under construction), designed by Charles Garnier. Destruction of old buildings to form the Avénue de l'Opéra, 1868.

322–24. *Coppélia.* Costume designs by Alfred Albert for czardas dancers and Dawn divertissement (Act III), 1870.
Paris, Musée de l'Opéra.

325. Marius Petipa, St. Petersburg, c. 1895.

326, 327. *La Belle au Bois Dormant.* Costume sketches by I. A. Vsevolozhsky for fairies and pages, 1890.
Moscow, Bakhrushin Museum and Library.

328. *La Belle au Bois Dormant.* Pen and ink sketch of composite action, 1890.
Annuals of the Imperial Theaters.

329. *La Belle au Bois Dormant,* Act I, St. Petersburg, 1890. The christening of Aurora. Stage set by A. M. Shishkov.
Annuals of the Imperial Theaters.

330. *The Sleeping Princess.* Diaghilev's revival, London, 1921. Act II, finale: Aurora's wedding. Stage setting by Léon Bakst.

331. Lev Ivanov, St. Petersburg, c. 1890.

332. Peter Ilitch Tchaikovsky. Bust by Astrid Zydower, London, 1959.

333. *Le Lac des Cygnes*. Act I, Moscow, 1877. Entrance of the swans.
Moscow, Bakhrushin Museum and Library.

334. *The Swans' Lake*. Alhambra Theater, London, 1884, with choreography by Joseph Hansen, music by Georges Jacobi. Watercolor drawing from *The Ballet Called Swan Lake* by Cyril Beaumont, London, 1952.

335. *Le Lac des Cygnes,* St. Petersburg, 1895.
Annuals of the Imperial Theaters.

336. *Swan Lake,* Act II, restaged by George Balanchine, New York City Ballet, 1951.
Photograph Fred Fehl.

337. *Swan Lake,* Act II, Bolshoi Theater, Moscow, 1960.

338–41. *Le Pavillon d'Armide*. Michel Fokine as Le Vicomte de Beaugency, Paris, 1909.

342. Nijinsky as Armida's Slave (scene 2). Drawing by Frank Haviland for *The Illustrated London News,* 1909.

343. *Le Pavillon d'Armide*. Design for scene 2. Watercolor drawing by Alexandre Benois.
Hartford, Conn., Wadsworth Atheneum (Lifar Collection).

344. *Le Pavillon d'Armide,* Théâtre du Châtelet, Paris, 1909.

345. Costume design for Armida, scene 2. Watercolor drawing by Alexandre Benois, 1909.
Hartford, Conn., Wadsworth Atheneum (Lifar Collection).

346. *Le Pavillon d'Armide*. Anna Pavlova and Vaslav Nijinsky, St. Petersburg, 1908.

347, 348. *Le Pavillon d'Armide*. Vaslav Nijinsky as Armida's Slave.
Photographs Bert, Paris, 1909.

349. Michel Fokine, St. Petersburg, 1905.

350, 351. Dalcroze dancers. Free movement. Photographed in Hellerau, c. 1910.

352. *Salammbô* by Alexander Gorsky, Moscow, 1910. The heaviness that Fokine left behind (see illus. 309, 433).
Annuals of the Imperial Theaters.

353. Nijinsky costumed for *Les Sylphides* (Alexandre Benois). Detail of watercolor drawing by Dorothy Mullock for *The Art of Nijinsky* by Goeffrey Whitworth, London, 1913.

354, 355. *Les Sylphides*. Performance photographs at Théâtre du Châtelet by Bert for *Le Théâtre,* Paris, 1909.

356. *Les Sylphides*.
Photograph White's Studio, New York, 1916.

357. Nijinsky dressed for *Schéhérazade with Diaghilev*. Pen Sketch by Jean Cocteau, Monte Carlo, 1912.

358. Variant costume design, watercolor drawing by Léon Bakst, 1915.
Ex collection Martin Birnbaum.

359. Head of Sardanapalus (detail), which inspired Bakst's Shah. Pen sketch for *La Mort de Sardanapale* by Eugène Delacroix, 1826.
Paris, Louvre (Cabinet des Dessins).

360–66. *Schéhérazade*. Pen sketches of rehearsals and performances, by André Dunoyer de Segonzac, Paris, 1910.

367. *Narcisse,* ballet by Michel Fokine, Paris, 1911. Pencil sketch by Fokine.
Moscow, Bakhrushin Museum and Library.

368. Dancer. Hellenistic bronze, c. A.D. 260.
Baltimore, Walters Art Gallery.

NOTES

369, 370. Vaslav Nijinsky as Petrouchka.
Photographs Eliot & Fry, London, 1911.

371. Nijinsky. Plaster sketch by Auguste Rodin, 1912.
Paris, Rodin Museum.

372. Diaghilev and Nijinsky. Pen sketch by Jean Cocteau, Paris, 1913.

373. "Street Fair, Butter Week, Petersburg." Colored aquatint by John Augustus Atkinson from *Représentations Pittoresques des Russes,* St. Petersburg, 1803.

374. *Petrouchka,* scenes 1 and 4. Watercolor drawings by Alexandre Benois, 1911.
Hartford, Conn., Wadsworth Atheneum (Lifar Collection).

375. *Petrouchka.* Scene 1, with Orlov as the Moor; Karsavina as the Ballerina; Nijinsky as Petrouchka. Paris, 1911.

376. *Petrouchka.* Costume sketch for peasant woman by Alexandre Benois, 1911.
Hartford, Conn., Wadsworth Atheneum (Lifar Collection).

377. Watercolor costume design for Petrouchka by Alexandre Benois, 1911.
Hartford, Conn., Wadsworth Atheneum (Lifar Collection).

378. Watercolor costume design for the Ballerina by Alexandre Benois, 1911.
Hartford, Conn., Wadsworth Atheneum (Lifar Collection).

379. Dionysus with Silenus and Maenads. Greek vase by the Brygos Painter, c. 500–480 B.C.
Berlin, State Museum.

380. Helmeted hoplite runner. Greek marble grave stele, c. 510–500 B.C.
Athens, National Museum.

381. *L'Après-Midi d'un Faune.* Watercolor costume design for the Faun by Léon Bakst, 1912.
Hartford, Conn., Wadsworth Atheneum (Lifar Collection).

382–84. *L'Après-Midi d'un Faune,* New York, 1916. Note bare feet; sandals worn in the original production have been discarded.

385. Vaslav Nijinsky in the uniform of the Imperial Ballet School, St. Petersburg, 1907.

386. *Jeux.* Vaslav Nijinsky in stage costume (adapted from practice clothes of the Imperial School). Paris, 1913.

387. Serge Diaghilev, Paris, c. 1914.

388. *Jeux.* Rejected costume designs for Nijinsky as a soccer player.

389. Léon Bakst. Pencil drawing by Pablo Picasso, Paris, c. 1917.

390. *Jeux* with Ludmilla Shollar, Vaslav Nijinsky, Tamara Karsavina, Paris, 1913.

391, 392. *Jeux.* Nijinsky.
Photographs Bert, Paris, 1913.

393, 394. *Jeux.* Shollar, Nijinsky, Karsavina. Paris, 1913.

395. *Le Train Bleu,* with Sokolova, Dolin, Cocteau, Woizikowsky, Bronislava Nijinska. A decade after *Jeux,* Nijinsky's sister uses the motif of the sport it first introduced; Paris, 1924.

396. Marie Rambert (Miriam Rambach), c. 1930.

397. *Le Sacre du Printemps.* Tribal maidens, with Roerich's drop for scene 1.

398–401. *Le Sacre du Printemps.* Tribal elders and maidens. Paris, 1913.

402. "Nijinsky's choreography for *Le Sacre du Printemps.*" Caricature by "Joel" for *Le Théâtre à Paris en MCMXIII,* 1913. An accompanying scurrilous quatrain notes that several parts of the human body, notably head and tail, are transposed.

403. *Stravinsky at His Piano Summons the Ancestors.* Pencil drawing by Jean Cocteau, Paris, 1913.

404, 405. *Le Sacre du Printemps* in performance. Pen sketches by Emmanuel Barcet, Paris, 1913.

406. Jean Cocteau. Pencil drawing by Léon Bakst, Paris, c. 1914.

407. *La Parade (Invitation to the Side Show)* by Georges Seurat, 1887. Oil.
New York, Metropolitan Museum (bequest of Stephen C. Clark, 1960).

408. *Parade.* Stage set by Pablo Picasso, Paris, 1917.

409. *Parade.* The New York Manager. Costume construction by Pablo Picasso, Paris, 1917.

410. *Parade.* The Parisian Manager. Costume construction by Pablo Picasso, Paris, 1917.

411. *Parade.* The Chinese Magician (Léonide Massine). Costume by Pablo Picasso, Paris, 1917.

412. *Parade.* The Little American Girl (Marie Chabelska). Costume by Pablo Picasso, Paris, 1917.

413. *Triadic Ballet.* Conceptual organization of the three parts. Pen drawing by Oskar Schlemmer, Weimar, 1922.

414. *Triadic Ballet.* Costume designs for Ambulant Architecture, Marionette, Technical Organism, Dematerialization.
Pen drawings by Oskar Schlemmer, Weimar, 1922.

415. *Triadic Ballet.* Photomontage and gouache by Oskar Schlemmer, 1921–23.
New York, Museum of Modern Art (Gift of Mr. and Mrs. Douglas Auchincloss).

416. *Universal Space Concept.* Drawing by Oskar Schlemmer, Weimar, c. 1922.

417. *Pas de Deux,* choreography by Kazian Goleizovsky, Leningrad, c. 1922. Anastasia Abramova and Mikhail Gabovich.

418–20. *Tanzsynfonia.* Silhouette figures by Pavel Gontcharov from the libretto, Leningrad, 1923.

421. *Tanzsynfonia.* Pencil sketch for finale by Lopoukhov, Leningrad, 1923.

422. *Tanzsynfonia.* Silhouette of finale by Pavel Gontcharov, "the ultimate 'cosmogonic spiral' with all dancers linked."
George Balanchine kneels on the right; over him, Gusev; Lidia Ivanova is lifted in the center by Mikhailov; Leonid Lavrovsky kneels to his right; Alexandra Danilova, left, is supported by Ivanovsky.

From the libretto, Leningrad, 1923.

423. "Eurythmics." Pen sketches by Paulet Thevanaz illustrating *Méthode: Exercices de Plastique* by Émile Jaques-Dalcroze, Lausanne, 1916.

424. *Posidelki* ("marriage feast"). Russian popular lithograph, c. 1850.
Moscow, Bakhrushin Museum and Library.

425. *Les Noces.* Gouache design for stage set by Nathalie Gontcharova, 1923.
Hartford, Conn., Wadsworth Atheneum (Lifer Collection).

426. *Les Noces.* Groomsmen, pen drawing by Nathalie Gontcharova, 1923.
London, Victoria and Albert Museum.

427. *Les Noces.* Bride and bridesmaids. Rehearsal photograph, Monte Carlo, 1923.

428. *Les Noces.* Groom and groomsmen. Rehearsal photograph, Monte Carlo, 1923.

429. George Balanchine and Igor Stravinsky, New York, 1957.
Photograph Martha Swope.

430. *Apollo Belvedere.* Marble Roman copy of a Greek bronze, c. 320 B.C.
Rome, Vatican Museum.

431. *Apollo.* Costume engraving by J-B. Martin, c. 1750.
New York, Pierpont Morgan Library.

NOTES

432. The Bari Sisters. Freedom in dress, attained in the late 18th century, was lost again in the first years of the 19th, but finally won for good in the early 20th.
Steel engraving, Paris, 1796.

433. Corseted "Grecian" dancers attired as "The Three Graces" for the bacchanale in *Tannhäuser* at the Marinsky Theater five years before the arrival of Duncan in Russia. While they do not wear tarlatan ballet skirts, their costumes show the retardative taste of the late Romanov court against which Diaghilev, Fokine, and Bakst reacted.
Annuals of the Imperial Theaters, 1900.

434. *Apollo,* New York, 1965. Jacques d'Amboise, Karen von Aroldingen, Marnee Morris, Suzanne Farrell.

435. *Apollo,* New York, c. 1956. Jacques d'Amboise, Patricia Wilde, Diana Adams, Jillana.

436. *Apollo,* New York, c. 1956. Jacques d'Amboise and Diana Adams.

437. *Apollo,* New York, c. 1967. *Pas de deux* with Jacques d'Amboise and Suzanne Farrell.
434–37, photographs Martha Swope.

438. Antony Tudor, c. 1937.
Photograph G. Maillard Tessiere.

439–41. *Lilac Garden,* New York City Ballet, 1950, with Hugh Laing, Nora Kaye, Antony Tudor, Tanaquil LeClercq.
Photographs Walter E. Owen.

442. *Lilac Garden,* New York City Ballet, London, Covent Garden, 1950. Stage set by Horace Armistead.
Photograph Roger Wood.

443. *Lilac Garden,* New York City Ballet, 1950. Nora Kaye, Hugh Laing, Tanaquil LeClercq.
Photograph Walter E. Owen.

444. Russian sailor dance. Pen drawing for *Fundamentals of Character Dancing* by Andrei Lopoukhov, Leningrad, 1939.

445. *Fancy Free,* American Ballet Theater, New York, 1944, with Jerome Robbins, John Kriza, Harold Lang.

446. *The Fleet's In!* by Paul Cadmus, 1934. Oil and tempera.
Washington, The Alibi Club.

447. *Fancy Free,* American Ballet Theater, New York, 1944, with Lang, Kriza, Robbins, and Muriel Bentley.

448. *Fancy Free,* American Ballet Theater, 1945. Stage setting by Oliver Smith. John Kriza, Jerome Robbins, Michael Kidd.
Photograph Maurice Seymour.

449. *Fancy Free,* 1944. Jerome Robbins.
Photograph Alfredo Valente.

450. *Fancy Free,* 1944. Janet Reed and Jerome Robbins.
Photograph Alfredo Valente.

451, 453, 454, 456. *Orpheus* (Stravinsky-Balanchine-Noguchi), New York, 1947. Nicholas Magallanes as Orpheus; Francisco Moncion as the Dark Angel.
Photographs George Platt Lynes.

452. *Orfeo ed Euridice* (Gluck-Balanchine-Tchelitchew), New York, Metropolitan Opera, 1936.
Photograph George Platt Lynes.

455. *Orpheus,* New York, 1948. Scene 2: The Realm of Pluto. Diana Adams as Eurydice.
Photograph Fred Fehl.

457. The arabesque, schematic analysis. Pen drawing by Carluś Dyer from *The Classic Ballet* by Lincoln Kirstein and Muriel Stuart, New York, 1952.

458. *Agon* (Stravinsky-Balanchine), New York, 1961, with Richard Rapp, Melissa Hayden, Earle Sieveling.

459. *Agon,* 1961. *Pas de deux,* with Arthur Mitchell and Allegra Kent.

460. *Agon,* 1957. Ensemble.

461. *Agon,* 1963. *Pas de trois.*

462. *Agon,* 1957. Ensemble.
458–62, photographs Martha Swope.

463. Sir Frederick Ashton, London, 1934.

464. *Enigma Variations* (Elgar-Ashton-Oman), Royal Ballet, London, Covent Garden, 1968. Derek Rencher as Sir Edward Elgar; Deanne Bergsma as Lady Mary Lygon.
Photograph Houston Rogers.

465. *Sir Edward Elgar.* Bronze bust by Patrick Heady, 1927.
London, National Portrait Gallery.

466. *Enigma Variations.* Richard Mead as Richard P. Arnold; Vyvyan Lorraine as Isabel Fitton.

467. *Enigma Variations.* Brian Shaw as Richard Baxter Townsend; Stanley Holden as Hew David Steuart-Powell.

468. *Enigma Variations.* Finale: Elgar's friends celebrate his triumph by posing for a group portrait.
466–68, performance photographs Houston Rogers.

Front endpapers A. Choreographic notation for a social dance. Engraving from *Chorégraphie, ou l'Art d'Écrire la Danse* by Raoul Ager Feuillet, Paris, 1701.

Translated into English, 1706, the book served through the 18th century as a partial guide to movement, indicating floor pattern and sequences of steps.

B. *Amor,* ballet by Luigi Manzotti. Disposition of dancers in finale. Milan, La Scala, 1886.

Back endpapers C. Academic Ballet Positions. Engraving from *Traîté Élémentaire* by Carlo Blasis, Milan, 1820.

D. Academic Ballet Positions. Line drawings by Friederich-Albert Zorn from his *Grammatik der Tanzkunst,* Leipzig, 1887.

E. Academic Ballet Positions: The Human Body and Its Possibilities. Pen drawing by Carlus Dyer from *The Classic Ballet* by Lincoln Kirstein and Muriel Stuart, New York, 1952.

F. Feet Positions: System of Delsarte. Line drawings from *System of Expression* by Genevieve Stebbins, New York, 1885.

Concentro-concentric: despondent passion, prostration
Excentro-concentric: antagonism, defiance
Concentro-excentric: neutral, transitive
Excentro-excentric: excitement, explosive

BIBLIOGRAPHY

GENERAL BACKGROUND

AUDEN, W. H. *Secondary Worlds*. New York and London, 1968.
AUDEN, W. H., and PEARSON, NORMAN HOLMES, eds. *Poets of the English Language*. 5 vols.; New York and London, 1952.
BALDICK, ROBERT. *The Duel: A History of Dueling*, London, 1965; New York, 1966.
BALTRUSAITIS, JURGIS. *Aberrations: Légendes des Formes*. Paris, 1957.
BEZOMBES, ROGER. *L'Exotisme dans l'Art et la Pensée*. Brussels, 1953.
DESCARTES, RENÉ. *Discours sur la Méthode*. Paris, 1637; New York, 1965.
DICKEY, JAMES. *Metaphor as Pure Adventure*. Washington, D.C. 1968.
DIDEROT, D'ALEMBERT, et al., eds. *Encyclopédie Méthodique*. Paris, 1786.
ELIOT, T. S. *The Sacred Wood*. 7th ed., New York and London, 1950.
FOXE, ARTHUR N. *The Common Sense from Heraclitus to Peirce*. New York, 1962.
GOMBRICH, E. H. *Meditations on a Hobby Horse*. New York and London, 1963.
KENNEDY, RUTH WEDGWOOD. *The Idea of Originality in the Italian Renaissance*. Northampton, Mass., 1938.
KERMAN, JOSEPH, and JANSON, M. W. *A History of Art and Music*. New York and London, 1968.
OVID. *Metamorphoses*. J. F. NIMS, ed.; ARTHUR GOLDING, trans. New York, 1965.
PANOFSKY, ERWIN. *Meaning in the Visual Arts*. New York, 1955.
POUND, EZRA. *Guide to Kulchur*. New York and London, 1952.
RAYMOND, MARCEL. *From Baudelaire to Surrealism*. New York, 1950.

MIMICRY AND GESTURE

ANGIOLINI, GASPARO. *Dissertation sur les Ballets Pantomimes des Anciens . . . .* Vienna, 1765.
BODE, RUDOLF. *Expression-Gymnastic*. New York, 1931.
BRAGAGLIA, ANTON GIULIO. *Evoluzione del Mimo*. Milan, 1930.
BROADBENT, R. J. *A History of Pantomime*. New York, 1901.
DE JORIO, ANDREA. *La Mimica degli Antichi*. Naples, 1836.
DIDEROT, DENIS. *Lettre sur les Sourdes et Muets*. Paris, 1751.
ENGEL, J. J. *Ideen zu einer Mimik*. Berlin, 1785.
GRATIOLET, PIERRE. *De la Physionomie et des Mouvements d'Expression*. Paris, n.d.
HACKS, CHARLES. *La Geste*. Paris, 1892.
HOLSTRÖM, KIRSTEN GRAM. *Monodrama: Attitudes, Tableaux Vivants, 1770–1815*. Stockholm, 1968.
LAIRESSE, GÉRARD DE. *Groot Schilderboek*. Amsterdam, 1707.
LAMB, WARREN. *Posture and Gesture: An Introduction to the Study of Behavior*. New York and London, 1965.
LAWSON, JOAN. *Mime*. New York and London, 1957.
SIDDONS, HENRY. *Practical Illustrations of Rhetorical Gesture and Action*. London, 1822.
STEBBINS, GENEVIEVE. *Delsarte System of Expression*. New York, 1885.
WINTER, MARIAN H. *Theatre of Marvels*. New York, 1964.

ICONOGRAPHY

ANTAL, FREDERICK. *Hogarth and His Place in European Art*. New York and London, 1962.
ARNHEIM, RUDOLF. *Toward a Psychology of Art*. Berkeley and Los Angeles, 1966.
CLARK, KENNETH. *Landscape into Art*. London, 1949; New York, 1961.
Gallery of Modern Art. "A Survey of Russian Painting." New York, 1967.
HASKELL, FRANCIS. *Patrons and Painters*. New York and London, 1963.
HAUSER, ARNOLD. *The Social History of Art*. 4 vols.; New York and London, 1951.
HAWLEY, HENRY. *Neo-Classicism: Style and Motif*. Cleveland, Ohio, 1964.
HONOUR, HUGH. *Neo-Classicism*. New York and London, 1968.
HUGHES, ROBERT. *Heaven and Hell in Western Art*. New York and London, 1968.
PANOFSKY, ERWIN. *Studies in Iconology*. New York and London, 1962.
PRAZ, MARIO. *Neo-Classicism*. London, 1968.
SCHÖNBERGER, ARNO, and SOEHNER, HALLDOR. *Die Welt des Rokoko*. Munich, n.d.
VERMEULE, CORNELIUS. *European Art and the Classical Past*. Cambridge, Mass., and London, 1964.
WINTERNITZ, EMANUEL. *Musical Instruments and Their Symbolism in Western Art*. London, 1967; New York, 1968.

SCENERY AND COSTUME

BABLET, DENIS. *Esthétique Générale du Décor de Théâtre*. Paris, 1965.
———. *Le Décor de Théâtre*. Paris, n.d.
BOUCHER, FRANCOIS. *A History of Costume in the West*. London, 1965. Published in New York, 1966, as *Twenty Thousand Years of Fashion*.
FISCHER, CARLOS. *Les Costumes de l'Opéra*. Paris, 1931.
FLUGEL, J. C. *The Psychology of Clothes*. London, 1930; New York, 1966.
JULLIEN, ADOLPHE. *Histoire du Costume au Théâtre*. Paris, 1880.
LAVER, JAMES. *Drama: Its Costume and Décor*. London, 1951; New York, 1955.

READE, BRIAN. *Ballet Designs and Illustrations 1581–1940* (Victoria and Albert Museum). New York and London, 1967.
SCHOLZ, JÁNOS, ed. *Baroque and Romantic Stage Design*. New York, 1962.

THEATER

BAPST, GERMAIN. *Essai sur l'Histoire du Théâtre*. Paris, 1893.
DE L'AULNAYE. *De la Saltation Théâtrale*. Paris, 1790.
DUMESNIL, RENÉ. *Histoire Illustrée du Théâtre Lyrique*. Paris, 1953.
GASCOIGNE, BAMBER. *World Theatre: An Illustrated History*. New York and London, 1968.
HÜRLIMANN, MARTIN. *Das Atlantisbuch des Theaters*. Zurich, 1966.
KINDERMANN, HEINZ. *Theatergeschichte Europas*. Salzburg, 1957–68.
LEVIN, HARRY. "What Was Modernism?" *Massachusetts Review*, I, no. 4 (1960).
LOUGH, JOHN. *Paris Theatre Audiences in the Seventeenth and Eighteenth Centuries*. New York and London, 1957.
NAGLER, A. M. *Sources of Theatrical History*. New York and London, 1952.
NICOLL, ALLARDYCE. *The Development of the Theatre*. London, 1927; 5th ed.; New York, 1967.
OREGILA, GIACOMO. *The Commedia dell'Arte*. Stockholm, 1964.
SLONIM, MARC. *Russian Theater: From the Empire to the Soviets*. New York, 1961; London, 1963.
Theater in Österreich. Vienna, 1965.
The Theater of Don Juan: A Collection of Plays and Views, 1630–1963. With a commentary by OSCAR MANDEL. Lincoln, Nebr., 1968.
VALENTINI, FRANCESCO. *Trattato su la Commedia dell'Arte*. Berlin, 1826.
WELSFORD, ENID. *The Court Masque: A Study in the Relationship Between Poetry and the Revels*. New York, 1927; reprint, 1962.

MUSIC

BOULEZ, PIERRE. *Notes of an Apprenticeship*. HERBERT WEINSTOCK, trans. New York, 1968.
CARSE, ADAM. *The History of Orchestration*. London, 1925; New York, 1935.
COLLAER, PAUL, and VANDERLINDEN, ALBERT. *Historical Atlas of Music*. New York and London, 1968.
COOPER, MARTIN. *Opéra Comique*. New York, 1949.
COX, DAVID. *The Symphony: Elgar to the Present Day*. London, 1967.
ERICKSON, ROBERT. *The Structure of Music*. New York, 1955.
GOLDMAN, ALBERT, and SPRINCHORN, EVERT, eds. *Wagner on Music and Drama: A Compendium of Richard Wagner's Prose Writings*. New York, 1964.
LEONARD, RICHARD ANTHONY. *A History of Russian Music*. New York and London, 1956.
NETTL, PAUL. *The Story of Dance Music*. New York, 1955.
PIRCHAN, EMIL; WITESCHNIK, ALEXANDER; and FRITZ, OTTO. *300 Jahre Wiener Operntheater*. Vienna, 1953.
ROBINSON, MICHAEL F. *Opera Before Mozart*. New York and London, 1966.
SECOND, ALBERIC. *Les petits Mystères de l'Opéra*. Paris, 1844.
STEIN, JACK M. *Richard Wagner and the Synthesis of the Arts*. Detroit, Mich., 1960.
STRUNK, OLIVER, ed. *Source Readings in Music History*. New York, 1950; London, 1952.
VIGANÒ, SALVATORE. *Vita e opere*. Milan, 1838.
YORKE-LONG, ALAN. *Music at Court*. London, 1954.

DANCE HISTORY
General

AMBROSE, KAY. *Ballet Impromptu*. London, 1946.
BAKHRUSHIN, Y. A. *Istoriia Russkogo Baleta*. Moscow, 1965.
BALANCHINE, GEORGE. *New Complete Stories of the Great Ballets*. Rev. ed.; Garden City, N. Y., 1968.
BEAUMONT, CYRIL W. *Complete Book of Ballets*. London, 1937; New York, 1938.
BLASIS, CARLO. *The Code of Terpsichore*. London, 1830.
BORISO-GLEBSKI, MIKHAIL V., ed. *Materialy po Istorii Russkogo Baleta*. Leningrad, 1939.
CARRIERI, RAFFAELE. *La Danza in Italia*. Milan, 1946.
CAVLING, VIGGO. *Balletens Bog*. Copenhagen, 1941.
CHESNOKOV, P. G. *Klassiki Khoreografii*. Moscow, 1937.
CHUJOY, ANATOLE, and MANCHESTER, P. W. *Dance Encyclopedia*. New York, 1967.
Enciclopedia della Spettacolo. Milan, 1957.
GALLINI, GIOVANNI-ANDREA BATTISTA. *Critical Observations on the Art of Dancing*. London, 1770.
GREGOR, JOSEPH. *Kulturgeschichte des Ballets*. Zurich, 1946.
GUEST, IVOR. *The Dancer's Quest*. London, 1960.
HAGER, BENGT. *Ballet Klassik og Fri*. Copenhagen, 1948.
HALL, FERNAU. *Anatomy of Ballet*. London, 1953.
HOFFER, MARI RUEF. *Polite and Social Dances*. Chicago, 1917.
KARSAVINA, TAMARA. *Classical Ballet: The Flow of Movement*. London, 1962; New York, 1963.
KRAGH-JACOBSEN, SVEN, and KROGH, TORBEN. *Den Kongelige Danske Ballet*. Copenhagen, 1952.

BIBLIOGRAPHY

LAWSON, JOAN. *A History of Ballet and Its Makers*. New York and London, 1964.
————. *Classical Ballet*. London, 1960.
LEGAT, NICHOLAS. *The Story of the Russian School*. London, 1932.
LEVINSON, ANDRÉ. *Meister des Balletts*. Berlin, 1921.
LIFAR, SERGE. *Le Livre de la Danse*. Paris, 1954.
MOORE, LILLIAN. *Images of the Dance*. New York, 1965.
NOVERRE, JEAN GEORGES. *Lettres sur la Danse*. St. Petersburg, 1803; Paris, 1927. CYRIL BEAUMONT, trans., *Letters on Dancing and Ballets*. London, 1930; New York, 1966.
PARNAC, VALENTIN. *Histoire de la Danse*. Paris, 1932.
PLESHCHEYEV, ALEXANDER. *Nash Balet*. St. Petersburg, 1896.
PRIDDEN, DEIRDRE. *The Art of Dance in French Literature*. New York and London, 1952.
REYNA, FERDINANDO. *Histoire du Ballet*. Paris, 1964. Trans. as *The Concise History of Ballet*. New York and London, 1965.
ROOTZEN, KAJSA. *Den Svenska Baletten*. Stockholm, 1945.
SAINT-LÉON, ARTHUR. *La Sténochorégraphie*. Paris, 1852.
STRUNK, OLIVER, ed. *La Danza in Italia*. Milan, 1949.
SWIFT, MARY GRACE. *The Art of the Dance in the U.S.S.R.* South Bend, Ind., 1968.
VAN PRAAGH, PEGGY, and BRINSON, PETER. *The Choreographic Art*. New York and London, 1963.

Sixteenth Century

ARIOSTO. *Ariosto's Orlando Furioso*. RUDOLF GOTTFRIED, ed.; JOHN HARINGTON, trans. Bloomington, Ind., 1963.
BEAUJOYEULX, BALTHASAR DE. *Ballet-Comique de la Royne Louise*. Facsimile. Turin, 1965.
BRACELLI, GIOVANNI BATTISTA. *Bizzarie*. 1624. Reprint; Paris, 1963.
COHEN, GUSTAVE. *Ronsard: Sa Vie et Son Oeuvre*. Paris, 1956.
DENIEUL-CORMIER. *La France de la Renaissance*. Paris, 1962.
HEWITT, BARNARD, ed. *The Renaissance Stage: Documents of Serlio, Sabbatini, and Furttenbach*. Coral Gables, Fla., 1958.
JACQUET, JEAN. *La Fête de la Renaissance*. Paris, 1956.
KERNODLE, GEORGE R. *From Art to Theatre*. New York and London, 1944.
KLIBANSKY, RAYMOND; PANOFSKY, ERWIN; and SAXL, FRITZ. *Saturn and Melancholy*. New York and London, 1964.
PETRARCH. *Triumphs*. E. H. WILKINS, trans. Chicago, 1962.
TASSO, TORQUATO. *Gerusalemme Liberata*. Bologna, 1963. EDWARD FAIRFAX, trans., *Jerusalem Liberated*. Bloomington, Ind., 1962.
WIND, EDGAR. *Pagan Mysteries in the Renaissance*. New York and London, 1958.
WÜRTENBERGER, FRANZSEPP. *Mannerism*. New York and London, 1963.

Seventeenth Century

BAUR-HEINHOLD, MARGARETE. *The Baroque Theater*. New York, 1967.
BJURSTRÖM, PER. *Giacomo Torelli and Baroque Stage Design*. Stockholm, 1961.
CHRISTOUT, MARIE-FRANÇOISE. *Le Ballet de Cour de Louis XIV (1643–1672)*. Paris, 1967.
DE LAUSE, F. *Apologie de la Danse*. London, 1952.
FERNANDEZ, RAMON. *Molière: The Man Seen Through His Plays*. WILSON FOLLETT, trans. New York, 1958.
FLETCHER, IFAN KYRLE; COHEN, SELMA JEANNE; and LONSDALE, RODGER. *Famed for Dance (England: 1660–1740)*. New York, 1960.
JOSEPH, BERTRAM L. *Elizabethan Acting*. 2d ed.; New York and London, 1964.
LACROIX, PAUL. *Ballet et Mascarades de Cour*. Geneva, 1868.
LAWRENSON, T. E. *The French Stage in the Seventeenth Century*. Manchester, England, 1957.
McGOWAN, MARGARET M. *L'Art de Ballet de Cour en France (1581–1643)*. Paris, 1963.
MENESTRIER, CLAUDE FRANÇOIS. *Des Ballets Anciens et Modernes selon les règles du Théâtre*. Paris, 1682.
MOLIÈRE. *Oeuvres Complètes*. Paris, 1962.
NAGLER, A. M. *Theater Festivals of the Medici*. New Haven, Conn., and London, 1964.
PRUNIÈRES, HENRI. *Le Ballet de Cour en France avant Benserade et Lully*. Paris, 1914.
REYHER, PAUL. *Les Masques Anglais*. New York, 1909.
SILIN, CHARLES I. *Benserade and His Ballets de Cour*. New York and London, 1940.
THOMSON, ELIZABETH McCLURE, ed. *The Chamberlain Letters*. New York, 1966.
WORSTORNE, SIMON TOWNSLEY. *Venetian Opera in the Seventeenth Century*. New York and Oxford, England, 1954.

Eighteenth Century

ALGAROTTI, FRANCESCO. *An Essay on Opera*. London, 1767.
AND, METIN. *Gönlü yüce Turk*. Ankara, 1958.
ANTAL, FREDERIC. *Hogarth*. New York and London, 1962.
AUBRY, PIERRE, and DACIER, ÉMILE. *Les Caractères de la Danse*. Paris, 1905.
BARTEN, MARGARET. *Garrick*. New York, 1949.
CHOQUET, GUSTAVE. *Histoire de la Musique Dramatique en France*. Paris, 1873.

DACIER, ÉMILE. *Mlle. Sallé.* Paris, 1909.
DIDEROT, DENIS. *Paradoxe sur le Comédien.* Paris, 1965.
HILLESTRÖM, PER. *Gustaviansk Teater.* Stockholm, 1947.
JANNEAU, GUILLAUME. *L'Époque Louis XV.* Paris, 1967.
JULLIEN, ADOLPHE. *La Cour et l'Opéra sous Louis XVI.* Paris, n.d.
KIMBALL, FISKE. *The Creation of the Rococo.* New York, 1942.
LA METTRIE, JULIEN. *L'Homme Machine.* Paris, 1747.
LIFAR, SERGE. *Auguste Vestris.* Paris, 1950.
LUCIAN. *Della Danza, Dialogo di Luciano con Annotazioni.* Florence, 1779.
————. *Della Pantomima, Dialogo di Luciano, Traduzione con Note.* Venice, 1783.
OLIVER, JEAN-JACQUES, and NORBERT, WILLY. *La Barberina Campanini.* Paris, 1910.
OMAN, CAROLA. *David Garrick.* New York and London, 1958.
PILON, EDMOND, and SAISSET, FRÉDÉRIC. *Les Fêtes en Europe.* Paris, n.d.
RAMEAU, PIERRE. *Le Maître à Danser.* Paris, 1734.
SIRIS, P. *The Art of Dancing.* Paris, 1706.
SLONIMSKY, Y. *Tschetnaia predostorozhnost.* Leningrad, 1961.
VAN LOO, ESTHER. *Le Vrai Don Juan.* Paris, 1950.
WEAVER, JOHN. *Anatomical and Mechanical Lectures Upon Dancing.* London, 1721.
————. *An Essay Towards an History of Dancing.* London, 1712.

Nineteenth Century

ANDREWS, EDWARD. *The Gift to Be Simple.* New York and London, 1958.
BASSI, ELENA. *Antonio Canova.* Milan, 1957.
BEAUMONT, CYRIL. *The Ballet Called Giselle.* London, 1944.
————. *The Ballet Called Swan Lake.* London, 1952.
BIGGS, JOHN. *Tchaikovsky and the Five.* New York, 1959.
BLASIS, CARLO. *Traîté Élémentaire Théorique et Pratique de l'Art de la Danse.* Milan, 1820.
————. *L'Uomo Fisico, Intellettuale e Morale.* Milan, 1868.
BROWSE, LILLIAN, ed. *Degas Dancers.* New York and London, n.d.
CHAPUIS, ALFRED, and DROZ, EDMOND. *Automata.* Lausanne, 1958.
COOK, BRADFORD. *Mallarmé.* Baltimore, Md., 1956.
COOPERMAN, HASYE. *The Aesthetics of Stéphane Mallarmé.* New York, 1933.
DORÉ, GUSTAVE. *La Ménagerie Parisienne.* Paris, n.d.
GUEST, IVOR. *Fanny Cerrito.* London, 1956.
————. *Fanny Elssler.* London, 1970.
————. *The Ballet of the Second Empire.* London, 1955.
————. *The Romantic Ballet in England.* London, 1954.
————. *The Romantic Ballet in Paris.* New York and London, 1966.
HEATH, CHARLES. *Beauties of the Opera and Ballet.* Paris and London, 1845.
JARRY, ALFRED. *Selected Works of Alfred Jarry.* ROGER SHATTUCK and SIMON W. TAYLOR, eds. New York and London, 1965.
LIFAR, SERGE. *Carlotta Grisi.* London, 1947.
MOORE, LILLIAN, ed. *Russian Ballet Master: The Memoirs of Marius Petipa.* London, 1958; New York, 1959.
MORGAN, ANNA. *An Hour with Delsarte: A Study of Expression.* New York, 1889.
NEIIENDAM, ROBERT. *Lucile Grahn.* Copenhagen, 1963.
ROSLAVLEVA, NATALIA. *Era of the Russian Ballet.* New York and London, 1966.
SHAWN, TED. *Every Little Movement.* Rev. ed.; Pittsfield, Mass., 1963.
SLONIMSKY, YURI. *Didelot.* Leningrad and Moscow, 1958.
————. *Lebedinoe ozero.* Leningrad, 1962.
————. *Mastera Baleta.* Moscow, 1936.
VAILLAT, LÉANDRE. *La Taglioni.* Paris, 1942.
ZHITOMIRSKY, D. *Balety Tchaikovskogo.* Moscow, 1957.

Twentieth Century

ARTAUD, ANTONIN. *Collected Works.* Vol. I; London, 1968.
BEAUMONT, CYRIL. *Michel Fokine and His Ballets.* London, 1935.
————. *Petrouchka.* London, 1919.
BENOIS, ALEXANDRE. *Memoirs.* 2 vols.; New York and London, 1960.
BUCKLE, RICHARD. *In Search of Diaghilev.* London, 1955.
————. *The Adventures of a Ballet Critic.* London, 1953.
CHUJOY, ANATOLE. *The New York City Ballet.* New York, 1953.
COCTEAU, JEAN. *Journals.* Paris, 1965.
————. *Le Rappel à l'Ordre (Le Coq et l'Arlequin).* Paris, 1926.
————. *Le Foyer des Artistes.* Paris, 1947.

BIBLIOGRAPHY

————. *Poésie Critique.* Paris, 1959.

————. *Portraits-Souvenirs.* Paris, 1947.

COOPER, DOUGLAS. *Picasso Theatre.* New York and London, 1968.

CORLE, EDWIN. *Igor Stravinsky.* New York, 1949.

CRAFT, ROBERT. *Igor Stravinsky: The Rite of Spring.* New York and London, 1969.

CRAIG, EDWARD. *Gordon Craig.* New York, 1968.

CRAIG, GORDON. *Index to the Story of My Days.* New York and London, 1957.

DOLIN, ANTON. *Ballet Go Round.* London, 1938.

————. *Divertissement.* London, n.d.

DUNCAN, ISADORA. *My Life.* New York, 1927.

EHRENBURG, ILYA. *First Years of Revolution: 1918–21.* London, 1962.

ETKIND, MARK. *Aleksander Nikolaevitch Benois.* Moscow, 1965.

FOKINE, MICHEL. *Memoirs of a Ballet Master.* London, 1961.

————. *Protiv techeniya.* Moscow, 1962.

Gallery of Modern Art. "Pavel Tchelitchew." New York, 1964.

GRAY, CAMILLA. *The Great Experiment: Russian Art 1863–1922.* New York and London, 1962.

GRIGORIEV, SERGE. *The Diaghilev Ballet, 1909–29.* London, 1953; New York, 1960.

HASKELL, ARNOLD. *Ballets Russes: The Age of Diaghilev.* London, 1968.

HASKELL, ARNOLD, and NOUVEL, WALTER. *Diaghileff, His Artistic and Private Life.* New York, 1935.

JAQUES-DALCROZE, ÉMILE. *La Plastique Animé.* Paris, 1912.

————. *La Rhythmique.* Paris, 1916.

————. *Ritmo, Musica, Educazione.* Milan, 1925.

JOHNSON, A. E. *The Russian Ballet.* London, 1913.

KARSAVINA, TAMARA. *Theatre Street.* London, 1930; New York, 1961.

KOMELOVA, G. *Stseny Russkoi Narodnoi Zhizni.* Leningrad, 1961.

LAMBERT, CONSTANT. *Music Ho: A Study of Music in Decline.* New York and London, 1969.

LEVINSON, ANDRÉ. *Léon Bakst.* Paris, 1924.

LIEVEN, PRINCE PETER. *The Birth of the Ballets Russes.* London, 1936.

LIFAR, SERGE. *Serge Diaghileff.* Paris, 1940.

LOPOUKHOV, FEODOR. *Putiletmeistera.* Moscow, 1925.

————. *Shestdesiat let v balete.* Moscow, 1966.

MAGRIEL, PAUL. *Nijinsky.* New York, 1946.

MALLARMÉ, STÉPHANE. *Divagations.* Geneva, 1943.

MARGARSHACK, DAVID. *Stanislavsky: A Life.* London, 1950.

MARIN, FRANK. *Émile Jaques-Dalcroze.* Neuchâtel, 1965.

MASSINE, LÉONIDE. *Memoirs.* London, 1968.

NABOKOV, NICHOLAS. *Old Friends and New Music.* Boston, 1951.

NAYLOR, GILLIAN. *The Bauhaus.* New York and London, 1968.

NIJINSKY, ROMOLA. *Nijinsky.* New York, 1934.

NIJINSKY, VASLAV. *The Diary of Vaslav Nijinsky.* New York, 1936.

O'DEA, WILLIAM T. *The Social History of Lighting.* London, 1958; New York, 1959.

ONNEN, FRANK. *Stravinsky.* Stockholm, 1948.

OXENHANDLER, NEAL. *Scandal and Parade.* New Brunswick, N.J., and London, 1957.

PROPERT, W. R. *The Russian Ballet in Western Europe: 1921–29.* London, 1930.

READ, SIR HERBERT. *Stravinsky and the Dance.* New York, 1962.

RIVIÈRE, JACQUES. *Nouvelles Études.* Paris, 1947.

SCHLEMMER, O.; MOHOLY-NAGY, L.; and MOLNAR, F. *The Theater of the Bauhaus.* Middletown, Conn., 1961.

SHATTUCK, ROGER. *The Banquet Years: 1885–1918.* New York, 1955; London, 1959.

SOKOLOVA, LYDIA. *Dancing for Diaghilev.* London, 1960.

STRAVINSKY, IGOR. *An Autobiography.* New York and London, 1936.

————. *Poetics of Music.* Cambridge, England, 1947; New York, 1956.

STRAVINSKY, IGOR, and CRAFT, ROBERT. *Conversations with Igor Stravinsky.* New York and London. 1959.

————. *Dialogues and a Diary.* London, 1968.

————. *Themes and Episodes.* New York, 1966.

TAPER, BERNARD. *Balanchine.* New York and London, 1963.

VALOIS, NINETTE DE. *Invitation to the Ballet.* London, 1937.

VERONESI, GIULIA. *Into the Twenties.* London, 1966.

————. *Style and Design: 1909–29.* New York and London, 1968.

WHITE, ERIC WALTER. *Stravinsky: The Composer and His Works.* Berkeley, Los Angeles, and London, 1966.

INDEX

Numbers in parentheses refer to illustrations and their explanatory notes.

abstract ballet, 158, 194, 214–15, 218
academic dance: long issue sketched of, v; modern dance contributed little to, 4; arbitrary, 20; criterion for, 32; enlarging, 51; future of, 59; and threshold of tradition, 98; reforms of, 118
Académie Royale, 82–83, 91, 94, 98
academy: teaches positions and steps, 5; ballet masters transcend or overturn, 16; today's eclectic ballet based on, 23; divested of rhetoric and vulgarism by French, 32; absolute criterion of Russian, 32; French official professional, 59; provincial and peasant sources gave new vitality to, 103; "pure" French, 171; "gymnastic" Italian, 171; Diaghilev only retained disciplined dancers from, 198; revitalized, 207; extended by Lopoukhov, 218; *Apollon* synthesis of, transformed, 226; tenacious attachment of *Agon* to, 243; forced dancers into uniform, 252 (10)
Academy of Dance, 82–83, 91, 94, 98
acrobacy: attracts public, 4; sharp, rapid movements necessary for, 5; Rameau opened path toward, 30; little leeway in costume for, 35; toe-dancing device for, 142, 255 (48); disciplined displays of, 151, 158; Goleizovsky experimented with, 219
acrobats: influenced ballet masters, 22; at fairs, 210, 211; acrobat-athlete, 251 (2)
Actio, 20
adagio, 5
Adam, Adolphe Charles, 28, 31, 150–51, 170
Adams, Diana, 242, 272 (435, 436, 455)
Aeolian Harp, The, 266 (258)
aerial action, 5, 87, 131, 147, 253 (26)
Age of Anxiety, The, 234
Agon, 33, 242–43, 272 (458, 459), 273 (460–62)
Agrippa, Cornelius, 20
Aignan, Le Comte de, 110, 261 (139, 140)
air de danse, 29, 30
airs de vitesse, 29, 114
Aleotti, Giovanni Battista, 40, 258 (82)
Alexander, Grand Duke, 183
Alexander the Great, 34, 75, 87
Alexander III, 175, 183
Algarotti, Francesco, 107
allegory, 34, 50, 51, 54, 62, 74, 75, 82, 138
allegro, 5, 159
allemande, 30, 253 (24)
Amants Magnifiques, Les, 86–87, 118, 262 (153, 155, 157)
amateur, 34, 50, 55, 82, 86, 98
American Ballet Caravan, 239
Aminta, 54
Amphitrion, 75
Anacreontism, 130, 142
Analysis of Beauty, The, 11, 23, 251 (7), 254 (44)

anatomy, 17, 95, 194, 214, 223, 242, 252 (13)
Angiolini, Gasparo, 23, 26, 90, 103, 110; as choreographer of *Don Juan*, 30, 118–19; influenced by Hilferding, 106; supported by Durazzo, 107; replaced Hilferding, 115; recalled, 134, 135
Anne of Austria, 74, 257 (75), 260 (109)
anti-masque, 66–67, 70
Antoine, André, 46
Aphrodite, 66, 78, 107, 194
Apollinaire, Guillaume, 210
Apollo, 238, 246; and his lyre, 10, 211, 227; Louis XIV as, 62, 75, 78, 86, 260 (132), 261 (135, 136, 139); and Muses, at Sceaux, 91; contrasted with Pygmalion, 106; as lord of poesy, 150; Henry VIII as, 260 (131) (see also *Apollon Musagète*)
Apollo Belvedere, 271 (430)
Apollon Musagète, 33, 226–27, 239, 242, 272 (434–37)
Apologie de la Danse, 242
Appia, Adolphe, 39, 47
Après-Midi d'un Faune, L', 32, 198–99, 206, 223, 227, 270 (381–84)
archeology: influenced design, 26, 34, 38, 39, 46; correctness of, in costume, décor, 134, 268 (309); replaced Greek and Roman influence with Gothic, 154; Napoleon's Egyptian campaign precipitated, 162; influence of, set aside, 190; and restored color, 198; influence of, on posturing 255 (56, 57)
Archimedes, 55, 90
Argand, Aimé, 41
Ariosto, Lodovico, 59, 62, 75, 251 (1)
Aristotle, 90, 119
Arlequin poli par l'amour, 198
Armida, 63, 257 (77), 260 (105, 110) (see also *Pavillon d'Armide*)
arms: positions of, 5, 20, 23–27 *passim*; Duncan's use of, 26, 186; for pirouette, 71; regularized, 87; gestures of, 95; from folk dances, 127, 166; feathery movements of, 179; sign of folded, 215; impersonalization of, 242; balancing action of, 252 (20)
Arnheim, Rudolph, 214
Ars Poetica, 90, 122
Ashton, Sir Frederick, 27, 127, 230, 246–47, 273 (463)
Astaire, Fred, 234
asymmetry, 11, 16, 30, 35, 115, 206, 243, 253 (29–32)
athlete, 4, 5, 17, 86, 251 (2); dancer as, 202, 203, 226, 227, 246
Auden, Wystan Hugh, 17, 34, 234
audience: pleased by repertory, 10; placement of, 11, 28, 46, 55, 253 (35); commanded richer aural background, 31; of courtiers and diplomats, 50, 51; and familiarity with myth, 54; middle-class,

86; intellectual élite as, 90; in city, 98; in London, 110, 130; Diderot's opinion of, 118; Milanese, 134, 135; bourgeois, 138, 139; world, 142; blasé, 163; in St. Petersburg, 166; mindless but susceptible, 198; patriotic, 210; megalopolitan, Philistine, 211; shocked at *Apollon*, 226
Aumer, Jean, 138–39, 162, 174
automata, 170, 194, 242

Bach, Johann Sebastian, 28, 31
Bacon, Francis, 67, 170
Baiser de la Fée, Le, 33
Bakst, Léon Nikolaevich, 210, 247, 251 (8), 272 (433); background and work of, 39, 46, 47; recreated grandeur for *La Belle au Bois Dormant*, 175, 268 (330); strident décor of, for *Schéhérazade*, 190, 258 (80), 269 (358, 359); designed *L'Après-Midi d'un Faune*, 198–99, 270 (381); and *Jeux*, 202–3, 252 (11); Picasso's drawing of, 270 (389); and drawing of Cocteau, 271 (406)
Balanchine, George, vi, 154, 219, 246; credits Dalcroze method, 27; and revivals of *Orfeo*, 31; and use of Chabrier's music, 32; and Stravinsky, 33, 271 (429); and use of practice clothes in performance, 39, 252 (11); first role of, as monkey, 70; and *Night Shadow*, or *Sonnambula*, 139; distilled Act II of *Swan Lake*, 179, 269 (336); in *Tanzsymphonia*, 218, 271 (422); choreographed *Apollon Musagète*, 226–27; and final *Follies*, 234; and *Orpheus*, 238–39, 272 (451, 453–56); and *Agon*, 242–43, 272 (458, 459), 273 (460–62)
Balanchivadze, Georgei, 218 (see also Balanchine, George)
Balbi, Giovanni Batista, 71
ballerina, v; new race of, 31; sylph's dress of, 39; personality of, commented on, 46; toe shoes made development possible for, 131; as sleepwalker, 138; Romantic, 142; mystique of, 146–47; as judged on *Giselle*, 151; and restricted classical dancing, 151; tyranny of, 154; age of, 158; favorite role of, 163; dehumanized, 170; on Broadway, 234
ballet à grand spectacle, 62, 162–63, 182–83, 194
ballet-bourgeois, 127, 138–39
ballet burlesque, 102–3
Ballet Club, 230
Ballet-Comique de la Royne Louise, 28, 54–55; as recalled, 58, 62, 256 (63), 257 (73, 74), 258 (85), 259 (93, 95), 261 (137)
ballet d'action, 182; Noverre and, 11, 21, 22; exalts pantomime over dancing, 24; aims of, 30; precursor of, 90; Garrick's effect on, 94; replaced pastorals, 98; as seen all over Europe, 103; in Vienna,

Cavalazzi, Malvina, 253 (24)
Cecchetti, Enrico, 127, 195, 222, 230
Cellini, Benvenuto, 246
censorship, 38, 90, 163
centrifugal forms, 26, 174
centripetal forms, 26, 174
Cerrito, Fanny, 154, 158–59, 166, 267 (298, 301, 302)
Chabrier, Alexis Emmanuel, 28, 30, 32
chaconne, 30, 94, 119
Chagall, Marc, 47n, 218
Chamberlain, John, 70
Chaplin, Charlie, 211
character dancing, 16, 127, 256 (58)
Charcot, Jean Martin, 138
Chardin, Jean Baptiste Siméon, 23
Charles I, 66
Charles II, 78, 94
Chausson, Ernest, 230, 231
Chekhov, Anton, 230, 246
Chenier, M. J., 123
Chéret, Jules, 46
chinoiserie, 47, 102, 110, 264 (202)
Chirologia, 20, 262 (170)
Chironomia, 20
Chopin, Frédéric François, 28, 186, 187
Chopiniana, 186, 246 (*see also Sylphides, Les*)
Chorégraphie, 94, 273 (endpaper A)
choreodramma, 20, 134, 154
choreographers: ballet masters as, generals as, 4; distinguished from ballet masters, 16, 17; borrowed from exotic, 26; discovered means for mime, 27; as sight-readers, 28; scarceness of able ones, 31; as artist-choreographers who never appear, 106; supplied own plots, 138; acid test of, 159; attempted to invent new syntax, 214; can't invent rhythm, 227
choreography: as hero of this book, v, 48, 49; autonomous, vi; materials and structure of, 4-16; projected toward autonomy, 18; routine, 22; evolved from participant to spectacular, 28; did not keep pace with orchestration, 31; Russian-derived, 32; first extension in twenty years of, 33; enriched, stripped style of, 39; and decoration, 40, 62; geometrical arrangement, 55; rules of, 59, borrowed familiar movements of, 83; established on instrumentation, 98; suggested by Rameau's music, 114; *Giselle* milestone in, 150; cannot be taught, 154; revolution in devices of, 190; and strongest moment in *Schéhérazade,* 191; Stravinsky's influence on, 194; dominated in *Faune,* 199; for *Sacre du Printemps,* 206–7; for *Parade,* 210; bankruptcy of, 214; full orchestra basis for, 218; step toward autonomous, 219; Nijinsky and Nijinska as sculptors of, 223; credit given for, 234; projects steel skeleton, 243; of riding and fenc-

ing, 254 (38); with moralized patterns, 259 (101, 102); floor patterns of, 263 (181); caricatured, 270 (402)
choros, 207, 251 (8)
Christensen, Lew, 234
Cibber, Colley, 94
Ciceri, Pierre-Luc Charles, 46, 142, 266 (275)
Cicero, Marcus Tullius, 20
Circe, 54, 58, 59, 63
circus, 16, 214
Clairon, Mlle. (Claire Josèphe Léris), 21, 38
Cléopâtre, 190
Cochin, C. N., 263 (190, 191)
Cocteau, Jean: brought in Picasso, 47; quoted, 207, 210; on *Parade,* 211; produced *Oedipus Rex,* 226; philosophy of, reversed, 246; pen sketches by, 269 (357), 270 (372); and drawing of Stravinsky, 271 (403); and drawing by Bakst, 271 (406)
Cohan, George M., 234
Colbert, Jean Baptiste, 90
colors: symbolic, 34; in costumes, 35, 39; in stage design, 41; restored by archeologists, 198; in costumes of *Triadic Ballet,* 215; in *Orpheus,* 239
Columbine, 35, 103, 127, 194, 261 (148)
Comédie Française, 21, 22, 38, 90, 103, 262 (163)
comédie-muette, 75
commedia dell' arte: background and influence of, 22; as known by Lully, 29; as recorded by Callot, 35; influence of, on English pantomime, 66, 94; types of, in *Ballet de la Nuit,* 75; influenced Molière, 82, 90, 118; types of, in *La Guinguette,* 102; represented Théâtre Italien, 103; stereotypes replaced in comic ballet, 106; in *Koniok Gorbunok,* 166; influenced *Petrouchka,* 194; as illustrated, 253 (26), 256 (59–61), 260 (119), 261 (148), 262 (151), 263 (188), 264 (208)
contredanses, 30, 31, 51, 119
Cooper, Emil, 219
Copernicus, Nicolaus, 90
Copland, Aaron, 17, 234
Coppélia, 27, 32, 106, 170–71; as recalled, 182, 194, 198, 214, 268 (320, 322–24)
Coq d'Or, Le, 222
Coralli, Jean, 151
Corneille, Pierre, 21, 90, 91, 122, 255 (56, 57)
Corot, Jean Baptiste Camille, 186
corps de ballet: role of, v, 10; fragmented, 11; Lully's new uses for, 29; stage hands converted to, 54; courtiers as, 55; as trained in expressive gesture, 102; amplified, 110, 111; aerial, 131; demechanized, 134; participatory, 151; individuation in, 154; proletarian, 154; unisonal numbers for, 163; as many-

voiced instrument, 178; as notes of music, 189; antithesis of traditional, 194; vignetted, 195; enriched patterns for, 218; in asymmetrical alignment, 253 (29–32)
corsets, 34; and Duncan, 38, 39, 147, 256 (68); Petipa "laced ballet in," 163; set aside, 190; reforms "lost in," 251 (8), 256 (67), 272 (433)
costume: Duncan's license in, 16; reforms in, 21, 99; from *commedia dell' arte,* 22; for dancing, 34–39; heavy and padded, 63; Jones's wit and richness in, 67; difference in, between singers' and dancers', 87; barely theatricalized, 103; civil, 107; freedom in, 130, 272 (432); as ballerina's uniform, 142, 146, 159, 186, 215; as Romantic ballet skirt, 147; as pleated shifts, 198, 199; as peasant flannels, 207; as décor, 214–15; reduced to uniform, 218, 219, 223; by Chanel, 227; as practice uniforms, 243, 252 (11); for *Enigma Variations,* 247; of *choros,* 251 (8); exaggerated silhouettes of, 252 (10); Harlequin's, 256 (61); castanet dancer's, 256 (64); approached nudity, 257 (67); for *Armide,* 261 (345); as classic uniform, 262 (154); for *Ballet du Roi,* 262 (159), 263 (176); for Comédie-Française, 262 (163); and opera dancers as peasants, 263 (184, 185); designs for Noverre, 264 (217–19), 266 (249–52); for *Coppélia,* 268 (322–24); for *Belle au Bois Dormant,* 268 (326, 327); for *Petrouchka,* 270 (376–78); for *Parade,* 271 (409–12); for *Triadic Ballet,* 271 (414); Romanov taste in, 272 (433)
courante, 30, 75, 99
Courbet, Gustave, 46
court, ballet at: in Italy, 58–59; in France, 62–63; as English court masques, 66–67 (*see also ballet de cour* and court ballet)
court ballet: sixteenth-century entries in, 10; monumental plasticity in, 11; ceased being masquerades, 20; *commedia dell' arte* interludes in, 22; seventeenth-century, 28–29; beginnings of, 50–51; culmination of, 54–55; *Sleeping Beauty* as last of, 174 (*see also ballet de cour*)
Coysevox, Antoine, 261 (144)
Craft, Robert, 206
Craig, Gordon, 16, 27, 203; on Isadora Duncan, 39; and experiments with décor, 47; and complaint about *Sacre du Printemps,* his "Übermarionette," 214
Creatures of Prometheus, 134
Crusader, 62, 63, 251 (1), 257 (77), 260 (106)
Cubism, 47, 202, 206, 210, 211, 214, 218, 222
czardas, 171

Petipa, Lucien, 255 (50), 267 (283)
Petipa, Marius, 28, 171, 187, 190, 218,
222; and Tchaikovsky, 32–33; portrait
with monkey, 70, 268 (304); Perrot
rivals, 154; inherits Perrot's methods,
154; and *Fille du Pharaon*, 162–63;
taught by Saint-Léon, 166; and *Belle au
Bois Dormant*, 174–75; contrasted with
Ivanov, 178; and *Swan Lake*, 178–79;
consoled Kschessinska, 183; revived *La
Sylphide*, 186; as recalled, 198; *Sleeping
Beauty* revived, 226, 268 (307, 325)
Petrouchka, 27, 30, 33, 166; conspect of,
194–95; as recalled, 198, 210; Nijinsky
as, 270 (369, 370); scenes from, 270
(374, 375); costumes in, 270 (376–78)
philosophia moralis, 51
Picasso, Pablo, 17, 206; his ballet designs,
47; and *Parade*, 210–11, 215, 246, 271
(408–12); and *Le Tricorne*, and *Pul-
cinella*, 223; his monumental paintings,
226; as recalled, 239n
pièces à la muette, 19
Pierrot, 23, 194, 261 (148)
Pigmalion, 99, 102, 103, 106
Piranesi, Giovanni Battista, 134
Planck, Max, 214
Plato, 16
Playford, John, 94
Plutarch, 162, 251 (4), 256 (67)
Poggioli, Renato, 242
pointe (see toe-dancing)
polka, 127, 253 (28)
polonaise, 127
Pompadour, Jeanne Antoinette Poisson,
Madame de, 102, 103, 263 (190, 191)
Pompeii, 26, 38, 135, 198, 226
Pope, Alexander, 146
port de bras, 5, 23, 146 (see also arms)
Porte St. Martin (theater), 138, 139, 190
positions, five academic, 5–10, 71, 87,
119, 252 (12), 253 (23), 266 (271), 273
(endpapers)
Post-Impressionism, 46, 183, 190, 199,
202, 218, 258 (80)
Poussin, Nicolas, 31, 87, 227
Pozzo, Andrea, 41
Prélude à l'Après-Midi d'un Faune, The, 32,
199
Preobrajenska, Olga, 187
Prévôt, Françoise, 90, 91, 98, 99, 106, 263
(173)
prince absolu, le, 63 (see also divine right
of kings)
Prince Igor, 46, 178, 183, 206, 222
Prodigal Son, 47 (see also *Fils Prodigue,
Le*)
Prokofiev, Sergei Sergeevich, 17, 222
Pronuntiatio, 18
Propert, W. A., 207
proscenium arch: became permanent by
1640, 11; its effect on costume, 34; first,
40, 258 (82); formed frame for dancing,
41, 70, 254 (36); focused action, 87;
determined frontality, 254 (42)

Proust, Marcel, 202, 211, 230
Puget, Pierre, 90
Pugni, Cesare, 166, 167
Pulcinella, 33, 223, 226
Puppenfee, Die, 171
puppets, 27, 170, 194–95
Purcell, Henry, 246
Pushkin, Aleksander Sergeevich, 32, 130,
166, 222, 227
Pygmalion, 106, 107, 139, 170, 194, 246
Pygmalion, 263 (199); Rousseau's, 23, 263
(195); with De Hesse, 102; conspect
of, 106–7; book illustration of, 263
(198)
Pyrrhic dance, 94, 251 (5)
Pythagoras, 55
Pythian games, 86

quadrille, 51, 102, 246; horses in, 254 (39),
266 (265)
Quintilian, Marcus Fabius, 20, 23

Rachel (Éliza Félix), 27
Racine, Jean Baptise, 255 (56, 57); classicism of, 21; and *Phèdre*, 29; and
Britannicus, 86, 106, 262 (158); Hilferding's treatment of, 118; on Euripides'
Medea, 123
Ragtime, 33
Rambert, Marie, 198, 206, 230, 270 (396)
Rameau, Jean Philippe, 11, 28, 102, 110;
directions of, for "pantomime," 22;
work and importance of, 29–30; Delibes
and Tchaikovsky go back to, 32; quoted
on Ballon, 91; and *Pygmalion*, 107; may
have written *Les Fêtes Chinoises*, 110;
and *Le Turc Généreux*, 114–15; as recalled, 118, 135, 150, 211; echoes of,
226; and engravings from *Le Maître à
Danser*, 252 (12), 253 (28), 262 (171);
apotheosis of, 265 (221)
Rape of the Lock, The, 146
Ravel, Maurice, 32, 106n
realism, 90, 119, 122, 154, 155
Rebel, Jean Fery, 98–99
Red Poppy (or *Flower*), *The*, 154, 234
Redon, Odilon, 46
Reed, Janet, 234, 272 (450)
Regency of Louis XV (*Régence*), 35, 98
Renaissance, 23; costume, 34, 39; parade
entries, 40, 50; and Neoplatonists, 55;
dancing masters, 59; art, 62; codifica-
tion of steps in, 126; and imitation of
Anacreon, 130; and *nuvoli*, 131; court
spectacles of, 257 (73)
Renaud, 251 (1) (see also *Déliverance de
Renaud, La*)
Renoir, Pierre Auguste, 32
revivalism, 39, 75, 194, 227
Rhetoric, 18
Riccoboni, Luigi, 22, 102
Rich, John, 95, 99, 238, 255 (53)
Richardson, Samuel, 22
Richelieu, Armand Jean du Plessis, Duc
de, Cardinal, 40, 62, 63, 70, 257 (75)

Richter, Hans, 246
riding (see *haute école* riding)
rigaudon, 29, 30, 99
Rimbaud, Arthur, 198, 246
Rimsky-Korsakov, Nikolai Andreevich, 33,
106n, 163, 166, 190–91
Rinaldo, 63, 75, 251 (1), 257 (77), 260
(110)
Rivière, Jacques, v, 206
Robbins, Jerome, 27, 234–35, 272 (445,
447–50)
Robert der Teufel (see *Robert le Diable*)
Robert le Diable, 39, 142–43, 146, 151,
266 (272–74, 276)
Robinson, Bill "Bojangles," 234
Rococo: lighter gesture of, 23; costume
and décor, 35, 38; Benois in tradition
of, 47; aesthetic, 98; fussiness, 102;
coyness, 126; lighthearted taste of, 127;
contrasted with Baroque, 175; restored
in *Pavillon d'Armide*, 182–83; *Jeux* almost, 211
Rodgers, Richard, 234
Rodin, François Auguste René, 199, 215,
270 (371)
Roerich, Nicholas, 46, 183, 206, 270 (397)
Rogers, Ginger, 234
Roi Soleil (see Louis XIV)
Roman precedent: Abbé warned against
blind dependence on, 21; dominated
in Renaissance and Baroque, 34; for
triumphant processions, 50; and Augustan drama, 90; and English imitation of mime, 94; first "true revival"
of, 118; manners and architecture of,
universal models, 134; and evil act not
truly "Roman," 135; history of, exhausted, 142
Roman sculpture, 11
Romanov regime: isolation of, 162; last
of, 166, 218; and *ballet de cour*, 174–
75; farewell to Russia of, 194; Chec-
kov's Russia of, 246; retardative taste
of, 272 (433)
Romantic ballet: brought innovations, 16;
rise and fall of, 31–32; stereotyped
ballerinas of, 39; verge of, 138; and
Robert le Diable, 142–43; and *La Sylphide*, 146–47; and *Giselle*, 150–51; less
important than Diaghilev, 182; distilled
in *Les Sylphides*, 186–87 (see also
ballerina)
Romanticism: in arts, 16; and revivalism,
39; in scenery, 46; Gautier's, 131;
Gothic, 142; ballerina anomalous to,
147, 151; battle for, 207; replaced Neoclassic, 252 (16) (see also Romantic
ballet)
Rome, 62, 87
Romeo and Juliet, 32
Romney, George, 26
Ronsard, Pierre, 50–51
Rosati, Carolina, 162–63
Rossignol, 47

C

Fig. 1.   Fig. 2.   Fig. 3.   Fig. 4.

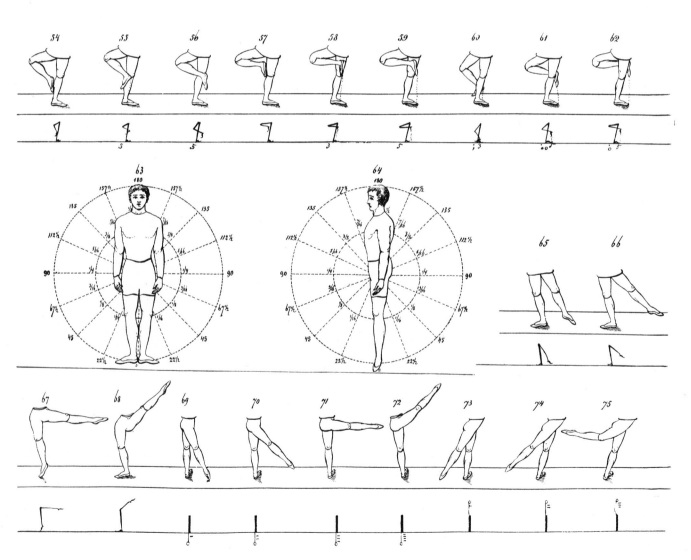

D